BLACK FOLK HERE AND THERE

Afro-American Culture and Society
A CAAS Monograph Series
Volume 7

The Academic Editor for this Monograph was
Claudia Mitchell-Kernan.

BLACK FOLK HERE AND THERE

An Essay in History and Anthropology

ST. CLAIR DRAKE

VOLUME 1

CENTER FOR AFRO-AMERICAN STUDIES
UNIVERSITY OF CALIFORNIA, LOS ANGELES

Library of Congress Cataloging in Publication Data

Drake, St. Clair.
  Black folk here and there.

  (Afro-American culture and society, ISSN 0882-5297 ; v. 7-)
  Includes bibliographies and index.
  1. Racism—History. 2. Blacks—History. 3. Blacks—Nile River Valley—History. 4. Nile River Valley—History. 5. Afro-Americans—Race Identity. I. Title. II. Series: Afro-American culture and society ; v. 7, etc.
CB195.D72 1987   305.8'96   86-16045
ISBN 0-934934-28-2 (set)
ISBN 0-934934-29-0 (pbk. : set)
ISBN 0-934934-20-7 (v. 1)
ISBN 0-934934-21-5 (pbk. : v. 1)

Center for Afro-American Studies
University of California, Los Angeles

Library of Congress Catalog Card Number:
ISBN: 0-934934-20-7
      0-934934-21-5 (pbk)
ISSN: 0882-5297
Printed in the United States of America

The following publishers are among those which have generously given permission to use quotations from copyrighted works: Reprinted from *Race Relations: Elements of Social Dynamics* (1976) by Oliver C. Cox, by permission of the Wayne State University Press. Copyright © 1976 by Wayne State University Press, Detroit, Michigan. From *Africa: Its Peoples and Their Culture History*. Copyright © 1959 by McGraw-Hill. Reproduced by permission from the publisher.

Designed by Serena Sharp
Maps by Kathryn Nirschl
Produced by UCLA Publication Services Dept.
Typography: Freedmen's Organization

In Memory of
ALLISON DAVIS
(1902–1983)

—distinguished social anthropologist and educator whose fiction, poetry, and essays of his youth inspired the students of the twenties and thirties to search for meaning in the Black Experience, especially "The Negro Deserts His People" [*Plain Talk*, 5(1929): 49–54] and "Fighters" [*Opportunity*, June 1928].

Fighters

These of the coal-black faces
Confide low-voiced,
Fisherman, washerwoman,
Quietly shutting themselves off
From the pool-room loafers.

Unbroken
By the salt spume of the sea,
Tight-lipped against the whispering fears of age,
He holds her laughing.

In his keen eyes
The gleam of one who knows he must endure
All shifting winds,
And hate
Of deep-embittered sons of slaving race,
Must outreach
The hunger of insatiate women,
And broken nets at sea.

Her brave face
Softens in a smile
And light of youth's long hopes and passion
Sunk away.
But she has seasoned in her proper time
And grown to mellow laughter.
Strong.
Like some far runner turning with new vigor
Home.

Now she is firm
Against the tearings of untimely births,
And sweating steam of clothes;
Firm now, at last,
Against the pleading smiles
Of brutal, melancholy,
Rich voiced men.

CONTENTS

ILLUSTRATIONS

Plates (following page 332)

PREFACE

Black Folk Here and There is part of a larger project that I began in 1977 with a Fellowship for Independent Study and Research granted by the National Endowment for the Humanities (Grant No. F77–41), under the title "Coping and Co-optation." The purpose of the project was to carry out *"an analysis of values and symbols that have emerged within Black communities in the Diaspora and to relate them to the 'coping' process at various periods in history and in diverse places where ecological and economic contexts present quite different options.* Since black communities have been, and are, relatively powerless, their cultural products are constantly being 'co-opted' for ends other than those they set for themselves."

Research and writing on the Diaspora was the primary focus of activity during the year, but the "various periods in history" and the "diverse places" selected for comparative purposes were not neglected. Near the end of 1977, the Center for Afro-American Studies of the University of California, Los Angeles, expressed interest in publishing a book that would utilize some of the comparative material. *Black Folk Here and There* is the result, an examination of the "coping" and "co-optation" processes over a wide expanse of time and space. Crucial in the Afro-Americans' coping process has been their identification, over a time span of more than two centuries, with ancient Egypt and Ethiopia as symbols of black initiative and success long before their enslavement on the plantations of the New World. Great myths are always part of group-coping strategies. The book begins with an examination of Nile Valley civilizations, after a brief discussion of "The Ambivalent Exiles" from Africa who found themselves evolving as part of North American societies.

The Black Experience after the Roman Empire's incorporation of Egypt on the eve of the Christian Era is conceptualized in volume 1 as a constant struggle by Nile Valley black elites to regain political power and cultural independence. Instead of autonomous development, co-optation by Roman, Greek, and Middle Eastern imperial rulers became their fate; however, they enjoyed a high degree of participation as equals in some situations. The sub-Saharan African population constituted a large pool of female domestic labor, concubines, and prostitutes; the males were valued as soldiers and workers in a variety of menial pursuits. Individuals were carried off into the Mediterranean and Middle Eastern Diaspora as slaves while the masses developed unique cultures in isolation from the artistic and intellectual currents prevailing elsewhere until a process of gradual Islamization began in the eleventh century A.D., followed by a massive economic and cultural European penetration after the middle of the nineteenth century.

From the eighth century through the fifteenth, the Arab-Berber slave trade siphoned off Blacks with military skill, political acumen, and intellectual and artistic talent for the benefit of Muslim cultures stretching from Spain to northern India. These gifted individuals were accepted as social equals and marriage partners and did not generate black communities in the Diaspora. The incorporation of their cultural contributions into European cultures without racial attribution began with the appropriation of Egyptian knowledge by Greek intellectuals soon after the Golden Age and continued through the Medieval period by absorption of Moorish contributions in Sicily and Spain. Meanwhile, the elites within black kingdoms became suppliers of slaves.

The transatlantic slave trade extending from the sixteenth century through the mid-nineteenth century brought thousands of Africans into the new societies which were established in the Western Hemisphere on the basis of *racial slavery*. Their descendants were forced to live under systems where color-caste and color-class kept them subordinated to whites. Volume 2 is especially relevant to the patterns of coping and co-optation that emerged in the Americas, presenting as it does the historical background of European conceptions of blackness to which Africans in the New World had to adjust.

A preliminary draft of *Black Folk Here and There* was prepared during the year that I was an NEH grant recipient. After a critical reading by the publication board of the Center for Afro-American Studies at UCLA, revision and refinement began, a process that extended over several years. I wish to express my appreciation to the NEH for the award that gave me the opportunity to think and write without distractions during the first year. Of course, that agency is in no way responsible for any attitudes or opinions expressed here.

The title selected for this book, *Black Folk Here and There: An Essay in History and Anthropology*, is obviously a variation on the title of a book by the eminent Afro-American scholar Dr. W.E.B. Du Bois, whose *Black Folk Then and Now: An Essay in the History and Sociology of the Negro Race* was published in 1941. Dr. Du Bois, born three years after the end of the Civil War, and among the first few black students to receive a doctorate from Harvard, was one of the founders of the American Negro Academy in 1897. One of the stated objectives of this organization of black intellectuals was "The Defense of the Negro Against Vicious Assaults."[1] The members considered themselves to be the inheritors of the "vindicationist" tradition, within which most educated black men and women had spoken and written during the previous two centuries against apologists for slavery who attempted to justify the "peculiar institution" with the argument that Negroes were an inferior animal-like breed of mankind unfit to be treated as equals by other people.

During the 1890s, in the third decade after Emancipation, such propaganda was revived and intensified to defend new interests. In the South the Ku Klux Klan and lily-white state legislatures used it to give sanction to racial terrorism and legislation designed to drive the newly freed slaves out of the political community and fasten caste and debt slavery upon them. In the North trade unions used anti-Negro racism to exclude Blacks in favor of job monopolies for white immigrants. Within the European powers, varied racist ideologies were elaborated and propagated to defend the conquest and plundering of Africa. Dr. Du Bois, who received his Ph.D. in history in 1895, was in the vanguard of the Afro-American, African, and West Indian intellectuals dedicated to "The Defense of the Negro Against Vicious Assaults."

The intellectual tasks of "the defense" involved a continuous searching criticism of the assumptions and facts used by some Darwinian evolutionists in an effort to prove that black people were "closest to the ape," and by those Social Darwinists who insisted that Negroes were doomed to disappear in the struggle for existence against superior Aryans, Nordics, and African "Hamites." The newly emergent field of Mendelian genetics was distorted by propagandists claiming that Negro physical traits—dark-brown skin, kinky hair, and thick lips—were an outward sign of an inner cognitive deficit, causally connected with inherited intellectual inferiority. The battle raged from the turn of the century to the outbreak of World War I, with pseudoscientists reinforcing the anti-Negro stereotypes then prevalent on the stage and in the popular press.

By 1910 Dr. Du Bois had begun to devote full time to the work of the National Association for the Advancement of Colored People and was editing its journal, *Crisis*. In 1915 another Harvard-trained black historian, Dr. Carter G. Woodson, founded the Association for the Study of Negro Life and History, whose *Journal of Negro History* each month for the next sixty-five years carried scholarly articles designed to set straight the oft-distorted record of the Black Experience and to fill in lacunae resulting from the conscious or unconscious omission of significant facts about black people. By coincidence Dr. Du Bois published a book entitled *The Negro* during the year of the founding of the Association for the Study of Negro Life and History. A quarter of a century later he revised and updated it with the new title *Black Folk Then and Now*. The vindicationist task still required attention on the eve of World War II. Du Bois, in his seventies, was still determined to make his contribution, and he did so.

In 1941, as in 1915, Dr. Du Bois chose to present a straightforward, tightly knit narrative of African history prior to the European overseas expansion, followed by an analysis of the slave trade and of colonial imperialism in Africa, and of antiblack discrimination throughout the world after the abolition of slavery. He contrasted the depressed state of twentieth-century Africa with the artistic, intellectual, and social creativity that existed in various parts of Africa prior to the massive social dislocations resulting from slave raids, the search for raw materials, the introduction of European and American trade goods, and the invasion of alien values suffused with demeaning and morally debilitating White Racism. It is this contrast that gives significance to his "then" and "now" frame of reference.

Du Bois stressed—as all vindicationists do—the role of ancient Egypt as an advanced *African* civilization, refusing to define it as *Near Eastern*, as many European scholars insisted upon doing. He pointed out that some of the early Egyptologists had stressed the essentially African character of Egyptian religious, familial, and political concepts, but that their work had been virtually suppressed by racist scholars who insisted that the creators of Egyptian civilization were "white," and that the impulses to their creativity had come from Palestine, Syria, and Mesopotamia. Some white scholars did not deny that Africans "of mixed blood" sometimes sat on the pharaonic throne, but they insisted that infusions of Negro blood led to the decline of Egypt. Others even claimed that no Egyptians, regardless of their appearance, should ever be called "Negroes."

Du Bois took a commonsense view of the Egyptian population controversy, pointing out that its people represented a mixture of genes from Negroes with those from many other peoples. He argued that ancient Egyptians spoke as respectfully of their indubitably Negro pharaohs as they did of those whose race was more problematic. However, Du Bois did not rest his argument for black participation in the development of early civilizations on the existence of a Negroid population in Egypt. He was one of the first widely read American scholars to call attention to beliefs, held by some ancient Egyptians and Homeric and classical Greeks, that the Ethiopians had originally "civilized" Egypt. And he also questioned why most contemporary scholars seemed to ignore both the Ethiopian kingdom of Meroë and the West African kingdoms of Ghana, Mali, and Songhay when discussing the capacities of black people for developing complex societies.

The students who inaugurated the Black Studies movement that grew up between 1967 and 1975 raised these questions anew, and their "discovery" of Du Bois was inevitable before he died at the age of ninety-five in Ghana in 1963. By then he had become an embarrassment to some and an enigma to many. Seeing no hope for an end to racism in the United States, still emphasizing his blackness and his Pan-Africanism, he joined the Communist party just before taking up his self-imposed exile in Ghana in 1961. Black Americans understood, even when they could not approve of his decisions. The Afro-American youth movement emphasized the value of Du Bois's early work not so much for its vindicationist effort to change white attitudes and behavior as for its value in fostering black consciousness and black solidarity.

Despite the ideological differences between Black Nationalists and various types of Marxists that existed within the field of Black Studies during the formative years, Du Bois was accorded a place of honor by all as a pioneer in the struggle to give legitimacy to "blackness." During the sixties Afro-American youth made the slogan "Black is Beautiful" a rallying cry, and thereafter the term "Negro" became an insult. A stream of books appeared with the word *Black* in their titles. Some were revised editions of old books with the word *Negro* changed to *Black.*

During the late nineteenth century, when Du Bois first began to publish, many educated Afro-Americans winced at the appellation "black." It excited shame. For others "Negro" was a pejorative term akin to "nigger." For still others the word COLORED was too color-*less* (and, moreover, southern Jim Crow signs read WHITE and COLORED), even though they supported the National Association for the Advancement of *Colored* People. Dr. Du Bois displayed a commonsense approach to this nomenclature question, which still has political significance and is, even now, occasionally a subject of controversy. He frequently used the word *Negro* in titles of books and articles but was also quite comfortable with *Black*, as illustrated in his

1903 classic, *The Souls of Black Folk: Essays and Sketches*. Two decades and four books later, both terms appear in a Du Bois book title: *The Gift of Black Folk: Negroes in the Making of America* (1924). Two years later he published an article in the *New Republic*, entitled "On Being Black." Then, in 1928, Dr. Du Bois considered it necessary to write an editorial in *Crisis* on the disputed question of proper nomenclature, under the title "The Name 'Negro'." Like Booker T. Washington and Marcus Garvey, Du Bois insisted that, if used, the word should be capitalized. The young Blacks of the sixties insisted upon burying *Negro* forever, and the word has virtually disappeared from both the print media and the visual media. For a work such as *Black Folk Here and There*, however, it is necessary to use the word in a number of specific contexts, one of which is in discussions of the anthropological literature. I also use it now and then for variety, believing that, having won the important struggle for self-definition of which this battle for a preferred designation was an essential part, we can be relaxed about the occasional use of the word *Negro* in scholarly works as distinct from the popular media.

In the struggle to have Afro-Americans called "black," it is ironic that, even as the fight went on, the word had lost any connection with a fixed skin-color referent. In fact, it may never have had one. During Shakespeare's time it could refer either to a dark English person, or it could be used, as in *Othello*, where the reference is obviously to a Negro. Taken literally, the word *black* was an absurdity when applied to Afro-Americans after the first hundred years of British colonization in North America. Miscegenation had produced some "Blacks" who were Caucasian in features, had blond eyes and hair, and skin-color usually referred to as "white." As late as the sixties, in some areas of the country a person was considered "black" by law or custom if he had, or was suspected of having, *any* African ancestry, however remote and small in degree. At the same time, in dealing with Africa some anthropologists refused to classify any Africans as "Negro" or "black" if they were known to have, or were assumed to have, any white Caucasoid ancestry! They were dubbed "Hamites," not "*true* Negroes." In some parts of the Islamic world and Latin America today, only people with pronounced Negroid features are called "black," and other terms are used to designate various degrees of racial mixture.

The Black Studies movement generated discussion of these inconsistencies, and of the racist implications of names used to designate Africans and people of full or partial African descent in Africa and various diaspora situations. When Black Nationalists conceded that

"Black is how you think," they were recognizing the problem of trying to apply the term literally to all people whom they wished to accept as "black." It is only recently, however, in a more quiet period of the liberation struggle in the United States, that most Black Studies programs have been prepared to examine the "absurdities" as well as the political utility and creative value of using "black" as a symbol of group solidarity. This book hopes to contribute toward such discussion. That I wrote it at all is one consequence of my having been drawn into the orbit of the Black Studies movement soon after it originated.

In 1969, after thirty years of teaching and research as a social anthropologist whose specialty was comparative race relations and urbanization in African societies, I accepted a position at Stanford University, where, in addition to teaching anthropology for the next seven years, I administered the Undergraduate Program in African and Afro-American Studies (Stanford's version of Black Studies) and the Committee for the Comparative Study of Africa and the Americas. The idea of writing a book in the field of comparative race relations had been germinating in my mind throughout my entire academic career, and the thought of a volume calling attention to themes first developed by Du Bois in *Black Folk Then and Now* had also been on my mind for some time. The decision to write such a book was directly related to my late-in-life experiences at Stanford. I was already at work on a comparative study of black communities in the New World, to be called "Africa and the Black Diaspora," when the compelling necessity became evident for a volume dealing with the Black Experience before European expansion into the Western Hemisphere, and that, in fact, comprises the thematic substance of *Black Folk Here and There*. This work has the double purpose of presenting factual data that should be more widely disseminated, and of using those data to test certain beliefs about the prevalence of prejudice and discrimination against dark-skinned people generally and "Negroes" in particular.

At Stanford I found myself working with one colleague in the humanities whose credentials as a dedicated liberal were impeccable, but who sneered at a book recently written by a distinguished black classicist pointing out the lack of prejudice against Negroes in Greco-Roman antiquity. This colleague insisted with sincere conviction that it was "natural" for all light-skinned peoples to be prejudiced against dark-skinned peoples. (Later I discovered that he had actually put this idea in print.) Another colleague, a Nobel Prize winner in physics, made no claim to be a liberal but reveled, rather, in the nationwide publicity he was receiving for his contention that persistent Negro average I.Q. scores below the white average could be explained only by causes that were 85 percent hereditary. His claims were based upon a dubious analogy with Cyril Burt's identical-twin studies, which were later proved to be fraudulent.

Considered beyond the intellectual pale by both of these men was a black colleague in the psychology department who, after joining the Nation of Islam (Black Muslims), became convinced that all white people are "Devils" by nature. He and some associates began to elaborate a theory that melanin is a substance that "tones up" the human nervous system, and because Blacks have an unusually large amount of it, they not only possess superior intellectual capabilities but also have potential paranormal powers that in some times and places have become highly developed but have been suppressed by Western culture. The traditional anthropology that I taught was constantly under challenge by some black students who were convinced that the superior inherited qualities of *Négritude* were shared by black people everywhere. Others, citing the British extreme diffusionists and nineteenth-century folklorists, accused Establishment anthropologists of suppressing data that proved black people were the civilizers of all mankind.

My previous teaching experience had not prepared me for dealing with colleagues and students who expressed such views, even though I suspect some of them had similar thoughts but had inhibitions about expressing them. In order to discuss these matters with devotees of the more arcane versions of the black mystique, I found it necessary to read a mass of esoteric literature about ancient Egypt, Mesopotamia, Greece, and India, publications that I might not otherwise have examined. At the same time I had to keep *au courant* with the conventional literature in the field of race relations, since students of all races in my Racism and Prejudice classes (later renamed Racism and Power) were perplexed by current controversies and constantly asking how much truth there was in what Shockley, Jensen, and Herrnstein were saying about the inborn incapacities of American Negroes. In this case I sent them off to read the dialogue between the experts in various journals.

I gradually realized that colleagues and students were forcing me closer and closer to a decision to write a book that might clarify some of the questions they were raising. In 1976, after I retired, I put "Africa and the Black Diaspora" aside for a while in order to think about the context within which these controversial questions had arisen in the first place. So I began writing *Black Folk Here and There*.

This book deals with only a few of the issues that arose during the Stanford teaching experience. It is my hope that some other serious students of the Black Experience, as well as a broader circle of readers, will be stimulated to read more widely than I did and to search for answers to some of the questions that neither I nor anyone else has yet found. While comparative history and anthropology make some contribution to this discussion, there are questions about attitudes toward blackness that require research designed by psychologists and psychiatrists. This exploratory essay, no doubt, raises more questions than it answers.

While Dr. Du Bois chose to develop a connected narrative portraying the broad sweep of the history of Negroes in Africa and the New World diaspora over five millennia, I have selected several problems for analysis and examined them through time in a number of localized situations in Europe, Africa, and southwest Asia. Some of these situations are also compared with each other in the same time period. This treatment of the data constitutes the ''here and there'' dimension, in contrast to Dr. Du Bois's ''then and now.'' My investigation ends with the sixteenth century, a historic watershed in global relations between black and white people. I argue that before that time neither White Racism nor *racial slavery* existed, although *color prejudice* was present in places. If ''Africa and the Black Diaspora'' is ever completed, the contrast between the Americas and the rest of the world in the confrontation of Negro Africans with other racial groups will be plainly evident.

It is hoped that *Black Folk Here and There* will stimulate a desire to read *Black Folk Then and Now*—and Dr. Du Bois's other books as well. Du Bois spoke for all who write in the vindicationist genre when he wrote in the preface to *Black Folk Then and Now*:

> I do not for a moment doubt that my Negro descent and narrow group culture have in many cases predisposed me to interpret my facts too favorably for my race; but there is little danger of long misleading here, for the champions of white folks are legion.

May the eventual end of racism make any such champions—for either side—unnecessary.

St. Clair Drake

Palo Alto, California
1986

ACKNOWLEDGMENTS

I wish to express my gratitude to the Center for Afro-American Studies (CAAS) of the University of California at Los Angeles for giving me the opportunity to prepare a volume in its monograph series that would address some problems over which I had been ruminating for several decades. Dr. Claudia Mitchell-Kernan, an anthropologist who had recently become director of the Center, extended the initial invitation in 1977 on behalf of the CAAS Publications Committee. What began as a modest task of revising drafts of manuscripts on hand and integrating them into a coherent volume grew into an ambitious enterprise demanding extensive research into unfamiliar territory. The Center has shown remarkable patience with an author whose manuscript kept increasing in size, and whose disconcerting changes in style and format extended over a period of nine years.

Professor Robert A. Hill, who was series editor for the Center when the project began, gave two drafts a thorough critical reading. Dr. Mitchell-Kernan, who had also read the first draft and made suggestions, subsequently became the academic editor for this work. Professor Hill had been supportive when I wandered off on unanticipated intellectual quests, and his tactful suggestions helped to keep the final product from becoming too unwieldy. Incisive editorial comments on each chapter by Dr. Mitchell-Kernan have checked my worst lapses into sloppy thinking and intellectual obscurity, while her constant encouragement to develop the book in my own way was a challenge I could not ignore. Of course, neither she nor Professor Hill bears any responsibility for the book's many deficiencies. If it is satisfactory in any respect, however, a great share of the credit is due to their editorial supervision.

Rick Harmon, assistant to the monograph series editor, scrutinized several drafts of the book line by line, detected errors of fact, raised queries about obscure passages and unclear intentions, suggested reorganization of material, monitored syntax and punctuation, and did the initial copy-editing. Well-read and appreciative of the author's point of view, as well as tolerant of his stylistic idiosyncrasies even when he questioned them, Rick Harmon was an editor with whom it was a pleasure to work. There would have been no book without his devotion to seeing it through, even when a change in employment made that inconvenient for him.

Nor would there have been any book without the professional skill and patience of the managing editor of the Center's publications unit, Marcelle Fortier. She retained a conviction that the task was worthwhile despite the anxieties inflicted by multiple revisions and broken deadlines, and she was invariably courteous when she had good reason to be exasperated. She gave the manuscript a thorough critical reading before the final copy-editing. Her editorial suggestions at this stage contributed greatly toward some necessary refinement.

In the final stages, the Center's editor, Sabrina Gledhill, prepared the manuscript for the press, expertly coordinating the work of the cartographer, Kathryn Nirschl, and the book designer, Serena Sharp, in addition to doing the final copy-editing and tying up manifold loose ends. The author's appreciation to all three is herewith expressed with a special acknowledgment of the role of Sabrina Gledhill.

A word of thanks is due, also, to two individuals whose efforts at an early stage made the work of all concerned somewhat less difficult: the former Gretchen Van Meter, who copy-edited the second draft prior to some drastic revision and expansion of the manuscript; and Lynda Lutz of Stanford University, who supplied us with a skillfully typed clean copy of that revision. In fact, her keen eye and intelligent queries helped to improve that version.

Several colleagues at Stanford have occasionally tendered welcome advice or steered the author toward valuable sources as the project developed: Professors Clayborne Carson and Kennell Jackson of the Department of History; Bridget O'Laughlin of the Department of Anthropology; Gregson Davis of the Department of Classics; and Sylvia Wynter of the Department of Spanish and Portuguese.

A number of graduate students at Stanford have suggested sources, caught errors of fact, and challenged some opinions and conclusions while agreeing with others. None was more enthusiastic about this project than Glenn Jordan, then completing his doctorate in anthropology at the University of Illinois, Urbana-Champaign. In teaching positions he has held from time to time, he has tried out portions of the text on his students and given me the benefit of their feedback as well as his own opinions. Others who have from time to time discussed with me ideas that were relevant to sections of the book are Dr. Ronald Bailey, currently the director of the Black Studies Program at the University of Mississippi in Oxford; and Mwesiga Baregu, Professor of Political Science, University of Tanzania, a candidate for the doctorate at Stanford. My good friends Dr. Tetteh Kofi from Ghana and Dr. Agibou Yansane from Guinea, both professors in California universities, have always been ready to give me an African perspective on problems discussed in this book.

I do not include the usual list of prestigious experts who are said to have read and commented upon chapters and thereby helped to shape their final form, and who require the comment that relieves them of responsibility for the author's errors, conclusions, and so on. I chose not to impose upon any specialists by asking them to read the writings of a nonspecialist who had been reading their works and commenting on them. Their verdict can be passed on the final product. The chips may then fall where they will.

Nor do I include the usual clichés about the wife who contributed to the book in various ways, ranging from research and writing to typing, or who just endured it all patiently. My wife, a sociologist, Dr. Elizabeth Johns Drake, and I have a joint investment of time and resources extending over a decade in an uncompleted volume, "Africa and the Black Diaspora." I owe a word of apology to her for putting aside that book and prolonging into a nine-year-long venture what was to have been a year-long interlude to do this one. The words of Ecclesiastes must have often echoed in her mind as she contemplated what seemed like an attack of monomania as I pursued the trail of "blackness" through antiquity and medieval times: "Much study is a weariness of the flesh and of the making of books there is no end."

The following publishers are among those which have generously given permission to use quotations from copyrighted works: From Roland Oliver and J. D. Fage, *A Short History of Africa* (The Penguin African Library, revised edition 1978). Copyright © Roland Oliver and J. D. Fage, 1962, 1966, 1970, 1972, 1975. Reprinted by permission of Penguin Books Ltd. From Gustav Ichheiser, "Sociopsychological and Cultural Factors in Race Relations," *American Journal of Sociology* 54(5): 395–398 (March 1949). Copyright © 1949 by The University of Chicago Press. Reprinted by permission of the publishers. From Louis Wirth, "Comment" on Gustav Ichheiser, "Sociopsychological and Cultural Factors in Race Relations," *American Journal of Sociology* 54(5): 399 (March 1949). Copyright © 1949 by The University of Chicago Press. Reprinted by permission of the publishers. From Carl Degler, *Neither Black nor White*. Copyright © 1971 by Carl N. Degler. Reprinted by permission of Macmillan Publishing Company. From Noel Chabani Manganyi, *Alienation and the Body in Racist Society, A Study of the Society that Invented Soweto*. Copyright © 1977 Nok Publishers International. Reprinted by permission of the publishers. From *General History of Africa*. Vol. II. Copyright © Unesco 1981. Reprinted by permission of Unesco. From Frederick L. Schuman, *The Nazi Dictatorship: A Study in Social Pathology and the Politics of Fascism*, 2d ed. rev. Copyright © 1936 Alfred A. Knopf Inc. Reprinted by permission of the publishers. From

H. Hoetink, *Caribbean Race Relations*. Copyright © Institute of Race Relations 1967. Reprinted by permission of Oxford University Press. Selected lines from the poem "Heritage" from *On These I Stand* by Countee Cullen. Copyright © 1925 by Harper & Row, Publishers, Inc. Renewed 1953 by Ida M. Cullen. Reprinted by permission of the publishers. Allison Davis, "Fighters," originally published in *Opportunity*, June 1928. Reprinted by permission of Allison S. Davis. From Phillis Wheatley, *Memoirs and Poems of Phillis Wheatley*. Reprinted by permission of Mnemosyne Press. From Norman E. Whitten, Jr. and John F. Szwed, *Afro-American Anthropology*. Reprinted by permission of The Free Press. From Henri Frankfort, *The Birth of Civilization in the Near East*. Reprinted by permission of the Indiana University Press. From Serge Sauneron, *The Priests of Ancient Egypt*. Translation copyright © 1969 by Ann Morrisset. Reprinted by permission of Grove Press, Inc. From Cyril Aldred, *Egyptian Art in the Days of the Pharaohs* (1980). Reprinted by permission of Thames and Hudson Ltd. From Edmund Leach, *Culture and Communication* (1976). Reprinted by permission of Cambridge University Press. From Philip D. Curtin, *The Image of Africa: British Ideas and Action, 1780-1850*, vol. 1 (1964). Reprinted by permission of the University of Wisconsin Press. From Hodge, Struckmann, Trost, *Cultural Bases of Racism and Group Oppression*. Reprinted by permission of Two Riders Press. From Charles Sumner, *White Slavery in the Barbary States*. Reprinted by permission of Mnemosyne Press. Gunnar Myrdal, *An American Dilemma*. Reprinted by permission of Harper & Row, Publishers, Inc.

INTRODUCTION

Black Folk Here and There is written from a point of view that, in recent years, has been frequently referred to as a "black perspective"—reality as perceived, conceptualized, and evaluated by individuals who are stigmatized and discriminated against because they are designated as "Negroes" or "Blacks." The tradition of vindicationist scholarship referred to in the Preface has, of course, always embodied that perspective whether those specific words were used to characterize it or not. Nevertheless, not all research and writing from a black perspective has racial vindication as its raison d'être. Some of it is purely expressive with no instrumental ends in view, as, for instance, much of the poetry and fiction.

The adoption of a black perspective in history, philosophy, or the social sciences deliberately restricts the frame of reference within which people and events are observed and evaluated. The focus is narrowed so as to concentrate on the Black Experience, with full awareness, of course, that social class, nationality, ethnicity, tribal affiliation, and/or religious orientation all make the experience different from person to person. In addition, the broader sociocultural context conditions it profoundly. But the derogation of "blackness" creates a residual common perspective despite the variations, and it is one example of what Karl Mannheim described as a "partial perspective" when he developed his theory of the sociology of knowledge in *Ideology and Utopia*. He writes, "perspective signified the manner in which one views an object, what one perceives in it, and how one construes it in his thinking . . . not only do the concepts in their concrete contents diverge from one another in accordance with differing social positions, but the basic categories of thought may likewise differ."[1] Such partial perspectives are not an obstacle in the pursuit of truth about social situations; in fact, they are necessary in order to know the *entire* truth. An approximation to total knowledge is impossible if data are not available that reflect ethnic, racial, national, class, and age- and gender-related special experiences. Some things can be known *only* by those who have experienced them in these social roles.

People who view reality from a partial persepctive, if they have the will to do so, with some training, can communicate the content, the

1

meanings, and the feeling tone of their experiences to others. Insofar as this is true, research from a black perspective has a vindicationist potential. It can serve as a corrective to biases, conscious or unconscious, that persist in studies of black people produced from other perspectives.

When a black perspective has vindicationist aims, it tends to assume a polemical tone. However, even when it is neither vindicationist nor polemical, mainstream historians and social scientists have, traditionally, looked askance at it. Scholars who utilized it were frequently dismissed as "biased" and charged with violating scholarly norms of objectivity and detachment. During the past decade, however, increasing self-criticism has laid bare the hidden agendas of so-called "objective" social science. These developments, along with dialogue initiated by professors and students from subordinated ethnic groups, as well as by feminists, Marxists, and Third World historians and social scientists, have contributed to a restructuring of professional norms. With the sanction of the now respectable sociology-of-knowledge frame of reference, validity has been conceded to a black perspective as well as to a number of other intellectual points of view.

Such validity was conceded by sociologists in the United States during the late sixties and early seventies. For example, in 1973 the American Sociological Association, for the second time, presented a Du Bois-Frazier-Johnson award at its annual meeting. The recipient (who was, incidentally, the author of this book) was cited for "sustained and vigorous efforts as teacher-scholar-essayist to advance the intellectual liberation of college and university students in the United States, Africa, and the islands of the Caribbean." This Pan-Africanist orientation being cited with approval was more characteristic of the scholar-activist Dr. W.E.B. Du Bois than it was of the other two black sociologists whom the award also honored: Dr. Charles S. Johnson and Dr. E. Franklin Frazier. The willingness to include Dr. Du Bois along with the two sociologists in establishing an award, and to include the politically charged word *liberation* in the 1973 citation, indicated a profound change in attitude on the part of the leaders of the American Sociological Association. In the past Du Bois had been considered too much of a partisan in his attacks on racial discrimination to be a "good" social scientist, even though *The Philadelphia Negro*, published in 1896, was generally recognized as a piece of outstanding pioneer work in urban sociology, and his publications while holding the chair in sociology at Atlanta University could not be ignored. Unfortunately, Du Bois was no longer living when the institution of the ASA award bestowed Establishment legitimacy on his intellectual contributions.

Frazier and Johnson, as protégés of Robert E. Park, founder of the Chicago School of sociology, won the respect of their peers between 1920 and 1960 through the high quality of their research and because of their contributions to an understanding of the dynamics of social and cultural change with special reference to race relations. These men were in continuous demand as consultants to governmental and private agencies on problems involving relationships between white Americans and their black fellow citizens. (Du Bois, meanwhile, was associated with organizations exerting pressure for change.) Although Frazier and Johnson were expected to interpret the black perspective to others, it was understood that, as social scientists, their scholarly writings would maintain a neutral and objective tone. They, like most other black scholars prior to the seventies, did not question the wisdom of working within the parameters set by the academic disciplines within which they had done their graduate work. (There were no interdisciplinary degrees in Black Studies in those days.) Each aspired to make some contribution to his discipline while, at the same time, carrying out research and publication on the Black Experience in such a way that it would, at least indirectly, contribute toward what a chapter heading in Drake and Cayton's *Black Metropolis* (1945) referred to as "Advancing the Race."

Among some Afro-American scholars who won academic distinction through this nonpolemical, discipline-oriented approach to the study of the Black Experience were Horace Mann Bond in the field of education; Allison Davis in social anthropology and social psychology; Ralph Bunche in political science; and Abram Harris and Robert Weaver in economics. Vindicationists made effective use of the work of such scholars in their own polemical writing (for example, Frank Snowden's outstanding contribution to Greco-Roman classical scholarship, *Blacks in Antiquity*). *Black Folk Here and There* is closer in tone to the style of Du Bois than was *Black Metropolis*, coauthored with Horace Cayton. That book was more similar to the Johnson-Frazier type of research, and to that of the above-mentioned group of discipline-oriented scholars.

In one field, however, in addition to such discipline-oriented scholars as Dr. John Hope Franklin, a group of Afro-American historians, under the leadership of Dr. Carter G. Woodson, developed what Engerman and Fogel in *Time on the Cross* refer to as "The Negro School." From 1915, when they established the Association for the Study of Negro Life and History, this group of historians frankly stated an explicit vindicationist aim: to challenge, correct, and supplement what was erroneously claimed to be the truth about Negroes, and to do it from a black perspective, using both detached scholarship and polemics. Their monographs and their periodical forum, the *Journal of Negro History*, won the respect of their peers. *Time on the Cross* points out that they made solid contributions through methodological innovations in historiography, although they were always considered marginal to the mainstream in the field of American history.

A survey of the great outpouring of works written from a black perspective during the sixties and seventies suggests certain pitfalls to be avoided when trying to set the historical record straight. Among these is the presentation of highly plausible possibilities as though they were "facts," and the imputing of racist motivations to individuals who lived in the remote past and whose actions that were disadvantageous to Blacks might be more appropriately explained in some other way. A few very race-conscious historians turned concepts such as *Négritude* and Black Power into mirror images of White Racism, a development as indefensible as it was extreme. However, when pursued with caution, vindicationist efforts need not be unscholarly although they may be unconventional. For instance, the criteria of relevance used in research from a black perspective will often lead to emphasis upon facts and personalities that others deem unimportant or even trivial. These may be crucial to a full understanding of the Black Experience; and, when integrated into meaningful patterns, even those who initially questioned their usefulness may recognize their value.

Emphasizing the Black Experience sometimes involves the idiosyncratic treatment of data. For instance, the more popular works of the self-trained historian Joel A. Rogers (e.g., *Sex and Race*) sometimes used photographs to "prove" the Negro ancestry of various important personalities in a manner that cannot be defended—as in the case of Beethoven. On the other hand, much of Rogers's work depends upon meticulous documentation to establish his claims. Thus the work of this particular vindicationist is valuable but must be used with caution. Other black scholars, such as Cheikh Anta Diop in *African Origins of Civilization* and Yosef Ben-Jochannan in *Black Man's Religion*, use unconventional approaches that those unsympathetic with their points of view will find disconcerting. When I am writing from a black perspective, I, too, occasionally indulge in peculiarities that might be proscribed in a publisher's manual of style, and are in contrast to the more conventional stance I assume in other contexts.

For instance, in order to emphasize previously neglected themes and facts I am not averse to the use of a more liberal sprinkling of capitalized and italicized words than conventional stylists prefer. In this book, however, I have refrained from anything so idiosyncratic as the device, used by Dr. Du Bois in *Black Reconstruction*, of appending to each carefully researched and soberly presented chapter a paragraph or two of passionately rhetorical opinion or judgment. I do, however, frequently mention the race of authors or participants in events, whereas presentation from some other perspective would make such designations unnecessary or even inappropriate.

This work is designated, as was Du Bois's *Black Folk Then and Now*, an "essay." This format allows for expression of opinion as well as the presentation of fact, and permits peculiarities of style that would not be acceptable in a scientific monograph. The book is called "an essay in history and anthropology." Scholars in both fields will, no doubt, decide that it has only a dubious connection with either discipline. If so, it will be because of my inadequate workmanship, not because the designation is unjustified. The late E. E. Evans-Pritchard, one of the founding fathers of British functional anthropology, noted upon one occasion that "Maitland has said that anthropology must choose between being history and being nothing." Evans-Pritchard pushed the point further by saying, "I accept the dictum, though only if it also be reversed—history must choose between being social anthropology and being nothing."[2] My view is closer to that of the distinguished American anthropologist Sidney Mintz, who wrote, "we need not accept the assertion that anthropology would ultimately be history or else it would be nothing at all in order to discover that the usefulness of history for anthropology, and of anthropology for history, is genuine and important." He warned, however, that "most of us who plunge today into problems that require the skills of both disciplines for their solution continue to feel with justice rather like the blind men charged with describing the elephant."[3] Yet, in his own work on the African impact on New World societies, Sidney Mintz has proved to be a craftsman of high merit in the development of concepts and methods for utilizing historical materials in anthropological investigations.

The use of the comparative method in analyzing historical data for an exercise in macrosociology or macroanthropology—as *Black Folk Here and There* is—becomes an especially hazardous intellectual enterprise when the anthropologist is, as I am, untrained in historiography. The result of such a venture runs the risk of being either superficial and anecdotal on one hand, or too heavily documented and ponderously pretentious on the other. If this work avoids either extreme and turns out to be at all significant, it will be, in large measure, the result of the fine work of specialists whose scholarship I have drawn upon. I have used written documents in place of the participant-observer notes usually brought back from anthropological fieldwork. My use of what some might consider excessive quotation from secondary sources is an attempt to adapt one of some anthropologists' preferred techniques of presentation, in which excerpts from interviews with informants are woven into the text. The authors of these authoritative works here act as my informants. I like to have them speak for themselves; I try to make it possible for the reader to savor some of the flavor of their words. This book, like Du Bois's *Black Folk Then and Now*, was not designed as a project that would examine primary source material. It is, rather, a critical review of a wide range of existing published data—text and photographs—that have relevance to the Black Experience, and an integration of such data into what I consider an interpretative pattern.

The claim of *Black Folk Here and There* to an affiliation with anthropology cannot rest upon the manner in which the raw data are assembled, analyzed, and presented. It is based instead upon the selection of concepts for organizing the data. These have been the study of acculturation under conditions of conquest, and of behavior and symbols associated with social stratification. The entire study might be considered an exercise in symbolic anthropology, broadly conceived. On another level the study deals with the traditional anthropological concern for the relationship between race and culture in human societies and the implications of studies of prehistory and physical anthropology for the Black Experience. Anthropology tempers ethnic chauvinsim by insisting upon an attitude of cultural relativism prior to passing judgment upon cultures different from our own.

One of the aims of this book is to give the reader an initial acquaintance with some relevant and potentially interesting published data that are not widely known and sometimes not readily accessible. One of its purposes, too, is the integration of familiar data into new patterns of relevance. Suggestions are included for additional reading and for possible future research, since some matters discussed herein remain obscure or confused while others merit more in-depth discussion and analysis. If, in addition to satisfying curiosity and answering a few previously unanswered questions, the book also has the effect of stimulating research that leads to an occasional master's thesis or doctoral dissertation, it will have more than justified the time and effort that went into it.

Black Folk Here and There deals with the Black Experience before White Racism emerged as a dogma to support a system of institutionalized practices designed to justify the transatlantic African slave trade and Western Hemisphere slave systems. Later, White Racism developed to reinforce colonial imperialism in Africa, Asia, and Oceania. The author has been working for several years on a book manuscript, entitled "Africa and the Black Diaspora," that analyzes the forces which brought White Racism into being and the counterforces which emerged concurrently in various parts of the world. *Black Folk Here and There* conceptualizes *slavery, skin-color prejudice,* and *racism* as three quite distinct phenomena, each of which had existed separately from the other prior to the period of the great European overseas explorations but which became intertwined and mutually interdependent in the African diaspora of the Western Hemisphere.

The empirical evidence presented here supports the view that prejudice and discrimination based upon skin-color existed for several centuries before the beginning of European overseas expansion but were not accompanied by any systematic doctrines of racial inferiority and superiority, that is, "racism" as we define it for the purposes of this study. Nor were color prejudice and discrimination institutionalized as structural principles defining systems of slavery, caste, or class. Slavery is a phenomenon that has existed in many times and places without any connection with either skin-color prejudice or racism. "Africa and the Black Diaspora" will consider in detail the relatively recent unique phenomenon of the institutionalization of skin-color prejudice in the form of *racial slavery*. It will also describe factors in the emergence of doctrinal supports for such a system, based upon theology and pseudoscience. From the outset *racial slavery* was systematically undermined by economic and noneconomic factors within the Western capitalist societies which gave birth to it. After it disappeared in the Americas during the nineteenth century, slavery *not* based upon racial discrimination continued to exist in various parts of Asia, the Middle East, and Africa.

Chapters 1 and 2 of this volume present the basic concepts that guide the examination of the empirical data in the chapters to follow. A distinction is drawn between generalized skin-color prejudice and prejudice against Negroes and Negroidness. The most crucial conception is the proposition that beliefs, attitudes, and behavior of others toward Negroes must always be understood as operating in relation to certain domains within any specific society. These are *esthetic, erotic, status conferring, moral-mystical,* and *utilitarian* (such as economic, military, and political). One or several of these domains may be dominant, insofar as skin-color evaluation is concerned, within a specific social situation. Though others exist, they are of lesser importance. Seemingly contradictory forms of belief and behavior with regard to skin-color may exist side by side within a single society.

As the study developed, it became clear that a distinction must be made between the following three objects of evaluation when contrasts between *Black* and *White*, *blackness* and *whiteness*, are made: (1) nonhuman objects and abstract ideas; (2) human beings defined as "colored" or "nonwhite"; and (3) human beings who have a Negro facial configuration associated with dark skin-color. "Blackness" is often a term that really means "Negroidness"; nevertheless, it is possible for societies to incorporate highly pejorative stereotypes and attitudes about "Negroes" without having similar reactions to other dark-skinned people, however "black" they may be. In formulating questions to be addressed in the examination of empirical data, these have assumed priority:

(1) Is the tendency universal to make the color *Black* symbolic of undesirable objects, situations, and emotional or psychological states?

(2) Does the devaluation of the color *Black* within the symbol system of a specific society necessarily lead to the expression of negative prejudices against people defined as "Black" within that society?

(3) If negative stereotypes are held, and negative attitudes are expressed, against people defined as "Black" within a society, does this necessarily result in discriminatory *behavior* toward them?

From a mass of secondary source material an attempt is made here to answer the above questions for each of several situations. The extent to which this is possible varies greatly with time and place. In many situations the data are not present in the written record to attempt an answer. The complexity of the problem extends beyond considerations of time and place, since the study of the record left by literates gives us an inadequate view of what the nonliterate segment of many populations felt—or how they acted, in instances where their alleged racial stereotypes and attitudes are presented by others. An attempt is made, however, to infer popular attitudes and behavior patterns from folklore, proverbs, and by analogy, comparing ancient situations with contemporary ones of similar societal type.

In addition to the three questions noted above, special attention is given to the following questions: *When, where, and why did pejorative connotations originally become attached to a specific kind of black person—the Negro physical type? Did these connotations diffuse to other areas and, if so, how and why? Did such connotations ever originate again independently and, if so, where and under what circumstances?* Scholars have given considerable attention to the question of why dark skin-color is frequently denigrated. Virtually none has attempted to explain why "Negroidness," prior to the transatlantic slave trade, bore the brunt of skin-color prejudice in some parts of the Mediterranean world and the Middle East.

All of the chapters, where the data are available, also try to address two other questions: (1) What are the factors that have been decisive in changes of attitude and behavior toward black people in various times and places? and (2) What are the factors that have been decisive in the change of attitude and behavior of black people toward themselves in various times and places?

Black Folk Here and There is presented in two volumes, the first of which includes the theoretical introduction to the analysis of cases, as well as one such analysis. The strategy for presenting the empirical data in a comparative frame of reference entails beginning with a chapter on the Black Experience in the ancient Nile Valley, the case presented in volume 1. Egypt provides the longest continuous documented record of relations between a variety of racial groups, including those defined as "Negro" by anthropologists and by customary usage. At times Blacks had military and political dominance in Egypt and in the upper Nile Valley, known to the ancient Greeks as Ethiopia. A study of the interaction between Egypt and Ethiopia provides valuable data for examining the self-concepts of diverse black groups when in contact with each other prior to periods of domination by lighter-skinned peoples. In addition, special emphasis is placed upon ancient Egypt because of the significance of that civilization in all vindicationist writing, past and present.

The need continues for correcting numerous errors that operate to obscure the role of the Negro people in the development of Egyptian civilization. Chapter 3 attempts to deal with some of these problems, which were posed in Dr. Du Bois's book *The Negro* in 1915 and have more recently been the subject of discussion at a symposium convened by UNESCO. In addition to the correction of errors it is important to treat in some detail certain aspects of Egyptian-Ethiopian history that have often been neglected in discussing relations between black and white people. One such theme is the close relations between the ancient Jews and the Nile Valley peoples.

The second volume consists of chapters 4, 5, and 6 and a concluding epilogue. Chapter 4 presents data on relations between black and white people in the Mediterranean world and the Middle East prior to the rise of Islam in the seventh century A.D. Emphasis is placed upon the fact that, after the sixth century B.C., two distinct Jewish traditions emerged—Palestinian and Mesopotamian—the former retaining historic connections with the Nile Valley peoples, the latter developing relations with Negroes from inner Africa through slaves imported into the Tigris-Euphrates Valley, and with Persian religious thought. The importance of the rabbinic scholars of the Mesopotamian diaspora in the development of myths about blackness and black people is examined and contrasted with the biblical tradition of Palestine. This latter tradition was close to that of the Greco-Roman world in its relatively favorable attitude toward the people whom the Greeks called "Ethiopians." Since European and American literate culture evolved from a synthesis of the Greco-Roman and the Judaic tradition as it took shape in early Christianity, the attitudes of the church fathers toward blackness in the Christian symbol system and toward Ethiopians is examined. Propositions about the transfer of color symbolism to social relations and to persons are considered in the light of data from the Mediterranean and Middle Eastern cultures. This is where the "roots," so to speak, of medieval Christendom are to be found. (A thorough examination of skin-color as it functions in the societies of the Indian subcontinent would be instructive, but this is not done because of limitations of time and space and in order to keep the focus on "Negroidness.")

Chapter 5 is entitled "The Black Experience in the Muslim World." Between the seventh century A.D. and the beginning of the Crusades in the eleventh century, the religion of Islam, drawing its initial impulse from Judaism and Christianity, became the most important social and political force throughout the Middle East and the African and European Mediterranean coasts, as well as in Spain and Portugal. Because the followers of Islam were in intimate contact with Negroes from below the Sahara and from the coasts of East Africa, and because of widespread misunderstanding about Muslim attitudes and behavior toward Blacks as compared with those of Christians, it was considered important to devote a chapter to the status of black people throughout the area in which Christianity had been dominant for five centuries but was replaced to a large extent by Islam, a new religion.

The data in chapter 5 confirm the proposition that widespread and deep-seated prejudice against Negroidness may prevail in some domains within a culture, even though there is no strong derogation of blackness in the abstract or of non-Negro black peoples. The conclusion also emerges that if slavery in a social system is not *racial slavery*, and if institutionalized racism does not exist, prejudice against

Negroes will not necessarily prevent a considerable degree of individual mobility based upon talent in some domains and upon the existence of favorable stereotypes in others.

Chapter 6 contrasts the Black Experience in European Christendom between the eighth and fifteenth centuries with that in the Muslim world during the same period. The key variable is slavery, which was omnipresent under Islam but absent from most of European Christendom after the tenth century A.D. In both cultures positive and negative values were associated with Negroidness. In neither were all slaves Negro. By examining the differences between the Iberian Peninsula and the British Isles on the eve of the sixteenth-century European expansion around the Atlantic basin, a baseline is set for studying the contrasting forms that *racial slavery* and White Racism took in areas settled by the British on one hand and those settled by the Spanish and the Portuguese on the other. Volume 2 ends with an epilogue entitled "The End of an Epoch in Black History," which discusses the historic turning point in black/white relations that occurred during the sixteenth century A.D., when the Black Diaspora into the Western Hemisphere began.

1. WHITE RACISM AND THE BLACK EXPERIENCE

The Black Experience began thousands of years before the phenomenon of White Racism appeared in human history, generated as it was by European economic and political expansion overseas beginning in the fifteenth century A.D. The roots of the Black Experience, as described in chapter 3 of this volume, lie deep in the prehistory and history of the Nile Valley, the Sahara Desert, and the northern savannah lands of Africa. It is a story that involves the extensive dispersion of black people, within the African continent and beyond it, and diverse contacts with other races.

To understand the complexity of the Black Experience in its full temporal and spatial amplitude, it is necessary to distinguish between White Racism and less drastic forms of prejudice through which colored people are sometimes stigmatized. These, although unjust and injurious to group welfare and individual personality development, are less devastating in their effects than White Racism. They are diffused negative prejudices involving stereotypes at the cognitive level and pejorative attitudes at the emotional level, neither of which are sanctioned with a systematic ideology or embodied in institutional structures. This chapter describes the manner in which anti-black, and especially anti-Negro, prejudices of some antiquity were mobilized as one part of the developing phenomenon of racism in Europe. It also describes the ongoing refinement of concepts dealing with racism.

The processes are outlined by which White Racism developed as a special type of nineteenth-century pseudoscientific racism, functionally related to the African slave trade and to colonial imperialism in Africa and Asia. It is noted that at some times and in some places, color prejudice against black people has existed without developing into White Racism. It should be noted that other forms of racism than White Racism exist, in which presumed ancestry rather than skin-color or other physical features is the criterion for invidious distinction.

Finally, this chapter emphasizes the need for distinguishing between prejudice against ''blackness'' in general and ''Negroidness'' in particular. Negative esthetic evaluations of "Negroidness," although rarely examined in detail, are here discussed because they persist tenaciously and reinforce negative beliefs about the intelligence and personality traits of black people, and thereby affect the life chances and self-esteem of people so evaluated. Prejudices of this type have a tendency to linger after racist dogmas have been widely discredited and public and private agencies have come into being to work actively against racial discrimination. They are deeply entrenched, even in some societies where the more blatant forms of institutional racism have never existed.

Some aspects of the Black Experience in eighteenth-century North America are presented as a significant historical baseline for considering ironies and inconsistencies, paradoxes and contradictions, that constitute elements of continuity and change in the expression of white attitudes toward "blackness" and "Negroidness."

COLOR PREJUDICE THEN AND NOW

In 1782, seven years after he had drafted the Declaration of Independence with a preamble declaring, "We hold these truths to be self-evident, that all men are created equal," Thomas Jefferson, the Virginia planter-scholar, rationalized the continuing enslavement of black people.[1] Of the men and women whom he and other white people owned, he wrote:

> This unfortunate difference of colour, and perhaps of faculty, is a powerful obstacle to the emancipation of these people. . . . I advance it therefore as a suspicion only, that the blacks, whether originally a distinct race, or made distinct by time and circumstances, are inferior to the whites in the endowments both of body and mind.[2]

After contrasting the slaves of classical antiquity with those in North America, to the disadvantage of the latter, Jefferson invoked a theory of biological inheritance to explain the suspected inferiority: "It is not against experience to suppose, that different species of the same genus, or varieties of the same species, may possess different qualifications."[3] Yet Jefferson believed that there was some hope for Blacks, because "the improvement of blacks in body and mind, in the first instance of their mixture with the whites, has been observed by everyone, and proves that their inferiority is not the effect merely of their condition of life."[4]

But Jefferson opposed further experiments in miscegenation and was sure that his countrymen would erect rigid barriers against intermixture if the slaves were ever emancipated. He proposed the deportation and colonization abroad of any freed Blacks, insisting that to let them remain would imbed an unassimilable mass of people in the nation's heart, about whose fate the "superior" governing race would become embroiled in bitter controversy and perhaps warfare. Black insurrection, too, was a specter that haunted Jefferson, and he was convinced that if the slaves were not eventually freed and colonized in Africa, the Caribbean, or the far western reaches of the continent, their continued presence would "produce convulsions, which [would] probably never end but in the extermination of the one race or the other race."[5]

Jefferson may have had only "suspicions" about the *intellectual* inferiority of Blacks, but he had no doubts about their *esthetic* inferiority.[6] The contrast between the black and white head and face helped to create an unbridgeable gulf.

> The first difference which strikes us is that of colour. . . . And is this difference of no importance? Is it not the foundation of a greater or less share of beauty in the two races? Are not the fine mixtures of red and white, the expressions of every passion by greater or less suffusions of colour in the one, preferable to that eternal monotony, which reigns in the countenances, that immoveable veil of black which covers all the emotions, of the other race? Add to these, flowing hair, a more elegant symmetry of form, their own judgment in favour of the whites, declared by their preference of them, as uniformly as is the preference of the Orangotan for the black women over those of his own species.[7]

Nearly thirty years after Jefferson's observations on "blackness" were circulated, a witty, clever, and skeptical reply to the Sage of Monticello was published anonymously. Historians attribute the piece to a fellow planter, George Tucker. The reply was written in the form of a letter from the Virginia planter to a fictitious French friend.

> I hasten to answer your question, whether the blacks here are really inferior to the whites by nature as well as by law. I have examined the passage in Jefferson's Notes, to which you direct me, and can assure you, that as far as I have seen, there is no just excuse for his remarks. I am afraid, indeed, that his opinion is but too popular here, as I have heard several masters ready to justify their severity to these poor wretches, by alleging that they are an inferior race, created only to be slaves. What a horrible doctrine, my dear D——, and what a pity that any gentleman of Mr. J.'s reputation for talents, should lend it the countenance of his name.

Jefferson's critic took special delight in responding to the observations imputing ugliness to black people. His comments, quoted below, on Jefferson's panegyric to Caucasian beauty show that even within the Virginia slaveholding planter class it was possible to assert the relativity of esthetic standards and to question the universality of a color symbolism that equated Black with evil. Thus, he continues:

> As to our author's remarks, indeed, upon the comparative beauty of the two races, I must certainly agree with him in taste, (tho' I own I was a little surprised at his decision after the stories I have heard of him). . . . I am not quite so satisfied, however, as he seems to be about making my own judgment the standard of taste for all the world. Their preference of the whites . . . can hardly be regarded as a concession of the point in our favour. . . . Nor is this supposed preference of theirs by any means universal. . . . In Africa, too, where artificial associations [i.e., slavery] do not influence their natural notions in the same way, the blacks appear to discover no such partiality for the beauty of the whites. On the contrary we are told that, in their rude pictures, they are always sure to paint their angels black and the devil white.[8]

In his letter Tucker referred also to accounts of intelligent travelers to England who reported that "women of the lower order seem to feel no great qualms of taste in associating with wooly-headed husbands."[9] He need not have gone to the Mother Country to find examples of this particular kind of miscegenation. It was frequent enough in Virginia and Maryland, when these colonies were first established, to induce the planters in both states to pass laws severely penalizing free white women who married African slaves, and later making all sexual relations between Blacks and whites illegal.[10] Such laws never inhibited white males of any social level from consorting with the "wooly-headed" women, a custom that persisted long after slavery was abolished in the South. Tucker's reference to stories he had heard about Jefferson concerned the allegation, widely discussed at the time, that Sally Hemings, a slave at Monticello, had borne him five children. Despite doubts expressed by earlier biographers concerned with protecting Jefferson's image, the authenticity of the story is accepted by some recent students of Jefferson's life.[11]

Tucker's remark is relevant to our discussion not only for the hint of this Founding Father's hypocrisy in practicing the miscegenation he loudly denounced, but also because of what it reveals about the contemporary use of the term *black* in referring to Africans and their progeny, pure and mixed. Latin American readers, if Tucker had any, would have considered irrelevant his allusion to Jefferson's inconsistency in deriding Blacks esthetically but having this slave woman as a mistress. Sally was very light in color and would not have been considered "black" by Latin American standards. That Tucker referred to these stories at all in discussing Jefferson's attitude toward "blackness" indicates that the North American custom of calling a person "black" when believed to have any "ascertainable trace" of Negro ancestry was already in existence. Some of the sources refer to Sally Hemings as "Black Sal," although contemporary gossips usually called the high-spirited quadroon "Dashing Sally."

Extending the term *black* to include Afro-Americans with "only a small amount of 'Negro blood'," as Tucker did by inference in the case of Sally Hemings, is a peculiarly North American practice. In Latin American countries, words that mean "Black" or "Negro" usually are confined to the so-called "extreme" or "pronounced" Negroid physical type, what some anthropologists call the "True Negro." This composite consists of several traits of the head and face: very dark skin-color, thick and everted lips, flat nose, frizzled ("kinky") hair, and projection of the lower face, technically known as alveolar prognathism. The tendency to characterize this configuration of traits as "ugly" and even "repulsive" is still prevalent throughout the Americas, as it was in Thomas Jefferson's day. Even many of the descendants of the African slaves have had a tendency to accept the white group's designation of this combination of physical features as "ugly," and to prefer a less Negroid physiognomy for themselves, their spouses, and their progeny. There was no effective challenge to such self-demeaning attitudes toward the Negro body image until the Afro-American youth of the 1960s flung forth a defensively defiant slogan—"Black is Beautiful"—and began wearing their hair "natural" and rejecting the use of skin-lightening preparations. (Marcus Garvey's Universal Negro Improvement Association had raised the issue some forty years previously, but without lasting effect.)[12]

It is important to note that it is "Negroidness," not dark skin-color alone, that has inspired esthetic derogation; very dark-skinned individuals with so-called "fine" or "delicate" features are sometimes defined as "*very* beautiful." In defining a "True Negro" type, some anthropologists have added refinements that Caucasians find unattractive, such as thin "shanks" of lower limbs and very narrow pelvis, or the opposite—steatopygy—in women. Insofar as their writings are popularized, they focus attention on anatomical differences that most laymen did not know existed, and they often raise disquieting questions about their significance. Occasionally, too, a physical anthropologist will smuggle in his personal esthetic biases. For instance, one well-known American anthropologist, the late Carleton

Coon, in an otherwise scholarly and relatively objective book, includes an idiosyncratic judgment of this type. In discussing an East African ethnic group, he praises the women for their beauty but does so with offensive insensitivity for the feelings of black professors and students who might use the book. He writes of the Somali people that they are characterized by "a degree of beauty seldom seen in Europe, with high conical breasts in the women, totally unlike *the pendulous negroid udders* so common among Gallas and Amharas [italics added]."[13] For an anthropologist to imply that hanging breasts constitute a racial trait distinguishing "Negroes" is unprofessional, to say the least. Furthermore, the author insists that Somalis are not "Negroes," although he notes that they carry some Negro genes and are often dark brown in skin-color. There is also a widespread related tendency to refer to some Asian and Oceanic peoples as "handsome," even though their skins are dark brown. In these cases straight hair and so-called refined features, not skin-color, are decisive in making the esthetic judgment.

Jefferson and Tucker expressed their esthetic preference for the Caucasian physical type—skin-color as well as hair type and other features—during a period when there were few literate black people outside the Islamic Arabic-speaking world. Carleton Coon wrote at a time when there were millions of potential black readers and probably hundreds of actual users of his book in colleges and universities. Although negative attitudes toward "Negroidness" still may be widespread in the United States today, they have to a great extent been repressed into the unconscious or remain unstated for reasons of political prudence or courtesy. In any event, few people would insult their Afro-American fellow citizens by publicly expressing a distaste, if they felt it, for "pronounced Negro features." Such sensitivity does not prevail in most of Latin America and the Middle East, or in Europe, for that matter. Derogatory jokes, cartoons, nicknames, epithets, patronizing endearments, and stereotyped roles on the stage and in music halls are prevalent there but would evoke protests from groups monitoring civil rights in the United States. Their disappearance here reflects some profound changes in American life.

A glance at magazine and newspaper display advertising, at athletic heroes and models, television performers and politicians, would suggest that the contemporary American public does not consider all persons with pronounced Negro facial traits to be unattractive. In fact, they never have; but now, for the first time, there is an open display of willingness to concede attractiveness in some cases. Afro-Americans have always been aware that often the same people who used the stereotype for selfish ends in one situation applied an esthetic norm in their personal relations with black people that distinguished between beautiful and ugly, attractive and unattractive, *within* the same "extreme Negro type" they demeaned.

It is significant that Tucker, in responding to Jefferson's comments about Blacks, made one commonsense judgment that has become the norm for most Americans: "*After all, whether the blacks are uglier or handsomer than the whites can prove nothing as to the inferiority of the endowments of mind* [italics added]."[14] This point of view has come to prevail, even though throughout the latter part of the nineteenth century and the first third of the twentieth century linkage between the esthetic devaluation of Negroes and the idea of intellectual inferiority was reinforced by the pseudosciences of phrenology and anthropometry. High-vaulted foreheads and perpendicular profiles became signs of high intelligence in the popular mind. The fight against Hitlerism between 1933 and 1945 discredited both of these props for a racism that itself became discredited.

Benjamin Franklin of Pennsylvania, a contemporary of Jefferson and Tucker, thought that Negroes were "not deficient in natural understanding." One of his reasons for opposing the slave trade, however, was motivated by a mild form of color prejudice fed by esthetic biases. On one occasion he wrote: "Why increase the sons of Africa by planting them in America where we have so fair an Opportunity, by excluding all Blacks and Tawneys, of increasing the lovely white and Red? But perhaps I am partial to the complexion of my Country for such kind of Partiality is natural to mankind."[15] His objection to "tawneys" extended to some Europeans, for he was disturbed by the fact that the Germans "are generally of what we call a swarthy Complexion." He remarked in despair that "the Number of white People in the world is proportionately very small." Franklin's sensitivity to skin-color was part of his own ancestral social tradition, and he was convinced that the English "make the principal Body of White People on the Face of the Earth." The English of his day and the North American colonists shared a type of prejudice against dark skin-color that included some Europeans, but it was focused most strongly on Negroes, whose bodies were important objects in their mercantile trade and whose labor was essential to the prosperity of their colonies. Some of the same European neighbors whom they considered their inferiors had also exhibited color prejudice against Negroes for centuries, but it was predominantly an esthetic judgment and did not result in social systems that consigned all Negroes to a special caste or to the lowest rungs of a class system, and did not equate "blackness" with slave status. The contrast between this pre–sixteenth-century type of Mediterranean and Middle Eastern color prejudice and that of societies permeated with racism, such as those in the Americas came to be, is as striking as it is significant. Yet some observers would call any manifestations of color prejudice "racism."

VARIETIES OF RACISM

Historian Philip Curtin, in discussing esthetic prejudices and some forms of ethnocentrism, insists that "any of these views may be labelled 'racism' of some variety but they need to be kept separate from the full-blown pseudo-scientific racism which dominated so much of European thought between the 1840's and the 1940's."[16] The term *racism*, until extended in recent years to include cultural chauvinism, referred to a form of racial prejudice that was justified by the dogma that some groups of people inherit characteristics—intellectual and temperamental—that make them inferior to others. A belief in biological determinism is at the root of all such racist thinking. Ideology used to justify systems that institutionalize domination of one racial group over another is referred to by many scholars as "*racist* doctrine," and some speak of "ideological racism" as distinct from more diffuse expressions of racial prejudices.

That American slavery generated racism is undeniable. Thomas Jefferson and his social stratum lived a way of life based upon *racial slavery*, a form of bondage that differed profoundly from systems of slavery prevalent in the Old World. In the new system the slave owner was expected to differ in physical type from the enslaved. The existence of a few exceptional cases of slaveholders who were allowed to rise from the "inferior black race" was considered an anomaly, and no whites could ever "fall" into a state of slavery. The system was justified by the deeply felt, and sometimes theologically sanctioned, belief that black people were born to serve white people. Benjamin Franklin's racial prejudices were typical of the North, where ideological racism was unnecessary since slavery was not an integral part of the socioeconomic system.

Anthropologist Ashley Montagu, commenting on the relatively recent emergence of ideological racism in human history, notes that it was not until the latter part of the eighteenth century that "the alleged inborn differences between peoples were erected into the doctrine of racism, . . . a melange of rationalizations calculated to prove that the Negro was created with articulate speech and hands so that he might be of service to his master the white man."[17] It was not until after the middle of the nineteenth century, however, that a full-blown, systematic racist ideology with "scientific" support took shape.

The concept of a hierarchy of ability based upon biological inheritance is at the root of the theory of ideological racism. It was used during the nineteenth century to interpret European national rivalries and class antagonism, as well as to defend the enslavement of Africans. It was integrated into the Darwinian concepts of "struggle for survival" and "survival of the fittest." So, in addition to races as anthropologists or laymen perceived them, ethnic groups (and even social classes) that could not be recognized by color and physiognomy were thought of as having a "racial" inheritance and were graded according to their presumed level of inborn intelligence and peculiarities of temperament. They were even called "races." In Europe, anthropologists placed "Nordics" at the top, "Alpines" in the middle, and "Mediterraneans" at the bottom in a racial hierarchy that depended mainly upon cranial measurements for distinguishing the groups, although blondness, or lack of it, was a criterion too. When this type of racial thinking—characteristic of some anthropologists and speculative historians—was applied globally, all Europeans were at the top, a superior group of Caucasoid whites with variations among themselves but superior to all "colored" peoples. Linguists, historians, and philosophers elaborated a theory that placed the hypothetical "Aryans" at the top of the list of Caucasian culture bearers.

The most widely read disseminators of these views placed Anglo-Saxon or Teutonic elites at the pinnacle—designating them the "Aryans" who served as the "guardians of civilization," protecting it not only for themselves but also for the benefit of "the lesser breeds without the law, half savage and half child," as Rudyard Kipling called them. Since most of these "lesser breeds" were colored people living in Africa, Asia, and Oceania, as well as Indians and recently freed black slaves in the Americas, the "civilizing mission" was called "The White Man's Burden." *Color prejudice thus became fused with beliefs in biological determinism to produce White Racism.*

The specific referent used to differentiate enslaved Africans and their descendants from their masters in the Americas was the dark color of their skin. Thus, the kind of racism associated with the systems of slavery prevailing throughout the Americas was one example of *White* Racism. Slavery had existed for millennia before 1492, when European settlement began in the New World. It had existed in various places since remote antiquity without the support of either color prejudice or racist theories. Blacks and whites frequently enslaved their own kind, as well as one another. Yet, until the transatlantic slave trade in black bodies began near the end of the fifteenth century, *racial slavery* did not exist, even though prejudice against the Negro phenotype can be documented as far back as the first century of the Christian Era. Racism, as we define it, came even later. But it is important to remember that *racism can exist without the reinforcement of color prejudice, just as color prejudice can exist apart from racism (and does within many black communities)*.

Once racism did appear in history, it was not always in the form of White Racism (that is, racism directed at colored people). The popularizers of racist theory, such as Count de Gobineau and Houston Stewart Chamberlain, graded all Europeans into the Aryan-Alpine-Mediterranean hierarchy. Jews and Gypsies were relegated to pariah status.[18] Even the system of ranking white people was suffused with color prejudice, for the darkness of southern Europeans as compared with northern Europeans symbolized inferiority, and suspected infusions of Negro blood in the past were sometimes inferred. Lothrop Stoddard, the American popularizer of de Gobineau's ideas, in *Racial Realities in Europe*, attributes cultural decline to what German Nazi theorists later called the "negrification" of parts of Europe. Stoddard wrote:

> To conquer and hold Portugal's vast colonial empire required great fleets and armies which took the very cream of the Portuguese stock. At the beginning of their heroic period the Portuguese were an almost purely Mediterranean stock, energetic, intelligent and with marked literary and artistic qualities. . . . And then, in a trifle over a hundred years, it was all over! . . . The drain on the Portuguese stock had been frightful and the resulting racial impoverishment was therefore even more lamentable. . . . Furthermore, upon this racially impoverished people fell a fresh misfortune—the incoming of inferior alien blood. The half-deserted countryside fell into the hands of great landowners who imported gangs of negro slaves drawn from Portugal's African colonies. This was particularly true of Southern Portugal, where a semitropical climate and a fertile soil made negro slavery highly profitable. *In time the population of Southern Portugal became distinctly tinged with negro blood, which produced a depressing and degrading effect upon the national character* [italics added].[19]

This kind of racist thinking reached its apogee under Hitler's National Socialism, culminating in German justifications for World War

II and the Holocaust. As one American political scientist summarized the Nazi ''race myth'' in 1935:

> The new Germany envisages world history as a conflict between races. The white or ''Aryan'' race is the source of all culture, the Negro is an inferior breed, and the Jew, as another representative of *Untermenschentum* or subhumanity, is the source of all corruption. The Germans represent the highest point of Aryan development.[20]

In 1933 a Nazi periodical carried the following recommendations for Nazi youth:

> Every Aryan hero should marry only a blonde Aryan woman with blue, wide-open eyes, a long oval face, a pink and white skin, a narrow nose, a small mouth and under all circumstances virginal. A blond, blue-eyed man must marry no brunette, no Mediterranean-type woman with short legs, black hair, hooked nose, full lips, a large mouth, and an inclination to plumpness. A blond, blue-eyed Aryan hero must marry no Negroid type of woman with the well-known Negro head and thinnish body.[21]

Racist ideology usually involves an esthetic appraisal of physical features, a mythology about traits of mind and personality correlated with physical features, and an almost mystical belief in the power of ''blood'' to elevate or to taint.

WHITE RACISM AND PSEUDOSCIENCE

The Unique Onus of ''Negroidness''

Racist thinking has victimized various European and Asiatic groups, and White Racism has functioned in the oppression of Asians as well as Africans. But since the sixteenth century black people everywhere have been subjected to the most sustained and severe racist assaults upon their bodies and psyches. The reasons for the extreme animus against ''blackness'' require an explanation separate from that which accounts for White Racism in general. The epoch of constant, relentless derogation of Africans and peoples of African descent is drawing to a close because of forces convergent since World War II, especially the emergence of a group of independent African nations. But in attacking the color prejudice that remains as a legacy of slavery and colonial imperialism, consideration must be given to the way in which Blacks became the central target of White Racism. The crucial factor, of course, was the traffic in black bodies, which flourished from the sixteenth century through part of the nineteenth century, and the enslavement of black people throughout the Americas. With the end of slavery, colonial imperialism on the continent of Africa shifted the scene of exploitation of African laborers to their home soil and reinforced antiblack ideologies that had emerged during the slavery period.

However, long before racist ideologies were systematized to defend the interests of those who profited from slavery and colonial imperialism, black people were being stereotyped. As mentioned above, derogatory appraisals of "Negroidness" existed in different parts of the world prior to the sixteenth century and were used in discrimination against and coercion of Blacks. By the mid-eighteenth century, intellectuals in Europe and the Americas were categorizing the Negro as an inferior creature in "The Great Chain of Being."[22] This philosophical concept of a universe with God at the apex and everything else in its place below, though not originally intended to function ideologically, was eventually used for justifying economic and political interests.

Racist thinking was also generated unwittingly by the activities of people who were interested in science for its own sake, especially the taxonomic aspects of it. They developed various kinds of hierarchical schemes that placed Africans "close to the ape."[23] At first this practice was based upon the obvious resemblance of certain species of anthropoids to all human beings in facial features. Winthrop Jordan, in a brilliant discussion entitled "Negroes, Apes and Beasts" in his book *White Over Black*, points out the unconscious anxieties that arise from this physical similarity in a culture with a Puritan bias. He felt that Negroes, especially, suffered from unconscious white negative emotions because "it is apparent, however unpalatable the apparency may be, that certain superficial characteristics of the West African Negro sustain (and perhaps helped initiate) the popular connection with the ape." Even Africans, in legends and folklore, speak of these resemblances, although it should be noted that some English writers have also thought they recognized a pronounced simian look in lower-class Irish faces! Darwinism, in its vulgarized forms, accentuated the idea that Negroes were *"closest* to the ape,"* and this implied inferiority as well as whatever derogatory esthetic appraisals Europeans might make.

Many of the early taxonomists should not be blamed for the use to which the defenders of slavery put their attempts at scientific classification, which in themselves did not imply racial inferiority. Others, however, were outright apologists for slavery and deliberately defamed and caricatured the Africans. Grist for the mills of intellectual speculation was supplied by taxonomists who sometimes accorded desirable attributes to Negroes, although usually in a patronizing manner. Negroes were sometimes said to have a gift for music, to be meek, gentle, forgiving, and long-suffering. Black people sometimes accept these appraisals of their "distinctive" nature.[24]

The Flourishing of Pseudoscientific Racism

Racist ideology burgeoned during the late nineteenth century when ethnocentric evaluations made by Europeans were merged with theories of biological determinism and anthropometry. Ethnic groups, nations, and tribes about whom judgments of inborn superiority and inferiority were made were now referred to colloquially as "races." Some anthropologists tried without success to restrict the term *race* to groups of human beings characterized by common anthropometric measurements of the cranium and the body and with certain combinations of hair type, skin-color, and eye coloring. However, journalists and politicians insisted upon applying the word *race* to nationalities, referring for instance, to the "British race" or the "French race," neither of which had enough anatomical homogeneity to meet anthropological criteria. The wide variation led to myths about some pure ancestral type that had once existed but had been diluted and sometimes "polluted."

There was a widespread tendency, too, to regard as "races" some ethnic groups that could not be defined by common anatomical traits, the Jewish people being the best-known example. Here the principle was to stress a presumed common heredity that resulted in distinctive behavioral traits and modes of thought and feeling, which were manifested despite the wide range of physical types in the group. Thus, among Jews, the Ashkenazim type from Eastern Europe, the Sephardic type from the Mediterranean, and the Falashas, or Black Jews, from Africa were all considered part of "the Jewish race." During the 1930s, when Hitler's Institute of Racial Biology set out to define Jews as those with at least one Jewish grandparent, it became evident that thousands of these individuals looked like any other Germans. Jews were made identifiable only by being compelled to wear yellow armbands and to use only Jewish names.

The term "race" was also applied to highly variable groups like the Afro-Americans and the Coloreds of South Africa, both products of known types of miscegenation. Some contemporary sociologists use the term *social race* to refer to any kind of group defined as a race in law or by custom that would not have enough anatomical homogeneity to be defined as a race by anthropometrists. On the whole, however, some degree of physical likeness is assumed or imagined when the word "race" is used to designate a group.

Widespread interest in the classification of plants, animals, and people concentrated attention upon Africans during the eighteenth century. Linnaeus, the great Swedish taxonomist, in his *Systema Naturae* (1735), grouped mankind into four "races" just below the species level: White, Yellow, Red, and Black, each associated with a major continent. The German naturalist Blumenbach introduced the concept of three major races: Caucasian, Mongolian, and Ethiopian. The names represented those geographical areas providing what Blumenbach considered the most esthetically pleasing examples of the races.[25] (It is significant that this principle was eventually abandoned when *Negro* replaced *Ethiopian*, a color designation superseding a geographical one. All of the pleasant associations with which Christendom had invested the highly romanticized Biblical kingdom of Ethiopia were lost when this change was made.)[26] The earliest classifications did not group the races into a hierarchy in which some were considered inferior to others, but this evenhanded treatment did not survive as taxonomy developed.

The American historian Philip Curtin is convinced that the principle of ranking groups used by the eighteenth-century taxonomists was motivated by an unstated ethnocentric assumption. *"All of them began by putting the European variety at the top of the scale. This was natural enough, if only an unthinking reflection of cultural chauvinism* [italics added]." Since these people were white, whiteness took on special characteristics and colored people were classed as inferior. How, then, to rank the others? *"One solution was to concentrate on skin color. If whiteness of skin was the mark of the highest race, than darker races would be inferior in the increasing order of their darkness* [italics added]."[27]

An integral part of racist thought among those who stressed anatomy as a social marker was the belief that external traits of physiognomy reflected inner states of mental ability and personality orientation. There was a deep stratum of popular belief that fostered the easy adoption of what was presented as "scientific" physical anthropology during the early nineteenth century. It was generally believed, for instance, that redheaded people were passionate and fiery, that "coarse" features indicated dull minds, and that "refined" features indicated sharp minds. Negro features were considered *very* coarse. Anthropologists, in classifying the people of Europe, placed a great deal of emphasis upon a single cranial statistic—the cephalic index—which expresses the relation between the length and breadth of the head. What the cephalic index was to the anthropologists, phrenology was to nineteenth-century laymen; thus it was easy to popularize ideas that spoke of dolichocephalic (long-headed) whites as superior to those who were brachycephalic (broad-headed).[28]

Anthropometrists gave a spurious aura of "scientific" authenticity to the process of defining races and assigning racial traits. *During the last decade of the eighteenth century, Peter Campier invented "the facial angle" for calculating the skull's degree of prognathism. This was a so-called diagnostic trait for determining whether a fossil skull or the cranium of a living person was "Negro." A "typical Negro" was supposed to have pronounced prognathism, which, according to Campier, signified the lowest variety of human being.* The French biologist Cuvier became the high priest of the anthropometrists during the early 1800s, and measurements made on the human body were vested with a mystique far out of proportion to their scientific worth.

In his sixteen-volume work entitled *The Animal Kingdom*, published between 1827 and 1835, Cuvier expressed certain unscientific conclusions along with his esthetic preferences. Thus, he wrote:

> The negro [sic] race is confined to the South of Mount Atlas. Its characters are black complexion, wooly hair, compressed cranium, and flattish nose. In the prominence of the lower part of the face [prognathism], the thickness of the lips, it manifestly approaches to the monkey tribe. The hordes of which this variety is composed have always remained in a state of complete barbarism.

He contrasted the Blacks to the Europeans:

> The Caucasian [race], to which we ourselves belong, is chiefly distinguished by the beautiful form of the head, which approximates to a perfect oval. It is also remarkable for variations in the shade of the complexion, and colour of the hair. From this variety have sprung the most civilized nations, and such as have most generally exercised dominion over the rest of mankind.[29]

Having sung the praises of "The Master Race," Cuvier proceeded to give grudging credit to the "Mongolian variety" for having formed "mighty empires," but noted that "its civilization has long appeared stationary." Curtin notes that only Blumenbach among the biological writers made a serious effort to correct the dominant tendencies of the science of physical anthropology. In some of his later writings,

Blumenbach not only moderated his own earlier racial chauvinism but tried to make a reasoned case for Negro equality.[30]

In his early works, however, Blumenbach had contributed to the derogatory stereotype of "*The* Negro" as ugly and repulsive.[31] He wrote that Caucasians had "in general the kind of appearance which *according to our opinion of symmetry* we consider most handsome and becoming [italics added]." Like Tucker, he recognized the relativity of esthetic evaluations. Although Blumenbach had selected the word *Ethiopian* (which had favorable connotations) to represent Africans, his description of the type was unflattering:

> *Colour black . . . forehead knotty, uneven, malar bones protruding outward; eyes very prominent; nose thick; mixed up as it were with the wide jaws; alveolar edge narrow, elongated in front; upper primaries obliquely prominent; lips very puffy, chin retreating; many are bandy legged* [italics added].[32]

He later changed the name to "Negro" to fit his unflattering description. Science now had begun to provide "authoritative" details to reinforce an emerging popular caricature of "*The* Negro."

This derogatory stereotype developed during the eighteenth century within a narrow circle of British and continental intellectuals, made up of clergymen, physicians, professors, and philosophers, who lived on salaries from the church or the university or from the largesse of patrons. The group also included a few people whose wealth permitted them to pursue natural history as an unpaid profession or hobby. The physical anthropologists among them contributed measurements made on skeletons and occasional living humans, but before the nineteenth century they, like the other naturalists, had rarely seen an African in their own countries and never in Africa. For details about the distribution of physical types and their customs, all were dependent upon accounts brought out of sub-Saharan Africa by explorers, sailors and soldiers, merchants, and missionaries since the time of classical Greece.

Propagation of the Negro Stereotype

Concurrent with the anthropometrists' and intellectuals' "scientific" abstraction, a popular image of "*The* Negro" was elaborated by journalists, dramatists and choreographers, racist orators, cartoonists, book illustrators, and in the theater and cinema.[33] Most of the black people whom white people actually knew had to be continuously explained as exceptions to the stereotypes. Yet this stereotyped image of "*The* Negro" shaped the basic attitudes of fear and contempt directed at Africans and peoples of African descent when they were considered in the abstract or collectively.[34] These stereotypes also became cues for treatment of individual black persons. A caricature of the Negro physique, which distorted reality and overgeneralized certain traits found at one extreme within a very diversified African population, was elaborated. The caricature was then invested with what were assumed to be inherited mental and temperamental qualities.

The stereotype was transmitted to the British and American masses by the popular press, the pulpit, the lecture platform, and the stage. The role of the blackface minstrel show is a case in point. Those in Africa and the Americas who were in continuous contract with black people may sometimes have used the stereotype for propaganda ends, but black individuals were at least recognized in their full range of personality types, daily behaviors, and roles. A wide variety of features and facial expressions was apparent among black people when they were treated as persons, not as abstractions. However, once the stereotype was rooted in the culture, people had an initial tendency to react to their preconceived ideas of what a black person was—or even looked like—rather than to the person in the flesh. Nevertheless, there was nothing about the tendency that absolutely determined the act. Other factors could offset the effect of the stereotype on actual face-to-face behavior.

West Indian planters, anxious to justify the enslavement of Blacks when under attack from humanitarians and religious sectarians in England, used the stereotype continuously, even when their own behavior belied any serious acceptance of it as a guide to conduct. For instance, Edward Long's *History of Jamaica* (1774) painted an extremely unflattering picture of Africans, and Philip Curtin states that Long was "expressing the common prejudice of the West Indies" when he wrote that Africans were a "brutish, ignorant, idle, crafty, treacherous, bloody, thievish, mistrustful, and superstitious people" with "a covering of wool, like the bestial fleece, instead of hair." According to Long, Blacks were inferior in "faculties of mind" and had a "bestial and fetid smell."[35] Such stereotypes did not inhibit extensive miscegenation or prevent white Jamaicans from becoming dependent upon the food grown and sold by enterprising slaves in their spare time. Derogatory images of this type were not deliberately fostered after the abolition of slavery (between 1834 and 1838) until the churches began to emphasize Christian missionary work in Africa during the latter part of the nineteenth century. Then, as a part of the powerful international missionary movement, West Indian preachers, as well as those in England and the United States, emphasized the "savagery" of the heathen in order to mobilize financial and moral support for their efforts to save souls and to civilize Africa.[36] They added to Long's list of undesirable attributes the idea that cannibalism and human sacrifice were ingrained Negro habits.

It is one of the ironies of the eighteenth and nineteenth centuries that a large proportion of the "friends of the Negro" who fought to abolish both slavery and the slave trade believed in the intellectual inferiority and esthetic repulsiveness of the people whose cause they espoused. Abolitionist Abbé Raynal, who inspired the great black Haitian liberator Toussaint L'Ouverture, wrote that "negro blood is perhaps mingled in all the ferments which transform, corrupt and destroy our people." Voltaire wrote that the whites were "superior to these Negroes, as the Negroes are to the apes, as the apes to the oysters."[37] Thomas Jefferson was thus not alone in his belief that Negroes had the right to be free but did not have the intellectual potential of other races. Until his experiences with black abolitionists and black soldiers changed his mind during the Civil War, Abraham Lincoln's attitudes were close to those of Jefferson, including the belief that once the slaves were freed they should be deported from the United States.[38]

THE CHANGING FUNCTIONS OF RACISM AND COLOR PREJUDICE

Ideology and Institutional Change

The coincidence of humanitarian and religious reform movements with a decline in the profitability of slavery in the Americas led to the abolition of the transatlantic slave trade and slavery. This occurred in British territories between 1834 and 1838, and earlier in much of Latin America. After a four-year Civil War in the United States, the contradiction between the sentiments expressed in the Declaration of Independence and actual practice was eliminated with the emancipation of the slaves in 1865. Brazil and Cuba, in the 1880s, were the last countries to give the quietus to *racial slavery* in the Western Hemisphere.

However, neither color prejudice nor racism disappeared with the end of slavery. In the United States, white workers found both to be useful tools in their attempts to restrict the competition of the ex-slaves who had become free workers, and employers used both race prejudice and racism in a policy of divide-and-rule toward the American working class. Racial hostility that might have slowly disappeared was now revitalized because of functional utility. Economic interests, racism, and color prejudice reinforced each other. The type of extreme vilification of black people represented by the Jamaican planter Edward Long was very rare in the United States until after slavery was abolished. Then competition between Blacks and poor whites elicited a kind of virulent stereotyping that the planter class had never found necessary in defending its interests in the South of the United States. While black people remained the primary target of White Racism in the United States, Orientals and Latin Americans were victimized too, and white immigrant workers became the objects of racism not reinforced by color. Antiracist countercurrents existed but had little influence. Then a halt in the escalation of racism occurred in the 1930s when the worldwide fight against Hitlerism began and institutional antiracist action emerged.[39]

Overt ideological racism has declined impressively everywhere since World War II except in the Republic of South Africa, and it is now in slow retreat there. More subtle forms of institutional racism have replaced ideological racism and, through policies of "tokenism" and "integration," have made color prejudice a less important force in North America than it was before the Civil Rights Revolution in the South and the Black Power upsurge throughout the country.

Twentieth-Century Forms of Racism and Color Prejudice

As slavery was disappearing in the Western Hemisphere, the partition of Africa was beginning. By the time of the outbreak of World War I, all of Africa except Ethiopia and Liberia had been divided into colonies or protectorates of some European power (along with one Afro-European condominium). Both color prejudice and racism were fused in these structures of domination to constitute a system of White Racism. At the ideological level, the so-called Hamitic Hypothesis emerged to explain that all advanced cultural development in Africa had derived from lighter-skinned, more Caucasoid, less Negroid people.[40] In French, Portuguese, and Belgian colonies in Africa, the favoring of mulatto progeny born out of wedlock to the consorts of administrators and settlers generated social strata in which light skin-color became an index of high status. Although World War II began a reversal of many of the processes that have sustained White Racism, that phenomenon has not been fully eliminated. South Africa is the last bastion of White Supremacy on the continent. Furthermore, color prejudice in favor of whiteness has persisted in some social contexts within new African nations, despite the fact that, in the political sphere, Africanization has often tipped the scales in the other direction.

Despite the disappearance of colonial imperialism in the Caribbean during the 1960s, color prejudice against blackness has remained strong in some areas and insidiously active in others. This is also true in many parts of Latin America. In some places it is functional only in the private sphere when people are choosing intimate associates and marriage partners. But in other areas there is widespread color discrimination in employment and political preferment.[41] There is reason to believe that in public situations Negroid physiognomy or even mere darkness of complexion can seriously limit individual opportunity throughout Latin America and much of the Muslim world. There is considerable disagreement as to the degree of persistence of color prejudice, especially against Negroid people, in areas where socialist revolutions have taken place and where official opposition to all forms of color prejudice as well as discrimination exists.[42]

BLACK PERSPECTIVES ON RACISM

Defining Racism

What came to be called "vindicating the Negro" emerged to counteract White Racism. It involved correcting stereotypes, setting the record straight, and substituting a more accurate picture of reality. This process, begun by literate white antislavery leaders and unlettered Afro-American preachers using Biblical arguments, was assumed as a duty by literate black ministers during the late eighteenth century. They developed a prepolitical ideology called "Ethiopianism." By the end of the nineteenth century, black historians had developed a Pan-African perspective as an important part of the "vindication movement," and the names of Edward Wilmot Blyden and W.E.B. Du Bois are well known in this regard.[43]

The first generation of black intellectuals who became concerned with the historical and psychological roots of racism utilized the concepts available to social scientists of their time.[44] By the end of World War I, the "vindicationist" focus was on the problem of changing the stereotypes and the conventional social attitudes clustered around them, of trying to alter those "overgeneralized prejudgments" that social psychologist Gordon W. Allport defines as always present in "racial prejudice." He, like others of his profession, stresses the point that "prejudice is not inborn but acquired," and that "throughout childhood and youth there are many opportunities for irreversible and unfavorable belief systems to become set." Prejudices operating as "inflexible, rigid and erroneous generalizations about groups of people" may express themselves in behavior that denies members of some stereotyped group full access to economic, political, and social opportunities. If the group is defined as a "race," such prejudice can give rise to *racial* discrimination. Although racial *discrimination* "ultimately rests on *prejudice*," the two processes are not identical. Individuals may harbor prejudices without expressing them if the sociocultural situation provides no reward for doing so or actually provides punishments for those who discriminate against another race.[45]

During the 1950s and 1960s Afro-American scholars became more concerned with refining the concept of racism, than with discussing either prejudice or discrimination, because racism is a concept that places emphasis upon underlying cognitive orientations that find expression in attitudes and behavior and affect systems of control. As used throughout the 1930s and 1940s, when Blacks became familiar with the term, *racism* was used almost exclusively to mean a systematic theory of innate and inherited inferiority or superiority of human beings. It was later used to emphasize differential power relationships.

Within the past two decades, the term *racism* has acquired many referents other than the system of ideas that grades people invidiously in a hierarchy. In fact, the term has become a useful propaganda stick with which to beat a variety of enemies. However, continued imprecision of definition will make it less and less useful in achieving black liberation goals. That is why black spokesmen have tended to cling to the restricted cluster of meanings subsumed in a definition proposed by Stokely Carmichael and Charles V. Hamilton in *Black Power* (1967): "*the predication of decisions and policies on considerations of race for purposes of subordinating a racial group* [italics added]."[46] They place emphasis upon the *actions* of one group as it attempts to dominate and control another, the subordinated group being a *racial* group, rather than upon racism as ideology. A few black scholars and leaders in liberation struggles display an interest, as intellectuals, in the constant refinement of concepts used by white scholars as they discuss the plight of black people, but most prefer to work with social science formulations that help them to clarify goals and to devise techniques for changing the status of black people vis-à-vis white power structures.[47]

Classifying Types of Racism

The Carmichael-Hamilton book drew a distinction between *individual racism* and *institutional racism* that quickly gained wide currency. The term *institutional racism* is now used to describe situations where, although there may not be deliberate intent to act in an unfavorable, discriminatory fashion, the objective result of various actions is reinforcement of subordination and control over a racial group and an inequitable distribution of power and prestige.[48] The term is used even in some cases where discrimination on the basis of race or color within a social system does not require the support of a body of racist theory and may persist in spite of prevailing antiracist ideology. For example, the rules, regulations, and norms for recruitment of personnel into a voluntary association, a bureaucracy, or an educational institution are sometimes set up in such a way that they automatically operate to the disadvantage of some racial group. In such a case, people whom Gordon Allport would classify as "unprejudiced discriminators" often enforce rules that have a racist outcome.[49]

Affirmative action programs are directed at coping with such forms of institutional racism, and this conceptualization has been of great value during a period in U.S. history when it has become unfashionable for whites to admit belief in the inherent inferiority of any racial or ethnic group, when some white people accept the idea that to be racist is to be "sick,"[50] and when the increased economic and political power of nonwhite peoples often makes expressions of overt prejudice counterproductive. In fact, reversal of the antiblack stereotype has actually become advantageous to some business enterprises in a period of consumerism, when display advertising directed at black people as a potential market utilizes attractive black images, and when multinational corporations publicize pictures of their black employees. But racism in more covert forms remains.

A South African Bantu scholar-psychiatrist, Noel Chabani Manganyi, reflecting upon these changes, has called attention to a distinction drawn by Joel Kovel, an American scholar, between *dominative racism* and *metaracism*, and sounded a warning.

> Popular opinion would lead us to believe that the end of the overtly colonial period in certain parts of Africa and elsewhere and the elimination of discriminatory practices against blacks in the Western world marked the end of racism against blacks. . . . The dominative racist thrived in the United States and in parts of Europe and Africa before independence when manifest social-political institutions existed to support racism and racist behavior. With the disappearance of these

structures, the metaracist, sleeker in his ways, made his appearance. . . . A metaracist may very well continue to be afflicted with unconscious racist fantasies that have survived the changes in manifest social organization. He remains a social risk because, in racially extreme situations, he can always be expected to regress into the dominative mold.

Concerned with the psychological dimensions of "white backlash," with what whites perceive as "reverse discrimination" in the United States, and with changes he foresees someday in his native South Africa, Manganyi continued:

> Institutional changes involving political, social and economic systems represent an essential beginning in the process of social change. To eradicate racism in the institutional life of a society it is not sufficient to demystify the unconscious ramifications involved in the fantasy social structure underlying such a system. But in clinical experience, patients in psychotherapy desperately resist the possible loss of their neuroses. On the collective level, the difficulties of working through the fantasy social structure supporting racism raises many practical problems which society prefers to ignore.

Manganyi is among those psychologists who are convinced that this "fantasy social structure" arises from a type of white child rearing that equates blackness with the devalued lower parts of the body (genital-anal). Subordinating black people serves certain psychological needs, related to "the alienation of man in industrial society," that have come from "elevating the mechanism of repression into a virtue in the organization of society."[51]

Some writers, among them Eldridge Cleaver in *Soul on Ice* and Frantz Fanon in *Black Skins, White Masks*, emphasize a view similar to Manganyi's neo-Freudian analysis, but most black intellectuals do not rank this kind of explanation very high. Whether Black Nationalists, pragmatic liberals, or Marxists, they usually share the prevalent social-environmental explanations provided by academic sociology and psychology. An extreme form of Black Nationalism rejects psychoanalytical explanations of White Racism but accepts even more deterministic theories, part mystical, part biological. For instance, the Black Muslims once defined all Whites as "Devils" whose inborn nature it was to oppress colored people. Such views have even penetrated Afro-American intellectual circles. For instance, in 1974, the *Black Scholar* published a debate between the Afro-American poet Madhubuti (once known as Don Lee) and Kalamu Ya Salaam, another Afro-American writer, on the issue of whether the white person is "by nature" antiblack. Madhubuti asserted that Blacks have had to bear the burden of inborn white racist propensities. Kalamu Ya Salaam objected, insisting that "what your color means and/or says about you varies directly from society to society, directly dependent on historical and contemporary conditions. The meaning of skin color, just as skin color itself, is also not static, but rather is relative, is dependent on time, place, and circumstances." This view has been elaborated by a number of black scholars engaged in reconciling Marxism with an ideology of black solidarity, and is taken for granted by most black scholars regardless of their politics.[52]

Racism and Capitalism

Oliver Cromwell Cox, an Afro-Trinidadian sociologist, has suggested that the concept of racism is so time-bound and culture-bound that it has no applicability beyond the past five or six hundred years, and only limited pertinence within that time span. He warns against confusing racism and race prejudice with the more general concept of ethnocentrism. *Cox insists that, unlike color prejudice and slavery, both of which antedated it, racism was uniquely associated with capitalist growth and expansion.* He wrote in 1976:

> Racism, like race prejudice, is a relatively recent human development; it did not always exist. . . . Racism, as we know it in modern times, is not merely verbal recognition of physical differences, ethnocentric comparisons among peoples, early mythological speculations about various known peoples in the design of creation, or invidious remarks by ancient conquerors about the physical and cultural traits of the vanquished. . . . Racism . . . provides Europeans with a moral rationale for their subjugation and exploitation of "inferior peoples."[53]

In an earlier work, Cox had stated his essentially Marxist view in stronger terms. After defining "racial antagonism" as a phenomenon that "had its rise only in modern times," he proceeded to state the hypothesis that

> racial exploitation and race prejudice developed among Europeans with the rise of capitalism and nationalism, and . . . because of the world-wide ramifications of capitalism all racial antagonisms can be traced to the policies and attitudes of the leading capitalist people, the white people of Europe and North America.[54]

Most Marxists would make a more cautious formulation today, stressing the point that while racism as a systematic doctrine and racial prejudice institutionalized in systems of caste, class, and slavery were products of capitalist expansion overseas, this did not apply to "*all* racial antagonisms." Yet Marxist scholarship has not seriously addressed itself to the special problem of the origins and functions of racial prejudice directed against Negroes and blackness (nor has non-Marxian scholarship done so, for that matter).

During the Depression years, as several varieties of Marxist thought became prevalent and popular, some historians and social scientists implied that "blackness" became a symbol of low status and undesirability only with the fifteenth-century expansion of Europe overseas, the subsequent rise of the transatlantic slave trade, and the later colonial imperialism in Africa. Derogation of blackness was seen as one aspect of an ideology elaborated to defend the exploitation of Africans and their descendants as well as to "brainwash" them into accepting their subordinate status. Such traditional Marxist analyses did not draw a clear distinction between color prejudice as a variable distinct from both racism and specific types of social systems such as slavery, caste, or class. Third World Marxists have, however, forced recognition of these distinctions. They stress that Africans and people of African descent have had to bear the heavy burden of being black in addition to the class burden of being slaves, peasants, and proletarians. Their insights have brought greater clarity to Marxist analysis.[55]

Color prejudice targeted against black people is only one form of racial prejudice and discrimination, and one aspect of White Racism. It existed long before the emerging capitalist system shaped the character of modern racism. Because skin-color prejudice is a specialized subset of attitudes and behaviors about race that affect the fate of all black people, it is the primary concern of this work. Our emphasis in this book is upon searching out the way in which skin-color prejudice against black people originated, describing how it became articulated to modern capitalism. Another, forthcoming book, "Africa and the Black Diaspora," explains where and why it persists in the Western Hemisphere in the form of postslavery systems of caste and class in which skin-color remains a significant factor in social stratification and social mobility.

Color prejudice appears in various forms in some of the socialist societies replacing capitalist economies in various parts of the world, although institutionalized racism is absent. In reacting to White Racism, currents of antiwhite feeling have arisen among colored people, and in some areas these have been incorporated into political movements for political independence or for the establishment of more egalitarian societies. Jean-Paul Sartre used the term *antiracist racism* to describe this phenomenon, but some black leaders refuse to accept the designation *racist* for their political use of antiwhite sentiments. This necessary mobilization of the oppressed around the issue of race has a reactionary potential, nevertheless, that must be resisted.[56]

An understanding of the dynamics of prejudice against "Negroidness" can be furthered by comparing early stages of single societies with later stages (diachronic approach), and by comparing different societies existing at the same time (synchronic approach). Both methods are used in the chapters that follow the discussion of race relations theory in chapter 2.

Bibliographic Essay

A widely read paperback by Harvard social psychologist Gordon W. Allport, published in 1954 by Addison-Wesley (Reading, Mass.), is probably the best introduction to the general field indicated by the book's title, *The Nature of Prejudice*. Eighteen years later, a discussion of the subject from a black perspective by James M. Jones, a young Afro-American psychologist on the Harvard faculty, was published as *Prejudice and Racism* (Reading, Mass.: Addison-Wesley, 1972). It is an excellent supplement to the older book, emphasizing institutions and power relations rather than attitudes and stereotypes as crucial in defining racism. The author presents also an informative discussion of the problems involved in refining old concepts and in relating research to social action. Both works contain extensive lists of books and articles that provide valuable leads for readers who wish to pursue the subject in greater depth. No new significant theoretical contributions have been made since these two books were written.

George W. Stocking, Jr., of the University of Chicago has skillfully integrated a mass of interesting and relevant scattered data in the topical chapters that make up *Race, Culture, and Evolution: Essays in the History of Anthropology* (New York: Free Press, 1968). Much of this history documents the development of ideological racism and the countermovement pioneered by the American anthropologist Franz Boas. Robert Froman has written a popular but well-researched small paperback for the Laurel-Leaf Library that introduces the reader to examples of racism that victimized various nonblack groups. The book is entitled *Racism* (New York: Dell, 1972). An erudite scholarly discussion of racism as used by some white groups to discriminate against other whites is provided by Leon Poliakov in *The Aryan Myth* (New York: New American Library, 1971). However, for an analysis of the type of racism most relevant to the theme of this chapter, and for a presentation of a theory to account for its emergence and persistence, see Joel Kovel, *White Racism: A Psychohistory* (New York: Pantheon Books, 1970). Other scholars choose to stress economic and social factors.

One of the first popular publications to provide a history of the emergence of racist thought was anthropologist Ruth Benedict's *Race: Science and Politics*, originally published in 1940 and reissued as a Compass Book paperback with an introduction by Margaret Mead (New York: Viking, 1959, with a fifth printing in 1964). A serious flaw in this otherwise excellent discussion is the author's failure to mention the role of the African slave trade in the development of European racist thinking. A thorough discussion of this facet of the problem is available in paperback in a two-volume University of Wisconsin edition (Madison, 1964) of historian Philip Curtin's *The Image of Africa: British Ideas and Action, 1780–1850*. A Pelican publication, *White Over Black: American Attitudes Toward the Negro, 1550–1812* (Baltimore, 1969), by historian Winthrop Jordan provides detailed documentation of the genesis of racism under conditions of *racial slavery*. A Harper Torchbook publication (New York, 1970) carries the story forward in George M. Fredrickson's *The Black Image in the White Mind: The Debate on Afro-American Character and Destiny, 1817–1914*. A collection of essays by a Marxist historian, Herbert Aptheker, including one entitled "The Mythology of Racism," was published in 1971 and reissued two years later as a paperback volume, *Afro-American History: The Modern Era* (Secaucus, N.J.: Citadel Press). It provides perceptive analyses of the forces that have led to significant changes in the status of black people and the attitudes of whites toward Blacks since World War I.

James Boggs's *Racism and the Class Struggle* (New York: Monthly Review Press, 1964) presents a thought-provoking discussion by an independent Afro-American Marxist. Afro–West Indian historian Eric Williams's *Capitalism and Slavery* (London: A. Deutsch, 1944) develops the thesis that plantation slavery preceded White Racism and was its primary cause. Black Nationalists have challenged this essentially Marxist analysis of anti-Negro prejudice without providing a convincing alternative explanation (see, for example, Haki R. Madhubuti [Don L. Lee], "The Latest Purge," *Black Scholar*, December

[1974]). A valuable overview of the rise of racism as seen from the perspective of another Afro–West Indian scholar can be found in the chapters entitled "Racism and Modern Culture" and "The Philosophy of Racism" in sociologist Oliver Cromwell Cox's book, *Race Relations*, published posthumously by Wayne State University Press (Detroit, 1976). Cox retained a Marxist explanation of the origins of White Racism while questioning doctrinaire Communist and Socialist views about conditions necessary for its eventual disappearance. One brilliant young scholar is writing from what he calls a "revolutionary Christian perspective . . . guided by the cultural outlook of the Afro-American humanist tradition informed by the social theory and political praxis of progressive Marxism." This is Cornel West in *Prophesy Deliverance! An Afro-American Revolutionary Christianity* (Philadelphia: The Westminster Press, 1982). An intellectually sophisticated analysis employing both Marxist and existentialist perspectives to interpret empirical data from many parts of the world, including modern France and the United States, is available in Professor Gilbert Varet's *Racisme et philosophie* (Paris: Editions Denoel, 1973). An important contribution by an Afro-American "mainstream" sociologist, William J. Wilson, is *The Declining Significance of Race* (Chicago: University of Chicago Press, 1977). This book served to widen the circle of discussants examining the relative importance of class and race in black/white relations in the United States. Several works by the crusading anti-Marxist, antiliberal economist Thomas Sowell have added a new dimension to this discussion—erudite Afro-American conservatism. These include: *Ethnic America: A History* (New York: Basic Books, 1981); *Race and Economics* (New York: D. McKay Co., 1975); (ed.) *American Ethnic Groups* (Washington, D.C.: The Urban Institute, 1978); *Black Education: Myths and Tragedies* (New York: D. McKay Co., 1972); and *Essays and Data on American Ethnic Groups* (Washington, D.C.: The Urban Institute, 1978).

An ingenious interpretation using non-Freudian, non-Marxian social psychology to explain the persistence of racism in the United States is put forward by an American university professor, Herbert Stember, in *Sexual Racism: The Emotional Barrier to an Integrated Society* (New York: Harper & Row, 1976). John Dollard, in *Caste and Class in a Southern Town* (New Haven, Conn.: Yale University Press, 1937) supplements his perceptive sociological analysis with Freudian theory to provide a convincing explanation of the persistence of institutionalized racism in a typical Black Belt community. For a more conventional social-psychological approach combining theory with vivid empirical data on Afro-Americans, Japanese, Chinese, Mexican, and Filipino immigrants, see Roger Daniels and Harry H. L. Kitano, *American Racism: Exploration of the Nature of Prejudice* (Englewood Cliffs, N.J.: Prentice-Hall, 1970).

White Racism was one of the consequences of *racial slavery*, as distinct from the kind of slavery where differences in race between master and slave were not crucial. Among many studies dealing with the origin and spread of *racial slavery*, the most scholarly synthesis is David Brion Davis's *The Problem of Slavery in Western Culture* (Ithaca, N.Y.: Cornell University Press, 1966). For a review of a more limited geographical area, see Duncan J. MacLeod's *Slavery, Race and the American Revolution* (London: Cambridge University Press, 1974). An excellent and succinct analysis of the relationship between *racial slavery* and other forms of labor in the Americas is presented, along with exhaustive documentation, in Immanuel Wallerstein's *The Modern World-System: Capitalist Agriculture and the Origins of the European World-Economy in the Sixteenth Century* (New York: Academic Press, 1974), pp. 86–93.

Readers interested in contrasting *racial slavery* with other types of slavery existing concurrently will find copious comparative data from various parts of the Islamic world in the brief but well-documented discussion entitled "Black and White Slaves" in Bernard Lewis's *Race and Color in Islam* (New York: Harper & Row, 1971). For Europe, see Marc Bloch's definitive, scholarly work, *Slavery and Serfdom in the Middle Ages* (Berkeley and Los Angeles: University of California Press, 1975), and chapter 2, "Medieval Slavery in Europe and Colonial Slavery in America," in Charles Verlinden's *The Beginnings of Modern Colonization* (Ithaca, N.Y.: Cornell University Press, 1970).

A thoroughly documented monograph on prefeudal European social systems, with some comparative data from Egypt and the Middle East, is available in William Linn Westermann's *The Slave Systems of Greek and Roman Antiquity* (Philadelphia: American Philosophical Society, 1955). At one point (p. 104), Westermann cites two factors that contributed toward great occupational diversity: "the accidental nature of slave recruitment from any social class" and the lack of "the fundamental race distinction which became a marked characteristic of American negro [*sic*] slavery in the eighteenth and nineteenth centuries." Further comparative data are given in Professor M. I. Finley's clear, succinct analysis of slavery in the Greco-Roman world—*The Ancient Economy* (Berkeley and Los Angeles: University of California Press, 1973)—and in chapter 3, "Masters and

Slaves,'' of the volume Finley edited under the title *Slaves in Classical Antiquity* (London: Cambridge University Press, 1968).

A vast literature exists on slavery, ancient and modern, and the analysis of racism has been carried out with diligence and thoroughness, as has the study of racial prejudice and discrimination in the United States. However, systematic discussion of antiblack prejudice in comparative perspective is very rare. One of few such studies is Pierre van den Berghe's *Race and Racism* (New York: John Wiley, 1967), which compares race relations in Mexico, South Africa, Brazil, and the United States, devoting some attention to the function of Negroid color, hair, and features in the status systems of these countries. George M. Fredrickson offers a brilliant comparative analysis of racism in the Republic of South Africa and the United States of America in *White Supremacy* (New York: Oxford University Press, 1981). Scholarly studies of the role of skin-color in single culture areas and civilizations, although very rare, are essential for any adequate comparative analyses. Those available when this work was begun are Bernard Lewis's *Race and Color in Islam* and Frank R. Snowden, Jr.'s *Blacks in Antiquity: Ethiopians in the Greco-Roman Experience* (Cambridge, Mass.: Harvard University Press, Belknap Press, 1970). Both are written for the general reading public but contain extensive citations to the specialist literature. In 1982, Belknap Press published a completely rewritten version of Snowden's book under the title *Before Color Prejudice*.

A book on the role of skin-color in the Indian subcontinent is yet to be written. However, an Afro-American anthropologist, Allison Davis, drawing upon Indian parallels, made a definitive study of *color-caste* in the United States in collaboration with white colleagues, producing Allison Davis, Burleigh B. Gardner, and Mary R. Gardner, *Deep South: A Social Anthropological Study of Caste and Class* (Chicago: University of Chicago Press, 1941; Phoenix Books [abridged], 1965. Reprint. Los Angeles: UCLA Center for Afro-American Studies, 1987).

2. THEORIES OF COLOR PREJUDICE: A CRITICAL REVIEW

Many centuries before White Racism emerged to justify the enslavement of Africans in the New World, some forms of color prejudice against black people had appeared in various places in the Old World. However, such prejudice did not arise in all situations where black people and those of other races came into contact. And where it was present, it was not institutionalized in systems of *racial slavery* or color-caste, nor was it a crucial factor in determining placement and mobility in class systems.

In order to understand the presence or absence of prejudice and/or discrimination against black people in specific, concrete situations, some familiarity with general race-relations theory is necessary. This chapter presents several theories that have been advanced to explain the origin and persistence of racial prejudice, with special emphasis on the prejudice of Europeans and Americans against Africans and peoples of African descent. Some European criticisms directed at the type of American race-relations theory that stresses situational factors and socioeconomic variables rather than the negative responses of whites to the skin-color and features of black persons are examined. Consideration is given to the influence of European thought on American race-relations theory—Freudian and Marxian ideas over a long span of time, existentialist and structuralist influences in recent years. The recent popularity of assertions that white prejudice against Blacks derives from innate predispositions or from universal childhood experiences is challenged on the grounds of faulty logic as well as lack of empirical validation. Other recent ideological and theoretical formulations advanced by black and white intellectuals in the United States are placed in their social settings. It is suggested that some aspects of American race-relations theory, although not all, may have explanatory value for situations other than those in the United States. Finally, the chapter suggests several specific approaches to research on color prejudice involving black/white relations that could test the validity of some of the generalizations that have been made about color prejudice, as well as fill in gaps in our knowledge through cross-cultural research in both the laboratory and the field.

AMERICAN "SOCIOLOGISTIC OPTIMISM"

Faith in Social Engineering

In 1944 two decades of research and theorizing about black/white relations in the United States culminated in the publication of *An American Dilemma: The Negro Problem and Modern Democracy*. The author was the distinguished Swedish scholar Gunnar Myrdal, who enlisted the assistance of virtually all the major scholars, black and white, who had been studying race relations in the United States since the mid–1930s. The book was widely acclaimed as the definitive explanation of why prejudice and discrimination against black people persisted in the United States, and how change could be "engineered." The only vigorously dissenting voices were among Marxists who objected to the book's emphasis upon noneconomic factors as crucial in the complex of forces that originated and sustained the system of color discrimination in the United States. The basic concept of *An American Dilemma*, the "struggle in the soul of America," struck these Marxists as a variety of philosophic idealism that denied the importance of class struggle.[1] These critics ignored the fact that Myrdal did not claim value conflict as the sole dynamic factor in American race relations; nor, in fact, did Myrdal deny that value conflict was rooted in economic and social conflict. But he did insist that it operated as an independent force.

Gunnar Myrdal utilized the relatively consistent theory of race relations developed by American social scientists between World War I and World War II, a theory that had been tested and refined by various governmental agencies and private agents of change during the Great Depression and World War II.[2] Its fundamental proposition holds that racial prejudice is neither inherited by individuals nor inevitable in group relations, even when pronounced physical differences exist between groups. A closely related axiom assumes that the socioeconomic system is the matrix within which institutionalized prejudice against racial groups develops, and that, since the sixteenth century, the worldwide capitalist-imperialist system has operated to keep people of African descent in the lowest economic, political, and social positions. However, the theory includes also the assumption that substantial changes can take place in race relations without transforming the capitalist system into a socialist system. The conviction was particularly strong that the color-caste subsystem, which existed as part of capitalist society in the United States, could be abolished because, as Gunnar Myrdal phrased it, in the United States "caste may exist but it cannot be recognized." He stated, further-more, that Afro-Americans

> in their fight for equality have their allies in the white man's own con-science. . . . He does not have the moral stamina to make the Negro's subjugation legal and approved by society. . . . *From the point of view of social science this means, among other things, that social engineer-ing will be increasingly demanded* [italics added].[3]

An American Dilemma was designed to aid the "engineers."

American social scientists from this milieu believed that intellec-tuals as well as ordinary people in society held *attitudes* toward black people that had been derived from the culture and that found expres-sion in both positive and negative *behavior* toward Afro-Americans. A negative *prejudice*, it was thought, involved a combination of nega-tive *attitudes* and negative *stereotypes*, or "pictures in the head."[4] It was assumed that individual attitudes and the images that formed stereotypes were products of cultural transmission, and the social scientist viewed them as being continually manipulated by interest groups. Furthermore, it was believed that any possibility of spontane-ous development of attitudes toward individuals of another race was constantly checked and controlled by considerations of status, which are defined by dominant prestige groups as well as by peer groups, reference groups, and role models. However, fads and fashions, cul-tivated through the mass media, are of greater importance than tra-dition in structuring attitudes. Advertisers and opinion makers were thus considered important in attitude formation.

The bureaucratic nature of American society made it possible for important decision makers in businesses, churches, unions, govern-ment agencies, law courts, and the armed forces to manipulate in-stitutional arrangements so as to generate new types of relations between black and white people. This was the so-called "social en-gineering." It became a truism that change should begin by eliminat-ing racial discrimination, not by trying to "preach out" or to "educate out" prejudices.[5] This paradigm for deliberately induced so-cial change was dominant until the mid–1960s, and must be credited with initiating far-reaching institutional changes in race relations (for example, desegregation of the armed forces and public interstate transportation). However, the model did not predict the advent of either the Civil Rights movement or the Black Power movement. In addition, the emergence of "white backlash" and Black Nationalist ideology as possibilities, or probabilities, was never considered as an example of "unintended consequences of purposive social action" meriting serious research.[6]

The "Somatic Norm Image" Critique

The theory of race relations developed by American sociologists in the interwar years to account for phenomena within their own society was still dominant in the 1960s when it was challenged by Dutch sociologist Herman Hoetink. Hoetink's own research on race relations had been carried out in the Netherlands Antilles, and he eventually served as director of the Institute of Caribbean Studies at the University of Puerto Rico. In his book *Caribbean Race Relations: A Study of Two Variants* (1962), Hoetink dubbed as "sociologistic optimism" the product of two decades of research and theorizing in the United States, and he dismissed this school of thought as biased social science expressing an ideological position characteristic of American liberals. After citing the Myrdal study and the works of a number of American students of race relations, Hoetink criticized their explanation of inequalities existing between white and black people in the United States for its use of the same factors employed in explaining inequalities between white immigrant groups. He wrote:

> With this approach, novel at the time, the "problem of race" was reduced to that of the social structure of a society with a heterogeneous population. The nature of the heterogeneity, whether religious, linguistic, cultural or racial, is irrelevant, for the problems are fundamentally identical. The unequal distribution of the different groups on the social ladder is maintained and supported by those on the higher rungs. The separation entailed by this unequal distribution gives rise to myths about the groups, myths which serve to maintain the *status quo. The colour of the skin, and other racial characteristics, are thus reduced to mere symbols of social status* [italics added].[7]

Convinced that these physical characteristics, forming a gestalt, must be more profoundly meaningful than "mere symbols of social status," Professor Hoetink argued that they should be considered as an independent factor in the creation of racial prejudice. Every ethnic group, he contended, has a "somatic norm image," that is, a "complex of physical (somatic) characteristics which are accepted by a group as its norm and ideal." According to Hoetink, skin-color becomes the most salient characteristic in the somatic norm image in New World societies. He noted that "preference for one's own appearance is not an individual psychological phenomenon but has a social component" and is "the yardstick of esthetic evaluation, an ideal of the somatic characteristics of the members of the group." Utilizing symbolic-interactionist theory, Hoetink made the important generalization that awareness of the norm is not *always* present, and "it is only continued social contact between groups with different somatic norm images which results in consciousness of a group's own socially determined somatic norm image."[8] But, given such prolonged contact, the somatic norm image then becomes a primary determinant in the development of negative prejudices and invidious discrimination against people who have a different somatic norm image.

Hoetink argued that so long as somatic norm images differ among groups of people in contact with one another within a single heterogeneous society, ethnocentrism, class consciousness, and differential distributions of power will survive, simply because the people involved "look different." Even when power relations are equalized substantially, physical difference remains the focal point of social tensions. Hoetink maintained that only through "homogenization" by miscegenation, or by the removal of one of the groups from the social system, can racial conflict be eradicated. The "sociologistic optimists" were naive to think otherwise, he insisted, as when they believed that

> if Negroes and whites in the Deep South were distributed evenly on the social and economic ladder—if, in other words, the Negro group were spread over the higher and the whites on the lower rungs in proportion to their numbers, and the socio-economic gap separating white and Negroes were to disappear—the race problem would cease to be a problem.[9]

Hoetink's assessment of the American scholars was summed up in his statement that "such optimism stems from a charming mixture of ardent idealism and excessive faith in the socio-economic foundation of psycho-social group phenomena."[10]

The Bases of "Sociologistic Optimism"

Even if Professor Hoetink was correct in his patronizing charge of naïveté, he was certainly incorrect in his analysis of where the faith of the American social scientists was grounded. It was not in the primacy of "the socioeconomic foundation" but rather in the concept of a continuously changing process of interaction between varied types of social formations and systems of social norms and values. Basic to what Hoetink called the "sociologistic optimism" of the Americans was their insistence that skin-color is only one of the salient attributes that set an individual Afro-American off from his or her fellows, and, therefore, skin-color *could* assume less importance than other attributes in some situations. The type of situation and the context were deemed all-important in determining the conditions under which other solidarities would crosscut color solidarity. The "sociologistic optimists" recognized, however, that under certain conditions, manipulators of crowds and mobs could focus hostility upon black people with such intensity that it resulted in race riots and lynchings. But such situations always returned to "normal," with interracial cooperation restored.

American social scientists had had firsthand experience with white and black people sometimes living together in the same neighborhoods, sometimes belonging to the same trade unions, clubs, and athletic teams, and sometimes interacting as members of the same occupational and professional groups—despite racism in the North and caste in the South. These social scientists were interested in answering the questions, "If sometimes, why not all the time?" and, "What are the specific conditions under which black people and white people cooperate or, alternatively, become involved in conflict?" They had never believed that preferred somatic norm images or even racial prejudice would disappear; to them, these were not the "problems." Rather, racial *discrimination* leading to racial conflict, sometimes violent, constituted the "problem," and the social scientists were confident that it could be eradicated, even though a residue of mild racial prejudice might remain.

The experience of the American social scientists led them to conclude that the concept of a unitary "racial attitude" was inadequate to explain behavior in many situations. By the time the Myrdal volume appeared in 1944, they were convinced that some seemingly contradictory behavior suggested that neither a "somatic norm image" nor a "prejudiced attitude" offered an explanatory cue. However, the concept of "segmentation of roles," meaning that people act out contrasting roles at different times and places, did offer an explanation. Thus, black and white individuals could walk picket lines together as workers during a strike and, at the same time, could belong to organizations in which they opposed each other in the roles of family heads competing for housing space. In the first instance the white worker might call the black worker "brother"; in the second, "nigger interloper running down the value of my property." Furthermore, it was hypothesized (and proved experimentally) that working together in equal-status relationships could make people forget physical differences or even "see faces in a new light," with the forming of personal ties of friendship, camaraderie, and even love.

Dr. Robert Ezra Park, a founder of the so-called Chicago School of sociology, which played a primary role in the development of race-relations theory, had lived for seven years in the Deep South of the United States as an associate of Booker T. Washington at the Tuskegee Institute in Alabama. Park was well acquainted with the rigid caste system of segregation existing between Blacks and whites, buttressed by law and custom, as well as with terrorization and lynching. Yet Park left the South in 1914 convinced that "interracial friendships cut across and eventually undermine all the barriers of racial segregation and caste by which races seek to maintain their integrity."[11] This is what might be called "long-run sociologistic optimism," but it did not rule out periods of intense racial conflict in the short run.

The strongest proponents of these views in the years between the two world wars were members of the Chicago School, founded by Park, W. I. Thomas, and their associates. During the 1920s, they carried out empirical studies of Negro and immigrant communities in Chicago, and they developed a body of theory on urbanism and ethnic and racial relations. These scholars witnessed profound changes in race relations during the Depression years of the 1930s when thousands of Afro-Americans became involved in the labor movement and in left-wing political activities as equals with whites. Analysis of observed new relationships led some social scientists to suggest deliberately induced changes in social arrangements to minimize opportunities for racial discrimination, as opposed to waiting for education and propaganda to eradicate racial prejudice and to change stereotypes. As advisers on social policy to local governments, some of these analysts were impressed, too, by the extent to which white police officers could be trained to act in their occupational roles, protecting the rights of black people even when they harbored personal prejudices against them.

Many of these social scientists were also inclined to feel that as people changed their behavior in order to act in a nondiscriminatory manner, their prejudices would "wither away." This hypothesis, no doubt, contained the greatest measure of naïveté; but it was not crucial to the main thrust of "sociologistic optimism," which viewed a certain amount of racial *prejudice* as "normal," even after social engineering had eliminated racial *discrimination*. Both positions, however, ignored the possibility of a strong "white backlash."

"High Visibility" and Assimilation

Park visualized a "race-relations cycle" and predicted a fate for racial and ethnic groups in America consonant with the "melting pot concept." It was observed that all such groups entered the urban order competing with one another for jobs, living space, political power, and prestige. The process of competition often led to conflict, both violent and nonviolent. Eventually, stabilized relations between the groups would result from a process Park called "accommodation," which allows for the borrowing and lending of customs and the ironing out of cultural differences. Thus, "assimilation" takes place. Implicit in this view, although seldom stated, was the belief that eventually even physical differences would disappear through the biological process of miscegenation, resulting in amalgamation. Insofar as black Americans were concerned, it was assumed that they too would be absorbed, although at a slower pace than white immigrants.

Over thirty years before Hoetink accused the "sociologistic optimists" of ignoring the importance of the somatic norm image, and five years after the Myrdal volume was published, another European scholar accused American social scientists of being so sure that cultural assimilation was inevitable that they ignored the fact that both Blacks and whites each cherished their own somatic norm image. Gustav Ichheiser, like Park, was acquainted with the South, having taught at a small black college in Mississippi. In March 1949 the *American Journal of Sociology* published an article by Ichheiser in which he charged that the reigning theory of race relations was "in a state of incredible confusion because certain obvious but highly important facts which determine the dynamics of race relations are either ignored, misinterpreted, or not taken adequately into account." He insisted that one such fact was physical difference between groups.[12] Ichheiser stated his position as follows:

> People who, in a significant way, look different to one another, have a tendency to consider one another as not only looking different but as being different. And they have this tendency because *our sociosensory perception of the physical appearance of other people is essentially symbolic in character; the external personality is immediately perceived as a manifestation of the inner personality.* . . . Since members of different racial groups, like white people and Negroes, look significantly different, they have a very strong tendency to consider each other not only as looking but also as being different and, consequently, as belonging to two different groups (the degree of disparity between the bodily appearance plays, as experience shows, an important role). . . . *This basic sociosensory perception of difference in physique plays a power-*

ful role in the conscious, and probably still more powerful role in the unconscious group identification. . . . In spite of Marxian theories, we are unconsciously more deeply identified with those who talk as we talk, behave as we behave, and look as we look than with those with whom we have identical economic interests. . . . *In terms of the sociopsychological reality, people who look different are different* [italics added].[13]

Professor Ichheiser was obviously interested in striking a blow at the Marxists and, at the same time, in centering his fire on the Chicago School of sociology, whose adherents he charged with trying to "talk away" both cultural and physical differences between Afro-Americans and themselves, as well as differences in the way black and white people view the world. Ichheiser did not feel that "race consciousness" or "color consciousness" or "color awareness" should be equated with race prejudice. He considered race consciousness a "natural" phenomenon:

The prejudice proper comes in only when the existing differences are interpreted and evaluated in terms of inferiority or other culturally determined stereotypes. Whereas the sociopsychological reaction to people of different physique as "being different" and "belonging to another group" seems to be more or less universal, the way this difference is interpreted and evaluated is specific and varies from culture to culture.[14]

It should be emphasized that the social scientists Ichheiser criticized were certainly in agreement with him on this point. Ichheiser must have known this and must have been aware, too, that the overwhelming majority of white Americans did believe that the physical differences of Negroes connoted inferiority of mind and character. He felt that Afro-Americans and their white friends had overreacted to the fact that most Americans held this view, and he singled out one of the professors at the University of Chicago, Dr. Louis Wirth, who wrote and spoke often on race relations:

Dr. Wirth does not make clear whether he thinks that white people are prejudiced only if they consider Negroes as being "different" (as belonging to "another group") or whether he thinks that white people are prejudiced only if they consider Negroes as being inferior. . . . Prejudiced is not he who admits that people who are different are different, but he who denies it, or even insists that people who are different are alike.[15]

Louis Wirth replied with an acerbic comment, ending with this statement:

As far as I know, no one with any sense in the field of race relations seeks to deny differences in physical characteristics or even in cultural characteristics. They do, however, object to the chauvinistic racialist suggestion that the two invariably go together.[16]

Wirth was correct about his colleagues: they did not deny the obvious physical differences. But they did minimize the importance of the somatic norm image, as compared with social and cultural factors, in determining relations between white and black people. And they *did* deny, with the backing of a large group of anthropologists, that there are innate, inherited group differences in intellectual ability or personality and temperament.

Long before this controversy erupted, Robert Park had abandoned a position he held in the 1920s, a position that his students had repudiated as an example of unjustifiable biological determinism. He had not only once stated his belief in profound racial differences but expressed also a conviction that such differences are inherited. He wrote that "racial temperament . . . consists in a few elementary but distinctive characteristics, determined by physical organization and transmitted biologically." Of Africans and people of African descent, Park said that "everywhere and always" they have possessed a temperament that "has been interested rather in expression than in action; interested in life itself rather than in its reconstruction or reformation."[17] Park declared that a Negro is

> by natural disposition, neither an intellectual nor an idealist like the Jew; nor a brooding introspective like the East Indian; nor a pioneer and frontiersman, like the Anglo-Saxon. He is primarily an artist, loving life for its own sake. His *metier* is expression rather than action. He is, so to speak, the lady among races.[18]

By the time of the Wirth-Ichheiser controversy, most of Park's students were questioning his conclusion that Negroes everywhere exhibit the traits that mark them off from Jews, East Indians, and Anglo-Saxons. *All* of his students rejected the idea that if any such differences exist, they are "determined by physical organization and transmitted biologically." They had accepted the conclusions of anthropologist Franz Boas and his influential band of students on this point.

Meanwhile, Wirth and his colleagues suspected that Ichheiser had not abandoned genetic explanations of differences in temperament and culture among ethnic groups. If Ichheiser had been content with charging that the American sociologists were simply not giving enough attention to the feeling of differentness that accompanies the fact of physical differentness, he would have been on safe ground. He left himself open to attack (and confirmed Wirth's suspicions), however, by an assertion in a footnote that one possible cause of personality differences between white people and Negroes "might have a biological basis." Park might have believed this in the 1920s, but none of the Chicago School did in 1949. Then, in a rejoinder that included an admonition, magisterial in tone, Professor Ichheiser revealed that the system of psychology that undergirded his sociology was very different from the Mead-Cooley symbolic interactionism that most of the Chicago School accepted:

> If Dr. Wirth would approach the problems of race relations not only in preconceived sociological terms but also in terms of the modern Gestalt psychology and psychology of depth, then I am sure the respective facts and issues would appear to him in a new and different light.[19]

None of the "sociologistic optimists" had ever denied that physical differences between black people and white people in the United States, or differences between racial groups elsewhere, play some part in generating and sustaining negative group prejudices. They refused, however, to accord the somatic norm image the primary role in the structuring of race relations anywhere. Wirth and Ichheiser agreed that racial awareness could exist without resulting in racial prejudice, but the difference of opinion about the inheritance of group characteristics was a gulf that could not be bridged.

The Chicago School of sociology developed its own body of theory about the role of physical differences in race prejudice and in the operation of the "race-relations cycle." It centered around the concept of "high visibility." Before bringing that factor into their analysis, however, they accepted as axiomatic several of Park's propositions: (1) racial prejudice does not arise everywhere among all peoples; (2) race prejudice is "inevitable when a hitherto isolated people migrates to an area where they confront another race which has interests to protect";[20] (3) such contact situations, coupled with conflict, are essential elements in the activation of prejudice between people who differ in physical type; (4) very pronounced physical differences—high visibility—make such prejudice more likely. Park used the concept of high visibility in the early 1920s when, reflecting upon immigrant populations in Chicago and on the Pacific Coast, he wrote:

> When a race bears an external mark by which every individual member of it can infallibly be identified, that race is by that fact set apart and segregated. Japanese, Chinese, and Negroes cannot move among us with the same freedom as other races because they bear marks which

identify them as members of their race. This fact isolates them. . . . Isolation is at once a cause and an effect of race prejudice.[21]

The term *high visibility* came into general use among sociologists to refer to the presence of the "external mark." Park's study of the prevalence of miscegenation and of the extent of interpersonal relations across caste lines in the southern United States convinced him that such external marks are eventually eroded, and that even while they persist they do not result in total social isolation. He and all of his students believed that the external marks impede assimilation but do not stop it. In defining racial prejudice as a special kind of ethnocentrism, Wirth discussed the role of high visibility in the social process:

> Racial prejudice is associated with the disposition on the part of virtually every human group to think of itself as superior to outsiders. The notion of chosen people is quite widespread. We know of primitive communities the members of which call themselves "men" or "human beings" to distinguish themselves from all outsiders, who are regarded as not quite human. We generally glorify the people whom we speak of as "we," whereas the "others" or outsiders are deprecated and suspected. Although strangers do sometimes have a romantic fascination for us, more often than not we fear them and remain at a respectful distance from them, ready to believe almost anything about them to which we would not for a moment give credence if it concerned a member of our own group. *Particularly where these strangers are distinguishable from our own group by such visible marks as color, the tendency to retain them in a category apart is persistent* [italics added].[22]

Whether Wirth saw this tendency to focus on color as universal or as restricted to Western societies is not clear from this passage.

Another sociologist, not connected with the Chicago School, seemed to consider high visibility as invariably resulting in prejudice, with European expansion being a special case:

> In a very basic sense, "race relations" are the direct outgrowth of the long wave of European expansion. . . . In a way the resulting so-called race relations had very little to do with "race"—initially it was an historical accident that the peoples encountered in the European expansion differed in shared physical characteristics of an obvious kind. But once the racial ideologies had been formed and widely disseminated, they constituted a powerful means of justifying political hegemony and economic control. . . . *Economic competition tends to arouse prejudice, once given a visible group and a definition of its members as different.* Such prejudice is especially likely to appear when a racially

or culturally recognized grouping is concentrated in highly visible occupations which involve direct contact with the public [italics added].[23]

The notion of high visibility, as an explanation of the low degree of assimilation and acceptance of Afro-Americans by white people in the United States, was elaborated into a formal generalization in 1945 by Professor W. Lloyd Warner and his student Leo Srole as one conclusion arising from the Yankee City studies: "The greater the racial difference between the populations of the immigrant and the host societies, the greater the subordination of the immigrant group, the greater the strength of the social subsystem, and the longer the period necessary for assimilation." In a summary of the Yankee City studies published in 1963, Warner and his associates presented an elaborate chart purporting to depict a timetable of acceptance of various ethnic groups for the whole United States by the high-status dominant whites of northern European origin, with Afro-Americans being the last on the list.[24]

Freudian and Marxian Approaches

Some of the members of the Chicago School of sociology built Freudian elements into their theories of race relations, but most did not. Yet all were influenced indirectly by this system of psychology. None were Marxists, yet no social scientist in the United States during the Depression years could avoid being influenced by Marxian currents of thought. The scholars who conceived of high visibility as a factor exacerbating invidious discrimination against black people, but only temporarily delaying assimilation, were inclined to ignore the neo-Freudian view that there are types of social systems that cannot exist without discrimination against some segments of the population, and that such a system exists in the United States.

Some psychoanalysts with an interest in sociology viewed modern capitalism as a social system that generates pressures resulting in groups of alienated individuals existing in anomic social situations. The survival of such a system requires "targets" against which built-up pressures can be discharged. Black people in the United States, the theory maintained, represent a special instance of an ethnic or racial target group against which the culture allows aggressions to be expressed without the degree of punishment that such aggression would elicit if others were so victimized. As psychoanalysts viewed the situation, the white *unconscious*, in this instance, expresses itself through projection and displacement of its repressed contents onto black people in culturally sanctioned actions. At the cognitive level, this same unconscious finds expression through the use of derogatory group stereotypes and through the sharing of a color symbolism that denigrates "blackness." At other times and places people other than blacks have been the targets—the Jews in nineteenth-century eastern Europe, for instance, or both Jews and Moors in late medieval Spain.

Yale University psychologist John Dollard integrated Freudian elements into a sociological model as early as 1937, in *Caste and Class in a Southern Town*, and psychoanalyst Harry Stack Sullivan participated in the research and wrote an appendix for *Growing Up in the Black Belt*, by Charles S. Johnson, in 1935. However, the psychological orientation of mainstream race-relations theory at that time was not psychoanalysis but rather the symbolic interactionism of George Herbert Mead and Charles Horton Cooley, as articulated by Herbert Blumer. During the first decade after World War II, the "sociologistic optimists" became involved in policy-oriented research concerned with inner-city–development planning and the monitoring of desegregation. While no new elements entered into race-relations theory between the wars, theory building was subsequently taken up by Freudian psychologists with an interest in social change as well as individual therapy. In the 1950s several classic studies utilizing psychoanalysis appeared whose primary focus was anti-Semitism. These included five volumes of the Studies in Prejudice Series, including *Dynamics of Prejudice* by Bruno Bettelheim and Morris Janowitz, and the highly influential *The Authoritarian Personality* by Theodor Adorno, Else Frenkel-Brunswik, Daniel Levinson, and R. Nevitt Sanford. Although research on anti-Semitism was central to these studies, their attempts to contrast prejudice against Jews with prejudice against Negroes had a significant impact upon subsequent theory and research.

In 1958 a synthesis of sociological and psychological points of view appeared in Gordon Allport's work. He used the "scapegoat" hypothesis as a popularized version of psychoanalytical concepts of displacement and projection, with Blacks and Jews as "targets."[25] *Allport's studies and other similar ones were somewhat less optimistic than those of earlier sociologists, for they implied that deep-seated prejudices might remain even if racial discrimination were prevented by law or other social sanctions.* This work suggested, too, that while most racial prejudice in the United States was "conformity prejudice," a significant number of people possessed "authoritarian personalities" that predisposed them to express racial prejudice.

The scapegoat theory was assimilated into virtually all analyses of racial and ethnic relations during the sixties, and it became a permanent aspect of American race-relations theory. More arcane and esoteric applications of psychoanalytic theory have remained confined to discussions among specialists at conferences and in journals. There have been, for instance, suggestions that aversion to dark skin-color is rooted in symbolic associations with anal and genital products, or that subordination of black males by white males is a form of symbolic castration.

Mention has been made of Marxist criticisms of Myrdal's *An American Dilemma*. Although more sophisticated Marxist analyses of ethnic and racial relations began to appear during and after the sixties, there had been a tendency among Marxist theorists (until Third World scholars joined their ranks) to subsume all racial oppression under analyses of class oppression. There was a tendency, too, to view skin-color prejudice against Africans and people of African descent as a historical accident related to the fact that modern economic and political power is in the hands of the Europeans, who happen to be white. At other times and in other places, they argued, skin-color prejudice in general and prejudice against Blacks in particular was virtually nonexistent. This position became increasingly unconvincing as knowledge about color prejudice in the Muslim world before the fifteenth century became more generally available. While it is possible to explain some aspects of this prejudice and discrimination in class terms, in the case of the growth of prejudice against black skin-color among Muslims and early Christians, other factors seem more relevant. These are questions that are addressed in chapters four and five of this book.

Freudian scapegoat theory and Marxist analysis reinforce each other in explaining some of the anti-Negro behavior in American labor history. Thus, Marxist theory conceives of the black population in the United States as part of a "labor reserve" operating to depress wages so that the rate of profit can be kept high. When Negroes are mobilized as strikebreakers or hired for lower wages than white workers, their skin-color becomes the symbol of "the enemy," and they become targets of aggression by white workers.[26]

The Rediscovery of Ethnicity

It is significant that while Ichheiser and Hoetink, two European scholars, had criticized the "sociologistic optimists" for ignoring the role of physical differences in the structuring of black/white relations in the United States, two American social scientists later accused these same social scientists of an unwillingness to face the reality of group differences in behavior and temperament. It was argued that, for the "sociologistic optimists," the "melting pot wish" was the father of distorted perception and analysis. Summarizing and evaluating nearly twenty years of research, Robert A. Levine and Donald T. Campbell published a book in 1972 calling for a realistic reappraisal of group differences:

> In social and educational psychology a literature amd teaching practice has grown up which says that all stereotypes or group differences are false, and implicitly, that all groups are similar. This social psychological literature was, perhaps, started by the excellent and classic study of Katz and Braly (1933) which showed that college students had stable and elaborate stereotypes of a wide variety of minority and nationality groups. They found no relation between the elaborateness and uniformity of these stereotypes and the amount of contact with the groups in question. . . . Certainly this literature did demonstrate that stereotypes can be completely false. . . . But . . . there was little or no comparison of the content of stereotypes with corresponding social statistics and anthropological data. . . . This summary is perhaps overdrawn, . . . but it is probably an accurate description of most teachings about prejudice and stereotypes in social psychology and education departments between 1935 and 1954.[27]

After 1954 events outside of the academic world led some social scientists to try to distinguish more carefully between what Gordon Allport called "the well-merited reputations" and the stereotypes of groups. Also, Blacks, Mexican-Americans, Puerto Ricans, Amerindians, and various groups of Asians began to express pride in their "roots," and to emphasize aspects of their subcultures in the United States that they considered unique and desirable. Some of these were traits that the white majority had stigmatized as "lower class," "primitive," "unscientific," and "backward." At the same time, white ethnics concentrated in the blue-collar strata, in response to the self-assertion of "colored" groups, began to emphasize qualities of their own that they considered unique and desirable.

That the situation described by Levine and Campbell became a focal point of scholarly interest is illustrated by the fact that, in the same year their book appeared (1972), a *Daedalus* conference on ethnicity, funded by the Ford Foundation, was held. Some of the papers from this conference were included in a volume published two years later that signaled the academic respectability of a new area of study. *Ethnicity: Theory and Experience*, edited with an introduction by Nathan Glazer and Daniel P. Moynihan, defined, as subjects for research, "all the groups of a society characterized by a distinctive sense of difference owing to culture and descent." These two Harvard University social scientists stated their belief that "the hope of doing without ethnicity in a society, as its subgroups assimilate to majority group, may be as utopian and questionable an enterprise as the hope of doing without social classes in a society." They quoted sociologist Daniel Bell in trying to explain why ethnicity had become important in both national and international affairs, and why it was more salient than class as an organizing focus: "It can combine an interest with an affective tie." This theoretical statement did not consider the role of color or of beliefs about biological inheritance as factors in the persistence of ethnic groups and their differential treatment. These were matters that had been the central focus of a conference under similar sponsorship seven years earlier. It is not surprising, therefore, that some Afro-Americans considered the new emphasis on ethnicity as one way of avoiding the serious problems posed by color prejudice and racism in the United States.

Black Studies programs had been established at over 200 predominantly white colleges and universities by the time Campbell and Levine and Glazer and Moynihan published books emphasizing ethnicity, and there was pressure on some campuses to transform them into Ethnic Studies programs. In some instances Black Studies publications were reconceived as Ethnic Studies publications (as, for example, at Brooklyn College and the Hampton Institute). One response to the Black Consciousness and Black Power movements in the United States was to try to deracialize them, to argue that the Black Experience was similar to that of European ethnic groups and that the passage of time would make race and color increasingly irrelevant, even if ethnic-group solidarity remained. Another approach was to emphasize the importance of the stigma of "blackness" and to insist that this made the Afro-American experience not only different in kind from that of European ethnics but also different from other colored immigrants. Conceptualizing Afro-Americans as an ethnic group was useful to advocates of both positions.

George Fredrickson, in his book *The Black Image in the White Mind: The Debate on Afro-American Character and Destiny, 1817–1914*, noted that liberals, black and white, had once accepted a "different but equal" philosophy, what he describes as "romantic racialism," and he traced this outlook to the German philosopher Herder. W.E.B. Du Bois and Robert E. Park, who had both studied in Germany and were profoundly impressed by nineteenth-century German thought, showed the influence of such "romantic racialism." This particular facet of German thought went out of vogue during the 1930s, however, and was considered reactionary during the struggle against Hitlerism between 1935 and 1945. It reappeared in the United States in the fifties among opponents of integration and assimilation, with the right-wing whites who espoused it evaluating

Anglo-Saxon traits as "better" and "best." Black Nationalists returned to "romantic racialism," too, but lauded the values of *Négritude* as superior, including Senghor's view that "emotion is Negro and reason Greek."[28]

Many social scientists were willing to abandon their assimilationist perspectives for the new ideal of a multiethnic pluralism in the United States if they were not asked to believe that group customs and ethnic temperament were inherited genetically. But it was precisely this characteristic that some of the proponents of "romantic racialism" advanced as its most salient distinction.

Although some Afro-American scholars participated in the exploration of ethnicity as a useful concept for understanding American society, most preferred to keep the spotlight on *race* relations. They saw the popularization of ethnicity as a focus of research as diverting attention from the discussion of Afro-American problems in terms of race and color. After all, Daniel Moynihan, one of the editors of *Ethnicity: Theory and Experience*, was the presidential adviser who had recommended a policy of "benign neglect" in the face of pressures emanating from the black community. When William J. Wilson, the black chairman of the prestigious Department of Sociology at the University of Chicago, published a book entitled *The Declining Significance of Race*, some black leaders felt that his optimism was premature and was, perhaps, related more to opportunities that had materialized for the small, well-educated segment of the Afro-American community than to the condition of the masses of black people. Interesting academic exercises in reconceptualizing the Black Experience, whether in terms of economic class or ethnicity, were thought by many observers to obscure the stark realities of the racial discrimination that still existed in the United States and to constitute a threat to the development of the black solidarity needed to struggle against it. During the 1980s much of this discussion revolved around the problem of a black "underclass" that seemed impervious to middle-class "uplift" overtures.

The Copenhagen Conference on Race

By 1965 "romantic racialism" was undergoing a strong revival among Afro-American artists and writers for the first time since the 1920s, and within a few years Black Consciousness and Black Power ideologies were dominant among Afro-American youth leaders and were affecting all aspects of black institutional life. In addition, the American black militant Malcolm X had become popular in Africa and the West Indies. Racial conflict in southern Africa escalated, in sharp contrast to the independence struggles in other parts of the continent where racial aspects of conflicts had been deliberately downplayed. But by 1965 these countries could not avoid seeing the African struggle as Black versus White. Increased immigration to Britain and France from Africa and the Caribbean exacerbated racial tensions. The *Négritude* and Black Power movements seemed menacing to white liberals, and attempts of white scholars and political leaders to focus attention on ethnicity and the class struggle instead of race could not prevent the burgeoning of color consciousness in the United States, Britain, and Africa. Discussion of the meaning of "high visibility" and "blackness" assumed a degree of urgency among intellectuals in the Black World.

In view of the international significance of race and race relations at the time—seven years before the ethnicity conference—it is not surprising that in September 1965 the Congress for Cultural Freedom, with the support of *Daedalus*, the journal of the American Academy of Arts and Sciences, convened a conference (funded by the Ford Foundation) in Copenhagen, Denmark, to discuss problems of race and color in the contemporary world. When *Daedalus* published the first group of conference papers, the editors noted that

> color and race remain decisive barriers to human associations—and that even those nations which pride themselves on their freedom from racial discrimination are rarely so impartial as they sometimes claim. . . . The concern of the group was both to document changing (and unchanging) attitudes toward racial differences and to consider the cultural, social, physical and political forces which contribute to the situation as it exists in the world at this time.[29]

The inclusion of the word *unchanging* in this statement was very significant, this was the first time during the twentieth century that any influential American social scientists had suggested that color prejudices might have the significance claimed by Ichheiser and Hoetink. Observing the phenomenon of white backlash and the disturbing upsurge of Black Nationalism, even liberal white scholars were now inclined to see something "primordial," as sociologist Edward Shils phrased it, about color prejudice, and perhaps even its inevitability, as other scholars argued. The conference papers represented the culmination of a gradually growing concern among intellectuals with the role of skin-color in human relations.[30]

The *Daedalus* report on color and race was first published in 1967, following a very optimistic *Daedalus* issue entitled "The Negro in the United States," published in 1965, the year of the Watts rebellion and the assassination of Malcolm X. The issue on color and race seemed to constitute a warning against overoptimism regarding the possibility of eliminating color prejudice, and it came in the midst of the "Black is Beautiful" campaign among young Afro-Americans. Some of those who contributed seemed to be saying to the assimilationists, "You are fighting a losing game." But for Black Nationalists these were welcome ideas, for they considered it "natural" to think of race as basic. Some of the contributors argued that "Black is Beautiful" was close to being a revolutionary idea.

The *Daedalus* conference papers reflected varied intellectual tendencies, and two of them attempted to make substantial theoretical contributions: Roger Bastide's "Color, Racism and Christianity" and Kenneth J. Gergen's "The Significance of Skin Color in Human Relations." Bastide, an anthropologist, had written often on black/white relations, combining Freudian analysis and the sociology of George Gurvitch in his interpretations. Now he wrote in *Daedalus*:

> The Christian symbolism of color is very rich. . . . But the greatest Christian two-part division is that of white and black. White is used to express the pure, while black expresses the diabolical. The conflict between Christ and Satan, the spiritual and the carnal, good and evil came finally to be expressed by the conflict between white and black, which underlines and synthesizes all the others.[31]

Bastide was convinced that interracial relations reflected this symbolism. This way of conceptualizing and interpreting race relations could be called "Manichaean."

After referring to the use, by Christians, of such phrases as "a black soul," Bastide suggested that *"thinking is so enslaved to language that this chain of associated ideas operates automatically when a white person finds himself in contact with a colored person* [italics added]."[32] As we shall see, Gergen went beyond Bastide to suggest that the Manichaean black/white contrast is not culture-bound but universal, involves dark-skinned people everywhere, and even forces black people to devalue themselves. The assertions of both men should be examined critically and should be subjected to testing against empirical data where possible.

THE MODERN MANICHAEANS: NEW WINE IN OLD BOTTLES

The Black/White Symbolic Metaphor

Social scientists, historians, and men and women of letters sometimes present evidence to show that the word for *black* in a specific language has numerous derogatory synonyms and referents. Some then add a comparative dimension by studying the meaning associated with *black* in a variety of contexts cross-culturally, contrasting these associations with those made with the word *white*. A few scholars have explored the extent to which black people themselves make negative appraisals of blackness. Some are convinced that not only is there a universal dislike of "darkness" in abstract symbol systems but also that invidious distinctions are made everywhere between light and dark people. A theory is then presented to account for (1) the existence of derogation of blackness in symbol systems and (2) the victimization of black people through these derogatory implications. In addition to a belief in the innate tendency of the human mind to polarize and dichotomize, a theory of unconscious associative learning is often employed in such explanations. Its proponents assert that all people contrast night and day, darkness and light. They argue that because of unpleasant associations with the night, day is preferred to night. Therefore, the argument continues, people will associate night and darkness with sin, evil, and impurity. Furthermore, these attributes will become associated with the dark skin of human beings, that is, "they will carry over to people." I have called scholars who make this kind of analysis of prejudice against blackness and black people the "Modern Manichaeans" because their thought style resembles, in some respects, that of the ancient religious cult of Mani, in which the eternal struggle between Light and Darkness is the focal point of both the cosmic and the human drama.[33] We use *Manichaean* here, of course, only as a secularized metaphor.

That Western conceptions of relations among black people involve Manichaean symbolism, implicitly or explicitly stated, has been suggested by Frantz Fanon, the West Indian psychiatrist who became well known after writing *The Wretched of the Earth* in 1961. In an earlier book, *Black Skin, White Masks,* Fanon had commented on a colored Caribbean woman in a novel who despised men of her own color and longed for a white husband: "It would seem indeed that for her white and black represent the two poles of a world, two poles in perpetual conflict: a genuinely Manichaean concept of the world."[34] What, in ancient Persia, was a religious world view of the struggle between Darkness and Light, here became a metaphor used by a black psychiatrist to explain a European thought style fraught with disastrous consequences for millions of other human beings. Fanon wrote,

In Europe, the black man is the symbol of Evil [Fanon's emphasis]. . . . The torturer is the black man, Satan is black, one talks of shadows, when one is dirty one is black—whether one is thinking of physical dirtiness or of moral dirtiness. . . . In Europe, whether concretely or symbolically, the black man stands for the bad side of the character. As long as one cannot understand this fact, one is doomed to talk in circles about the "black problem." Blackness, darkness, shadow, shades, night, the labyrinths of the earth, abysmal depths, blacken someone's reputation; and on the other side, the bright look of innocence, the white dove of peace, magical, heavenly light. A magnificent blond child—how much peace there is in that phrase, how much joy, and above all, how much hope! There is no comparison with a magnificent black child. . . . In Europe, that is to say, in every civilized and civilizing country, the Negro is the symbol of sin. . . . In the remotest depth of the European unconscious an inordinately black hollow has been made in which the most immoral impulses, the most shameful desires lie dormant. And as every man climbs up toward whiteness and light, the European has tried to repudiate this uncivilized self, which has attempted to defend itself. When European civilization came into contact with the black world, with those savage peoples, everyone agreed: Those Negroes were the principle of evil. . . . In Europe the Negro has one function: that of symbolizing the lower emotions, the baser inclinations, the dark side of the soul. In the collective unconscious of *homo occidentalis*, the Negro—or if one prefers, the color black—symbolizes evil, sin, wretchedness, death, war, famine.[35]

Fanon's conception of the black/white opposition was based on a combination of existentialist ideas and Marxian and Freudian explanatory theory. It also involved the non sequitur that all Modern Manichaeans perpetuate, namely, the notion that where a sharp opposition between *black* and *white* exists in the symbol system of a culture, it necessarily means opposition between black and white *people*, with the black people suffering from prejudice and invidious discrimination. This should be considered as a possibility, a hypothesis to be examined, not as dogma or as a foregone conclusion.

A few scholars working in the English and American traditions have used the Manichaean metaphor. Some of the most penetrating comments on the development of the Manichaean contrast within the English-speaking world, involving derogatory conceptions of "blackness" and the application of these conceptions to black people, have been made by historian Winthrop Jordan, in his book *White Over Black*. Jordan theorized that sixteenth-century Englishmen, experiencing close contact with Africans for the first time, suffered culture shock and tended to respond in terms of bipolar conceptualizations already embedded in British culture. Of taxonomists this was especially true. Jordan wrote:

By far the most common assumption was that the original color of man was white, an assumption which gave special sharpness to the question of why the Negro was black. It was not so much a matter of why the

Negro was black as why the Negro had become the very negation of white. Many commentators treated the Negro's blackness as a degeneration from original color. . . . For classifiers of mankind, the Negro's blackness was in itself sufficient reason for placing him in a distinct category.[36]

According to Jordan, the dramatic first contact between an Englishman and a West African elicited reactions unshared by Mediterranean peoples, who had been in contact with Negroid physical types for centuries. Curiosity, both morbid and scientific, characterized sixteenth- and seventeenth-century British writers, but Jordan argued that the contrast with a black "Other" had a much wider distribution:

> For Europeans in general, the Negro's blackness afforded a fixed polar position from which they could calculate the colors of all the peoples of the globe. Probably as much as any single factor the Negro's blackness lay at the root of the eventual European predilection for dividing the world's population into "white men" and "colored," a predilection more recently acquired by the "colored" people themselves. . . . Negroes were black, and Europeans, happily, were white. Black remained the opposite of white.[37]

The issue of whether this mode of response was a purely European phenomenon will be considered in the chapters that follow.

Before Fanon, Sartre and other intellectuals in the modern European tradition had begun to talk about black people as the "Other," against which white people formed a sense of their identity. Lewis Copeland, a graduate student at the University of Chicago in the 1930s, raised the question, in a dissertation, of whether or not the high visibility of black people might have deeper implications than Park, Wirth, and Warner believed. He suggested the possibility that white people used "*The* Negro" as a "contrast conception" against which to measure themselves. Thus, "blackness" in others symbolizes their vices, in contrast to what whites think of as their own virtues; furthermore, for whites to define Blacks as ugly is to emphasize their own positive self-image.[38] Copeland's suggestion that a group needs an "Other" against which to define its own existence was a novel one in the pre–World War II period in the United States, but after the war, with an upsurge of interest in existentialism, it became a widely discussed idea. During the sixties, Frantz Fanon and Eldridge Cleaver speculated about the consequences for black people of being the "Other" for whites, the necessary object for the realization of white identities. Black Muslims in the United States insisted upon reconceptualizing "blackness" by defining Caucasians as White Devils, in the role of their own "Other."

Western Metaphysical Dualism

Three California graduate students published a thoughtful book in 1975 entitled *Cultural Bases of Racism and Group Oppression*, in which they included a chapter called "Western Metaphysical Dualism as an Element in Racism." Citing Winthrop Jordan and Roger Bastide, Bruno Bettelheim and John Dollard, they documented the black/white conceptual opposition and related it to the tendency in Western thought to pose contrasts such as body versus mind, matter versus spirit, sensual expression versus disciplined will, the former, in each case, being "lower," the latter "higher." Furthermore, they argued, this type of dualistic thinking tends to associate Caucasians and Western culture with the "higher" pole, Africans and their cultures with the "lower" pole. Discussing the theme of "Domination and the Will in Western Thought and Culture," they suggested that Afro-Americans have suffered from this process of dichotomizing coupled with hierarchical evaluating:

> Just as Westerners typically consider a society or culture inferior which has not developed technological control over nature, so do they also consider inferior a society or culture which has not subordinated sensuality, emotionality, and bodily expression to the strictest control of the will. The cultures of West Africa, from which most American blacks originate, exhibited neither elaborate technology, nor rigid control over sensuality and bodily expression. The frequent association of black people with animals reveals the Western disgust with the sensual, with nature, and with the body—all three of which are generally considered related objects to be controlled. . . . Part of this African heritage remains in the culture of black America. We cannot fully understand racism in present-day America unless we understand it in part as a reflection of a Western bias against African culture.[39]

This discussion of metaphysical dualism can best be understood, perhaps, in terms of modern structural analysis. At the black pole, which contrasts with the white, the meanings attached to "blackness" undergo a series of transformations as attention shifts from physical type to culture and to nature, and each image suggests one of the others.

To Frantz Fanon, Winthrop Jordan, and these three American students, the Manichaean mode of categorizing black people is both culture bound and clearly a European intellectual mode. To Fanon it was specifically a product of modern colonialism and imperialism. Like most black intellectuals in Paris, Fanon had been profoundly influenced by Marxism, but his theories about race derived mainly from Freud. In the same year that Fanon published *Black Skin, White*

Masks, Claude Lévi-Strauss, an anthropologist whose concept of structuralism would eventually dominate broad areas of Western intellectual life, published a booklet under the imprimatur of UNESCO, *Race et Histoire*. Both Fanon and Lévi-Strauss had been influenced by Marx and Freud, as well as by a number of existentialist writers. Among the latter was Jean-Paul Sartre, whose essay "Orphée Noir," published in 1948 as an introduction to an anthology of black poetry, focused attention on the usefulness of the concept of the "Other" in understanding the development of self-awareness among colonized people, and on the implications of his provocative term *antiracist racism*.

By the mid-sixties these intellectual tools fashioned on the continent were beginning to have some impact upon British and American intellectuals. (*Black Skin, White Masks* appeared in translation in the United States in 1967.) As structuralism became fashionable in academic circles, it was inevitable that it would be applied to matters of race and color directly or in connection with studies in linguistics and semiotics. In 1963 the British anthropologist Victor Turner read a paper before the Association of Social Anthropologists of the Commonwealth, in which he spoke of the "marked revival of interest" in studying the "symbolism of laterality, of the opposition of right and left and its sociological implications and other kinds of isometrical relationships." His own paper was entitled "Color Classification in Ndembu Ritual; a Problem in Primitive Classification," and it concluded with a section on the white/black contrast and with a statement of theory as to why red/white/black triads turn up so frequently when cross-cultural comparisons are made. This paper appeared in the United States in 1966, in a collection of Turner's work published by Cornell University Press. This was one year after the conference in Copenhagen had convened to discuss the implications of race and color, and a year before the summer of race riots in the United States that led to the appointment of a national commission, which reported on the danger of a social and psychological separation between Negroes and the white majority more serious than the country had ever experienced.

The Degler-Gergen Propositions

The report of the Copenhagen conference, supported as it was by the Ford Foundation and the Conference for Cultural Freedom, and, when published as a book, with an introduction by the distinguished black historian John Hope Franklin, was widely cited and quoted as an authoritative document. Interpretations of race relations in most of the conference papers were in terms of quite conventional "sociologistic optimism," and many were purely descriptive. Two of them—those by Bastide and Gergen—however, provided support for the views of the "Modern Manichaeans." Social psychologist Gergen's views, in particular, were adopted six years later (1971) in support of some extreme Manichaean conclusions expressed by Professor Carl Degler, a Pulitzer Prize–winning historian on the faculty at Stanford University, in his book *Neither Black nor White: Slavery and Race Relations in Brazil and the United States*. An excellent work blending history and sociology, the study was nonetheless marred by an excursion into social psychology, a field with which the author was not thoroughly familiar. Degler was not therefore in a position to deal critically with Gergen's ideas, which he adopted and presented more dogmatically than Gergen himself had done. Degler also used some of anthropologist Victor Turner's observations about the Ndembu people in Africa without adopting that scholar's caveats. Degler wrote:

> If the culture of peoples with pigmented skin as well as that of white Europeans is permeated with a preference for white as a color and in skin, then perhaps we are in the presence of an attitude that is universal and not simply the consequence of mere history. It is surely more than a coincidence that in Africa and Asia as well as in Europe, black is associated with unpleasantness, disaster, or evil. Black undoubtedly evokes recollections of the night. . . . White, on the other hand, is the color of light, which emanates principally from the sun, which, in turn is the source of warmth and the other conditions that support life. Night is not only dark, but cold and therefore a threat to life. Is it any wonder that white is seen *everywhere* as the symbol of success, virtue, purity, goodness, whereas black is associated with evil, dirt, fear, disaster, and sin? . . . For our *purposes the conclusion to be drawn from this brief excursion into color symbolism is that perceptions of dark color are not only universally made, but that dark color is generally denigrated. It would seem that color prejudice is a universal phenomenon, not simply North American or Brazilian* [italics added].[41]

Insofar as Professor Degler spoke of *white* as "the color of light," he was on shaky ground, since most students of color carefully distinguish between hue and brightness. They do not equate the brightness of the sun with the hue, or color, *white*.

In another context, Degler states categorically:

> It is my conviction that blacks will be recognized as different and discriminated against whenever nonblacks have the power and an incentive to do so. So long as men perceive identifying physical differences that can be used to discriminate against another group, they will do so.

The tendency is especially likely to manifest itself if there are strong historical reasons for singling out a particular group, like Negroes, who are not only identifiable, but who have also been held in the degrading position of slaves for a long time. . . . *This tendency to discriminate, to be sure, is not irresistible or uncontrollable, but it seems to be universal* [italics added].[42]

To support his belief in the universality of prejudice against *Black* as a color and therefore prejudice against black people, as well as to provide a theory accounting for it, Degler accepted the views of Gergen.[43] For both men, Negroes and white people represent the polar opposites in a sharp Manichaean contrast; but both also conceptualized a more generalized type of color discrimination in which "perceptions of dark color are not only universally made, but . . . dark color is generally denigrated." The notion of a gradient from very dark to very light is implicit in the larger concept of black and white as polar opposites.

The first question posed by Gergen in his *Daedalus* article was not confined to contrasts between blackness and whiteness but rather opened up a discussion of color prejudice in its most general form. He asked, "*Given no other information about persons whose skin differs from one's own, are there psychological processes that tend to cause one to evaluate such persons in a less favorable way?* [italics added]"[44] He was convinced that "evidence from a number of domains suggests an affirmative answer to this question."[45] Gergen first explained why one likes one's own skin-color best, not why one dislikes darker skin-colors or even, perhaps, lighter colors. He, like Hoetink, used a Freudian term, *narcissism*, and modified the meaning slightly to explain the psychological phenomenon involved in preferring a specific "somatic norm image." Both men recognized a social component in the individual's formation of the norm, and both indicated that this tendency toward narcissism can become a complex social attitude that may, nevertheless, disappear with training buttressed by positive reinforcement. Gergen suggested also that the tendency itself needs constant reinforcement, and he drew upon one specific variety of learning theory and combined it with a neo-Freudian model to make generalizations about how childhood gratifications from feeding and maternal affection influence later behavior. Gergen concluded: "*To the extent that the person's major gratifications have been received within a social group delineated by a particular skin color, his future choice of friends, colleagues, or compatriots may be expected to fall within the same category. His evaluating persons outside the category will be much less positive* [italics added]."[46]

There is an apparent contradiction between this assertion and one introduced later that stated that Blacks as well as whites dislike dark skin-color. Thus, the question of why Blacks are not also subject to the narcissistic tendency immediately arises; their "major social gratifications" are received within a black group, not a white one. Gergen did not discuss this point but did introduce a footnote indicating his awareness of its importance.[47] He implied that, in the case of people with very dark skin-color, the natural tendency to cherish one's own somatic norm image is overridden by some other factor or factors. Using the adjectives "compelling" and "unsettling" to describe the phenomenon, he observed that "Negroes themselves seem negatively disposed toward those among them with dark skin." He indicated that research has shown "Negroes' self-esteem" to be "greatly impaired" as a result of pining to look white, and the "accompanying self-hatred may be generalized to hatred for the entire Negro race."[48] All of the literature he cited refers to Afro-Americans, despite the fact that this is an issue where comparative, cross-cultural studies in time and space would seem to be crucial. (Ancient Egypt and Ethiopia, for instance, constitute important test cases for determining the universality of black self-hatred, in addition to the many contemporary independent African nations.)

Hoetink stressed the desire to resemble the people who wield power and have prestige as a sufficient cause for rejection of a black body image by black people in a racist society. For him this social fact was "compelling" and "unsettling" enough. But not for Gergen, who argued that *all* people reject darkness of skin, and particularly "blackness," because of certain experiences common to all human beings. He sought scientific grounding for this view in an area where he and his students had done research: the emotional effect of various colors. Gergen stated that serious students of "the impact of color on communication" hold that individual colors "have the capacity to elicit certain types of feelings or emotions."[49] The literature on this subject is voluminous, but there is no unanimous agreement as to which colors elicit which emotions or why. Given the fact, however, that different colors do arouse different emotions, Professor Gergen contended that explanation of this general effect derives from the principle of "associative learning." For instance, if a given color is usually present when a child is frightened or sad, through processes of associative learning such a color may come to elicit such feelings at a later point in time. These associations may develop prior to the acquisition of linguistic abilities, and unless extinguished—and they *can* be—they may continue throughout the individual's life. In Gergen's view, prejudice against people because of skin-color is thus a conditioned response. This particular social-psychological theory grounds the Manichaean dichotomy between *Black* and *White* in a realm of early childhood experience rather than in the innate structure of the mind or in the existence of archetypes, as some structuralist or Jungian psychologists maintain.[50]

Gergen suggested that all children—including black ones—undergo experiences that generate adverse reactions to blackness (whether defined as a color or the absence of all color). He presented evidence that the color *Black* is widely disliked and even feared in cultures so disparate that diffusion cannot account for the similarity. Since some explanation other than diffusion must be given, Gergen hypothesized that some type of common early associative learning experience must be present in the widely separated situations. He is convinced that he knows what that common experience entails: *"Two such experiences seem especially germane: the meaning of night versus day for the child and the training he receives in cleanliness* [italics added]."[51] It is not difficult to believe that children everywhere fear the darkness associated with night, although they can be taught to overcome such fear. However, the assertion that children everywhere are taught that dirt or excreta are "bad" does not survive cross-cultural scrutiny. The Nuer of the upper Nile, for instance, coat themselves with mud as a protection against mosquitoes, and children in India learn to collect cow dung to burn and to use for plastering walls. That a generalized fear of Black and "blackness" originates in such childhood experiences even in situations where cleanliness training *does* lay a taboo on dirt and feces has not been proved.

While both Gergen and Degler stressed the universality of prejudice against dark skin-color, the former scholar was more cautious and tentative in his generalizations than the latter. However, Gergen's use of comparative history and anthropology was as weak as Degler's use of social psychology. Degler's argument would have been more convincing if, instead of relying upon statements by a single social psychologist, he had raised one question and sought the answer within the framework of his own discipline: *Does comparative history actually show that preference for light skin-color is universal and that darkness of skin is generally denigrated?* Only by asking this question can we judge the veracity of his conviction that prejudice against dark skin-color is not the consequence of "mere history." (Obviously, some specification of degree of darkness is mandatory. "Hawaiian bronze" is admired, not disliked.) To answer such a question about the universality of a polar opposition between *Black* and

White in abstract systems of color symbolism, both scholars would also have to rely upon the findings of anthropologists and comparative historians.

Degler and Gergen cited the work of anthropologist Victor Turner to buttress the universality claim, but neither discussed the exceptions that Turner cited to generalizations about negative associations with "blackness," and neither scholar criticized Turner's unproved and unprovable use of Freudian symbolism, resulting in these equivalences: whiteness ≅ milk ≅ semen ≅ white people versus "blackness" ≅ feces ≅ black people. The distinguished social anthropologist Edmund Leach of Cambridge, in a recent work on "the use of structuralist analysis in social anthropology," did put forward such a critique. Not ignoring associative learning as a process that might set up equivalences between feces, dirt, and aversion to people who call up these associations, Leach nevertheless maintained that nonstructuralists make a fundamental error:

> It is possible that early childhood experiences may "imprint" particular emotional attitudes toward particular colours. Milk and semen are white; blood is red; faeces are brown. Blood and faeces both turn black with age. These body products are of personal importance to every individual and they are all elements which appear repeatedly in the symbolic coding of colour discriminations. *But there do not seem to be any universals* [italics added].[52]

Leach then presented a case of a reversal of the expected black/white symbolism:

> There are many chains of association by which: white/black = good/bad, but sometimes "black is beautiful." For example among the Lolo of West China the aristocrats were distinguished from the serfs as "black boned" versus "white boned," not the other way round.[53]

Leach explained the absence of a universal Manichaean black/white symbolism by using the concept of "deep structure," as developed by Lévi-Strauss. He suggested that "symbols occur in sets and that the meaning of particular symbols is to be found in the contrast with other symbols rather than in the symbol as such." Thus, we have sacred versus profane, high status versus low, ugly versus beautiful, and so forth. The universal tendency is to conceptualize in terms of the oppositions, but *any* colors can symbolize the contrasts. As Leach pointed out,

> because all objects in the visible external world possess attributes of colour, colour difference is always an available means of classification.

But an indefinitely large variety of things will fall into any one colour class, so the social metaphors of colour are always potentially polysemic. Even when it is evident that the colour of something has symbolic significance, we can never be sure what it is. Each case must be investigated in its particular context.

Leach, unlike Degler, felt that "Victor Turner's extensive analysis of colour symbolism among the Ndembu of central Africa demonstrates this point in great detail,"[54] and that it does not prove an invariable connection between the color *Black* and undesirable events, persons, and things.

Leach's observations were directed toward the problem of general color symbolism. This includes the question of what the color *Black* and "blackness" as an attribute mean in the abstract. He did not consider another problem of interest to us, namely, the extent to which meanings attached to *Black* and *White* "carry over" to people. Although Professor Gergen did argue for universality rooted in early childhood fears, he counseled caution, pointing out that although a great deal is known about emotive reactions to specific colors, no firm experimental evidence is available to answer the crucial question: *"Are the basic emotional reactions triggered by various colors generalized to the domain of social interaction?* [italics added]"[55] Gergen maintained, however, that the evidence supports an affirmative answer to a more limited and, for us, more crucial question: *"Does the person whose emotional reaction to black is negative also feel antipathy for people whose skin is dark?* [italics added]"[56] He pointed out the difficulty of devising experimental research to answer this question and fell back on another type of evidence, commenting: "The supposition that attitudes toward color generalize to attitudes toward people, in this case, working toward the detriment of the Negro, gains credence when one peruses various accounts of experience in non-Western cultures."[57] However, this attempt to use the comparative method is not really very convincing.

Gergen, in fact, conceded that his data from non-Western cultures were scanty and that his conclusions must be tentative. Nevertheless, he presented what he called "a systematic examination of a randomly selected group of cultures." Actually, less than half-a-dozen cases were examined, and none of these is from classical antiquity or ancient Egypt and Ethiopia, theoretically important areas that will be examined, along with others, in this book in testing the Degler-Gergen hypotheses. In considering these cases and others, it is relatively easy to describe the differential evaluations placed upon "whiteness" and "blackness" in various contexts, but it is difficult to demonstrate carry-over from the domain of abstract systems to human interaction. *To a striking extent, in fact, derogatory attitudes toward "blackness" as a color exist in cultures side by side with favorable connotations and with the absence of invidious discrimination based on "blackness" of skin-color.*

Both Gergen and Degler were interested in a wider problem than the Manichaean contrast between the extremes of white and black skin-color. They were convinced that skin-color, viewed along a gradient, always predetermines that darker people will look up to lighter people and lighter people will look down on the darker varieties of mankind. Gergen presented very few examples of black/white contacts, although extensive literature is available. Rather, he cited (1) Cortéz and Cook in Mexico and Oceania, respectively, claiming that the people they met thought they were gods because they were white; (2) novelist Herman Melville, who claimed that Marquesan males regarded white women as "some new divinity"; and (3) India, where all Brahmins were said to be light and all Sudras black (an error of fact).[58] (This discussion also ignored the cult of the suntan, in which "Polynesian beauties" are used to advertise various products.)

Gergen's shakiest assertion, however, was his claim that *"whenever there are distinctively different color lines within a society, there will be a pronounced tendency toward strife between the light and the dark* [italics added]."[59] No data were presented to substantiate this very broad generalization tinged with Manichaean assumptions of an almost classical type, and the statement remains a non sequitur. Why the mere presence of the color difference inevitably generates *conflict* was not made clear. The presence or absence of such conflict requires a sociological explanation. In fact, there are existing situations where exactly the reverse of "strife between the light and the dark" occurs, where color prejudice operates to inhibit strife! In most Latin American societies, for instance, the most Negroid portion of the population is impacted at the poverty-stricken bottom of the socioeconomic ladder, and the social status of people in the middle varies with shade of color. Through the mystification of ideology and a feeling among very dark people of individual personal inadequacy and the worthlessness of being Black, any "pronounced tendency toward strife" between white, black, and numerous color shades has long since disappeared. Some Latin Americans prefer such systems because conflict between racial *groups* and color categories is absent and people are preoccupied with seeking whatever individual advantage comes, for example, from being a mulatto instead of a Black, or from being a White instead of a *morena*. Intermediate types operate as a stabilizing force and serve as "proof" that complete amalgamation can eventually take place, with the Black as a physical type disappearing from the system. "Blackness" is openly devalued, and black people in such systems may experience rejection and ridicule even by members of their immediate families.[60] Furthermore, they rarely organize as Blacks to demand the end of racial discrimination.

The theories of the Modern Manichaeans, when used to explain antiblack prejudices against people, ignore or discount historical explanations of why the people of any group may have negative attitudes toward people darker than themselves—or toward their own body images if they are dark. Such theories tend to be tinged with pessimism, yet they are not necessarily deterministic. For instance, Gergen concluded that since early socialization makes children prejudiced against dark-skinned people, "they may have to be taught not to be prejudiced."[61] While Gergen argued that such training is necesssary before prejudice can be eliminated from society, like Ichheiser and Hoetink he maintained that prejudice *could* persist so long as color differences remain. Therefore, Gergen wrote that while "the hurdles of racial equality may be high ones, indeed, and great preparation may be needed for the jump, . . . the ultimate solution may reside in the domain of racial homogenization." Professor Hoetink seems to agree with Professor Gergen and used the same term, *homogenization*. Many black people feel that such a position is racist however liberal the proponents of the solution may be, since it says in effect that it would be desirable for the Negro phenotype to disappear and that multiracial, multiethnic pluralism is neither feasible nor desirable.[62]

CRITICAL DOMAINS IN TRANS-RACIAL EVALUATIONS

In the modern world, skin-color provides a stimulus-cue to thoughts and emotions in some domains of interpersonal relationships. Psychologists have studied these responses in a few controlled experiments, but research on emotions aroused, images evoked, and meanings connected with the visual stimulus of a black person in various contexts has been less frequent than word-association tests designed to elicit reaction to the written or spoken stimulus of the words "Negro" or "Black." The few cross-cultural studies that have been made in a broad time-space framework, some content analyses of literary and biographical works, and discussions of educational and political philosophy suggest at least four significant domains of evaluation of the color *Black* as a symbol and of people designated as Black. These might be termed the *esthetic*, the *erotic*, the *moral/mystical*, and the *status-allocating*. In addition, a *cognitive* dimension exists that affects, and is affected by, these domains. Appraisals by others are sometimes internalized by black people, and this area of behavior merits extensive research cross-culturally. Research on evaluations in each of these domains within various types of societies is especially necessary to test the Degler-Gergen position that negative evaluations of "blackness" are universal, that these evaluations carry over to people, and that Blacks downgrade "blackness" in their own symbol systems and with reference to their own body images. In the sections that follow, some observations are made about the state of knowledge with regard to each of these domains that serve as guidelines in the organization of some of the data in the chapters about specific geographical areas.

The tendency among some Caucasoid and Mongoloid groups to define the Negroid physical type as "ugly" is one of the most significant reactions to be noted in comparative studies. In Middle Eastern and Mediterranean lands where Africans have been used as domestic slaves for over 2,000 years, there has been a tendency for erotic stereotypes of black men and women to arise. Protestant-Christian cultures, during and after the period of the slave trade, have associated moral deficiencies with "Negroidness"; but these, like many other cultures, also attribute some positive moral and mystical values to "blackness" and black people. During the past 500 years European and American societies have associated the concept of cognitive deficit with "Negroidness." Since such evaluations as these are not made everywhere and at all times, the situational components that affect these appraisals must be defined if their presence is to be understood. Personal evaluations in terms of skin-color are always made within some specific sociocultural context.

The Esthetic Dimension

At the Copenhagen "Color and Race" conference in 1965, several of the participants stressed the extent to which Caucasians and Asians historically defined dark skin-color within their own societies as an undesirable trait for women, or thought of alien black peoples as "ugly." In an article entitled "The Social Perception of Skin Color in Japan," for instance, one author noted:

Long before any sustained contact with either Caucasoid Europeans or dark-skinned Africans and Indians, the Japanese valued "white" skin as beautiful and deprecated "black" skin as ugly. Their spontaneous responses to the white skin of the Caucasoid Europeans and the black skin of Negroid people were an extension of values deeply embedded in Japanese concepts of beauty.[63]

One Japanese scholar writing in the eighteenth century confused the people of India with those of Africa, remarking about servants used by the Dutch:

> Black ones are impoverished Indians. . . . As their country is in the South and the heat is extreme, their body is sun scorched and their color becomes black. Their hair is burned by the sun and becomes frizzled, but they are human and not monkeys as some mistakenly think.[64]

The word *black* is loosely applied today to several varieties of mankind, including Indians and Australian aborigines ("Black-fellows"), but in its application to sub-Saharan Africans and their descendants—"Negroes"—the derogation has been most intense. Throughout the 400 years of slavery in the Western Hemisphere, possession of dark skin-color, kinky hair, flat nose, and thick lips subjected millions of people to ridicule, abuse, and vilification. Stereotypes have become fixed as visual images and have been correlated with a nomenclature including such derogatory epithets as "nigger," "blue-gummed nigger," "darky," "Sambo," "coon," "bongo man," "burr head," "*grito*," "*jabao*," and "*nègre*." It is evident from the contemptuous and patronizing tone of these abusive terms that they exceed mere expressions of a mild preference by whites for their own somatic norm image. Their use clearly serves some other psychological function. To reiterate constantly that some group is "ugly" and yet simultaneously to miscegenate with members of that group calls as much for psychiatric explanations as social-scientific ones. Stereotyping also has served the needs of socioeconomic interest groups that profit from the process. It has lowered the self-esteem of those exploited and abused, and has divided the more Negroid among them from the less Negroid. Reference was made in chapter 1 to the role of esthetic evaluation in racist ideology. When young Afro-Americans shouted, "Black is Beautiful!" during the 1960s, they meant it literally as well as metaphorically. An assertion of worth demanded the repudiation of centuries of ridicule of the body image of black people.

The esthetic dimension of black/white relations does not involve reaction to skin-color in isolation from the factors that create a total gestalt of body image. Black skin-color is only one element in an image that includes type of hair, shape of nose, thickness of lips, and alleged racial characteristics of pelvis, buttocks, and breasts, feet and gait, and perceived or imagined body odor. "Negroidness" is usually the concept associated with "blackness," but not always. Winthrop Jordan pointed out the negative attitudes that literate seventeenth-century English people expressed toward "blackness" and toward Africans, but he also quoted a playwright describing her hero to indicate that, for some people, facial features were more important than skin-color in making a beauty assessment:

> The most famous Statuary could not form the Figure of a Man more admirable turn'd from Head to Foot. His Face was not of that brown rusty Black which most of that Nation are, but a perfect Ebony or polished Jet. . . . His Nose was rising and *Roman* instead of *African* and flat: His Mouth the finest shaped that could be seen; far from those great turn'd Lips which are so natural to the rest of the Negroes. The whole Proportion and Air of his Face was so nobly and exactly formed that bating his Colour, there could be nothing in Nature more beautiful, agreeable and handsome.[65]

The figure described was *Oroonoko*, the black prince, who could have been either East Indian or African. The appraisal is that of a connoisseur and is similar to one made by a seventeenth-century British artist, Richard Ligon, who wrote of his admiration for beautiful black women, if they did not have Negroid features.[66]

That hair posed problems for some sixteenth-century Englishmen is suggested by one of Shakespeare's sonnets to the Dark Lady, in which these lines occur: "If hairs be wires, black wires grow on her head."[67] In the late nineteenth century, the expression "Molly Glosters" was used by some Afro-Americans to refer to very dark individuals with long, straight hair. They were considered attractive. Although the type may have resulted from admixture with Amerindians, it is likely that the name is a corruption of "Malagasy," for some slaves were landed from Madagascar. It is not unusual to hear words of admiration expressed by Africans and Afro-Americans as well as by whites for East Indian women with very black skin and Negroid lips, but who have long, glossy black hair. (Is it possible that there is a general tendency among human beings to value "sleekness" and "smoothness" in animal and human integumental cover because of a pleasant tactile sensation when the hand passes over it? Cross-cultural research could be designed to answer this comparative-esthetic question.)[68] It is significant that both the ancient Greeks and some Latin American groups use both skin-color and hair type in defining varieties of Africans and people of partial African descent. Herodotus, for instance, defined two types of Ethiopians, distinguishing between those who were Blacks with straight hair and those who were Blacks with frizzled hair. He, unlike the Latin Americans, made no esthetic judgment based upon the type of hair.

That it was not color per se but the total configuration of "Negroidness" that most Europeans perceived as ugly is given greater plausibility by the insistence in some quarters that Negroes resemble apes. Evolutionary theory during the nineteenth century popularized the idea that Negroes are "closest to the ape" on the evolutionary scale. Well into the twentieth century, anthropologists have been patiently explaining that apes have straight hair, thin lips, and pale skin. But insofar as it has served psychological needs for some people to believe that Negroes resemble apes, they have been perceived that way, and the belief has been manipulated by self-serving interest groups.[69]

It is important to note that these stereotyped esthetic appraisals have not completely controlled interaction between individual white and black people. Within all racial and ethnic groups, people sustain friendly and warm relations as well as less intimate ones with people they conceive of as ugly (including mating and marriage) and they also do so across racial lines. The proverb that "beauty is only skin deep" has applied in interracial as well as intraracial relations. Familiarity also dissipates appraisals of ugliness based upon strangeness, and sociologist Hoetink has reminded us that where Negroes have not been considered a threat to a status order that subordinates them, they have sometimes been prized as exotic. A consideration usually ignored in discussing attitudes of one race toward another is the fact that harmoniousness of features tends to override considerations of color when esthetic appraisals of facial beauty are made. (See current issues of *Ebony* and *Essence* magazines and occasional advertisements in *Newsweek*.) People learn to appreciate various kinds of esthetically pleasing combinations of color and features in people different from themselves. (It is recorded, however, that on the first encounter some Asians had difficulty in seeing beauty in Caucasian noses that, to them, "stood out like the beak of a ship.") Defining women as ugly has never been a barrier to miscegenation, as the case of the initial contact between the Dutch and the southern Africans graphically illustrates. The invaders considered the steatopygous women of the people they named "Hottentots" (the Khoi people) unattractive, but mated with them nevertheless.[70]

Evaluations in terms of "ugly" and "beautiful" have implications that extend beyond esthetic appraisals of ethnic groups. So long as a stereotype of Negro ugliness persists within a culture, it reinforces the subordination and the exploitation of the more Negroid portion of any collectivity defined as "black" with a wide skin-color range. And it generates in-group tensions. Its effects are particularly insidious because esthetic evaluations become intertwined with appraisals of intellectual capacity. Sometimes there is a simple tendency to think of "ugly" people as "dumb."[71]

The Erotic Dimension

The erotic implications of being Black in some of the societies of medieval Europe and of the Western Hemisphere after the fifteenth century have been detailed by numerous writers, historians, and social scientists. Black intellectuals have made observations as insiders, and American blues singers and West Indian calypsonians have added their lyrics to the jokes and the folklore. Psychoanalysis has lent an aura of presumed scientific legitimacy to a wide range of theorizing on the subject.[72]

Students of Latin American and Caribbean cultures have noted that specific African tribes gained a reputation for having women who made attractive concubines for their masters during slavery, and in these cases the Caucasian norm of physical beauty was not always the most highly valued.[73] Some stress, too, the extent to which the cult of the mulatto woman became widespread in French and Latin American areas. The mulatto combined esthetic and erotic appeal, and devotion to the concept of "the divine mulatto" depressed the status of the black woman to that of a mere sexual object. Professor Degler, in *Neither Black nor White*, quoted a nineteenth-century Brazilian aphorism suggesting that the process of degradation could be even more extreme than that entailed by being made a sex object:

> White women are for marrying;
> Mulatto women are for fornicating;
> Black women are for service.[74]

In his article "Dusky Venus, Black Apollo" (1961), Roger Bastide argued that the institutionalized miscegenation of Brazil reduced the entire female black population to the status of prostitutes.[75] It is striking, however, that despite such aphoristic appraisals or anthropological labeling, these interracial sexual relationships were as complex and variegated during slavery as they are throughout the Caribbean and in Latin America today. Some Negroid women were defined as both beautiful and sexually attractive. Some were loved as mistresses, others respected and cherished as wives. Personal choices of female companions were never completely determined by stereotypes.

The scholarly literature on the erotic component in race relations is vast, much of it cast in a Freudian idiom that considers the Negro an id symbol in those Western Christian societies where a high degree of sexual repression is considered desirable. Unconscious wishes to participate in forbidden sexual practices are thought to be projected onto the Negro, who then excites guilt and may be punished to avoid punishing oneself. Certain special twists are applied in analyzing the southern United States, where some males may have had permissive black women as wet nurses or surrogate mothers, and therefore may have developed deep affection for brown-skinned women in contrast to women like their more remote and austere biological mothers. The prevailing caste system then imposed the demand that such feelings be repressed as males grew older.

A southern white novelist, Lillian Smith, in *Strange Fruit*, elaborated a plot involving a middle-class white male and a college-educated black woman. In another work, *Killers of the Dream*, she called attention, as a Freudian might do, to what she saw as an intricate link binding the "three S's" in the South: sin-sex-segregation. Novelist Alan Paton, writing of South African society in *Too Late the Phalarope*, developed a similar theme. In this case, a churchgoing, Calvinistic family man succumbs to the attractions of a black Bantu girl. Being a police officer, his career and his reputation collapse in ruins when the affair is discovered. John Dollard's *Caste and Class in a Southern Town* (1937) attempted to state the nature of what he called the "sexual gains" that accrue to white males of the dominant caste at the expense of black males in the system of the American South, for sexual repression there did not prevent clandestine affairs.[76]

According to Freudian explanation, the dogma that fornication with Blacks is sinful results in repression, which, in turn, augments systems of segregation that are justified as necessary to preserve the "purity" of white society. But fantasies as well as compulsive behavior result from such repression, and perhaps not among white males only. Afro-American Calvin Herndon, in *Sex and Race*, postulated a generalized desire by black males in the United States to experience sex relations with white women—the forbidden object. A more recent work by a white American sociologist suggested that white males fear that white women have a suppressed desire for black males, whether or not it actually exists. In the southern United

States, the challenging question, "Would you want your daughter to marry a nigger?" could intimidate proponents of the most innocuous social reforms.[77]

For reasons to be discussed in the chapters that follow, Negro men and women became sexual symbols long before European feudalism emerged, and they still possess erotic significance throughout the Middle East. It is doubtful, however, whether Freudian and neo-Freudian theories have the same explanatory plausibility outside of the Western world, which has always had a strong tendency toward metaphysical dualism. Emphasis upon a struggle between the "lower" urges of the body and the "higher" aspirations of the mind and spirit not only stigmatizes Africans and their cultures but leads also to rigorous suppression of the desire for the sexual freedom they are believed to possess as "a more primitive people." With the so-called sexual revolution in the West, occurring after World War II, it is possible that the negative attitude toward alleged Negro sensuality is diminishing in some circles while being reinforced in very conservative religious circles. In Islamic societies there is no such sharp dualism, and sexuality has been more frankly accepted,[78] but the erotic implications of "Negroidness" work to the disadvantage of Africans in other ways.

Some doubt is thrown on the existence of a Manichaean belief in a malevolent "blackness" rooted deeply in the European psyche by the popularity of the so-called Black Madonnas in various parts of Europe. One of the most popular shrines of this type is located in the city of Czestochowa, where the image of the "Queen of Poland" is located, the famous Black Madonna. Why are the hundreds of thousands of worshipers who stream to this shrine every year not deterred by the Manichaean dichotomy? The Polish icon is dark brown, but with somewhat Caucasoid features; so, while this is a good example for studying attitudes toward "blackness," it is less useful for assessing reactions to "Negroidness." The Black Madonna near Zurich is unmistakably Negro.

The Stereotype of Immorality

Nowhere is comparative research more important than in carrying out an investigation of the origins, provenance, and content of the stereotype of "Negro immorality." There has been a persistent attempt for centuries to define the Negro as an immoral and corrupting influence within Christian societies. Occasionally, demons have been portrayed as Black, but more often the derogation has resided in

the vague feeling that Africans are "oversexed" and that their dancing and music are too sexually seductive. Catholic fathers in the
Caribbean preached against the dancing of the *calinda* by the slaves
a full century before the Puritans settled in Massachusetts. It is significant that New Englanders who went to the southern United States
to establish schools for the ex-slaves after the Civil War did not feel
that their students were handicapped by a cognitive deficit, but they
did feel that they had a significant *moral* deficit, perhaps inherited.
The emphasis upon "character training" at Tuskegee, as stressed by
Booker T. Washington, was based upon assumptions that black students had to struggle against tendencies toward slothfulness, dis-
honesty, pleasure-loving pursuits, and laziness. The Phelps-Stokes
Fund, which was influential in shaping the educational policy in
English-speaking Africa during the 1920s, approached its tasks with
similar beliefs about the character traits of black students.[79]

Criticism of the morality of black people in North America originated in white Protestant circles and was accepted as a "racial weakness" by the black middle class, which had its earliest base in the
churches of the Free Negroes in northern cities. Education and conversion were needed to "redeem the race." These beliefs about Negro
"immorality" became stereotypes that shaped attitudes of European
immigrants entering the American social system during the
nineteenth and twentieth centuries. The caricature of the chicken-
stealing, watermelon-stealing yet churchgoing black man, whose
preacher was a woman chaser, became the stock-in-trade of the great
black entertainer (from the Bahamas) Bert Williams, as well as of
numerous white entertainers. Changing attitudes toward the work
ethic since World War II and changing standards of sexual behavior
throughout the Western world have helped to lessen criticism of
black men and women for behavior deviating from white, middle-
class norms. Some fundamentalist Christian circles in the United
States, however, insist that Blacks have corrupted the whole of society by popularizing the blues, jazz, and a variety of black dances.

The stereotype of black immorality exists side-by-side with the belief that Negroes possess special mystical powers and produce an unusual number of individuals with ethical and moral insight. In some
cultures an individual's endowment with such power and insight is
not diminished by sexual behavior that in Judaeo-Christian societies
is evaluated as "immoral." Public sexuality was present in religious
ritual in the ancient Near East, and left-hand Tantric rites still take
place in modern India. In the United States, Negroes are thought to

have special gifts that find expression in spirituals and gospel songs, as well as in the blues. Their religiosity is proverbial, as well as their roistering. A similar two-sided stereotype of Negroes existed in ancient Greece and Rome, with Blacks excelling in oracular pronouncements as well as certain kinds of erotic entertainment. A similar duality was present in Medieval Islam, while Medieval Christianity had its Black Madonnas as well as its black images of the devil. Evaluation in *the moral/mystical domain* operates to create and reinforce both positive and negative prejudices against black people.

The Myth of a Cognitive Deficit

The association of Negroes with slavery in the Western world has brought an almost automatic assumption that they lack the same degree of intellectual ability that whites possess. Comparative studies of both the stereotype and the fact, in varied times and places, are needed to put this question in perspective. Esthetic and erotic evaluations of "Negroidness" typically include considerations of moral approval or censure and sometimes entail estimates of intellectual ability as well. In Anglophone areas, much of this is an unconscious aspect of English-language usage. The use of adjectives like "coarse," "refined," and "keen" to characterize human features (even when discussing Caucasians) leads inevitably to "keen minds" being associated with "keen features" and "dullness of mind" being connected with "coarseness of features."[80] Research is needed to discover how prevalent this tendency is within other language communities.

It has been noted, in the discussion of Thomas Jefferson in the previous chapter, that the conception of a cognitive deficit among Negroes was present in eighteenth-century American culture. It was probably present in a vague way in what might be called the "folk anthropology" of the country, but it was not generally accepted as "proven by science" until the use of intelligence tests became general during and after World War I. Racist publicists such as de Gobineau and Stoddard had, of course, proclaimed the low intelligence of Blacks as a "fact" proved by evolution. But the Boas school of anthropology in the United States, backed up by a group of social psychologists at Columbia University, carried on the battle against the idea of a genetic cognitive deficiency, facing a formidable array of biologists, psychologists, and educators. The struggle against Hitlerian racism that accompanied the fighting of World War II weakened the belief in the scientific objectivity of the biological determinists, and a worldwide campaign by UNESCO during the 1950s spread widely the views of modern social scientists on the question of racial cognitive deficits.

Further research in the 1950s indicated that, even in the South, Americans were rapidly dropping their belief in the inborn intellectual inferiority of black people.

With the beginning of the Civil Rights movement in the southern United States in the mid-fifties, there ensued a revival of the concept of a cognitive deficit by those opposed to school desegregation. The names of Arthur Jensen, William Shockley, and Richard Herrnstein became well known as representatives of an influential minority of American scientists who called for a return to earlier views about the innate ability of Negroes. An upsurge in immigration from Africa, Asia, and the West Indies to Great Britain threw Hans Eysenck and Sir Cyril Burt into opposition against most psychologists and sociologists on this same question. These biological determinists were again in the ascendancy until evidence released after Sir Cyril's death showed that some of his research data had been fabricated either by himself or his assistants. South African defenders of apartheid have come increasingly to argue that they believe biological differences make a single, multiracial society impossible, but that these differences do not imply discrepancies in intelligence.

The literature on both sides of this argument about black intellectual capacity is voluminous, but the position of the defenders of the view that Blacks are genetically inferior becomes increasingly weaker. Of some significance is the effort of one group of young black psychologists to shift the argument to another plane, to accept the concept of inborn differences in *types* of intelligence but to argue that Blacks inherit a superior kind of intelligence that IQ tests do not measure.[81]

Situational Components in Black/White Relations

The esthetic and erotic components of prejudice, and beliefs about moral and cognitive deficiencies, as well as mystical/religious virtues, operate within social systems that are, in turn, articulated to specific modes of production that reflect ecological and demographic particularities. These situational components are decisive in generating and sustaining changes in race relations.

Even if associations with "blackness" at the level of abstract symbolism do prove to be more negative than positive, and if further research demonstrates that the Negro physical type functions as an id symbol regardless of the culture, the influence of such factors upon racial relations would still vary according to the framework of social institutions and social situations within which Blacks and Whites interact. Two well-known scholars, Bruno Bettelheim and Morris

Janowitz, in publishing research into the question of the scapegoating of Blacks and Jews in the Western world, have noted that "no claim is made that these hypotheses are universally applicable." They emphasized the point that their hypotheses are relevant only to a specific type of society, namely, "modern industrialized communities which are characterized by a complex division of labor." As researchers attempting to combine a neo-Freudian system of psychology with sociological analysis, they wrote:

> Group hostilities take on different aspects in primitive cultures, in predominantly agricultural societies, and in cultural areas which are in a period of particular transition. Under those conditions other hypotheses might be required for understanding the particular forms in which group hostility may operate.[82]

What is true of group conflict is true also of racial prejudice generally and prejudice against Blacks particularly. Color symbolism, group stereotypes, attitudes, and the *content* of the superego will vary according to the type of society within which they exist. For instance, the precapitalist but nontribal societies of the Middle East have traditionally incorporated large numbers of Africans into their communities under a system of domestic slavery, as contrasted with industrial slavery. Very few Blacks have been employed in production, whether in the fields or in urban artisan workshops. Stereotypes have derived from their occupational roles, exemplified by eunuchs, concubines, and servants in the households of the wealthy, as well as by soldiers in the armies of rulers and feudal lords, and singing girls and dancers in public places. White slaves have been used in similar capacities. After the coming of Islam, many Blacks attained free status, being replaced by freshly captured pagans of both races. Except in rare cases, the only direct cause of interracial conflict among the ordinary people was when Blacks operated as soldiers that oppressed some segment of the population, or occasional slave rebellions. Race relations in the Middle East, therefore, might be expected to have a different character from race relations in the Caribbean or in the southern United States, where slaves were a primary factor in the economic life and white free labor was competing against black slave labor. Color prejudice against Blacks has existed in all of these situations, but *racial slavery* and institutional racism were not present.

Hoetink, in *Caribbean Race Relations*, and other scholars, have emphasized the study of the characteristics of "initial contact" situations in generalizing about the results of contact between groups that differ in race or culture. It is almost impossible to find contemporary first-contact situations for study, but a mass of literature generated by travelers, explorers, missionaries, and imperial administrators in the past, not to mention some literature produced by the "natives" themselves, is available for analysis. Sociologist Herbert Blumer, like Robert Ezra Park, after examining such material, concludes that contact between different races does not inevitably generate racial prejudice. He noted that "frequently racial prejudice may not appear in racial contacts; if present it may disappear; or although present, it may not dominate the relations. Instead of thinking of racial prejudice as an invariant and simple matter, it must be viewed as a highly variable and complex phenomenon." Blumer believed, however, that when it does appear, "the chief feeling in racial prejudice is usually a feeling of dislike or an impulse of aversion." Yet he stressed that

> it is a mistake to regard such a feeling or impulse as the only one or even necessarily always the main one. Instead, racial prejudice is made up of a variety of feelings and impulses which in different situations enter into the attitude in differing combinations and differing proportions. Hatred, dislike, resentment, distrust, envy, fear, feelings of obligation, possessive impulses, guilt—these are some of the feelings and impulses which may enter into racial prejudices.[83]

Social psychologist Gordon Allport added a dimension that Blumer neglected, namely, the possibility of *positive* prejudices—prejudice in favor of another group.[84] The conceptualization of group differences as *racial* does not always occur upon first contact, and even when the groups are viewed as races, color does not necessarily emerge as the most relevant distinguishing marker. However, a fifth domain of skin-color evaluation, that of *status-evaluation*, sometimes emerges within this context as an aspect of status-allocation. In examining any concrete situation where skin-color differences do exist, a model based upon Blumer's and Allport's observations about the more general phenomenon of race prejudice may be useful (see chart 1), always keeping in mind the question, "Does the presence of color difference increase the tendency of relations to develop in the direction of psychological rejection rather than positive identification?" Let us assume a situation in which two races in contact are differentiated by skin-color. During the initial contact there is a natural *awareness* of difference, and the definition of the group difference is couched in terms of color. According to the Blumer-Allport paradigm, a range of attitudes is then possible, moving away from indifference

CHART 1. Types of Institutionalization: Attitudes Expressed in Initial Contact Between Individuals of Different Racial Groups

Basic Cognitive Reaction	Range of Possible Attitudes when Initial Contact Occurs (Individual)	Types of Possible Group Reactions after Contact	Possible End Results of Contact (including Institutionalization)
	Psychological rejection	Extirpation of one group	No incorporation into a single social system
	Evaluation according to some esthetic, ethical, and utilitarian norms and values *(cultural component)*	Expulsion of One Group	
		Enslavement	Systems of Color-Caste
Awareness of Difference in Skin-Color	Fear / Disgust / Repugnance / Dislike / Curiosity / Indifference / Curiosity / Exotic Appeal / Admiration / Confidence	Acceptance with Inferior Status, but not in Kin Groups	Systems of Color-Class
	Evaluation according to some esthetic, ethical, and utilitarian norms and values *(cultural component)*		Systems Where Color is Not a Status Marker
	Positive Identification	Acceptance with Inferior Status in Kin Groups	Disappearance of differences due to complete amalgamation
		Egalitarian Acceptance	

SOURCES: Blumer, ''Nature of Race Prejudice''; Allport, *Nature of Prejudice.*

toward either rejection or positive identification. Color may or may not assume symbolic and emotional significance in addition to being a mere indicator of the existence of two separate groups.

Subcultural reactions can be characterized by such expressions as curiosity, dislike, repugnance, or fear leading toward rejection, as well as curiosity, eroticism, admiration, or confidence leading toward positive identification (chart 1). The culture provides some cues according to esthetic, ethical, and utilitarian norms and values, both positive and negative. Various situational factors, as well as idiosyncratic psychological factors, enter into the acceptance and operation of one set of cues as opposed to another. Insofar as attitudes find expression in behavior, racial discrimination (which in some societies will be on the basis of skin-color) can lead either to extirpation or to expulsion of the discriminated-against persons from the society. However, if it leads to societal incorporation, a wide range of types of unequal status is possible, in addition to egalitarian incorporation. The right-hand column of chart 1 indicates possible structural results of the interaction, ranging from systems of color-*caste* through systems of color-*class* to amalgamation with disappearance of differences.

Blumer, like most American sociologists and anthropologists between the two world wars, was impressed by the tendency of people to prefer the customs of the societies in which they have been socialized and often to be so narcissistic—and prejudiced—about it as to call themselves "the men" or "the people." That is, they are *ethnocentric*. But he insisted that it is incorrect to equate ethnocentrism with *racial* prejudice, or even to allot it first place in explaining why race prejudice sometimes arises:

> *There seems to be little doubt that ethnocentrism must be reckoned with as a nucleus around which an attitude of racial prejudice may develop. . . . Yet, however important ethnocentrism may be as a factor in racial prejudice, it does not seem to be the decisive factor. Of more importance is what amounts to a primitive tribal tendency in the form of fear of an attack, or displacement, or of annihilation* [italics added].[85]

The concept of ethnocentrism was originally developed from the observation of small, isolated communities. In considering complex, multiethnic, stratified societies, Blumer substituted other notions for "the primitive tribal tendency," but he retained the concept of group fear of attack, displacement, or annihilation as the necessary cause in triggering attitudes of racial prejudice. Color differences sometimes become the primary symbol of the racial differences perceived by the members of such complex, hierarchically organized societies. When groups differentiated from one another by color develop structured relations toward one another in the form of a hierarchy, race prejudice is likely to flourish. The following proposition, then, expressed Blumer's basic theory of race relations: *"It is the sense of social position . . . which provides the basis of race prejudice* [italics added]." He considered all explanations given by people involved in such situations to be rationalizations of the relative social positions in which they functioned. Blumer described four particular social situations where race prejudice is likely to be most acute.[86]

(1) When two or more ethnic groups live together within a single society

(2) When one or more ethnic groups are subordinated, segregated, and subject to invidious discrimination

(3) When a dominant ethnic group fears that a subordinate group is not keeping its place and threatens to claim the opportunities and privileges from which it has been excluded

(4) When critical incidents occur, resulting in a dominant group's feeling that its relative position is being jeopardized and its security threatened

Attitudes, Ideology, and Social Structure

In the four types of situations noted above, any cultural or physical difference between groups can be emphasized and used as counters in the game and as weapons in the struggle—that is, they can function as ideological supports. Skin-color and other anatomical traits are among these. One of Herbert Blumer's critics, Afro–West Indian Marxist sociologist Oliver C. Cox, in presenting a section entitled "Theory of Race Prejudice and Racism" in his own book *Race Relations*, took issue with Blumer's social-psychological emphasis upon prejudiced attitudes, insisting that *"the critical factor is not the type of feeling, but the type of society which causes the addition of the fourth element* [see preceding list] *to result in race prejudice* [italics added]." Cox suggested that "perhaps our first realization should be that race prejudice is a peculiar socio-political attitude." His own view is that "the source of race prejudice . . . emanates from a powerful, elite interest group which also orients the society on all significant questions. It could not exist in opposition to the wishes and ideology of the class."[87] Cox maintained that race prejudice as well as racism are the result of the racial discrimination introduced by a specific elite group—the European capitalist class—as it expanded after the fifteenth century. This statement is not consistent with the facts. It would be more useful for our purposes to stress that although the prejudice of white people toward colored people ante-dated Western capitalist expansion, *racial slavery* and White Racism are products of that European overseas expansion, including the in-auguration of the transatlantic African slave trade.

Both Herbert Blumer and Oliver Cox were more interested in the general phenomenon of racial prejudice than in its more limited, specific expression in the form of skin-color prejudice. There has been no organized attempt since the Copenhagen conference in 1965 to ex-amine the role of color discrimination in the modern world. It is pos-sible that negative associations with "blackness" have become so entrenched in the national culture of the United States that hope for eventual equality of Afro-Americans is an illusion, but Cox, writing in 1976, reminded us that *"in the study of race relations the critical data are not to be sought in the biological stability of color but rather in its changing cultural definition* [italics added]."[88] Studies in com-parative history and comparative anthropology are necessary to un-derstand this process. To this end, we shall attempt to examine, against a broad background in time and space, the following hypotheses about modern societies:

(1) Negative characteristics associated with *Black* as a color are widespread but may exist at the abstract level without being *so-cially* salient.

(2) Negative attitudes toward black people may be held by seg-ments of the white population, when both reside within a single culture, without institutionalized racism resulting.

(3) Constant contact at work, worship, play, and in other cooper-ative efforts may operate to offset negative appraisals of "black-ness" and of black people that are propagated by certain segments of a culture.

(4) Dominant groups may denigrate the skin-color of a subordinate group in order to try to weaken that group's sense of self-esteem and social solidarity.

(5) Dominant groups may denigrate the skin-color of a subordinate group in order to implement a policy of divide and rule within the lower ranks of the social order, and to heighten the morale of those below them who share their own physical traits but are themselves socially subordinated.

(6) Since skin-color is only one of many personal attributes, insti-tutionalized racism is a necessary tool for elites to use in order

to prevent solidarities from arising among those below them along dimensions of similarity other than color, for example, economic class.

(7) Under some conditions, subordinated groups utilize color solidarity in their own struggle for survival and status.

THE NEED FOR COMPARATIVE RESEARCH

A survey of the work of psychologists, sociologists, and social anthropologists studying race relations since World War II reveals the acceptance by individual scholars of some or all of the following beliefs about general processes that underlie the prejudice and discrimination of members of one human group against those of other groups who are phenotypically different (the evidence is presented from studies in comparative history and anthropology, as well as in Freudian psychology):

(1) A tendency among members of groups to prefer their own somatic norm image and thus to reinforce ethnocentrism with incipient racial prejudice (Hoetink)

(2) A tendency to utilize physical differences, as well as various other kinds of differences, in boundary formation between groups (Wirth, Warner, Blumer, Hoetink)

(3) A tendency to utilize physical differences in ideology formation during power struggles (Blumer, Cox)

(4) A tendency to project repressed psychic content from the id onto culturally approved groups (targets); and, in more general situations, a tendency to act out frustration and aggression (Freud, Dollard, Bettelheim, Manganyi, Allport)

Acceptance of these propositions does not, however, explain why black people, specifically, become the objects of prejudice and discrimination. In addition to the historical and cultural explanations that will be discussed later, several existing influential theories might be subjected to experimental testing. Very little research of this type has been attempted.

(1) Psycho-physical causation without any assumptions that associative learning is involved:

(a) Black skin-color acts as a direct negative stimulus on the human nervous system, as experimental psychology shows some colors do (not taken seriously by any current experimenters)

(b) Innate tendency to think in bipolar oppositions, of which the black/white opposition is one

(c) Presence of black people as frightening Jungian-like archetypes, presumably perceived by all people

(2) Psycho-physical causation operating only through associative learning processes (conditioning):

(a) Universal association of blackness with various natural phenomena such as night, dirt, and feces, which are evaluated negatively by children (with or without parental pressures) and then, through conditioning, become associated with the somatic image of black people

(b) Process mentioned in (a) but not occurring at all times and in all places

(c) Carry-over to people of emotions associated with verbalizations about blackness and with *Black* as a color in the abstract symbol system

Theories currently dominant among social scientists consider prejudice and discrimination against black people to be the result of historical processes that have thrown black people into contact with nonblack people, resulting in either of two phenomena: (1) existing evaluations of blackness as a color symbol have been transferred to people, or (2) the interracial contact has generated evaluations that did not exist before. In either case, black skin-color and black people have assumed a symbolic character, that is, they have come to stand for ideas, not emotions, and they serve as cues to action and trigger emotional responses. The symbolism is sociocultural in nature; the meanings are not intrinsic but imputed. "Blackness," as applied to people, takes on meanings at several different levels:

(1) *Mystical symbolism*, as in the case of the Egyptian deity Osiris, Black Madonnas in Europe; devils, in some cultures

(2) *Ethnocentric symbolism*, where "blackness" of skin-color functions to define the boundaries between in-group and out-group, subject to change in degree of importance

(3) *Social-stratification symbolism*, where within a given society skin-color prejudices are used to reinforce systems of slavery, caste, class, estates, etc.

(4) *Power-struggle symbolism*, where in contests for economic and political power or territory, color solidarity is evoked as a mobilizing device, that is, functions as ideology

Two processes always proceed simultaneously: (1) the appraisals and evaluations made by black and nonblack individuals interacting spontaneously; and (2) the structuring of the interaction by those segments of society that wield power and that are in a position to use institutions of education and propaganda to define what ideas and emotions associated with "blackness" are approved of. A sociocultural analysis of these processes might well include both Freudian and Marxian perspectives, but by its nature would exclude a psychophysical determinism locating prejudice against black people in the structure of the mind, the nervous system, or the unconscious. The idea of a socially defined target for projection of the unconscious contents of the id is acceptable; Jungian archetypes are not. The concept of an innate tendency to think in binary oppositions is acceptable, but the idea of this process necessarily involving a black/white contrast is not. Historical materialism is acceptable; economic determinism is not.

Intensive social-anthropological investigations within a range of carefully selected societies are necessary to test the several hypotheses suggested here, as well as the Degler-Gergen propositions. Analysis of a group of especially significant cases treated within the framework of comparative history should also be carried out. Very little research of this type has been attempted. The chapters that follow combine social anthropology and comparative history in an attempt to examine the propositions listed earlier, and we propose to test, with a few selected cases, the Degler-Gergen generalizations against empirical data of a type these scholars of the Black Experience chose not to utilize. We begin with the Nile Valley in antiquity.

Bibliographic Essay

Rigorous scientific analyses of the causes of prejudice against "blackness" in the abstract and against black people are rare compared to the number of books and articles dealing with racial prejudice in general. References to the basic literature dealing with both of these aspects of racial prejudice in the United States have been cited in the endnotes to this chapter. It is important, however, that a broader, comparative review of the literature be provided if the suggested problems for research are to be seriously considered.

British empire builders and missionaries have contributed a mass of raw data on Africa, India, and the West Indies that documents reactions of white people to black people. Only since World War II, however, have British social scientists begun to develop theories to explain racial prejudice.

Sir Alan Burns's *Colour Prejudice: With Particular Reference to the Relationship Between Whites and Negroes* (London: Allen and Unwin, 1948; Westport, Conn.: Negro Universities Press, 1971) is an examination of the roots of prejudice against black people, written by a liberal British colonial administrator. This book is worth reading both for its historic interest and for the raw data presented, despite the inadequacy of the explanations. Serious research on race relations by English scholars began during the decade following Sir Alan's book. Increased African, West Indian, and Asian emigration to Britain not only increased racial tensions there but also created problems in areas throughout the multiracial Commonwealth, where expressions of racial prejudice in Britain were resented. New types of scholars with new perspectives were needed. The historian Arnold Toynbee, in his monumental work *A Study of History*, combined an eloquent plea against racism with a type of perceptual distortion that led him to state that the black race was the only race on earth that had never made any contribution to the development of civilization! The works of Kenneth Little, Anthony Richmond, Richard Banton, and John Rex should be consulted for examples of modern British race-relations theory, which leans toward what Hoetink has called "sociologistic optimism." *Race and Class: A Journal for Black and Third World Liberation* (a quarterly publication of the Institute of Race Relations and the Transnational Institute) publishes scholarly articles utilizing a Marxian approach.

During the early sixties the Ford Foundation made funds available to the Institute of Race Relations in London for a series of studies that would deal with "the development of relationships between ethnic groups in the Spanish-speaking parts of America, in the Caribbean, Brazil, India, Africa, and South-East Asia." The conclusions were to be summarized by Sir Philip Mason, the director of the institute. Some of the special monographs were completed, but the director decided to make a more broadly comparative study and to organize the data around one significant guiding theme. The Ford Foundation made it possible for him to do so, and in 1970 he published *Patterns of Dominance* with data drawn from Sparta and Athens, the Incas and Aztecs, the African empires, India, southern Africa, Spanish America, the Caribbean, and Brazil. It is an erudite and thought-provoking book well worth reading. (The chapter entitled "Sexual Attitudes" has something fresh to say about a continuously discussed aspect of race relations.) He endorsed without criticism, however, the unproved "Modern Manichaean" assertion that in ancient Greece and Rome, in Judaism, Christianity, and Islam, and "in much of Africa," there is an "association of moral qualities with light and brightness, while passions that are deplored and disliked are linked with darkness. This metaphorical use of language . . . has been confused with the biological fact of skin colour."[1]

The most important scholarly publication to date on the color-prejudice dimension of race relations viewed in worldwide perspective is the special issue of *Daedalus* entitled "Color and Race" (96, 2 [Spring 1967]), referred to in chapter 2. (Dr. W.E.B. Du Bois had been contending for seventy-five years that "the problem of the twentieth century is the problem of the color line.") The *Daedalus* issue contained seventeen articles, thirteen of which had been prepared for the conference sponsored by the Congress for Cultural Freedom and the American Academy of Arts and Sciences, which met in Copenhagen in September 1965 to "study attitudes toward race and color in as many dimensions as possible." A special theoretical article was commissioned after the conference for inclusion in the volume. This article, authored by Professor Kenneth Gergen, who was then an assistant professor of psychology at Harvard, was entitled "The Significance of Skin Color in Human Relations." The papers were republished in 1968 with an introduction by the Afro-American historian Dr. John Hope Franklin, who had been chairman of the Copenhagen conference. Franklin observed that no single point of view emerged at the conference on the question of how deeply rooted skin-color prejudice is and whether or not it is universal.

The greatest weakness of the *Daedalus* issue is that readers are left with the impression that the key to understanding the origin and persistence of color prejudice lies in psychoanalytical and social-psychological analysis. The need for studies involving comparative history and anthropology, or semiotic analysis, was not stressed. Very little research or speculation on the origins of color prejudice, and particularly of anti-Negro prejudice, has appeared since the Copenhagen conference. The *Daedalus* papers are interesting and thought provoking despite the theoretical inadequacy of most of them.

The only systematic comparative study by a sociologist of racial prejudice in several situations where black people have been present in considerable numbers is Pierre van den Berghe's *Race and Racism: A Comparative Perspective* (New York: Wiley, 1967). Van den Berghe contrasted Mexico with three other situations: Brazil, which is closest to it in type; South Africa, which is most unlike it; and the United States, which falls in between. He then offered a theory to account for some of the differences in degree of segregation and discrimination involving Africans and peoples of African descent. The dominance of patriarchal as contrasted with competitive relations within a society emerged as his key to understanding the differences.

Other observers have stressed differences in *cultural* type rather than *societal* differences. A now almost forgotten book, *The Negro in the New World* (London: Methuen, 1910), by Sir H. H. Johnston, a prominent British colonial administrator and self-trained anthropologist, presented vivid data from his own travels in the early twentieth century to emphasize racial differences between French, Spanish, and British colonies in the Americas. Since World War II several in-depth comparisons of slavery in culturally different areas of the Western Hemisphere diaspora have been made.

Frank Tannenbaum, in *Slave and Citizen; the Negro in the Americas* (New York: Knopf, 1947), attempted to systematize casual observations that had been made for decades on differences between the status of black people in Anglo-Saxon Protestant areas and in Latin Catholic areas. His book initiated research and controversies that still continue. These issues were summarized and a critical analysis made by H. Hoetink in *Caribbean Race Relations: A Study of Two Variants* (London: Oxford University Press, 1971). More limited geographical areas were compared in two very readable volumes that supplement each other: Herbert S. Klein, *Slavery in the Americas: A Comparative Study of Cuba and Virginia* (Chicago: University of Chicago Press, 1967); and Franklin Knight, *Slave Society in Cuba during the Nineteenth Century* (Madison: University of Wisconsin Press, 1970). The latter book analyzed a period of slavery in Cuba later than the one studied by Klein and cast doubt on the proposition that Catholic Iberian culture necessarily meant a less severe form of slavery. The introduction to Knight's book made a major theoretical contribution to discussions about the relative importance of economic and noneconomic factors in shaping the status and treatment of black people. Carl Degler's excellent and unique study, *Neither Black nor White: Slavery and Race Relations in Brazil and the United States* (New York: Macmillan, 1971), presented a wide range of valuable and interesting empirical data, despite the fact that the author's theories to account for racial prejudice in general are untenable. Monographic literature and a wide variety of secondary sources are available for comparative study of the status of black people in various parts of the British Commonwealth and in the French Community, and for examining situational versus cultural factors within broad areas.

No systematic comparisons of differences in the perception and treatment of black people *within* specific cultural areas, such as the Spanish, French, or Anglo-Saxon, have been made, although such comparisons are necessary in order to ascertain what effects specifically are related to the cultural factor as opposed to other influences (for instance, in Brazil versus Angola). Nor have careful studies been made of much broader groupings—"civilizations," as Toynbee calls them. The worlds of Buddhism, Islam, and Christianity prior to European expansion overseas should be examined for constants and variables in ethnic and racial relations. Comparisons within one specific segment of the Islamic world, that of the Arabic cultural domain, have been made by the English scholar Bernard Lewis in his book *Race and Color in Islam* (New York: Harper & Row, 1971), but the author did not compare this extensive area with non-Arabic Muslim countries such as Java or Nigeria.

Black scholars have, of course, been deeply interested in these questions that concern them and their people so directly, and their perspective is certainly necessary in gaining a rounded view of the subject. During the entire sixty-eight years of its existence, the *Journal of Negro History* has provided an outlet for scholars of all races to publish in the field of comparative race relations, and the founder, Dr. Carter G. Woodson, was especially interested in encouraging research on the Black Experience in areas of the world where non-Anglo-Saxon European cultures prevailed. (See his own well-informed, perceptive article in the April 1935 issue of the *Journal* entitled "Attitudes of the Iberian Peninsula in Literature.") There is a wealth of too often neglected material in past issues of the *Journal of Negro History*.

Since World War II a number of young black scholars have contributed valuable monographic studies based upon comparative analyses that will eventually form the basis for generalizations about the Black Experience. Among these are: Joseph E. Harris, *The African Presence in Asia: Consequences of the East African Slave Trade* (Evanston, Ill.: Northwestern University Press, 1971); and Knight's *Slave Society in Cuba during the Nineteenth Century*. No discussion of comparative race relations would be complete without consideration of the work of the highly motivated, self-trained historian Joel A. Rogers. While Woodson, also the founder of the Association for the Study of Negro Life and History, and Associated Publishers, took a doctorate at Harvard, Rogers had only the equivalent of a secondary-school education. Endowed with unusual talent, Rogers advanced from the menial pursuits he first engaged in as an immigrant to the United States from Jamaica to become one of the best-informed individuals in the world on black history, writing and publishing his own books without any kind of organizational or foundation support. Solid scholarship combined with considerable speculation based upon photographic evidence appeared in the interesting and informative three-volume work *Sex and Race: Negro-Caucasian Mixing in All*

Ages and All Lands (vols. 1 and 2 [New York: J. A. Rogers], vol. 3 [New York: H. M. Rogers], 1942–67). Much of the data was presented in a more popular form in *Nature Knows No Color-line: Research into the Negro Ancestry of the White Race*, 3d ed. (New York: H. M. Rogers, 1952). Two substantial, well-documented volumes constitute *World's Great Men of Color: 3000 B.C. to 1946 A.D.*, first published privately, but then by Macmillan during the 1960s. One book by Rogers used the format of an argument between a black Pullman porter and a southern senator to present much of the data from his other books, and a small pamphlet, *100 Amazing Facts about the Negro, with Complete Proof: A Short-cut to the World History of the Negro*, 23d revised and enlarged edition (New York: H. M. Rogers, 1957), made a great deal of his scholarship available in capsule form. A preface to volume one of *World's Great Men of Color*, entitled "How and Why This Book Was Written," not only described the author's intellectual development and how he decided to write in the vindicationist genre but also revealed a temperate, sophisticated approach to the use of sources, which unfortunately was sometimes not strictly adhered to in his handling of the biographies (as, for example, in the somewhat feeble evidence presented for Beethoven's "blackness" in comparison with the more scholarly treatment of the evidence about Cleopatra). Whatever the weaknesses of Joel A. Rogers's work, it merits serious study.

J. A. Rogers's industriously collected facts constitute an important complement to the work of Carter G. Woodson and W.E.B. Du Bois. Although Rogers's books were written for a popular audience, they contain valuable data for students and provide leads for further research. His work stands in sharp contrast to much of the social science literature that attempts to provide Marxian or psychoanalytical explanations, with Rogers advancing what he considers certain "commonsense" explanations of discrimination and segregation. For example, in *Nature Knows No Color-line*, Rogers simply presented an "opposites attract each other" theory to explain the prevalence of miscegenation.

Nearly all black social scientists work within mainstream paradigms, but there are some significant exceptions. Some black college students find explanations of color prejudice among white people to be plausible which many of their black fellow students, and most black professors would accept only as hypotheses for testing, but not as already validated propositions. Among these is the theory proposed to account for White Racism by an Afro-American medical doctor trained in psychiatry as well as pediatrics, Dr. Frances Cress Welsing.

Psychologist Cedric X. Clark, in the July/August 1975 issue of *The Black Scholar*, called her widely discussed argument "The Genetic Jealousy Hypothesis."

Dr. Welsing (using her maiden name in the title) had published an article in the May 1974 issue of *The Black Scholar* on "The Cress Theory of Color Confrontation." Going beyond the "narcissism" concept used by Hoetink and by Degler and Gergen, Dr. Welsing utilized Freudian concepts of repression, reaction formation, and projection to account for "an uncontrollable sense of hostility and aggression" that has "continued to manifest itself throughout the entire historical epoch of the mass confrontation of whites with people of color." A "deeply sensed inadequacy" finds expression in White Racism. "Is it not true," she asks, "that white people represent in numerical terms a very small minority of the world's people? And more profoundly, is not white itself, or the quality of 'whiteness' indeed, not a color but, more correctly, the very absence of any ability to produce color?" Envy of those who can produce the skin-color which places them among the world's majority results in psychological problems for white people. One basic cause of tension lies in "the great fear that the white male has had of the black male's capacity to fulfill the greatest longing of the white female—that of conceiving and delivering a product of color." No convincing proof from psychiatric records to document both "the great longing" and "the great fear" have been presented. Dr. Welsing insists, furthermore, that "The quality of whiteness is indeed a genetic inadequacy or a relative genetic deficiency state or disease based upon the genetic inability to produce the skin pigments of melanin which are responsible for all skin coloration." This generalization involves a value judgment about biological matters rather than a conclusion from psychiatric research.

Several black psychologists and a medical doctor who shares their views contend that the "genetic inadequacy" referred to by Dr. Welsing has resulted in cognitive and emotional deficiencies among white people. Black people, on the other hand, have enhanced mental powers and superior emotional endowments because of a greater output of melanin in their bodies. One psychologist writes that "there has been virtually no research into the skin color producing substance melanin by modern race intelligence theorists despite the fact that the absence of such is known to be related to certain brain diseases such as PKU and Parkinson's disease" (Cedric X. Clark, "The Shockley-Jensen Thesis: A Contextual Appraisal," *The Black*

Scholar, 6, 10 [July–August 1975], p. 6, citing C. Philip McGee, "Melanin and Brain Diseases," unpublished manuscript, Stanford University, 1972).

During the eighties, Dr. Welsing and members of what might be called "The Melanin School" were frequently invited to speak by black student groups, but no results of controlled experimental research design had been produced to bolster their bold, far-reaching assertions. Richard King, the medical doctor interested in research on melanin, has published a book on the subject as a by-product of his National Institute of Mental Health (NIMH) research project on calcification of the pineal gland: *Black Dot Melanin, The Black Experience, A Holistic View: Selected Annotated References, 1945–1974*, Fanon Center Publications (announced in *Research Bulletin*, Fanon Research and Development Center, Los Angeles, 1, 1 [October 1979]). (See also "An Interview with Richard King, M.D., on the Study of the Pineal Gland," in the same issue of *Research Bulletin*.) The Fanon Research and Development Center had also published a volume on *African Philosophy: Assumptions and Paradigms for Research on Black Persons* that contained an article by psychologist Philip McGee on "Psychology: Melanin, the Physiological Basis for Psychological Oneness."

These black scholars are significant for their decisive rejection of the environmentalist orientation that has prevailed in the study of race relations since the thirties, and for turning back toward pre-Boasian biological determinism. They are a minority among black scholars, but are in the vindicationist tradition.

Novels and essays about the Black Experience in the United States, Latin America, the Caribbean, and Africa (especially southern Africa) provide indispensable aids to understanding the impact of White Racism. Frantz Fanon's *Black Skin, White Masks: The Experiences of a Black Man in a White World* (New York: Grove Press, 1967) is a classic statement on White Racism by an Afro–French West Indian who had studied in France. Fanon mobilized the resources provided by Adlerian, Jungian, and Freudian psychology, as well as by existentialist and Marxist philosophies, in his own quest for meaning. Essays such as this, as well as novels, autobiographies, and biographies by persons who have experienced racial prejudice under White Racism, provide rich material for highlighting contrasts, as well as a baseline from which to look backward, as we do in this volume, to the period before White Racism began.

The type of literature reviewed up to this point does not approach the problem of "blackness" within the framework of a systematic body of theory susceptible to statistical controls or that generates experimental designs. Before mentioning some selected works that do so, the following comments are relevant.

It is usually taken for granted in discussing the status of black people in English-speaking areas of the world that there is a direct connection between derogatory connotations of the word *black* and negative attitudes toward black people. Similar certainty about negative associations in other languages is also sometimes expressed. Such a connection *may* be present, but how close it is and precisely how associations with the word *black* when it is seen or heard carry over to people have never been clearly demonstrated. Whatever the situation has been since the fifteenth century, when the massive transatlantic African slave trade began, it should not be assumed that, in all times and places, the word *black* and the concept of "blackness" have had only unsavory and pejorative associations, or that when such associations exist in a culture they will necessarily affect the interactions of people. Each culture presents semantic puzzles to be solved. These are matters for empirical research, not dogmatic assertion. They have been a stimulus to the comparative enquiry attempted in this book. Controlled experimental research is also needed.

Meanings associated with words referring to "black," and the emotions that accompany them, presumably existed within many cultures prior to the use of the word *black* to refer to groups of people. Such a word and its connotations would already have had referents other than people, and, presumably, the meanings and the emotions associated with them, that is, the "affect," would have differed as the word was variously applied to persons, places, or things, or to qualities, conditions, or other abstractions.[2] *Black* is polysemic with multiple referents. In all cases, the context in which the usage occurs is extremely important. The relationships between the word *black* as a visual or auditory cue, and its referents other than people, as well as the kind of people referred to, require research using methods developed in the fields of semantics and semiotics as well as social psychology. Chart 2 is a crude device for examining some of the dimensions of the problem.

The word *black* (or its equivalent in languages other than English) is a spoken or written symbol (note central box in chart) that has many different kinds of referents. In English, as in a number of other languages, *black* is frequently paired as a polar opposite with *white*, and the words serve as metaphors for sharply contrasted ideas and values.[3] Insofar as the basic referent of the word is to a color, an ideal conception of that color (A) exists, for example as in the idea of something being "jet black." Most often the definitive hue is symbolized by some nonhuman object or being described by the color name (C), as for example, "sable." In several modern schemes for studying color, "chips" or charts are used to standardize color hues, and these include *Black*, although not all students of color call either *Black* or *White* a color.

Insofar as specific characteristics are associated with the color *Black*, they appear in the formulation of abstract concepts and may or may not have distinct empirical referents. In section B of the chart, it will be noted that classification of characteristics may be made in terms of cultural values embodied in concepts or that evoke a culturally defined appropriate affect—positive, negative, or neutral. Thus, at the abstract concept level, we can say that *Black* is BEAUTIFUL, or that *Black* is EVIL. In the former case, the story *Black Beauty* exemplifies the positive value at the empirical level in which a horse is the favored object. Conversely, in the negative, in some European cultures a black cat is considered a symbol of bad luck and witches are sometimes portrayed as black. One of the three Wise Men was portrayed as black, but so was Black Peter who whipped bad children on Christmas Eve as the companion of Santa Claus.

A cursory examination of usage in European and American societies will suffice to indicate that esthetic meanings are not always negative. For instance, a sable coat, an ebony statue, a black bird are sometimes not considered "ugly." This is true even when the referent is a person. For instance, in England or the United States, when a person has Caucasoid features, straight hair, and very dark skin, one might hear this evaluation expressed, "Isn't she a beautiful black woman?" And although the Black Hole of Calcutta, the black flag of anarchism, and the "black night of despair" conjure up emotions of foreboding, on the other hand, in some historic periods, the black flag, for important segments of Islam, has been a symbol eliciting sentiments of piety and loyalty. It can also be demonstrated that positive *esthetic* evaluations of *Black* as a color may function within a culture coterminously with negative *moral* evaluations. *It is obvious that all evaluations involve internal contradictions and attitudes of ambivalence that merit some attention if "blackness" is to be understood as both a descriptive term and as metaphor or metonym.*

Insofar as specific colors are used to symbolize values, and the same terms are used to describe the skin-color of various individuals or groups, the possibility exists within a given speech community that

CHART 2. THE NAMES OF COLORS AS VERBAL SYMBOLS
WITH MULTIPLE REFERENTS

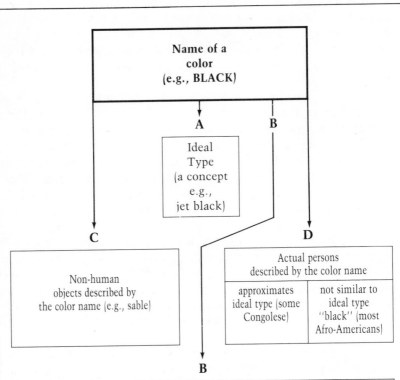

Name of a color (e.g., BLACK)		

A   B

A — Ideal Type (a concept e.g., jet black)

C — Non-human objects described by the color name (e.g., sable)

D — Actual persons described by the color name

approximates ideal type (some Congolese)	not similar to ideal type "black" (most Afro-Americans)

B

A number of referents associated with the word "BLACK"					
Positive Value		Neutral Value		Negative Value	
"Black is Beautiful" or "Black is spiritually powerful" or "in the black" (accounting)	Black Beauty, a horse in a story — Black Madonnas in Europe	"Black as Night" or black as absence of color in color spectrum	color of an auto or a dress — "Black Holes" in space	"Black is Evil" or "Black is Ugly"	Black cat in European folklore — Some devils — Some human races
abstract concept	empirical referent (in a context)	abstract concept	empirical referent (in a context)	abstract concept	empirical referent (in a context)

1. The term *Black*, in the chart above, has as referents:

   (A) an ideal type concept of what *"Black"* is
   (B) a number of referents that are imputed to the word, *"Black,"* and that presumably evoke emotions, sentiments, etc. (connotations)
   (C) inanimate objects described by the name of the color
   (D) individuals or groups of people referred to by the color name; they may, or may not, approximate the ideal type in actuality

2. The crucial question is: "When one referent of the color-name is a characteristic or group of characteristics, is it possible that these characteristics are not necessarily imputed to *people* who may be called by the color name?" Is it possible that a distinction is drawn as between color to designate abstract qualities and color to designate skin-color?

derogatory connotations, as well as more positive ones, will carry over to human beings.

The use of a single color term to designate an entire human group in which there is likely to be a range of skin-color with an average or typical color that changes over time complicates the problem of making generalizations about the carry-over of color meanings to people. A case in point is the existence of very light-skinned American Negroes. It is also important to recognize the fact that a verbal or written symbol for a color, or its use in a banner or a similar sign, is often applied to groups of people without any reference to their "racial" status or origin, implying absolutely nothing about the color of the skin. Thus, the members of an athletic team can be referred to as "The Reds," or a nonliterate society can be divided into two moieties, one labeled *White* and the other *Black*. In one Amerindian group, the division is between Red Bones and White Bones. In such cases these may be mere labels that do not imply any associated mental or emotional traits. In our culture we are familiar with patronyms of this sort. Thus, a Mr. Black is not thought to have any characteristics that distinguish him from a Mr. White, and either of those surnames may be borne by a racially white or a racially black person. An Indian informant has pointed out to the author that Krishna is a very popular name in India and that while people may know that the word means "black," existing feelings about "blackness" are not carried over to individuals named Krishna. Also, to call a person Mr. Black in the United States arouses none of the same emotions that are evoked when a ghetto dweller is called "*a* Black." The study of symbol, referent, and affect is thus a very complicated process where the color *black* and "blackness" are involved.

Visual and auditory cues evoking responses associated with "blackness" or "whiteness" as concepts, or with black and white objects, or people classified as Black or nonblack, may exist as a part of a nexus of seemingly contradictory rules within a specific culture. The contradictions are sometimes associated with experiences of earlier phases of an individual's life cycle. Both pleasant and unpleasant experiences may be repressed. Groups of people occupying similar social positions may have similar repressed content in the unconscious involving "blackness" from earlier reactions to symbols, ideas, and people. This content sometimes finds expression in dreams and fantasies or in aspects of the "acting out" process that gets defined as deviant behavior. Accounts of clinical interviews, their psychoanalytical interpretations, and the mystical literature of Christianity, Islam, and Manichaeism often involve symbolic oppositions of white and black, light and darkness, that may or may not have some reference to interpersonal relations. At the present time, fiction may offer some of the most fruitful insights into the subtleties of black-white relations and the effect of appraisals of "blackness" in Western cultures. Social science has, as yet, little to offer in explaining inconsistencies in attitudes toward "blackness."

The connection between attitude and behavior of individuals and the existence of some word in a language that means *black*, whether it stands alone or in a compound noun or functions as an adjective, and whether it is considered as an auditory or a visual stimulus, is not a simple "Skinner box" relationship. Intervening between the cue word and the response are multiple layers of meaning learned by the individual participant in a culture, and these are always differentiated as to context and referent. And these, too, are undergoing constant change. The research problem is confounded by the fact that persons designated as "Black" themselves become stimuli or cues, eliciting reactions when observed or referred to, and their responses are, in turn, conditioned by the meanings of "blackness" that suffuse the culture.

Any study of color evaluation applied to people must first acknowledge that human beings normally react to a gestalt in assessing the bodies of others—not to skin-color alone. Facial features and type of hair, as well as skin-color, assume importance in the making of evaluations. Of prime significance in making an esthetic judgment, is the perceived "harmoniousness" of the combination. No adequate research techniques are available for distinguishing between the cultural components and the noncultural ones, if they exist, that enter into concepts of "harmoniousness" or the evolution of desirable body images.[4] Comparative racial esthetics is an underdeveloped field.

Color words such as *Black* or *Yellow* or *White* or *Red* are used as shorthand symbols for configurations of physical traits, not for skin-color alone; but they may also apply to the assumed heredity of a person not immediately manifest visually. For instance, the culture of the United States is frequently cited as one in which the color terms have become detached from the actual appearance of individuals when they are used to provide cues for discriminatory behavior. The state of Virginia carried a law on the books for many years that defined a "Negro" as anyone with "an ascertainable trace of Negro blood." *Thus, many ostensibly "white" people are "Black," showing that people react to the presumed ancestry—to a concept—not to the actual phenotype.* Jokes and apocryphal tales are legion as well as a few documented cases of how behavior changes when a white person has been treating another as white and, then, becomes aware that the person has some Negro ancestry. Sinclair Lewis's novel *Kingsblood Royal* (New York: Random House, 1947) is based on this theme.

Despite the difficulty of designing relevant research to deal with those complexities, a number of questions susceptible to imaginative research efforts will, no doubt, eventually attract the attention of some graduate students or established social scientists. Among the questions are these:

(1) What are the conditions under which darker colors elicit unfavorable associations within individual cultures, and what hypotheses can be advanced to explain this?

(2) How do responses to the word *black* when spoken differ from responses when *black* is presented as a written word or in the form of chips or pictures in experimental situations, and what hypotheses can be advanced to explain these differences?

(3) In what contexts does conditioning to the spoken or written word *black* evoke negative attitudes and behavior toward people who are so designated, even if phenotypically these people are not Negroid in their physical attributes?

(4) Is it possible for a person designated as *Black*, whether recognizable as such or not, to hold negative feelings toward "blackness" in the abstract without making derogatory appraisals of himself or herself?

(5) How far-reaching are the changes in meanings and affect associated with *black* and "blackness" as it refers to people since World War II, and especially since the 1960s, when viewed in a comparative perspective within and across cultures?

The last two questions have a degree of contemporary relevance that suggests the need for a more concentrated research effort than has occurred. What has been done merits study as an index to dynamic social change and to suggest future research problems.

The Civil Rights movement (1954–1965) and the Black Power movement (1965–1970) stimulated research on the last question, and during the 1970–1980 decade some of the most important journal articles were these:

1970   "The Changing Attitudes of Black Students," by W. M. Banks in *Personality and Guidance Journal* (48): 739–745.

"Black is Beautiful: A Re-examination of Racial Preferences and Identification," by J. Hraba and G. Grant in *Journal of Personality and Social Psychology* (16): 398–402.

"The New Ghetto Man: A Review of Recent Empirical Studies," by N. Caplan in *Journal of Social Issues* (26): 69–86.

1972 "Black Power Ideology and College Students' Attitudes Toward Their Own and Other Racial Groups," by E. Lessing and S. Zagorin in *Journal of Personality and Social Psychology*: 61–73.

1976 "Racial Self-Identification and Self-Concept by Means of Unobtrusive Measures," by Dan M. Smith and Michael B. Mazis in *Journal of Social Psychology* (90): 221–228.

"Ethnocentrism in Black College Students," by Edward C. Chang and Edward H. Ritter in *Journal of Social Psychology* (100): 89–98.

1978 "The Sensitivity of Black and White Americans to Nonverbal Cues of Prejudice," by Steven A. Rollman in *American Journal of Social Psychology* (105): 73–77.

1979 "Scars of Bondage: Black Americans as Subjects in Behavioral Science Research," by Hoyt Alverson in *Journal of Social Psychology* (109): 187–200. (A thorough critique of deficit models and "blame the victim" models.)

"Color Connotations and Racial Attitudes," by Douglas Longshore in *Journal of Black Studies* 10(2): 183–197, December 1979.

1980 "Interracial Behavior in the Prisoner's Dilemma," by Douglas Longshore and Robert Beilin in *Journal of Black Studies* 11(1): 105–120, September 1980.

An important doctoral dissertation should also be consulted:

1971 "The Mythical Negative Black Self Concept," Ph.D. dissertation by Elmer Eugene Wells at the University New Mexico. (An excellent, much-needed, study to correct long-standing research biases.)

The Black Power movement that emerged after 1965 was a *youth* movement to a greater extent than the Civil Rights movement had been. American social scientists interested in problems of identification, self-esteem, and attitudes toward skin-color have concentrated their attention for almost fifty years on subadolescents. An exception was the Depression period. Then, during the fifties and sixties, changes among high school and college students and ghetto drop-outs assumed such social significance that a shift in focus occurred. But research on children continued. Two publications appeared in 1971 that represented the traditional focus:

> S. Harris and J. R. Braun, "Self-esteem and Racial Preference in Black Children," in *Proceedings of the 79th Annual Convention of the American Psychological Association* (summary on pp. 259–260).
> M. Rosenberg, "Black and White Self Esteem," in *The Urban School Child* (Washington, D.C.: Sociological Association).

The results of a pioneering study documenting the fact that black children in the United States rejected their body images in favor of a Caucasian somatic norm had appeared in 1939 and 1940, in a report by an Afro-American husband-and-wife team, Kenneth and Mamie Clark, on their studies of preschool children who were given a choice of dolls: "The Development of Consciousness of Self and the Emergence of Racial Indentification in Negro Pre-School Children" (*Journal of Social Psychology* [10], 139, 591–599). Three decades later, in 1974, P. A. Katz and S. R. Salk raised questions about the Clarks' research technique in their article "Doll Preferences: An Index of Racial Attitudes?" in *Journal of Educational Psychology* (66) 1974: 663–668. In 1977, R. H. Winnick and J. A. Taylor published "Racial Preference—36 Years Later" in the *Journal of Social Psychology* (102): 157–158. One study of kindergarten children using a refinement of the Clark technique, reported upon in 1979, found that only 40 percent of the black children chose black dolls while 70 percent of the whites chose white dolls. Fourteen years of raising Black Consciousness had had little effect on this sample. (See also Prina S. Klein, Esther Levine, and Margaret Marcus Charry, "Effects of Skin Color and Hair Difference on Facial Choices of Kindergarten Children," *Journal of Social Psychology* [107] 1979: 287–288.)

The literature just cited was reporting on attempts to study what Hoetink calls "the somatic norm image." But there has also been sustained interest in the United States for nearly fifty years in a problem broader than that of black self-concept and self-esteem, namely, the study of racial attitude formation by young children of all races. Such research is highly relevant to testing the "conventional wisdom" that childhood conditioning is a crucial determinant of later attitudes toward "blackness" of skin:

> 1939 "Racial Aspects of Self-Identification in Nursery School Children," by R. E. Horowitz, *Journal of Psychology* (7): 91–99.

1946 "Evidence Concerning the Genesis of Interracial Attitudes," by M. E. Goodman, *American Anthropologist* (48): 624–630.

1950 "Children's Perceptions of the Social Roles of Negroes and Whites," by M. Radke and H. G. Trager, *Journal of Psychology* (29): 3–33.

1953 "Young Children's Responses to a Picture and Inset Test Designed to Reveal Reactions to Persons of Different Skin Color," by C. Landreth and B. C. Johnson, *Child Development* (24): 63–79.

1958 "A Developmental Study of Race Awareness in Young Children," by H. W. Stevenson and E. C. Stewart, *Child Development* (29): 399–410.

1963 "Racial Self-Identification: A Study of Nursery School Children," by J. K. Morland, *American Catholic Sociology Review* (24): 231–242.

1969 "Racial Recognition by Nursery School Children in Lynchburg, Virginia," by J. K. Morland, *Social Forces* (37): 132–137.

1975 "The Development of Racial Attitudes in Young Black and White Children," by R. M. Lerner and C. J. Buehrig, *Journal of Genetic Psychology* (127): 45–54.

1980 "Role of Cognitive Development in Children's Explanations and Preferences for Skin Color," by A. Clark et al., *Developmental Psychology* (16): 332–339.

A search of the journals in which these articles appeared, for the 1975–1985 period, will reveal the extent to which school integration has offered new opportunities for examining this problem.

Research during the sixties and seventies on race and color was not confined to children. A sampling of some of the other literature reveals the types of problems addressed among other age groups:

1959 "Stereotyping and Favorableness in the Perception of Negro Faces," by P. E. Gecord, *Journal of Abnormal and Social Psychology* (59): 309–314.

1963 "Skin Color Perception and Self-Esteem," by Hugh F. Butts, *Journal of Negro Education* (32): 122–128.

1966 "Color Gradation and Attitudes among Middle Income Negroes," by Howard Freeman, J. Michael Ross, David Armor, and Thomas Pettigrew, *American Sociological Review*.

1971 "Age, Sex, Race, and the Perception of Facial Beauty," by J. F. Cross and J. Cross, *Developmental Psychology* (5): 433–439.

1972 "The Effect of Skin Color and Physiognomy on Racial Misidentification," by A. George Gitter, David I. Mostofsky, and Yoichi Satow, *Journal of Social Psychology* (88): 139–143.

After the upsurge of the Black Power movement in the mid-sixties, increasingly greater attention was given to the racial attitudes toward self and others of older age groups. This was reflected in large-scale research projects. A definitive book-length volume about Blacks, based upon extensive research, was Patricia Gurin and Edgar Epps, *Black Consciousness, Identity, and Achievement: A Study of Students in Historically Black Colleges* (New York: John Wiley and Sons, 1975). A similar study of Blacks in predominantly white colleges has not yet been published. A number of less extensive studies have been reported upon, too, that were concerned with changes in attitudes and conceptions of both white and black respondents in controlled experimental situations. Some of these merit special study and evaluation.

Controlled research on meanings associated with skin-color began in the mid-sixties. Douglas Longshore's 1979 article "Color Connotations and Racial Attitudes," cited above, is of considerable value because it summarizes the findings of an important series of articles reporting on the use of the semantic differential approach to the study of concepts and attitudes to which his own work was an added increment. All of the articles Longshore reviewed were by J. E. Williams:

1964   "Connotations of Color Names among Negroes and Caucasians," *Perceptual and Motor Skills*: 399–410, establishing the fact that black and white students evaluated the color *White* more favorably than the color *Black*.

1966   "Connotations of Racial Concepts and Color Names," *Journal of Personality and Social Psychology*: 531–540, reporting that black and white college students, in experimental situations, rated the term "white person" more favorably than the term "black person"; that whites rated the term "Caucasian" more favorably than the term "Negro"; *and* Blacks rated the term "Negro" more favorably than the term "Caucasian," thus demonstrating that, *"Apparently the introduction of color-codes [i.e., Black instead of Negro, and White instead of Caucasian] into racial designation pulls the evaluations toward the connotation of the colors themselves, rendering attitudes less favorable to Black person than to Negro and more favorable to White person than to Caucasian."*[5] Williams expresses doubt that any reversal of the "conventional symbolism" could take place among

Afro-Americans by "associating black with goodness and bad with whiteness" as the Black Muslims were doing.[6]

1969   "Individual Differences in Color Name Connotations as Related to Measures of Racial Attitudes," *Perceptual and Motor Skills*: 383–386.

1971   "Changes in the Connotations of Color Names among Negroes and Caucasians: 1963–1969," *Journal of Social Psychology*: 222–228, reporting that although black college students generally rated the color *White* more favorably than *Black*, Negro students with a black separatist orientation displayed the reverse reaction. The interpretation poses problems, however, since this could be a peer pressure reaction and not a real change in attitude.

In 1974, Douglas Longshore confirmed the Williams findings of 1971 in a draft of his master's paper for the Department of Sociology at the University of California, Los Angeles (UCLA): "The Effect of Black Power on Racial Self-Esteem and Reference Group Orientation among Blacks." This study also included responses from a group of white teachers enrolled, along with black teachers, in a course on problems relating to the education of minority children. Longshore found that changes were apparent among white students as well as among Blacks, a finding that went beyond Williams's 1971 report for his sample. Longshore concluded that,

> Black respondents rated all black color adjectives (Black people, most Black people, and Black man) more favorably than they rated the corresponding white items. The White respondents were not so consistent. In two sets of color adjectives, they rated the black adjectives more favorably than the white adjectives. . . . In all three sets of color adjectives, high approvers [of Black Power] rated the black items more favorably and the white items less favorably than the low approvers did.[7]

Five years later, Longshore, after continuing his research in this field, published his considered judgment that, despite numerous plausible assertions based upon uncontrolled observations, "The theoretical basis for inferring a causal relationship between Black Power and color connotations has not been elaborated by appropriate research methods. . . . Elaboration should include (1) controls for age, sex, skin-shade, and SES; and (2) quasi-experimental manipulation of relevant variables."[8] He reported on his own recent work employing semantic differential scaling that led him to conclude that "high approvers of Black Power rated White people less favorably and Black people more favorably than low approvers did."[9] Only some of the above variables were controlled, however. In any event, as he notes, this is a result that "conventional wisdom would suggest."

Longshore and Beilin's 1980 article, "Interracial Behavior in the Prisoner's Dilemma—The Effect of Color Connotations," was based on imaginatively designed experimental methods. It resulted in a conclusion about white UCLA students that, if confirmed elsewhere, has considerable theoretical significance: *"Perhaps the Black Power movement has rendered whites more favorable to black when used as a racial designation, without similarly affecting the feelings which are conjured up by the color black itself* [italics added]."[10] That is, attitudes to the color do not necessarily transfer from people to the abstract level. Within a few years, Longshore had embarked upon a new area of research. See his "School Racial Composition and Blacks' Attitudes toward Desegregation: The Problem of Control in Desegregated Schools," *Social Science Quarterly* (63): 674–687, December 1982.

Two frames of reference recently utilized by American social psychologists in studying inter-ethnic relations and differences in racial and ethnic groups, merit mention: (a) social comparison theory and (b) studies of the relation between type of internal control and race. Neither has been used, however, for studying the influence of differential degrees of "Negroidness" on judgments about self and others.[11]

A large amount of research has been carried out by psychologists on color symbolism and color preferences in the abstract, but very little has been centered on questions such as those listed earlier in this essay. *Our primary concern is not with color symbolism per se, but with how it affects social interaction, social structure, and psychological states, that is, how the designation of some people as Black and their relegation to an inferior position in socioeconomic hierarchies has affected individuals and groups.* The approaches of both comparative anthropologists and of social psychologists interested in cross-cultural research are vitally necessary. Controlled research on race and color in the Muslim East and Latin America are especially needed. Such research should also include a number of groups other than those usually referred to as "Negroes"—among them many on the Indian subcontinent, the indigenous peoples of Australia and Melanesia, and black Africans and their descendants living in diasporas everywhere.

3.   NILE VALLEY BLACKS IN ANTIQUITY

The continent of Africa, 11,759,000 square miles of land, largely savannah and desert but also including extensive high plateau and mountain areas and a small amount of equatorial rain forest (so-called jungle), is inhabited by over 300 million people of many colors, tongues, and tribes (see map 1). Most of them, however, would be classified as "Black" according to American convention. Africa provides a crucial case in examining the Degler-Gergen proposition that the color *Black* is always contrasted negatively with *White*, that such evaluations carry over to social relations, and that all people everywhere—including black people themselves—are prejudiced against dark skin-color. Archaeological evidence and written documentation covering several millennia of contact between Negroid and Caucasoid people in the northern portion of the continent are available, and these data can be utilized in the study of these important questions.

As the Nile Valley provides us with the oldest documented cases of cooperation and conflict involving "Negroes" and other races, that region is of great importance in examining the reactions of black people to themselves and to other people. Furthermore, the Blumer and Cox generalizations about the linkages between race relations and various kinds of social situations can be examined utilizing Nile Valley data from long time spans, as can changes in the significance of skin-color differences. This chapter therefore concentrates upon the Nile Valley portion of the continent.

The Nile Valley, as one of several geographical locations chosen for discussing "black folk here and there," not only provides data of importance for anthropology and comparative history; it also constitutes a specific portion of Africa that Afro-American religious, political, and educational leaders invested with great significance during the nineteenth century and that still carries high symbolic import. These leaders wrote and spoke to slaves and their descendants, whose African backgrounds lay in western and central Africa, where people had been captured in raids, shackled, stripped naked for the voyage across the ocean, and then sold on the auction block after being inspected like animals. Their captors thought of them as immoral savages

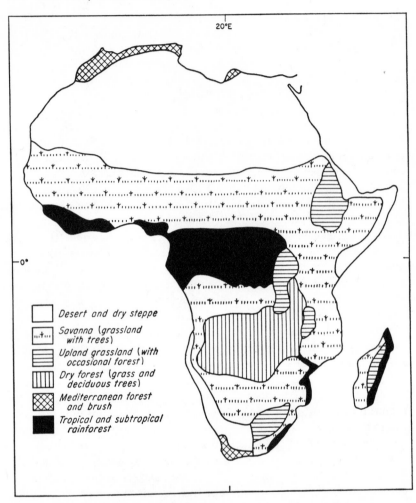

MAP 1. VEGETATION ZONES OF AFRICA. Reprinted, by permission, from George Peter Murdock, *Africa: Its Peoples and Their Culture History*. Copyright © 1959 by McGraw-Hill Book Company.

whose customs included exotic (and erotic) rituals frequently connected with the worship of "idol gods." They were heathens. Nudity, bodily scarification, and occasional cases of cannibalism and human sacrifice were cited as evidence of a general degradation of black people that justified their enslavement by a "more advanced race."

By the beginning of the nineteenth century, without denying the existence of some of these practices, which they too considered deplorable, Afro-Americans who had managed to secure some education questioned whether *all* tribes *everywhere* in Africa exhibited any or all of these characteristics. They sought satisfying nonracist explanations for the presence and distribution of traits and practices that Westerners disapproved of. They expressed confidence in the ultimate triumph of "civilization" and Christianity in what Europeans called the "Dark Continent," but which was their Ancestral Homeland, however unsavory its reputation or deplorable some aspects of its reality. "Blackness" referred to a sociocultural condition as well as to the color of their bodies. Their self-esteem was at stake.

This chapter begins with examples of an ambivalence toward Africa, which was generated by the constant derogation of the continent from which Afro-Americans could not dissociate themselves, however uncomfortable the association. Some leaders assumed the role of defending Africa against its detractors and developed that genre of speaking and writing which has been referred to as "vindicationist" (see preface).

We then move on to the critical "test case" of Egyptian history, which is discussed with an emphasis on the declining role that black elites played after conquests by Assyrians, Persians, Greeks, Romans, Arabs, and Turks. Some attention is given to the controversy over whether or not *any* Egyptians—and even some prominent Ethiopians—were "Negroes." Copious use is made of illustrations so that readers can make judgments of their own in some crucial cases. The chapter also includes a general discussion of the meaning of "blackness" in ancient Egypt. The Kingdom of Meroë in Ethiopia, and its implications for African history, are discussed. And the chapter concludes with some observations on the consequences, for the African psyche, of repeated confrontations between Africans and Asians and Europeans.

AMBIVALENT EXILES

About 697,000 Africans and individuals of African descent were being held in slavery by white colonists in North America when the Declaration of Independence from the British crown was proclaimed in 1776. Thomas Jefferson, who drafted it, included a preamble that spoke of inalienable rights to life, liberty, and the pursuit of happiness, although he himself owned slaves. A small group of approximately 60,000 "Free Negroes" had emerged by 1776, and among them were a few intellectuals who shared the enthusiasm and the hopes of the white radical republicans and took their promises seriously. One of them, a young woman from Senegal, had been bought as a slave at the age of eight by a devout New England family. Fortunately, her owners encouraged what they recognized as young Phillis Wheatley's literary talent, and she eventually emerged as America's first black poet to receive public recognition. It is not difficult to understand why, although she opposed slavery, she held such an image of herself and Africa as is here expressed in one of her poems, "On Being Brought from Africa to America":

> 'Twas mercy brought me from my *Pagan* land,
> Taught my benighted soul to understand
> That there's a God, that there's a *Saviour*, too;
> Once I redemption neither sought nor knew,
> Some view our sable race with scornful eye,
> "Their color is a diabolic die."
> Remember, *Christians*, *Negroes*, black as Cain,
> May be refined, and join th' angelic train.[1]

This African girl, reared in a New England household, rejected Africa, although she stated her opposition to slavery in other poems. For thousands of slaves, on the other hand, nostalgic memories of the Africa from which they had been forcibly carried away were a source of pleasant contemplation. Indeed, for some of them, life in Africa seemed preferable to life in North America. For instance, two years before the Declaration of Independence was signed, a group of North American Negroes of such mind sent a petition to the British governor of Massachusetts. They asked to go back to Africa, and they complained of being "held in a state of Slavery within the bowels of a free and Christian country," stating that they had been "unjustly dragged by the cruel hand of power from our dearest friends and sum [sic] of us stolen from the bosoms of our tender Parents and from a Populous Pleasant and plentiful country."[2] Unlike Peter Salem, Prince Hall, and other Free Negroes who fought at Lexington, Concord, and Bunker Hill, these were native-born Africans existing as slaves in an alien land. They wanted to go home. In contrast to them Phillis Wheatley identified with the Free Negro supporters of the Revolution and wrote a poem extolling George Washington!

After the revolutionary war, slavery was not abolished by the new nation. Free Negroes were denied citizenship and equal rights. They were able to maintain a sense of positive identity only by calling themselves "African" and giving their churches and societies such names as *African* Methodist, Free *African* Society, *African* Lodge 459 of the Prince Hall Masons. At the same time, they decisively rejected African *culture* and the idea of emigrating to Africa. In fact, they began sending missionaries to convert their kinsmen, just as the white churches did.[3]

About 150 years after Phillis Wheatley wrote the poem about her "pagan" fatherland, another black poet, Countee Cullen, who grew up in an African Methodist Episcopal Church (AME) parsonage as an adopted child, expressed a very different attitude in his poem "Heritage." First, he raised a pertinent query:

> What is Africa to me
> Copper sun or scarlet sea,
> Jungle star or jungle track,
> Strong bronzed men, or regal black,
> Women from whose loins I sprang
> When the birds of Eden sang?
> One three centuries removed
> From the scenes his fathers loved,
> Spicy grove, cinnamon tree,
> What is Africa to me?

The poet then bemoaned his being forced, as a Christian, to "Quench my pride and cool my blood." He wrote this lament:

> My conversion came high-priced
> I belong to Jesus Christ. . . .
>
> Not yet has my heart or head
> In the least way realized
> They and I are civilized.[4]

Ambivalence toward Africa has been characteristic of literate black people throughout the Western Hemisphere diaspora. The poems cited above represent polar extremes of feeling about African cultures that have existed in North American Afro-American communities for over 350 years. During some periods shame about the Ancestral Homeland has been the dominant mood among intellectuals as well as among devout Christians. In other periods negative attitudes have been challenged by romanticists in revolt against Puritan values and bourgeois norms of behavior, to which they counterposed other values, such as those expressed in the concepts of *Négritude* and *soul*.[5]

The persistence of this ambivalence merits study as a source of the desire for "vindication." One of the most insidious aspects of the system of slavery as it developed in the Western Hemisphere was the concerted and deliberate attempt to convince black people that they were inferior "by nature" and an "ugly" variety of mankind. Remnants of these ideas still exist. Within the last two decades, in the midst of the black struggle against such "brainwashing," some "friends of the Negro" have begun to suggest that dark skin-color generally, and black skin-color in particular, are *universally* considered undesirable. They consider this "natural" and a burden that Blacks must face up to. These "Modern Manicheans," as chapter 2 points out, *insist that Africans themselves dislike (and perhaps despise) dark skin-color, even when they themselves are dark, and they assert that all Africans idealize "whiteness," both at the level of abstract symbolism and as a preferred "somatic norm image."* Objective examination of the generalizations that Africans dislike dark skin-color and experience negative associations with "blackness" in the abstract did not become historically urgent until after the fifteenth and sixteenth centuries, when European invaders for the first time exercised White Power in their relations with Africans and Western explorers invaded Africa as well as the Americas and Oceania.

There have been ideological reasons for popularizing the conception that "colored" natives were welcoming white men as long-expected supernatural beings. Many discoverers and explorers also inflated their own egos and justified their abuse of "native" women by convincing themselves that they were the ideal lovers whom the women preferred to their own men. They may have been honestly self-deluded in some cases; in others it was quite likely that some of their trusted informants during the period of initial contact told the white foreigners what they thought these powerful newcomers wanted to hear. Yet, while some Europeans were stressing the advantage they assumed their "whiteness" gave them, others reported that they had made contact with Africans who conceived of the "Devil" as white and who preferred their own black skins, flat noses, and kinky hair to the European norms of beauty.[6] No satisfactory explanation of these contradictory accounts has yet appeared in the literature on race relations and the black self-concept. What seems clear is that when Europeans (i.e., "white" people) exhibited superiority in firepower and other technical developments during their expansion after the fifteenth century, some of the peoples of Africa, Asia, the Americas, and Oceania (i.e., "colored" people) were overawed. A mystique of whiteness sometimes developed, but what it meant and how long it lasted varied from time to time and from place to place.

In seeking to explain the presence of skin-color prejudices in some parts of the world, there is no need to invoke theories about a primordial dislike for dark skin. Specific historical and anthropological studies suggest alternative explanations. Instead of speculating, as the Degler-Gergen propositions do, about human propensities to contrast light and dark, black and white, or the universality of early life experiences that lead to the derogation of "blackness," a reassessment of the empirical evidence, based on cultural comparisons, is necessary.

Africa is the logical place to begin such a comparative study. Is it true, for instance, that all Africans, even those not influenced by contact with white people, dislike "blackness" in the abstract and idealize a lighter body image than their own? If so, has this been true in all historical periods? This is a matter for historical and anthropological research, with special attention given to early periods and with an emphasis upon the "Negro" as a physical type, because "Negroes" have been most viciously derogated.* The questions of when and where so-called Negroes first appeared in human history and what relations they had with other people at the time are relevant to such an enquiry.

NEGRO ORIGINS AND AFRICAN PREHISTORY

Vindicationist scholars welcomed the increasing consensus among anthropologists during the second half of the twentieth century that it was neither in Java nor in China that the first true men, as distinct from other anthropoids, had appeared during the process of evolution.[7] The idea that mankind originated in eastern or southern Africa seemed, to the vindicationists, to have a strong antiracist potential. They soon had to contend with the suggestion from some physical anthropologists, however, that this did not necessarily mean that the early men were dark skinned, and it certainly did not prove that they were "Negroes."[8] Although some cogent reasons have been cited for believing that *Homo habilis* and other African hominids *were* dark

---

*Although "Afro-American" and "Black" are currently the terms preferred in referring to North Americans of African descent, the term "Negro" has a specialized meaning in the anthropological literature that requires its use in the discussion of African populations in this book.

skinned, the oldest human fossils do not meet the anthropometric criteria for Negroes, or any variety of modern man, for that matter.[9] As to where and when the Negro type first appeared with the distinctive combination of skin-color, facial features, lip form, and hair type used to distinguish it from the Caucasoid and Mongoloid stocks, modern physical anthropologists have no certain answer. Nor do they offer any convincing explanations about why similar physical types exist today in what must be some very old societies in Oceania and Southeast Asia.

Most anthropologists lean toward the view that the Negro physical type appeared late in the process of evolution in Africa, as a variation on a more generalized, probably dark-skinned human type.[10] The oldest fossils classified by anthropologists as "Negro" are approximately 10,000 years old, these coming from both the eastern and western Sahara regions, where they were associated with bone harpoons and fishhooks. These are the remains of people who lived in this area before it became a desert—when it was well watered, lush, and green. The ultimate origin, in time and place, of this oldest known "Negro" type is unknown. Such people may certainly have lived in other areas where soil and climate did not permit fossilization of bones.[11]

British Africanists Roland Oliver and John Fage present the prevailing theory of a late emergence of the Negro physical type in Africa in their widely used *Short History of Africa*. At the same time, the authors stress the point that "in *pre*-historic times—at least through all the long millennia of the paleolithic or 'Old Stone Age'—Africa was not even relatively backward; it was in the lead." In speaking of the elaboration and spread of improved tool styles, Oliver and Fage maintain that "*there is little doubt that throughout all but the last small fraction of this long development of the human form, Africa remained at the center of the inhabited world* [italics added]"; and with regard to the earliest type of stone tools, "the centre of their distribution appears to be the woodland savannah region of tropical Africa." Since Oliver and Fage believe in a late date for the appearance of Negroes in Africa, this scenario presumably places the dynamic early African prehistory sometime before the emergence of any Negroes![12]

Polemicists who stress what they believe to be distinctive inherited mental and temperamental traits that differentiate one race from another usually postulate an early divergence of white and black people from a common ancestor. The late Carleton Coon, an American anthropologist, achieved the same end by arguing that Negroes emerged late from an ancestral line that began developing *separately* over 200,000 years ago. Moreover, this separate line certainly was *not* "in the lead." Few of his colleagues took him seriously, then or later, when he wrote in his book *The Origin of Races* (1962) that "as far as we know now, the Congoid [i.e., Negro] line started on the same evolutionary level as the Eurasiatic ones in the Early Middle Pleistocene and then stood still for half a million years, after which Negroes and Pygmies appeared as if out of nowhere."[13] An anthropologist of liberal persuasion, Ashley Montagu, in a critical analysis of *The Origin of Races*, commented:

> Since according to Coon, the Negroes were the last of the subspecies of *Homo erectus* to be transformed into *sapiens* (pp. 655–666), the level of civilization attained by them is "explained." They simply do not have as long a biological or genetic history as *sapiens*, as we whites or Caucasoids.[14]

A theory of late emergence could, logically, mean either that Negroes are the most highly evolved or that they are "retarded," depending upon what one has to say about their progenitors. Oliver and Fage, who believe in a late appearance, do not concern themselves with this argument between "racists" and "vindicationists."

With such little fossil evidence on hand, discussion of the *late prehistory* and *early history* of Africa's Negroes is more rewarding than arguing about *early prehistory*. That portion of the Negro African population living on the savannah land south of the desert and in the Nile Valley certainly participated in and contributed to the great food-producing revolution of about 7,000 or 8,000 years ago, based upon the domestication of grain, sheep, goats, pigs, and cows. This agricultural revolution led to a population explosion of both the Caucasian and black populations that occupied northern Africa. The rest of the continent remained sparsely populated for several thousand years, although some of its peoples gradually increased in number as they adopted new sources of food, or as they domesticated some plants themselves. Extensive migration of the expanding northern populations into central and southern Africa occurred after iron tools made it possible to clear forests and as new crops suited to new ecologies became available (map 2). Oliver and Fage expressed the dominant view among Africanists in the fifties when they wrote:

> Six or seven thousand years ago . . . at the end of man's purely parasitic existence as a hunter and gatherer . . . Africa was already inhabited by the ancestors of the four main types recognized as indigenous in historical times [i.e., Caucasian "Hamite," Bushman, Pygmy, and

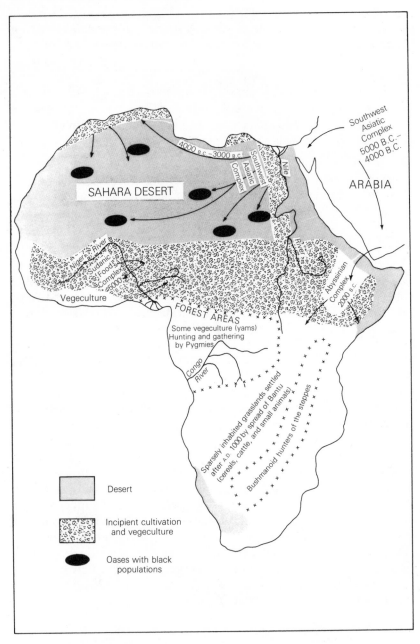

MAP 2. DIFFUSION OF FOOD COMPLEXES IN AFRICA.
Cartography based on a concept by the author.

Negro]. . . . *The Negro appeared on the scene even later than the other three types, and his present predominance was certainly achieved during the modern food-producing period* [italics added].[15]

This food-producing period began with what some archaeologists call the Neolithic Revolution in the Middle East. The major technical advances of that "revolution" involved the domestication of plants and animals, innovations that made possible the substitution of settled village life for existence in hunting and gathering bands, and thereby laid the foundation for the emergence of cities and the "civilization" associated with them. (Some groups continued to prefer a nomadic existence but it was now based upon pastoralism.) The Middle Eastern Neolithic began in the highlands of eastern Africa and southwestern Asia when some innovative peoples domesticated various cereal grains, small animals, cattle, a few vegetables, and some fruits. Coffee is regarded by American anthropologist George Peter Murdock as one of the contributions of the East African highlands. The "Southwest Asiatic food complex" and the "East African food complex" were transferred to the Tigris-Euphrates river valley,[16] to the Fertile Crescent between that area, and to the Nile Delta, as well as into the Nile Valley itself (map 3).

Improved nutrition and sedentary patterns of living led to population explosions in some areas. The food cultivators in the Nile Valley and the savannah of northern Africa soon outnumbered the hunters and fishers in these areas and later displaced the Pygmies and Bushmanoid peoples farther south. Oliver and Fage here comment on an ongoing controversy:

> There are those who would argue the case for an original and independent invention of agriculture in this sub-Saharan region [i.e., "the light woodland savanna which stretches from Senegal to the upper Nile"]. Against this, however, there is at present a lack of any firm archaeological evidence for the existence of truly cultivating communities to the south of the Sahara earlier than the end of the second millennium B.C.[17]

The first to argue that case, George Peter Murdock, saw no need to rest his case on archaeology. He used a sophisticated method of analysis, developed by the Russian botanist Vavilov, to demonstrate that certain wild strains of plants had first been domesticated by Mande-speaking Negroes in the area near the big bend of the Niger River, in what is now the Mali Republic.

Murdock insists that while North Africa was borrowing the crops of the Southwest Asian food complex, first introduced into Africa

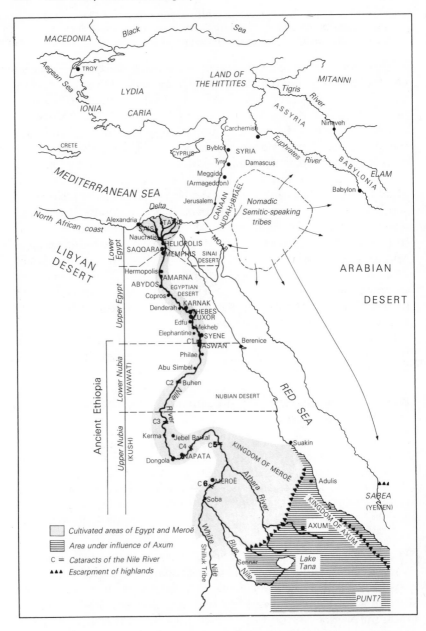

MAP 3. ANCIENT SETTLEMENTS AND POLITICAL DIVISIONS IN THE NILE VALLEY.
Cartography based on a concept by the author.

through the Egyptian delta by immigrants from the Fertile Crescent of Asia Minor, and while some of these crops were being adopted by oasis dwellers in the desert, a West African food-producing revolution may have been under way in the area near the present-day city of Timbuctoo. Murdock assigns a date of about 5000 B.C. for the time when these innovations began to spread eastward toward the Nile Valley. In what he calls the "Sudanic food complex" were included several types of yams, one variety of rice, and watermelon; but, above all, there was cotton, which had previously been considered an Indian contribution.[18]

Although Murdock espouses his point of view with crusading fervor and dedicates the book in which he presents his evidence to "Americans of African Descent," a leading Afro-American Africanist, Professor Joseph Harris, has advised caution regarding Murdock's vindicationist conclusion, noting that "support for [his] position is minimal because the confirming evidence is slight." Since Harris wrote, however, some experts whose opinions cannot be discounted have rallied to the support of portions of Murdock's argument.[19] Murdock insists that racism prevented earlier recognition of "West African Negroes as one of mankind's leading creative benefactors." He is convinced that early anthropologists fell victim to "the vulgar assumption, widespread among Asiatics as well as Europeans, that the Negro is an inferior race incapable of making any substantial contribution to civilization," and that "all complex manifestations of culture in Africa south of the Sahara must have emanated from some other and 'higher' race like the Caucasoid 'Hamites'."[20]

The population explosion among the Negroes of the savannah lands in western Africa between 8000 and 5000 B.C., resulting from the adoption of agriculture, precipitated a population spread throughout central and southern Africa into territory occupied by Pygmies and Bushmen. Some of these hunters and gatherers were absorbed; others retreated into inaccessible forest, desert, and mountainous areas to become "marginal" peoples. A cattle-keeping people with some Bushmanoid and Negroid affinities evolved into the Hottentots of South Africa (see map 2).

During the massive movements of peoples in Africa in response to climatic and demographic changes extending over a long period of time, small, previously isolated groups were thrown into contact with one another. When such groups met, they not only fought one another occasionally but also mixed genetically. This is evident from the archaeological record as well as from the physical appearance of the existing populations of central and southern Africa.[21] They borrowed cultural traits from one another, too. For example, the "clicks" of Bushmen and Hottentots occur now in Bantu speech. Alan Lomax, the distinguished musicologist, came to a surprising conclusion after an exhaustive comparative analysis of African and Afro-American musical styles:

> As Negro tribes moved east and south into the jungle, they displaced, often absorbed, or established symbiotic relationships with the African Hunter bands, at the same time, acquiring their musical style. Evidence is everywhere at hand to support this notion. . . . *This Negro-Pygmy style was kept alive by the black slaves in America and now forms the baseline for the entire Afro-American [musical] tradition* [italics added].[22]

Large numbers of Africans from the Congo-Angola region were brought to North America as well as to the West Indies and Latin America and were probably the culture bearers of this musical style that links Africa and the diaspora.

We know nothing about the extent to which color or other physical traits symbolized ethnicity or group solidarity for the people involved in the migrations of African prehistoric times. Rock paintings in the Sahara and predynastic artifacts in Egyptian tombs reveal a keen awareness of differences in physical type, but what meanings were attached to them—esthetic, erotic, mystical, or status allocating—we have no way of knowing.[23] If relations between some of the peoples of contemporary eastern Africa (e.g., the Watutsi, Wahutu, and Watwa, or Ba-Twa, pygmies) are studied for clues to the past, relative height emerges as a status attribute of considerable antiquity.[24] There are legends, too, of "red" people, the Bachwezi, who came as invaders and were invested with mystical significance. However, among other people in the same region, "redness" was considered within the normal ethnic range of a number of tribal populations, not as evidence of miscegenation with Caucasians. And "red" was not a word that signified superior esthetic status.[25]

"Prehistoric" times for most of the peoples of Africa existed until Islamic penetration after the ninth century A.D.; for some, "prehistory" ended only after the massive invasion by Europeans in the sixteenth century. Some Africans never saw white people until World War I! Attitudes toward skin-color differences can only be inferred from relations observed after conflict began, or from folklore and legend or sociolinguistic analysis. Objective research of this type has been neglected, but a group of British racist anthropologists confused the situation during the late nineteenth century by elaborating the

"Hamitic myth," which has played the same role in African studies as the "Aryan myth" has played in European pseudohistory. They assumed that wherever lighter-skinned "Hamitic" Africans met darker-skinned Africans, the former scorned the latter and made serfs or slaves of them, and that the Blacks, an inferior breed biologically, deferred to these lighter-skinned peoples. That myth has almost been destroyed, but remnants of it linger in the literature on eastern and southern Africa. The term "Hamitic" is still used by Africanists whose attempts to purge it of racist implications have not yet been entirely successful.[26]

The Nile Valley alone, of all the regions of the Ancestral Homeland, provides an ideal situation for examining race relations in the earliest historic periods of the continent. The vast expanse of North Africa now occupied by the Sahara, Libyan, and Egyptian deserts was well watered and grassy up to about 2500 B.C. and was occupied by Negroes and Bushmanoid peoples as well as pastoral Caucasians. As desiccation began after 2500 B.C. in response to climatic changes, many of these people, with their cattle, small animals, and rudimentary agricultural practices, moved southward into the savannah, with some of the Blacks remaining on the oases as agriculturalists or cultivators of date palms. Others of this racially mixed Sahara population wandered eastward into the fertile Nile Valley, augmenting an agricultural population already there and adding new racial elements to a basically Negro indigenous population. Increases in population density created a challenge to the ingenuity of the political leaders of the Nile Valley to bring new land into cultivation through expansion of irrigation schemes. A similar process of concentration of population resulting from desiccation was taking place in the Tigris-Euphrates Valley.[27]

The two river valleys became centers where "civilization" developed under the aegis of priestly hierarchies. That is, a type of society emerged with writing, a calendrical system, mathematics and astronomy, religious cults administered by a priesthood, and property relations that resulted in the emergence of wealthy leisured classes existing on a share of the surplus provided by serfs, slaves, and taxable peasant-freemen. Armies used for defense and conquest grew up as an integral part of these systems of "civilized" living. Immediately south of Egypt several Kushitic, or Ethiopian, kingdoms developed also as a part of the Nile Valley "civilized" complex, surrounded on both sides by the barbarian peoples of the desert. The early Nile Valley civilizations have always been considered important in vindicationist arguments (see map 3).

The Roles of Egypt and Ethiopia in Black History

By the time the interracial abolition movement was organized in the United States in 1831, Afro-American leaders had developed a network of institutions devoted to self-help, aid to runaway slaves, and protest against slavery and racial discrimination suffered by Free Negroes. In their speeches, sermons, tracts, newspapers, and books, they referred frequently to Ethiopia, and the ministers made their congregations familiar with the prophecy in Psalms 68:31: "Princes shall come out of Egypt and Ethiopia shall soon stretch forth her hand unto God."

In February 1829, one Robert Alexander Young applied for a copyright for his pamphlet entitled *The Ethiopian Manifesto, Issued in Defense of the Black Man's Rights in the Scale of Universal Freedom*. The next year the most militant of the pamphleteers, David Walker, in his *Appeal . . . to the Coloured Citizens of the World*, wrote: "Though our cruel oppressors and murderers may (if possible) treat us more cruel, as Pharaoh did the children of Israel, yet the God of the Etheopeans, has been pleased to hear our moans in consequence of oppression; and the day of redemption from abject wretchedness draweth near." Later, despite his denunciation of the oppressive pharaoh, he wrote of other Egyptians who were "wise legislators," and produced pyramids, also "turning the channel of the Nile." He called them "sons of Africa or of Ham, among whom learning originated, and was carried thence into Greece where it was improved upon and refined."

Young and Walker were Free Negroes who had read widely and knew something of history and geography.[28] The less sophisticated slaves did not fix their attention on Ethiopia and had little reason to admire Egypt which, for them, was the country where lived the pharaoh who had oppressed "God's chosen people." When the spirituals grew up on the plantations, some of them expressed identification with Moses and "the mixed multitude" that he led "out of the house of bondage," with an Ethiopian wife at his side. The Egyptian pharaoh who pursued the Jews fleeing slavery was the villain. The slaves sang: "Go down Moses; / Way down in Egypt's Land; / Tell Ol' Pharaoh / Let my people go." They exulted in his defeat as Jehovah showed his hand, singing, "Oh, Mary don' you weep; / Oh Mary, don' you moan; / Pharaoh's army got drownded." It was only after Emancipation that Egypt could become a master symbol in Afro-American liberation mythology and racial advancement ideology.

Both slaves and Free Negroes knew that Egypt and Ethiopia were said to be in Africa, the place where some of them had been born and from which some of the ancestors of all of them had come. Those who became familiar with the Bible knew that both places were somewhere in the vicinity of "the Holy Land." (The Creation story referred to a "river of Ethiopia" as being one of the boundaries of the Garden of Eden.) But the exact geographical location of Ethiopia, prior to the late nineteenth century, was never a matter of much concern to Afro-Americans. Ethiopia was both the name of a place—whose location somewhere in Africa was vague—and a metaphor for a widely scattered diaspora people, as was the term "Israel." However, by the end of the nineteenth century, better-educated Afro-Americans were becoming interested in the fate of the specific areas in Africa referred to by Jews, Greeks, and Romans as Ethiopia, the land inhabited by "the people with the burnt faces." In the 1980s, the old historic Arab name, "Abyssinia," and "Ethiopia" were both being applied to the kingdom in the East African highlands that had fought off the Muslims and remained Christian in the sixteenth century and that defeated Italy in 1896 at the Battle of Adowa, thus preserving its independence during the European "scramble for Africa." Black people everywhere identified with the victor in that battle, and some thought that prophecy was being fulfilled—that Ethiopia was now about to "stretch forth her hand unto God."

By the middle of the nineteenth century, most literate black leaders in the United States were aware that the ancient Greeks and Romans had made favorable remarks about Ethiopians, since abolitionists, Black and White, used quotations from the *Iliad* and the *Odyssey*, from Herodotus, Dioscorus, and Strabo to defend black people when involved in polemics about their inborn capabilities.[29] Some knew that Dioscorus had repeated stories told to him by Egyptians who said that their country was originally a colony of Ethiopia. Most who knew this knew that *ancient* Ethiopia was in the Nile Valley. They were also, no doubt, familiar with a statement by Herodotus that, in some translations, described Egyptians as having black skin and kinky hair.[30] They did not begin confidently to claim Egypt as part of the black world, however, until they became familiar with the findings of some of the French Egyptologists that appeared in the early nineteenth century. After that, Egypt became a cherished symbol for many vindicationists, along with Ethiopia. Devout Afro-American churchgoers were ambivalent, however, because their image of cruel and blasphemous pharaohs, gleaned from the Bible, tarnished the image of Egypt and made it difficult for them to embrace Egypt with pride. The more sophisticated black intellectuals had no such conflict. It satisfied them that Egypt had been powerful.

The transatlantic African slave trade and the use of black slaves in the Western Hemisphere were practices being challenged by the growth of humanitarian sentiment in Britain and France at the same time that Egyptology was coming into being as a serious discipline. The first scholars to describe the Egyptian antiquities noted that some of the high-status individuals had Negroid features.[31] Some apologists for slavery accepted these reports but insisted that an unfortunate Negro infusion into a fine white strain of Egyptian leaders had caused Egyptian civilization to decline, and they warned against letting such miscegenation occur in the United States. Others argued that these Negroid Egyptians were not really "*True* Negroes" of the type brought to the New World as slaves but were a different, more intelligent breed of dark-skinned people.

The founding fathers of the American School of Ethnology, Josiah C. Nott and George R. Gliddon, became involved in this discussion in the 1840s, giving legitimacy to a recently published book, *Crania Egyptica*, written by physician S. G. Morton, that reported on the author's hobby of collecting skulls. Combining Morton's amateur anthropometry with biblical folklore, Nott and Gliddon suggested that the Egyptians were gifted *dark-skinned Caucasians* descended from Noah's son Ham. These people had developed writing, mathematics, astronomy, and lofty philosophical conceptions, and with tautological naïveté Nott and Gliddon pointed out that this would have been impossible had they been Negroes. They claimed that later, however, Egyptian civilization was debased by miscegenation with Negroes, who came from a quite different Noaic line of descent and who were also the ancestors of the Blacks enslaved in the American South. Unless the United States preserved a rigid color line in its dealings with enslaved and Free Negroes, they argued, Anglo-Saxon civilization would disappear as pharaonic civilization had.[32] Such ideas were widespread until the 1930s, and Afro-American leaders felt duty-bound to combat them.

Egyptology thus became a crucial arena in the persisting struggle between antiblack racists and those black intellectuals who considered themselves to be vindicationists. The latter were not prepared to leave the arguments of the Notts and the Gliddons unchallenged. One of their basic strategies was to call attention to the fact that the early dynasties of Egypt, including some of the most creative ones, included a number of pharaohs who would be considered "Negroes" by white Americans if they were asked to judge their race on the basis of photographs not designated as "Egyptian." But black scholars were not the first to point out this similarity to New World Negroes.

Among the first Europeans to reflect upon the race of ancient Egyptians was Count Constantine de Volney (1757–1820), who visited Egypt between 1783 and 1785. He wrote of the brown-skinned Christian Copts, who formed a great part of the nonurban population, that "all have a bloated face, puffed up eyes, flat nose, thick lips; in a word, the true face of the mulatto." The count was surprised and puzzled at finding in Egypt this physical type with which he was familiar in Europe, where it had resulted from matings between white people and Africans or Blacks from the Caribbean. After viewing the Sphinx, he was convinced that a similar process of miscegenation had been at work in Africa, but with Blacks as the majority population and whites the minority in the initial mixture. This led him to write about the Sphinx in words that were disconcerting to the proslavery forces of his day:

> On seeing that head, typically Negro in all its features, I remembered the remarkable passage [of Herodotus]. . . . The ancient Egyptians were true Negroes of the same type as all native-born Africans. That being so, we can see how their blood mixed for several centuries with that of the Romans and Greeks, must have lost the intensity of its original color, while retaining nonetheless the imprint of its original mold. . . . What a subject for meditation, to see the present barbarism and ignorance of the Copts, descendants of the alliance between the profound genius of the Egyptians and the brilliant mind of the Greeks! Just think that this race of black men, today our slave and the object of our scorn, is the very race to which we owe our arts, sciences, and even the use of speech! Just imagine, finally, that it is in the midst of peoples who call themselves the greatest friends of liberty and humanity that one has approved the most barbarous slavery and questioned whether black men have the same kind of intelligence as Whites![33]

This sounds like a volley being shot at one of the count's famous contemporaries, Thomas Jefferson, the American politician-intellectual. The count is, of course, including mulattoes and quadroons and octoroons in his concept of "Negroes" and "Blacks," as did the Sage of Monticello when it suited his purposes to do so.

Baron Vivant Denon, a contemporary of Count Volney, who accompanied Napoleon's army to Egypt as an artist making sketches, wrote of his journey to Cairo:

> I had only time to view the Sphinx, which deserves to be drawn with a more scrupulous attention than has ever yet been bestowed upon it.

> Though its proportions are colossal, the outline is pure and graceful; the expression of the head is mild, gracious and tranquil; the character is African; but the mouth, the lips of which are thick, has a softness and delicacy of execution truly admirable [see plates 1 and 2].[34]

Following Volney and Denon, a century of savants tried to prove that Egyptians were, and always had been, white! There were always a few Egyptologists, however, who took an objective position and claimed that some pharaohs were Caucasian, some Negro, and some mixed; and that the average degree of admixture within the general population varied from period to period, but was, in a general sense, "mulatto."

Black vindicationists, as did Volney and Denon, used the Sphinx as a symbol of the Negro presence in Egypt. Believed to have been modeled on the head of a prominent pharaoh from Old Kingdom times, when the basic outlines of Egypt's future greatness were set, the Sphinx evoked the following comment from the distinguished Afro-Caribbean nineteenth-century scholar who is sometimes called the "Father of Black Cultural Nationalism," Edward Wilmot Blyden:

> Her [sic] features are decidedly that of the African or Negro type, with "expanded nostrils." If, then, the sphinx was placed here—looking out in majestic and mysterious silence over the empty plain where once stood the great city of Memphis in all its pride and glory, as an "emblematic representation of the king"—is not the inference clear as to the peculiar type of race to which that king belonged?[35]

In commenting on the Sphinx, the contemporary Afro-American historian Chancellor Williams, of Howard University, here refers to Pharaoh Chefren [Khafre], who is reputed to have had the monumental sculpture carved from a rock in the desert:

> As though he intended to settle the question of his racial identity for all ages to come, he had his African features so boldly and clearly carved into a portrait statue that not even a fool could seriously doubt that this mighty monarch was a "Negro."[36]

Arthur Weigall, an Englishman, former inspector general of antiquities for the Egyptian government and a distinguished Egyptologist, agrees that the Sphinx portrays Pharaoh Chefren and states that "the features of the face bear a decided resemblance to those of the statues of about this period."[37] However, comparison of the Sphinx with the most widely publicized portrait statue of Chefren reveals the latter as presenting less Negroid features.[38] But this fact itself has significance in examining the Degler-Gergen propositions, for it reveals no reluctance on the part of the pharaoh to have whatever degree of Negroidness he did possess emphasized in a highly public situation on the borders of the Delta, the most non-Negroid part of Egypt, gateway to the country. Since the Sphinx signified wisdom, it follows that neither Egyptians nor foreigners saw anything incongruous in symbolizing wisdom by Negroidness. Egyptologist Weigall, certainly no partisan of Negro Africans (a chapter in one of his books refers to the Twenty-fifth Dynasty as "an astonishing era of nigger domination"),[39] suggested the following about the Sphinx:

> Probably it was originally an actual representation of the Pharaoh Khafre [i.e., Chefren] in his aspect as an incarnation of the sun-god, and gradually it came to be regarded as the embodiment of the collective Pharaonic spirit.[40]

Racism has put such blinders on people of the contemporary Western world that most tourists visiting Cairo today can take their camel rides around the Sphinx without ever noticing what struck Volney and Denon so forcefully, namely, that an ancient pharaoh of Egypt was physically the same type of person as the slaves who toiled on plantations in the Americas and the Caribbean. If these tourists were to relate what they saw to their own experience, they would notice that the pharaoh was the same type of man who today walks the streets of Kingston, Harlem, Birmingham, and the South Side of Chicago. Likewise, most of the Arab population of Egypt is probably unaware that millennia before their ancestors arrived on the scene after A.D. 700, most of the Egyptians resembled the Sphinx, and that Blacks, not Arabs, were once the dominant type in Egypt. Today Aswan, far up the Nile, or even Khartoum in the Sudan, presents a more accurate picture of early Egypt's population than does Cairo.

Count Volney was somewhat less than scientific in inferring from the Sphinx alone that the entire population of Egypt had been Negro during the Old Kingdom. (Perhaps only the ruling class, or a portion of it, was Negro!) Volney ignored the fact, too, that ancient Egypt included barbarities to match those of the southern planters. Nevertheless, his scholarly intuitions were more soundly based than those of Thomas Jefferson, who refused to accept evidence from either the Bible or the classics, both of which he knew well, that refuted the argument that no black person at any time, anywhere, had ever shown intellectual capacities equivalent to those of whites. Almost a century later, W.E.B. Du Bois commented that, "in recent years, despite the work of exploration and interpretation in Egypt and Ethiopia, almost nothing is said of the Negro race. Yet that race was always prominent in the valley of the Nile."[41] He tried to fill in this gap with his own writing, publishing a book, *The Negro*, in 1915, in which he summarized, in an accurate and clear manner, all that was then known about the role of various racial groups in ancient Egypt. Twenty-five years later he published *Black Folk Then and Now*. Du Bois evaluated the data objectively, in an effort to set the record straight about the participation of Blacks in the building of Egyptian civilization, but made only modest claims for their contributions.

During the years between Count de Volney's visit to Egypt and Dr. Du Bois's book, a mass of data had accumulated, for Egyptology had emerged as a professional discipline based in a few European and American university departments and museums. French academics kept tight control of the Cairo Museum under an agreement with the Turkish rulers. In discussing his sources, Du Bois wrote, "The works of Breasted and Petrie, Maspéro, Budge, and Newberry and Garstang are the standard books on Egypt. They mention the Negro but incidentally and often slightingly."[42] There were as yet no black Egyptologists in either Africa or the diaspora. (Including a few Egyptians, there are less than a dozen even today.) However, these men, and another, Arthur Weigall, not mentioned by Du Bois, despite their biases, were enthusiasts for preserving antiquities and were industrious scholars who learned to decipher hieroglyphics. Thus they provided the necessary "raw materials" that vindicationists needed for fashioning a more acceptable account of Egyptian history.

Du Bois attempted to evaluate the classical Greco-Roman sources and the material published by Egyptologists—translations of texts, reproductions of temple frescoes, photographs of sculpture—and came to a conclusion that, with some minor modifications and reservations, is surprisingly close to that of contemporary mainstream Egyptology:

> Of what race, then were the Egyptians? They certainly were not white in any sense of the modern use of that word—neither in color nor physical measurement, in hair nor countenance, in language nor social customs. *They stood in relationship nearest the Negro race in earliest times, and then gradually through the infiltration of Mediterranean and Semitic elements became what would be described in America as light mulatto stock of Octoroons or Quadroons.* This stock was varied continually: now by new infiltration of Negro blood from the south, now by Negroid and Semitic blood from the east, now by Berber types from the north and west [italics added].[43]

What Du Bois called a "light mulatto stock of Octoroons or Quadroons" has been dubbed "Hamite" when found in Africa but is classified as "Negro" or "Black" in the United States, and is treated accordingly. It is a matter of taxonomical irony that, by the time Du Bois wrote *The Negro*, anthropologists had taken a word that was used during the period of slavery to mean "an *inferior* breed of humanity descended from Ham, that is, a Negro," and transformed it to mean "a light-skinned African with Caucasian features, definitely *superior* to darker Africans, especially Negroid ones." Du Bois assailed the use of the term " 'Hamite,' under cover of which millions of Negroids have been characteristically transferred to the 'white' race by some eager scientists."

Black Americans with an interest in this issue asked two perfectly logical questions that drew evasive answers from physical anthropologists, wrapped up in technical jargon: "Why are people who look like us called 'white' or 'Hamite' if they live in Egypt but 'Negroes' if they live in this country?" and "Why, if someone of that type turns up among the Egyptian pharaohs is he classified 'white,' but if he lived in Mississippi he'd be put in the back of the bus?" Du Bois and other vindicationists were led to adopt a simple basic strategy. *They called for consistency in the use of the term "Negro." They pointed out that failure to do so automatically removed virtually all of Egypt's achievements from the realm of the Black World.* They challenged Egyptologists to face up to the inconsistencies of their terminology and to realize the racist uses to which their inconsistencies were being put. Some did, and were Du Bois now living, he would be pleasantly surprised at some of the modern publications on Egypt. But the inconsistency still remains unresolved—and usually unrecognized —particularly among historians who have not yet assimilated the latest results of research in Egyptology.

The attack on semantic sleight of hand reached its peak during the sixties in the work of Dr. Cheikh Anta Diop, a professor at the University of Dakar in Senegal, West Africa. This French-trained African savant had specialized in history, linguistics, Egyptology, and the use of scientific tests for determining the approximate age of some archaeological finds. The leading vindicationist was now an African, not a diaspora Black. He was also a scholar who could meet the Egyptologists on their own ground.

During the 1960s, Diop and a group of African scholars convinced UNESCO that it should sponsor the research for, and the writing and publication of, a definitive history of Africa, most of which would consist of contributions by African scholars but would also include the work of non-Africans approved as collaborators by an editorial committee with an African majority. The first two volumes of what is to be a nine-volume work appeared in 1981, published jointly by

UNESCO, the University California Press, and Heinemann of London. Some of the historical articles deal with Egypt and Ethiopia. Several explicitly consider the question of the race of the early Egyptians, including an annex that summarizes the discussions that took place in 1974 at a conference that had been arranged at the urging of Diop. Dr. G. Mokhtar, editor of volume 2 of *A General History of Africa*, called attention in an overview to the implications of that conference:

> Already in 1874 there was argument about whether the ancient Egyptians were "white" or "black." A century later a Unesco-sponsored symposium in Cairo proved that the discussion was not, nor was likely soon to be closed. It is not easy to find a physical definition of "black" acceptable to all.

Mokhtar, himself an Egyptian, had put his finger on the crux of the problem.

The official report of the 1974 symposium stated that much of the activity turned out to involve a "successive and mutually contradictory monologue" between individuals opposing Diop's views and either Diop himself or a Congolese linguist and historian, Dr. Theophile Obenga, who supported him. Only these two scholars and a Sudanese represented "Negro Africa," as contrasted with six Egyptians, one Canadian, one representative from the United States, and eight from Europe. No one from England participated. The most vocal and energetic opponents of Diop's views were Professors Jean Vercoutter and Serge Sauneron, both French Egyptologists. The rapporteur stated that the "disagreement was profound" on the question of whether or not the ancient Egyptians were Negroes, but some unity was achieved on three other issues: (1) desire to see careful studies made of the relationship between the ancient Egyptian language and other African languages; (2) support for more thorough studies of Egyptian mummies; (3) desire for clarification of terminology and methodology used by anthropologists in racial classification.

Egyptians objected to the obvious enthusiasm of Diop to see the point firmly established that the ancient Egyptians were "Black." The Sudanese participant said he "did not think it important to establish whether the ancient Egyptians were black or negroid; what was most remarkable was the degree of civilization they had achieved." The Sudanese scholar had a lively exchange with Diop on linguistic methodology and on the proper semantic values to place on ancient Egyptian words sometimes translated as "black people." Professor Jean Leclant, a French savant, leaned a bit toward Diop's view that the ancient Egyptians were not Caucasians, but was inclined to say they were "neither white nor negro." It was obvious that much of the polarization at this conference came because Diop and Obenga insisted upon a definition of "Negro" that included a very wide range of skin-color and features, whereas the other participants clung to a concept of "Negro" that was essentially a holdover from traditional physical anthropology. Those who used the narrow definition did not deny that such physical types had been present in every period of Egyptian history, but they questioned their predominance at any given period. In considering ancient Egyptian populations, they also refused to call "Brown" (or "Red") and "Yellow" people "Black," as Diop, using North American criteria, insisted upon doing. Maurice Glele, a program specialist in the Division of Cultural Studies, UNESCO, remarked that

> if the criteria for classifying a person as black, white or yellow were so debatable, and if the concepts which had been discussed were so ill-defined and perhaps so subjective or inseparable from habitual patterns of thought, this should be frankly stated and a revision should be made of the entire terminology of world history in the light of new scientific criteria, so that the vocabulary should be the same for every one and that words should have the same connotations, thus avoiding misconceptions and being conducive to understanding and agreement.

Diop and Obenga insisted upon using the current physical anthropological data, along with iconographic inquiry and linguistic analysis, to characterize the ancient Egyptians as "Black" in both a technical anthropological sense and in terms of popular usage. The rapporteur states that Diop dismissed his critics summarily as being so conditioned that they could not face facts:

> He was, therefore, in no doubt: the first inhabitants of the Nile valley belonged to the black race, as defined by the research findings currently accepted by specialists in anthropology and prehistory. Professor Diop considered that only psychological and educational factors prevented the truth of this from being accepted. . . . Professor Diop was not in favor of setting up commissions to verify patent facts which, at the present time, simply needed formal recognition.

None of the participants other than Diop and Obenga was willing to accept the "Negroness" of the early Egyptians as a "patent fact." Instead of "formal recognition" of what were regarded as "facts" by Diop and Obenga, other participants did recommend the establishment of several commissions to study the problem in more detail. Most insisted that the Egyptian populations had been "mixed" from the earliest times. They did not discuss whether such "mixed" populations would be characterized as "black" or "Negro" if current social definitions in Europe and North America were used; nor did they discuss usage in other contexts where political ends would be served thereby. For Diop, these were crucial questions that were ignored by the symposium.[44]

In Mokhtar's summation of the findings of the symposium, he noted that while some of Diop's arguments had been adopted as expressing the consensus of the group, there had been no unanimous agreement upon any point except that what laymen or political personalities mean by "race" is not what geneticists and most contemporary anthropologists mean. Diop's rejoinder was that specialists should remember that laymen do not react to genotypes and blood types but to phenotypes, that is, to what old-fashioned anthropologists call "races." Diop argued that the question we must answer is, "Did Egyptians resemble what ordinary people, today, call 'Negroes'?" not "What do skull measurements and blood types show?"[45]

Some scholars lash out at those who write about Egypt from a black perspective, with displays of amazing insensitivity to motivation. Fortunately, this did not occur at the symposium. However, one of the most distinguished contemporary British Africanists, Roland Oliver, of the London School of Oriental and African Studies, previously quoted and cited, in reviewing the chapter by Diop entitled "The Origins of Ancient Egypt" in the UNESCO *General History of Africa* for the *Times Literary Supplement*, dismisses this highly trained scholar as being not "serious" and ridicules him for having "made a life-long hobby of the thesis that the Ancient Egyptians were black." The disagreement between Oliver and Diop, in part, involves the issue of how broad a definition of "black" or "Negro" should be used by scholars. Yet, since the British scholar felt impelled to deride the African savant as a "rumbustious Senegalese museum director," and to dismiss his work by saying that "of sixty-odd contributions there is only one which is a total nonsense," we can only assume that the emotion behind the contemptuous tone suggests that more than semantics is involved.[46] Diop's occasional overstatement of his case and his tendency sometimes to treat folklore as fact, as well as his use of oral tradition without fully adequate controls in a previous work, had been criticized by a French university professor. But that scholar did so in a temperate tone and accorded some respect to a learned African colleague. In fact, Diop published these criticisms along with his answers to them. There was far less for a conventional scholar to quarrel with in the 1981 article criticized by Oliver than in the earlier work that brought on the controversy with the French scholar. Yet Oliver seemed more inclined to "destroy" Diop than to "correct" him.

Oliver also accused Diop of flogging a dead horse, commenting that "Edward Wilmot Blyden held the same view but that was a century or more ago." Then, in trying to argue that some Negroid admixture in the Egyptian population is now generally accepted (introduced through slavery, according to him), he states that it is ridiculous to call the ancient Egyptian people as a whole "Black." Here Oliver revealed the gulf between a British liberal academic perspective and a black perspective. He missed Diop's whole point, since black scholars see inconsistency (if not hypocrisy) in the English practice of calling the children of African and West Indian fathers and British mothers "Black" but sneering at those who use the same designation for similar types among the ancient Egyptians. These black scholars have never been willing to accept a definition of "Negro" or "Black" that includes a wide range of physical types when Anglo-Africans, Afro-Americans, or Afro–West Indians are classified, but uses totally different criteria of classification for Egyptians.

A portion of Diop's book, *The African Origin of Civilization,* argues for a definition of "Negro," in dealing with ancient and modern Africa, that would include the same range of physical types represented in the Afro-American population of the United States. He argues that no Egyptian term for "black race" existed that would be equivalent to "Negro," and that the word *Nehesi,* frequently translated as "Negro," actually means "people of the south." A wide range in color and physical type existed among these Nehesi, who lived above the first Nile cataract.[47] *Within* the Egyptian population, classifications on the basis of skin-color do not seem to have been the custom. The only foreigners who were so classified seem to have been some of the inhabitants of the African area west of Egypt, who were referred to by a term that meant "Yellow" and who were usually called "Libyans" by the Greek historians.[48] There is some evidence that the Egyptians called themselves "Black," that is, *khem,* although some scholars insist this word meant "people who live on the black land," not "people with black skin." Despite the acceptance of people of all colors as Egyptians, there was undoubtedly a somatic norm image. It may or may not have been the same as that *conventionally* represented in the painting of males as dark reddish-brown or red and females as very light brown or lemon color, but it was not so dark as that of Negroes among the Nehesi. After the Eighteenth Dynasty, artists frequently attempted to portray various physical types of foreigners by showing a wide range in skin-color and facial features, but the written record makes no reference to the significance of the differences.[49] Prisoners of war are shown bound and beaten without regard to race or color. The somatic norm image seems to have changed over a long span of time from "Negro" to brown with Caucasoid features.

Although Du Bois's assessment of the racial situation in ancient Egypt foreshadowed the progressive modern view, his statement about the culture stressed external influences to an extent that has been abandoned by most Egyptologists. Du Bois wrote of Egypt that

> like all civilizations it drew largely from without and undoubtedly arose in the valley of the Nile, because that valley was so easily made a center for the meeting of men of all types and from all parts of the world. At the same time Egyptian civilization seems to have been African in its beginning and in its main line of development, despite strong influences from all parts of Asia [italics added].[50]

The statement that Egypt "drew *largely* from without" was the standard view when Du Bois wrote. This is no longer the consensus among Egyptologists. There was some borrowing of ideas and technology, but the emphasis today is on the point that the "main line of development" was African. *The best of the modern Egyptologists consider the Egyptian culture a specialized, refined variant of Nile Valley cultures, which in turn are a variant of a broader continental African type.*

Recent research supports the vindicationist argument that the early Egyptians did not "borrow" or "adopt" a basic culture from Blacks to the south—that is, from "Negroes"—but were themselves part of a continuous Negro population extending from the mouth of the Nile up beyond the sixth Nile cataract into what is now the Republic of Sudan. Both the physical type of the people and the details of the culture in the portion of the Nile Valley that is now Egypt changed over many millennia, but the basic "Negroidness" of both is discernible despite miscegenation and acculturation.

Egyptian religious systems and ethical codes were elaborations and refinements of a common core of African beliefs and practices that were widespread south and east of Egypt. Students of the Book of the Dead point out that beneath the esoteric symbolism and the residue of magical spells from predynastic times, the versions of the text used during the Fourth and Fifth Dynasties—indubitably Negroid dynasties—contain philosophical ideas and ethical codes that are alien neither to the Judeo-Christian values cherished by Western civilizations nor to Indian, Chinese, or Persian religious values. Passages

such as the following—in the Book of the Dead—from the so-called
Negative Confession, existed long before the Ten Commandments,
Buddha's Sevenfold Aryan Path, or the Confucian maxims:

I have not committed evil in the place of truth.
I have not defrauded the poor man of his goods.
I have allowed no man to go hungry.
I have made no man to weep.
I have slain no man.
I have not encroached upon the fields of others.
I have not taken away the milk from the mouth of the babes.[51]

PERSPECTIVES FOR VIEWING EGYPTIAN HISTORY

The reconstruction and interpretation of Egyptian history is always
carried out from some socially conditioned perspective. The basic
data have been gathered by professional Egyptologists, and their ethnic and racial biases are often evident in their presentation and analysis of results. These researches have not, however, seriously affected
the traditional scheme of periodizing Nile Valley history that was
written down by the Egyptian priest-scholar Manetho for the benefit
of Greek enquirers between 300 and 200 B.C. He recorded that the
northern portion of the Nile Valley (see map 3), below the first
cataract, had been ruled by thirty-one "dynasties" or "royal families." Each ruler was known as a "pharaoh," and Manetho provided
a list of these sovereigns. With the advent of professional Egyptology
in the late eighteenth century, the process began of examining the validity of Manetho's scheme against archaeological data and written
records, of reconciling contradictory bits of evidence, and of assigning dates to the dynasties and the periods during which specific kings
reigned. Egyptian chronology then had to be coordinated with Near
Eastern and continentwide African chronology as it slowly became
clear from the archaeological record.[52]

The result of nearly 200 years of research is now a substantial measure of agreement among Egyptologists to use some date between 3200
and 3000 B.C. as the approximate time when the first Egyptian dynasty was established. Furthermore, the first two dynasties are
usually called the Early Dynastic, or Archaic Period, ending between
2600 and 2800 B.C., after which four dynasties form the Old Kingdom,
followed by four more, usually called the First Intermediate Dynasties, and then a Middle Kingdom. After another Intermediate, or
"low," period, the New Kingdom begins. It includes the Ramesside
kings. The New Kingdom, or New Empire, was followed by six other

dynasties preceding foreign conquest by Persians, Greeks, and Romans. (See chart 3 for a summary of some of the significant events during the first twelve dynasties.)

The thousand-year period prior to the rule of the First Dynasty is referred to as the Predynastic period, behind which the Chalcolithic, Neolithic, and Paleolithic periods, in that order, stretch far back into the past. "Prehistory" ends and "history" starts sometime between 3500 and 3000 B.C., when scribes and priests began to make written records, with the Egyptians being, perhaps, the first people in human history to do so in a systematic fashion.[53] Over the next 500 years a civilization was emerging in the Nile River Valley and the Nile Delta concurrently, with similar developments in the Tigris-Euphrates Valley and the Indus River Valley. *This anthropological frame of reference is of value to students of Egyptian history regardless of their political or ethnic perspectives.*

From *a black perspective*, three periods of Egyptian history have special significance: dynasties three and four of the Old Kingdom (2750 B.C.–2200 B.C.); dynasty eighteen of the New Kingdom (1550 B.C.–1305 B.C.); and dynasty twenty-five, sometimes referred to as the Ethiopian, or Kushitic, Dynasty (715 B.C.–656 B.C.), also of the New Kingdom. The first high point of Egyptian creativity occurred during dynasties three and four, and since Negroid pharaohs, priests, and intellectuals were prevalent then, these dynasties are important for vindicationist purposes. What is sometimes called the "Glorious Eighteenth" is discussed herein as "The Eighteenth Dynasty: Leaders of a National Renaissance." It has been selected because, according to North American social criteria, it was a "Negro" dynasty. The Ethiopian, or Kushitic, Twenty-fifth Dynasty was composed of pharaohs from above the first cataract of the Nile and ruled Egypt and Kush as a single empire for seventy years. The significance of this dynasty from a black perspective is obvious, and it is therefore considered in some detail.

There is still some debate among Egyptologists about the setting of dates for important events in ancient Egyptian history, including those that mark the beginning and end of specific dynasties and pharaonic incumbencies. What might be called a revised standard chronology was presented in 1980 by Cyril Aldred in *Egyptian Art in the Age of the Pharaohs.* Most Egyptologists are in general agreement with his scheme. The dates used throughout this book (including chart 3), however, are those presented by the scholars who produced volumes 1 and 2 of UNESCO's *General History of Africa,* published in 1981. This represents the first attempt by African scholars, and Egyptologists in whom they reposed confidence, to establish a system of periodization and dating that is satisfactory from a black perspective. Therefore, it seems appropriate to use their dates in this book. Those scholars accepted the standard periodization but, in some instances, have chosen dates that vary slightly from those put forth by Aldred. I have not adopted their most striking deviation, which involves substituting a minus sign (–) for b.c. and a plus sign (+) for a.d. This was done out of deference to those Africans who are Traditionalists or Muslims, and for whom Anno Domini ("Year of our Lord") is both ethnocentric and offensive, with Before Christ ("the Anointed One") conferring a status upon Jesus that they do not concede. (Some Jewish and UNESCO publications use b.c.e.—Before the Common Era, and c.e.—Common Era, to achieve this same, less ethnocentric, result.) At the risk of being considered insensitive, I have retained the more familier b.c. and a.d., recognizing at the same time why the usage has been abandoned by some scholars. No insult is intended nor any ethnocentric claim for the superiority of the Christian religion made. I have discussed the matter at some length because it is essential to an understanding of the only important revision in periodization that this particular black perspective entails.

From *the perspective of students of interracial relations*, all of the dynasties are useful for examining attitudes toward "Negroidness" and for testing Blumer's theory of race relations as well as the Degler-Gergen propositions. However, the period of the seven dynasties that existed between the end of the Ramesside Age (between 1085 and 1070 b.c.) and the conquest of Egypt by the Romans in 31 b.c. presents a crucial case of a situation likely to generate racial prejudice. For the first time since an earlier invasion by Southwest Asians, Egyptians were dominated by an alien ruling class that differed from them by being "white" in skin-color. This period of domination came after they had themselves operated as an imperialist power in the Middle East. Resentment against the invaders was strong and conflict frequent. The extent to which the dominant foreigners used the difference in color to justify their rule, or the Egyptians used it to justify rebellion, merits study. The extent to which the somatic norm image of the conqueror influenced the self-concept of the Egyptians, as Hoetink's theory suggests it would, can be observed during this period.

CHART 3. ETHNIC INTERACTION DURING PREDYNASTIC PERIOD AND
DYNASTIES ONE THROUGH TWELVE

Time-Periods and Dynasties	Significant Internal Events	Relations with Asians and Europeans	Relations with Peoples of Wawat and Kush (i.e., ancient Ethiopia)
MIDDLE KINGDOM— Dynasties Eleven through Twelve 2150–1780 B.C.	Theban princes from Upper Egypt re-unify nation.	Widespread trade relations with Crete and Asia Minor.	"Nehesi" repulsed; then Nubia invaded in search for gold. Temple of Amon erected at Cataract Four.
FIRST INTERMEDIATE DYNASTIES— Seven through Ten 2200–2150 B.C.	Monarchy weakened by local feudal lords during sixth led to disorder.	Asian nomads, taking advantage of disorders, infiltrate delta provinces.	While Asians are harassing the delta, the "barbarian" Blacks attack at Cataract One, but trade continues.
OLD KINGDOM —Dynasties Three through Six 2750–2200 B.C. Era of "The Pyramid Builders" and great intellectual growth	Petrie says Fourth Dynasty is "of Nubian origin." King as "god" who unifies and is also symbol of Osiris, the culture hero and god. Building in stone after Dynasty Two.	No invasions from Asia; fruitful trade and exchange of ideas with Mesopotamia. Some danger of nomadic invasion from north after Dynasty Five.	"Barbarian Blacks" impel "civilized" Egyptian Blacks to counterattack and erect a barrier at Cataract One against incursions by the "Nehesi" (southerners). Tradition of Punt as "the sacred land" being recorded on walls of some tombs.
EARLY DYNASTIC PERIOD— One, Two 3000–2750 B.C. Beginning of writing	Upper and Lower Kingdoms united by Menes (Narmer) under Red and White crowns.	Archaeology indicates indicates trade with Mesopotamia.	Limited amount of trade with people in Nubia beyond Cataract One.
PREDYNASTIC PERIOD— Before 3000 B.C.	Teter-Neter, and the Anu, march down the Nile from Theban area.	Asians bring domesticated plants and animals into delta area.	West Africans introduce food crops near Cataract VI; people from Punt (Somalia?) probably entering Nile Valley.

EGYPT BEFORE THE PHARAOHS

The unique ecological setting in which Egyptian civilization arose is frequently cited as decisive in the shaping of the culture over several millennia. Like the culture of the Sumerians and the Akkadians, it was a river valley culture; but the Nile Valley was very different from the Tigris-Euphrates Valley in Mesopotamia. The Nile flows for over 4000 miles from Lake Nyanza in what is now Uganda down to the Mediterranean Sea, being joined along the way by two important tributaries from the East African highlands. Near the Mediterranean it fans out into several branches to form the broad fertile delta that constitutes Lower Egypt. Six rocky obstructions, called "cataracts," lie between Aswan (500 miles from the sea) and modern Khartoum, near ancient Meroë and part of a land the Egyptians called Upper Nubia or Kush (see map 3). What the Egyptians called Lower and Upper Nubia the classical Greeks called Ethiopia. It embraced the modern Republic of Sudan but not the modern state of Ethiopia, which in antiquity was called Axum and then somewhat later, Abyssinia. Because the Nile overflowed annually and deposited fertile soil on its banks, a high degree of confidence in nature was generated, unlike the moods evoked by the desert, where sandstorms, drought, and mirages gave life a harsh edge.

Egyptian civilization developed in the 600-mile narrow valley between the first cataract (near modern Aswan) and the Mediterranean Sea, a fertile strip averaging ten miles in width with the Nile in its center, and in the broad delta where the mouths of the river entered the sea. Arthur Weigall, the British Egyptologist previously referred to as having called the Twenty-fifth Dynasty pharaohs "niggers," wrote about this ecological setting, and the culture that emerged within it, with a degree of appreciation and understanding that makes the use of his work desirable despite some of his racist language and attitudes. I quote at some length. He notes that during historic times,

> the Nile branched into seven separate streams, and poured into the Mediterranean from seven mouths, situated along some two hundred and fifty miles of coast-line. These streams were supplemented in very early times by artificial canals, and thus Lower Egypt was a well-watered triangle of flat and seemingly boundless fields, which merged into marsh-land before the sea was reached. Slightly to the west side of the middle of this triangle stood the city of Sae, the modern Sa, called by the Greeks Sais, and, nearer to the sea, the city of Peutho, the Greek Buto.

This delta attracted migrants from Asia and Europe as well as periodic invaders from the sea. It also encouraged extensive maritime trade. This was "the North," "Lower Egypt." Southward from the Delta, "Upper Egypt" stretched into the distance, the most remote part of which, including the Thebaid, was called "the South."

Weigall, in describing the climatic situation of the valley, which retained excellent fertility despite little rain, stressed the uniqueness of the geographical setting:

> Early in June every year the waters of the Nile began to rise, owing to the rainfall in Central Africa, and in the second half of July the rise became very rapid, until, in August, the river overflowed its banks, and the whole valley of Upper Egypt was transformed into one great lake, the cities and towns rising like islands above the placid surface of the water, being connected one with another only by embanked roads. The highest flood-levels were reached at about the middle of October, after which the river rapidly subsided, and the sowing of the crops began in the wet mud, almost as soon as the ground was visible. In Upper Egypt the first harvest was gathered by the middle of February; and then began the sowing of the second crop, which was reaped just before the floods poured on to the fields. In the Delta, however, the inundation did not cover the land in the same manner, and a third crop was grown while Upper Egypt was under water.
>
> With three crops in the year, Egypt was always a land of plenty, where hunger was hardly known, except in the rare event of a series of bad Niles. Great herds of cattle and goats were maintained, and the Nile abounded in fish. The vast gold-mines in the eastern desert, moreover, were worked from the earliest known times; and thus the wealth of the country was enormous. *Its geographical position—shut in between the deserts—saved it in early days from attack; and therefore, whenever the somewhat restless and intrigue-loving inhabitants were firmly governed, the prosperous and peaceful life of the nation was able to be developed and maintained in a manner unknown in other ancient lands.* The dry, sunny climate, too, was ideal, except during the summer in the south, when the heat was great. Transport by river was always a simple matter, for, going northwards, the rapid stream carried the vessels down without any labour, and, going southwards, the bracing north wind, which blows almost continuously, filled the great sails of the ships and brought them upstream at a fine speed and with the minimum of trouble. *Under such favourable conditions the active-minded and happy race of Egyptians, in spite of innumerable revolutions and changes of government, produced their civilization at so remote a period that its beginnings are lost in obscurity, and maintained it with surprising tenacity and conservatism for thousands of years* [italics added].[54]

This romanticized description is nevertheless basically accurate, although it obscures the role of the constant hard work involved in digging irrigation ditches and in maintaining earthworks to prevent floods. Egypt's prosperity was possible only because a group of disciplined village agriculturalists learned to cooperate under regional leaders who displayed remarkable intelligence and who, thereby, won power and prestige. The people called their country "The Black Land" to distinguish it from the menacing desert, "The Red Land."[55] As the valley communities grew more prosperous, they attracted bands of marauders who lurked in the desert and raided the villages and the caravan trails. The disciplined activity that made civilization in the valley possible began during what Egyptologists call the Predynastic Period, and the knitting together of the village communities into a nation extending from the Mediterranean to the first cataract also began in predynastic times, that is, before king lists were kept. Egyptian prehistory ended sometime during late predynastic times, when writing was adopted by priests and scribes.

A recent definitive discussion of Egyptian prehistory and early history suggests that experience gained from flood control was used by Egyptian leaders as the basis for an elaborate engineering system to distribute Nile flood water efficiently:

> It is sometimes forgotten that the overflowing of the Nile is not solely beneficial; it can bring disaster, and it was no doubt for themselves that the valley's inhabitants learned to build dikes and dams to shield their villages and to dig canals to dry out their fields. . . . Using the dike-building and canal-digging techniques which they had perfected over the centuries, the Egyptians little by little developed the system of irrigation by basins (hods), thus securing not only their survival in a climate increasingly desert-like, but even the possibility of expansion.

Embankments and drains were devised to fill and empty the basins and to distribute the water equitably over wide areas.

> It is no exaggeration to say that this unique system of irrigation is at the very root of the development of Egyptian civilization. It explains how human ingenuity slowly managed to overcome great difficulties and succeeded in changing the valley's natural ecology. . . . Egypt is not only *a gift of the Nile*; it is above all, a creation of man.

It was necessary to repair the embankments, strengthen the cross-dams, and clear the canals each year after the Nile flood.

> It was a continual collective task, which in primitive times was probably carried out at the level of the village. In the historic period it was conducted and supervised by the central government. If the latter failed to ensure in due time the detailed maintenance of the entire system, the next flood might carry it all away, returning the valley to its original state.[56]

The central government stored grain in warehouses set up through-out the country to provide food when there were either excessive or inadequate Nile floods. Priests and scribes made up the corps of ex-perts who maintained the complex accounting system that was necessary for efficient social control. They also kept records of past climatic conditions and possessed the knowledge of astronomy needed for guiding the farmers through their yearly cycle of agricul-tural activities. Writing was essential for carrying out these activities.

A strong central government was necessary to give cohesion to this complex system geared toward survival in the Two Lands—Delta and Upper Egypt. The pharaoh, in his person, symbolized both the collec-tive leadership and the beneficent forces of nature. To understand the magnitude and significance of the role of the king, or pharaoh, a com-ment by John A. Wilson of the Oriental Institute of the University of Chicago is relevant:

> Physically and culturally the land of Egypt breaks into the narrow trough of the Nile Valley and the spreading Delta. . . . These two regions were then disparate, and they were traditionally and continu-ingly competitive. Yet they were a unity in their isolation from the rest of the world, and they were a unity in their dependence upon the Nile. *It was a function of government to make Upper and Lower Egypt an ef-fective single nation. This was done by incorporating authority and responsibility for both regions in a single figure, the god-king . . . the wearer of the double crown which symbolizes the union of the two regions* [italics added].[57]

The white crown or *hedjet* symbolized the South; the red crown or *deshret*, the North.

Egyptologists are convinced that the concept of the "god-king" was elaborated in predynastic times among people living above the first cataract of the Nile, in Wawat or Kush, and was associated with the function of rainmaker chiefs, who assured fertility to the earth, animals, and human beings.[58] These functions were retained by the pharaoh. But in dynastic Egypt his primary role was to symbolize the unity of a nation composed of numerous small political units—*nomes* (presided over by *nomarchs*); centers of power vested in colleges of priests—Memphis, Thebes, Heliopolis, and Hermionopolis; and, in some periods, kings who thought of themselves as being rulers of either Lower Egypt or Upper Egypt. By 4000 B.C., priests, feudal lords, and nomarchs were extracting enough economic surplus from the production of peasant labor to indulge in some leisure-class refine-ments. Then, within 500 years, the characteristics associated with early "civilization" could be discerned. Within another 500 years military leaders were beginning to make attempts to unify Upper Egypt and Lower Egypt into a single kingdom.

Sometime between 3500 and 3200 B.C. agricultural productivity and Neolithic skill in tool and weapon making began to support a stable, socially stratified society along the banks of the Nile between the first cataract and the point where the river now splits into several separate branches to form a delta. The Delta was divided into twenty-two nomes, each of which had an animal totem and a body of local tradition as well as local religious shrines. Property owners, sometimes referred to as "feudal lords" in the literature, were, ethnically, a very mixed group after the pharaohs began to parcel out estates to mercenary soldiers. It is thought that, from earliest dynastic times, a racially mixed population lived side by side with an older, more Negroid stratum in the Delta, with continuous accretions of "Libyans," "Sea People," and Asiatics.

The string of nomes south of the Delta constituted Upper Egypt and extended to the first Nile cataract at Aswan. One power center was at Hermopolis, close to the edge of the Delta and sometimes thought of as representing "Middle Egypt." The other center was far to the south at Thebes. Of the twenty-six southern nomes, those near Thebes and the Nubian border contained numerous legendary sacred shrines, including Abydos, where the head of the culture hero Osiris was said to be buried. The people of the southernmost nome were not only of the same physical type as the people across the border in Nubia, but the nome itself was sometimes called Ta-Meri, the Egyptian word meaning "Land of the Bowmen," or "Nubian Warriors."

Some Egyptologists have a tendency to think of Upper Egypt, near the southern extremity, as "black" Egypt, and the Delta as "white," or "near-white." Although Egyptians spoke of the "Two Lands" and the "Two Kingdoms," there is no evidence in any hieroglyphic inscriptions or papyrus writings that Egyptians thought of this in terms of a color difference, although they recognized subcultural regional differences, reflected in speech.[59] *If the difference between the Delta and the South was conceptualized as a color difference, it was not reflected in discrimination based on skin-color in the political and religious life of Egypt or in mating and marriage, as the subsequent analysis will indicate.*

Race and Color in Predynastic Egypt

Since Egypt is generally regarded as one of the two "cradles of civilization," Mesopotamia being the other, students of the Black Experience have continually raised questions about the extent of Negro participation in the Neolithic "food-producing revolution" that preceded "civilization." What kind of people were the original Egyptians? Were the first Egyptians who practiced agriculture Blacks or Asians? Did the Egyptians domesticate plants and animals themselves, or did they borrow the techniques and the crops from the peoples of the Fertile Crescent? Is it possible that the Mesopotamian peoples and the Arabians were themselves Black, and therefore that borrowing from these areas meant one black group borrowing from another? Is it possible that several different racial groups have lived together in Egypt from prehistoric times? These matters, except for the last question, are still in dispute.

Egyptologists, in studying predynastic Egypt, rely heavily upon archaeology, in addition to drawing conclusions from myths, folklore, and oral tradition. There is no way to assess the "race" of human remains found in the various sites without playing the "numbers game" that anthropologists play. When Dr. Du Bois wrote *The Negro* in 1915, both the racists and the antiracists had been at each other hammer and tongs for decades citing figures on cephalic indices, cranial capacities, skull shape, facial angles, nasal structure, and so on. The rules of the game involved accepting some fundamental ideas about the meaning of cranial statistics, of which the most relevant was: "The greater the degree of alveolar prognathism (i.e., forward projection of the lower face), the more Negroid the skull" (fig. 1). A certain combination of skeletal measurements was used to define an ideal type, the "True Negro," among living Africans; when bones approximating this norm were found, the fossil was assessed as "Negro," despite the absence of skin and hair. Skeletal material, particularly cranial, was defined as "white" in a similar fashion. Limbs and pelvis measurements were also used.

In carrying on the dialogue, most black scholars have not criticized the entire field of anthropometry. The majority of them have preferred, rather, to accept the premises and to argue within them, although the assumptions and techniques themselves are vulnerable.[60] However, after two decades of using anthropometric data to substantiate his arguments about the race of predynastic Egyptians, Cheikh Anta Diop, writing in 1981 in UNESCO's *A General History of Africa*, revealed his feeling of frustration:

> The arbitrary nature of the criteria used, to go no farther, as well as abolishing any notion of a conclusion acceptable without qualification, introduces so much scientific hair-splitting that there are times when one wonders whether the solution of the problem would not have been nearer if we had not had the ill luck to approach it from this angle.

Yet he proceeded immediately to say, "Although the conclusions of these anthropological studies stop short of the full truth, they still speak unanimously of the existence of a negro race from the most distant ages of prehistory down to the dynastic period."[61]

Diop was careful not to say that the *only* race detectable among ancient Egyptian fossil finds and mummies was "Negro," as anthropologists use the term. He presents statistics he had used in earlier works to give a generalized summary based upon available studies of about 2,000 predynastic skulls. These indicated that Egyptologists had classified 36 percent as "definitely Negroid," 33 percent as "Mediterranean," and 11 percent as "Cro-Magnon." (An earlier study had suggested that only 25 percent were Negroid.)[62] In view of the fact that the "Mediterranean Race" was called the "Brown Race" by Sergi, the Italian anthropologist who first described it, Diop would be on firm ground if he merely argued that most of this skeletal material was *probably* covered by an integument that would have led to the individuals' being classified as "nonwhite" or "colored."[63] But since such "brownness" in populations of African descent in Europe and the United States is enough to define them as "Negro," Diop insisted upon doing so as well. In addition, since adding the Mediterraneans to the group of skeletons defined as "Negro" increases the proportion of Blacks and browns to 56 percent of the total, he felt justified in calling the entire population "Negro." The African, Diop, would seem to have as much justification for doing this as a British Egyptologist had for describing the predynastic population without mentioning a possible Negro component.[64]

The pro-Negro American anthropologist George Peter Murdock avoids a definitive statement about these predynastic fossils found in Egypt by making the matter contingent upon the racial assessment of data from subsequent periods. He wrote of the Egyptian Neolithic cultures that they were "borne by people indistinguishable in physical type from the later dynastic Egyptians," whom he calls "Caucasoid."[65] Although Murdock is aggressively antiracist, he uses a very narrow definition of "Negro" in his book *Africa*. For example, a number of black ethnic groups are classified as "Caucasian" because their skeletal traits are similar to those of Europeans. In dealing with fossils, Murdock, like all the other archaeologists and anthropologists, has only bones—without any skin or hair—to work with in deciding whether or not a fossil is "Negro." The term "Caucasoid" cannot be equated automatically with "white," but the skeletal features in this case preclude calling the fossils "Negro."

In his 1981 UNESCO article, Diop challenged Egyptologists, as he

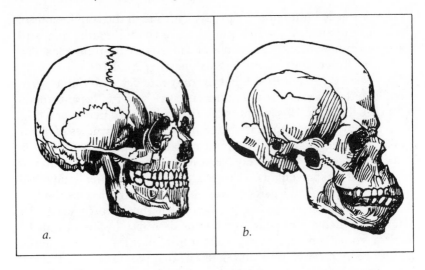

FIGURE 1. ALVEOLAR PROGNATHISM IN TWO SKULLS. Reprinted from
Nott and Gliddon, *Types of Mankind* (1855).
a. GREEK SPECIMEN
b. WEST AFRICAN SPECIMEN

had done previously, to use a system he had devised for measuring the
amount of melanin present in the skin of mummies. However, because predynastic mummified remains are so rare, the method would
be of limited use for that period.[66] In any event, it could determine
only the degree of "blackness," not the extent of "Negroidness." The
predynastic Egyptians could have been Black but more similar in features to the Dravidian and Veddoid peoples of India than to the people of Central Africa. (Indeed, portraits of some dynastic Egyptians
have the "Indian look.")[67] *Arguments about fossils and mummies,*
like arguments about the living, revolve as much around the question
of how broadly the term "Negro" or "Black" should be extended as
they do about the collection, manipulation, and evaluation of empir-
ical data.

The question of the race of the early Egyptians is bound up with the
question of where predynastic movement toward civilization in the
Nile Valley began. Some anthropologists think the archaeological evidence supports a theory of direct evolution of the dynastic regimes
out of a predynastic civilization that grew up among the Delta peoples. They assert that this advanced culture, like the practice of
agriculture, diffused north to south, *up* the Nile. Diop argues against
this view by pointing out that there was no delta until near historic
time, the Mediterranean coast, before then, extending almost as far

inland as the city of Memphis is today. Diop also cites archaeologists who have presented impressive data to support the position that the valley civilization originated in Neolithic cultures of southern Egypt, near the border with Nubia or perhaps in Nubia itself.[68]

All students, despite these differences of opinion, agree that a relatively high level of efficient cultivation was necessary to sustain the emergent kingdoms, and that by 3100 B.C. this foundation had been laid by predynastic people living in small groups on both sides of the Nile, from its mouth southward through an area extending beyond the first cataract into Nubia. They cultivated some crops that were first domesticated in Southwest Asia—wheat, barley, and a variety of fruits, melons, and vegetables. They also used animals from that area—goats, asses, and cattle. From the East African highlands came plants supplying essential oils such as castor and safflower, and from West Africa they received cotton, gourds, and watermelon. The flax used for linen they probably domesticated themselves. These predynastic Egyptians were thus participants in what archaeologists began to call the "Neolithic Revolution" in the early post–World War II years, or, alternatively, the "food-producing revolution."[69] The Nile Valley was not one of the centers in which the domestication of plants and animals occurred at the beginning of the Neolithic Revolution, but it provided a fertile area for the new economies to take root.

Because the northern area (Lower Egypt) was the region where crops and animals introduced from Southwest Asia first appeared, there has been considerable discussion about the probable race of the inhabitants. Were they immigrants from the Fertile Crescent or an indigenous Nile Delta population that adopted innovations from beyond their borders? Or were they a mixed racial group coming in from the deserts? A number of northern sites containing skeletons and artifacts have been excavated. Given the emphasis that physical anthropologists have placed upon alveolar prognathism as a diagnostic trait in assessing a skull as "Negro," it is significant to note that Sir Arthur Keith (who, incidentally, believed in the innate inferiority of black people) found "prevalence of alveolar prognathism" in the so-called Natufian type that some scholars feel was the first to cultivate plants and animals in northern Egypt. This was the same breed of man who had made the basic innovations of the Neolithic Revolution somewhere in the Middle East.

If the early Delta population was Natufian, even Carleton Coon, an anthropologist whose racist statements sometimes embarrassed his colleagues, would concede a Negroid tinge. On one occasion he wrote of Natufians that "the wide, low vaulted nose, in combination with prognathism, gives a somewhat negroid cast to the face." But he hastened to conclude that these people were *really* "white," that "these late Natufians represent a basically Mediterranean type with minor Negroid affinities."[70] These same people would probably be classified as "Negroes" in the United States, where such *minor* Negroid affinities are always enough to tip the scales. In the Middle East, however, they remain "white." Such inconsistencies have evoked charges against the professional taxonomists ranging from hypocrisy to racism, by those Blacks who are aware of their operations. They see a definite attempt to insist that the Neolithic innovators who developed agriculture, pottery, metallurgy, and weaving could not possibly have been what we now call "Negroes."

Even in dealing with the prehistoric southern population of Upper Egypt, close to Nubia, Coon was reluctant to designate the people as "Negroid" despite the presence of traits usually considered definitive. Thus he writes of the Badarian Neolithic people that "while the prognathism and nose form would suggest a negroid tendency, this cannot be established since the hair form is definitely not negroid." (In this case mummified remains were available.) Coon referred to the Sebilians in the southern area with esthetic approval as being of "a fine Mediterranean type," although in another context he notes that "Mediterranean proper often carries a slight Negroid tendency." As to the Naqada skeletons, which had "less prognathism than the Badarians," it was Coon's opinion that they represented people similar to the contemporary Coptic population in Egypt, who "probably represent the ancient Egyptian type more faithfully than the Muslim population."[71] This was the type that Count Volney compared with the Sphinx and decided that ancient Egyptians had Negro features. Thus Coon uses the words *somewhat, minor,* and *slight tendency* to minimize the importance of traits that he himself calls "negroid" in the prehistoric southern population of Egypt and its probable descendants. These are the people whom black scholars consider most crucial in assessing possible Negro contributions to early Egyptian civilization. (It might be noted that Coon used similar language to minimize the extent of "Negroidness" in Natufian fossils.)

Those who consider the North—Lower Egypt—to be the important center of prehistoric innovations usually stress the probability of an Asian origin for the inhabitants. But they, too, have to contend with traits anthropologists call Negroid in the fossilized or mummified human remains, whether they be Natufian or the so-called "Northern Race" that came later. Thus, as late as 1964, one of the most eminent of the American Egyptologists argued for the superiority of some presumably non-Negroid populations that were assumed to have been present in Lower Egypt; and he hinted, during a period when most anthropologists had abandoned the idea, that intelligence was correlated with cranial traits:

> The early northern Egyptian, wherever we encounter him—Merimda, El-Omari, Maadi North, Maadi South, and Heliopolis—appears to have been somewhat taller and more sturdily built than his Upper Egyptian contemporary and to have been endowed with a broader and better formed skull and a generally greater cranial capacity.[72]

Despite the fact that most anthropologists usually pounced upon prognathism as almost conclusive evidence of "Negroidness," this scholar did not wish to admit that the "purity" of a Northern Race he sought to define was compromised, although he had to concede that it might be: "The prognathism observed in the skulls from Maadi South and Heliopolis may or may not indicate the infiltration of a negroid strain into the northern region."[73] He was anxious to draw a sharp line between the inhabitants of Lower Egypt, near the Mediterranean, and those farther south:

> Generally speaking, however, the prehistoric northerner seems to represent a type distinct in race and physique as well as in culture from the people of the south. In him, rather than in some intrusive group of outlanders, we may perhaps recognize, with Junker, the ancestor of the so-called Dynastic Race, or Giza type, of Early Dynastic and Old Kingdom times.[74]

Arnold Toynbee, an erudite British scholar, in describing what he calls the Egyptiac Civilization in his monumental work, *A Study of History*, was more inclined to accept the idea of a racially mixed population as the originator of Egyptian civilization than some hypothetical special northern "Dynastic Race." Nevertheless, explicitly antiracist though he was, Toynbee was not able to break out of his conservative British intellectual mold. The result was ambiguity about racial terminology and reliance upon a narrow range of sources. In the final analysis, his thought-provoking work is flawed. Toynbee argues cogently against those who would explain the origin of *any* civilization in terms of some genetic predisposition or theory of racial superiority. Yet he unwittingly lends support to the racist camp by restricting the term "Black Race" to "Australian Blackfellows, the Papuans and Melanesians, the Veddahs of Ceylon and the Todas of Southern India, as well as the Negro population of Africa south of the Sahara." After presenting this definition, he makes the categorical statement that *"the only one of the primary races . . . which has not made a creative contribution to any one of our twenty-one civilizations is the Black Race"*; and, in another context, *"the Black Race has not helped to create any civilization* [italics added]." These sweeping conclusions about the unique lack of creativity on the part of black people, slightly modified in phrasing, received very wide dissemination in the Book-of-the-Month Club abridgment of Toynbee's nine volumes.[75] They must have confirmed the prejudices of thousands of Americans and reinforced stereotypes about their neighbors.

Toynbee's argument that black people did not even "help" in the development of the one African civilization he analyzes—the "Egyptiac"—is predicated upon excluding all mixed-blood Egyptians from the category "Black" and ignoring the contributions of individual full-blooded Negroes who appeared throughout Egyptian history and who were particularly prevalent during the late predynastic period and the first four dynasties, when Egyptian civilization took form and flowered. He accepted the standard view of Egyptologists that both Caucasoid and Negroid genetic strains were represented in the Egyptian population; but, in repudiating biological explanations of creativity, he did not consider this mixture important except as an index to the fact that Egyptians, unlike most other Africans, had not been isolated from people bearing other cultures.

Sometimes Toynbee seems to be referring only to contributions made by *entire* ethnic groups, not isolated individuals, meaning that no *groups* of relatively unmixed Negroes in Africa had developed civilizations or "helped" to originate artifacts and ideas that went into them. Thus, in discussing why Blacks had made no contributions in Africa, he proceeds to discuss inhabitants of specific geographical areas. He quotes French anthropologist Maurice Delafosse, in order "to suggest certain features in the Negro's circumstances which convincingly account for his failure to take an active part in the enterprise of Civilization during these first five or six thousand years."

Neither scholar imputes any genetic deficiency to Negroes, but Delafosse, who was an expert on West African societies, stressed a single factor: isolation from Mediterranean cultural innovations that were carried into Europe, through force and persuasion, by Roman legions and, later, by Roman Catholic priests. As Delafosse phrases it, "the Gauls, our ancestors," were constantly in contact with "more evolved" peoples, while "the unfortunate Negroes were *during the same period* almost completely isolated from *the rest of humanity* [italics added]."[76] The enthnocentrism in the Delafosse statement is revealed in the word *unfortunate*. The fortunate people were those conquered by Roman troops. Delafosse ignores the Negroes of eastern Africa, where the kingdom of Meroë developed between the fourth and sixth Nile cataracts. His isolation theory is certainly somewhat less applicable there. Delafosse ignores also the role of these Negroes in the development of Egyptian civilization over many centuries and misconstrues their choice to disengage from the Mediterranean power struggles. Rome was not *able* forcibly to "civilize" Meroë, although it had treaty relations and diplomatic intercourse with this black kingdom.

Europe was conquered and Mediterranean civilization was imposed upon it. Meroë, in contrast, preserved its independence and seems to have borrowed more from India and Persia than from the Greeks and Romans. In any event, the crucial issue raised by historian Toynbee does not concern the period with which the Delafosse quotation deals. It concerns, rather, the fourth and third millennia B.C., before the Roman "civilizers" of Europe had themselves been "civilized" by the Greeks. It deals with a period in which important ideas in philosophy, mathematics, and religion were developed in Egypt, ideas for which both Greeks and Romans would later admit they were indebted to the Egyptians. Even Toynbee's sources indicate black participation in these developments. And despite Toynbee's insistence that Blacks did not "help" to create any civilization—including the "Egyptiac"—he presents a quotation from an archaeologist that demolishes the foundation of his own argument. V. Gordon Childe was his authority for a remark pointing out that the ancient Egyptians resembled a group of contemporary Africans: *"On the upper Nile there dwell today people allied to the oldest Egyptians in appearance, stature, cranial proportions, language and dress* [italics added]." The reference was to the Shilluk, a very Negroid people whether judged by the criteria of the anthropologist or the layman! Perhaps the learned British historian did not know this, or was using such a narrow definition of Negro as to exclude the Shilluk.[77]

The beginnings of Egyptian civilization can be discerned from artifacts found in a late predynastic village called Naqada, just south of Thebes in Upper Egypt. The culture, of which Naqada was part, extended across the border into Lower Nubia as far as the second cataract of the Nile. It was in contact there with another culture, which the specialists call Nubian-A, that extended as far as the sixth cataract. There were no sharp differences at that time in either the physical type of the people or the cultures in what became the border area between Egypt and Nubia in dynastic times. In fact, there is increasing evidence that these two cultures, Nubian-A and Naqada, shared many traits and that the peoples were essentially of the same physical type.

The question immediately arises as to why the Naqada people developed what Toynbee calls "Egyptiac civilization" between 4000 B.C. and 3000 B.C., whereas the Nubian-A people, in what later became Kush, did not. Their "civilization" emerged much later, only after extensive Egyptianization. Aspects of Toynbee's "challenge and response" theory are more relevant than the isolation hypothesis in explaining why one segment of a black group on the Nile developed a "civilization" whereas a closely related group did not.

Some Egyptologists make the plausible suggestion that as desiccation became more widespread on both sides of the Nile large masses of people moved into the fertile valley north of the first cataract, where their existence depended upon working out the technical and social problems posed by the annual flooding of the Nile. The more sparsely populated areas south of the first cataract, especially where pastoralism rather than agriculture provided the main subsistence mode, did not make such demands upon the leadership. What we call "civilization" emerged as an adaptation in the former situation, where ecological pressures dictated technological and social innovation.

In the Egyptian case, as in Mesopotamia, a priesthood received a portion of the agricultural surplus in return for knowledge and leadership in the development of irrigation and flood control, as well as the religious sanction it provided to the government. These religious ideas were shared by people living in areas between the first cataract and beyond the sixth, but there was no pressure in that region for religious leaders to supply social leadership. Recent archaeological excavations in Nubia confirm the existence of burial customs similar to those in predynastic Egypt, and Egyptian tradition points to the "uncivilized" black lands as the source of Egypt's religious concepts and rituals. Students of the Book of the Dead see hints of an older stratum of beliefs shared with inner Africa embedded in the Pyramid Texts.

Speaking of the similarity of the cultures in southern Egypt and northern Nubia at approximately 5000 B.C., Aldred notes that

> the essentially African culture of the early Predynastic period might have remained sterile at this level as it did apparently in the Sudan, where a Badarian type of culture persisted for a much longer time, if it had not been fertilized by contacts with a different civilization coming from Asia. . . . All these innovations, however, have no appearance of having been imposed by conquests.[78]

Not all scholars accept the "fertilization" theory, but most do.

Undoubtedly the factor that made the crucial difference in the late Predynastic Period between black cultures above the first cataract of the Nile and those below it was that the latter group, living in Egypt, adopted or invented metallurgical techniques for working copper and gold, and that they developed mathematical systems and writing. Some Egyptologists are inclined toward the view that the stimulus, and perhaps the models, were supplied through contact with peoples from Mesopotamia, and that these contacts were useful in solving the problem of developing a system of agriculture in the Nile Valley. The significant fact, however, is not that these Africans borrowed ideas and techniques from outside, if they did, but that they reworked them, integrated them into their own distinctive cultural matrix, and used them to serve their own cultural values. They added to the stock of common knowledge in such a way that aspects of Egyptian thought were eventually incorporated into the intellectual heritage of Europe by way of the Greeks. Egyptian history is consistent with Toynbee's theory that civilization flowers when cultures meet. His blind spot lay in an unwillingness to concede the black contribution to the process that occurred in the Nile Valley.

Diop has pointed out traditions among the Egyptians themselves concerning the adoption of metallurgy that indicate the technology came from outside of the valley culture. One of the oldest legends refers to a group of metal workers in predynastic times who came to the Nile Valley as "invaders" and proceeded to build forges from the first cataract to the edge of the Delta. The southern Egyptian version of the story, recorded on the walls of a temple at Edfu after the Greek conquest of Egypt, speaks of the god Harmachis, who reigned in Nubia, presiding over conquest of the valley by his son Horus, who settled his companions, the "blacksmiths," with him throughout the valley. The Egyptologist Gaston Maspéro accepted the legend as reflecting a historic event and referred to the innovators as "Negro blacksmiths." A French Egyptologist, Alexandre Moret, cited by Diop, interprets the legend in one of its other versions as indicating that the smiths began their journey in the north and carried the innovation to the southland. Regional pride, as well as changes in the prestige of Kush, may account for the variations in the story. The contradictory legends may, however, represent two distinctly different events widely separated in time: one being the adoption of metallurgy involving gold, copper, and silver from the Middle East; the other the adoption of iron-working techniques, possibly introduced centuries later, during late dynastic times, from Meroë, near the sixth cataract of the Nile.

The problems in interpreting these stories about the smiths are compounded by the ambiguity concerning the meaning of the hieroglyphics. Does the glyph translated as "blacksmiths" mean "workers in iron" or "black" (i.e., Negro) smiths? Diop has insisted upon the latter interpretation. Both versions of the legend, however, derive the rituals presided over by the priests at Heliopolis in the north from the impact of smiths, for whom the worship of Re, the sun-god, was important. Professor Vercoutter, writing in 1981, states that copper, gold, and silver were diffused widely throughout the Nile Valley before the pharaonic era. No theory of an outside origin of metallurgy is necessary to account for the use of these metals. However, only meteoric iron was used until the eighth century B.C. After that time, iron was mined and smelted and tools, weapons, and technique diffused widely from Meroë.[79]

The pioneer among British Egyptologists, Sir Flinders Petrie, who excavated in the Thebaid, was convinced that the basic elements of Egyptian predynastic cultural development came into Egypt from the southeast, near the Red Sea, but that the rulers of the highly creative Old Kingdom dynasties were of Nubian origin.[80] If this view is accepted, the question still remains of precisely where the predynastic migrants came from and how long they had been settled within the borders of Egypt before political unification of the area between the Red Sea and the first cataract occurred. Archaeologists now know that fine ceramics were being made near the sixth cataract of the Nile just prior to the dynastic period and societies based upon cattle breeding and mixed agriculture were in existence there, but no movements northward from this area have yet been traced.[81] Nor have population movements been traced from Nubian areas closer to Egypt during the period when dessication was probably forcing people into the valley and then northward as the area between the first and third cataracts—Lower Nubia—became less habitable.

Two locations were considered "holy" from late predynastic times on into later Egyptian history. One was the Thebaid, the area from the vicinity of the city of Thebes southward to the first cataract. The shrine of Hathor, the Nubian mother-goddess, was at Denderah, and that of Hapi, the god of the Nile, at the first cataract itself. The other sacred spot, "God's Land," or the "Holy Land," was located vaguely somewhere to the south. From there, it was said, the original Egyptians came and the rituals for worshiping the gods originated. This was "the land of the ancestors." By the time the Greeks first visited Egypt, Ethiopia was being referred to by the priests as "that sacred land of origin," but its boundaries were stated with imprecision. At an earlier period, God's Land was called the "Land of Punt" and because of the crops grown there, the oils and incense characteristic of the country, early Egyptologists assumed the reference was to the area around the Red Sea near what is now Somalia, or even across the sea in southern Arabia.[82] When the priests told Greek and Roman enquirers that Egypt was a colony of the Ethiopians, European and American scholars have usually assumed that they must have meant the less Negroid areas in the Horn of Africa. The ancient Greeks and Romans, however, took for granted that they were referring to the Kingdom of Meroë, up the Nile.

Petrie was one of the Egyptologists who was convinced that the people who established the predynastic civilizations were invaders from Arabia or Mesopotamia who, coming across the Red Sea at some point, moved over to the Nile Valley near Thebes and then marched northward to Memphis (near present-day Cairo). Diop notes that the proponents of this view refer to a specific group of people, the Anu, following a specific culture bearer, Teter-Neter, as the "civilizers" marched down the Nile from the south. He has reprinted from Petrie portraits of Teter-Neter, the predynastic leader of the Anu, and Narmer, who is by tradition considered the founder of the first dynasty. Both had physical characteristics that anthropologists call "Negroid." *Thus, regardless of whether the Anu migrated from Asia or were an indigenous African people coming in from eastern Africa or from areas farther up the Nile, the archaeological evidence suggests that their leader was Negroid.*

The possibility that the "civilizing thrust" spread down the Nile northward into Egypt and eastward into Somalia and Arabia should not be ruled out. There is increasing archaeological evidence to support this view. In considering the location of the area referred to as the Egyptian ancestral land or the sacred land, it should be remembered that the entire landscape between the Nile Valley and the Red Sea may have been very different during the millennium prior to 3000 B.C., when the first dynasty of kings emerged in Egypt. What is now desert between the Nile and the Red Sea may have been grassland across which people moved easily, just as they moved freely deep into what is now the Sahara Desert. Links by water southward around the Ethiopian highlands to the Red Sea may even have existed. These lands may not have been as impassable as they are today.[83]

In any event, recent archaeological work reported by scholars from the Oriental Institute at the University of Chicago suggests that viable and prosperous Nubian kingdoms may have existed between the fourth and sixth Nile cataracts, that is, between the old capital of

Kush and the later one at Meroë prior to the development of the first Egyptian kingdoms.[84] This lends some credence to stories preserved by priests that Egypt, in late predynastic times, was established as a colony of the Ethiopians—that people were moving northward beyond the first Nile cataract carrying the rudimentary elements of what would become Egyptian civilization. According to this reconstruction, changes in climate and terrain between the first Nile cataract and the third later broke the connection between the Ethiopian "mother kingdom" and Egypt. The Ethiopians being isolated from contact with Mesopotamia and the countries of the Fertile Crescent did not have the stimulus that comes from intensive intercultural contact. A few black scholars have suggested that Ethiopia during this period may have been the "civilizer" of both southern Arabia and the Nile Valley below the first cataract. Some Arabian and Jewish legends, in fact, suggest that conquering armies from Ethiopia wandered about in Arabia and other eastern lands in remote antiquity.[85] The question of predynastic cultural origins remains in the realm of speculation, possibility, and probability, not irrefutable fact.

Black vindicationists have never concentrated their efforts on trying to explain why Nubians did not develop advanced mathematics and calendrical systems as their kinsmen below the first cataract of the Nile did; or why they did not develop the common stock of religious beliefs into elaborate metaphysical and cosmological systems as the priests in Thebes, Memphis, and Heliopolis did. Most, including Du Bois, have taken satisfaction from the fact that Negroes were well represented in the populations of the Egyptian dynasties of great accomplishment, and were, therefore, "helping" to create a civilization, to use Toynbee's word. Others, such as Diop, have argued that the early Egyptians *were* Negroes and, therefore, that Egyptian civilization of the first four dynasties *was* a black civilization. The basic problem with Toynbee's argument lay in his neglect of evidence, which was at hand when he wrote, indicating that many of the Egyptians of the Predynastic and the Early Dynastic periods in Egypt were, in fact, "Negroes" as anthropologists use the term, and many more were Negroes or "Black" in the broader sense of the term, as it is employed by custom in the United States. However, insofar as the valley absorbed populations from what are now the Libyan and Sahara deserts, Bushmanoid and Caucasoid types, as well as "Hamites" and Negroes, were all represented in the Nile Valley population. The proportions of one physical type as compared with another varied over time, and from place to place, and in relation to the size of the component groups.[86]

The rock paintings of the Sahara Desert leave no doubt that one dark, but non-Negroid, population coexisted there with a considerably darker variety of mankind during the millennium preceding the emergence of dynastic Egypt. It is assumed that both of these physical types, as well as more Caucasoid peoples, drifted into the Nile Valley as desiccation gradually took place, producing the Sahara and Libyan deserts. Petrie refers to a painted tomb at Hierankopolis that portrays "combats of black men overcoming red men." He is convinced that this painting, as well as a scene carved on an ivory knife handle, support archaeological evidence that early settlements in Egypt were "the result of the mixture of half a dozen races fighting for supremacy." Diop considers all of these early peoples to be within the normal range of variability of a basic Negro physical type. In these dynastic scenes some observers see post-Neolithic "racial" conflict between "Libyans" and "Blacks," but whether the antagonists conceptualized their relations as "interracial" we have no way of knowing. There are scenes, too, of early Egyptian kings exulting in victory over people whose beards mark them out as "Asiatics."[87] Did these conflicts result in prejudice structured along a color line? Most Egyptologists are inclined to say no, because in later periods such conflicts were never written about by Egyptians in terms of race and color.

In later periods physical traits distinguishing groups of captives from one another are depicted on numerous victory monuments. Modern conventional wisdom would suggest that over a period of time skin-color and physical features would emerge as cues eliciting unfavorable attitudes and generating stereotypes. But if we try to specify the nature of conflicts, especially for periods so remote as the predynastic, we run the risk of reading our own customary reactions back into ancient Egypt.

Whether evaluations of blackness in general and dark skin-color in particular differed in dynastic times from such evaluations in predynastic times we shall never know. However, folklore during dynastic times reveals a willingness to accord high status to black mythological figures such as Osiris, whose origins were predynastic. This is relevant to a discussion of the Neolithic Revolution that took place during the Predynastic Period. Osiris, who became Judge of the Dead during Old Kingdom days, was previously a culture hero associated with the food-producing revolution. A tradition exists suggesting that other peoples in Africa and the Middle East, during Egypt's Predynastic Period, considered Osiris a culture hero as well.

Osiris in Religion and Folklore

The anthropologists' version of the Egyptian late Predynastic Period has just been presented in brief outline. More information can be gleaned by reading works that present basic archaeological data and that make interpretations of some of the folklore. The Egyptian people themselves cherished a version of their own predynastic history that was embodied in legend and mythology. It has relevance to our inquiry into the connotations of color. It was a story cherished in many varied versions throughout Egyptian history until it was obliterated by the Near Eastern origin myths that Christianity and Islam imposed upon Egypt. The emergence of civilization was attributed to a culture hero of Upper Egypt in the sacred land near the first cataract of the Nile. He was a god in a complex theological system as well as a culture hero—Osiris, worshiped in fertility rituals and as Judge of the Dead.

The British Egyptologist E.A.W. Budge relates the story of how priests and scribes developed a legend from folktales to account for the fact that civilization emerged in Egypt whereas Africans in other areas remain "uncivilized":

> The Egyptians generally believed that a god made himself incarnate, and that an immediate ancestor of the first pharaoh of Egypt was a being who possessed two natures, the one human and the other divine [i.e., Osiris]. As a man he performed the good works which his divine nature indicated to him, he abolished cannibalism, he improved the manners and morals of men, he taught them to live according to law, to worship the gods, and to practice the arts of agriculture.[88]

This mythological ancestor of the first Egyptian pharaoh was said to have civilized areas outside of Egypt: "Filled with love for man he set out to travel over the whole world so that he might teach all non-Egyptians to embrace his beneficent doctrine and enjoy the blessings which accrue to God-fearing and law-abiding peoples."[89] Budge, in relating this Egyptian appraisal of their own role in history, points out that by the time of the late Roman Empire, when Christianity was emerging, the belief in Osiris as the ancient culture bearer was widespread. One classical writer, Plutarch, specified the places where Osiris went, "by way of the Coast of Arabia into India where he built many cities." Osiris was then said to have journeyed westward and brought his armies through the Hellespont into Europe. In Thrace he was said to have killed the king, who refused to adopt civilization.[90]

These Greco-Roman traditions regarding Osiris obviously combine stories of many different heroes into the figure of Osiris and incorporate ancient Egyptian and Near Eastern legends that may have already been fused and transformed through the telling. Significantly, however, they speak of a culture bearer from the Nile Valley who brought enlightenment to other areas of the world after first "civilizing" a part of the African continent. From Homeric times until the Twenty-fifth Egyptian Dynasty riveted the concept of Ethiopia-on-the-Nile into the minds of poets, prophets, and historians, the term "Ethiopian" had covered all of the peoples with "burnt faces" in India, Mesopotamia, Arabia, and the Fertile Crescent. Not all of these, of course, were what anthropologists would later call "Negroes," but many were what North Americans would classify as such. Even some eminent early twentieth-century British scholars were inclined to describe the earliest non-African peoples of this broad area as "Negroid." Thus Sir Harry H. Johnston, who believed that "the Negro sub-species" originated in India, writes: "The Elamites of Mesopotamia appear to have been a negroid people with kinky hair and to have transmitted this racial type to the jews [*sic*] and Syrians." He notes an "evident Negro element" in the features of Babylonians and Assyrians depicted in ancient sculptures. Archaeologists such as Petrie saw in the Anu an ancient group of Negroid civilizers moving into the Nile valley from the east, perhaps from Mesopotamia via Arabia.[91]

Ancient folklorists kept alive legends of Ethiopians from the upper Nile Valley conquering the entire Middle East in remote antiquity. Nineteenth-century English folklorists, such as Gerald Massey in his *Book of the Beginnings* and Godfrey Higgins in *Anacalypsis*, developed elaborate theories of black civilizers moving about from India to the Mediterranean. Groups of Afro-American vindicationists have generated renewed interest in these theories, which fell out of favor with the academic Orientalists between the two world wars. The Osiris story as Plutarch told it serves as a reminder that Greeks and Romans saw nothing strange in the concept of Africans as the primal civilizers and accepted both myths—that of the imposition by force and that of peaceful persuasion when Osiris was the culture bearer.[92]

Greek and Roman visitors, after the establishment of Greek Ptolemaic rule in Egypt, were told that Egypt was founded by a colony of Ethiopians who had originated the improved ways of living that Osiris was reputed to have spread throughout the world. Budge notes that some Greco-Roman writers recorded a quite different story: "Having taught the Ethiopians the arts of tillage and husbandry, he [Osiris] built several cities in their country, and appointed governors over them." He raised levees along the banks of the Nile in Ethiopia and established a system of flood control. This could be a garbled version of a story about what Osiris was supposed to have done before he moved north from Ethiopia to "civilize" Egypt, or it could be another legend denying the civilizing influence of Ethiopia on Egypt and reversing the cause-and-effect relations. It might also be a legend referring to a different period, when a powerful Egypt had invaded Ethiopia. One account gives Ethiopia a quite subordinate role in the Osiris civilizing process, stating that he carried a group of musicians, singers, and dancers with him everywhere and that Ethiopian rulers gave him a company of satyrs to join the band of entertainers.[93] Whether or not Osiris was considered Egyptian or Ethiopian in his earliest manifestation, he eventually became the most popular god among both peoples, and the Greeks and Romans adopted him and proceeded to "whiten" him. The Egyptian versions of the civilizing mission do not emphasize Osirian military conquests as Plutarch's does, but indicate rather, according to Budge, a highly idealized, beneficent being:

> He forced no man to carry out his instructions, but by means of gentle persuasion and an appeal to their reason, he succeeded in inducing them to practice what he preached. Many of his wise counsels were imparted to listeners in hymns and songs which were sung to the accompaniment of instruments of music.[94]

As a number of scholars have pointed out, the earliest conceptions of Osiris associated him with the fertility of the soil rather than with being the Judge of the Dead. They identified him with the growth of seeds rather than, as in a later conception, with human resurrection. Budge emphasizes the point that the wife of Osiris, Isis, played an important role in the civilizing process before her husband became the traveling culture bearer:

> In the earliest times we find him [Osiris] identified with the spirit of the growing crop and the grain god, and he represented the spirit of vegetation in general. His chief assistant was his wife, Isis, who taught men to prepare the grain which her husband had given them. . . . As a great god of agriculture he controls the order of the seasons.[95]

Sir James George Frazer, in *The Golden Bough*, was primarily interested in Osiris and Isis as examples of gods connected with the agricultural cycle. The following is his summary of the basic legend as the Roman author Plutarch attempted to reconstruct it:

> Reigning as a king of earth, Osiris reclaimed the Egyptians from savagery, gave them laws, and taught them to worship the gods. Before his time the Egyptians had been cannibals. But Isis, the sister and wife of Osiris, discovered wheat and barley growing wild, and Osiris introduced the cultivation of these grains amongst his people who forthwith abandoned cannibalism and took kindly to a corn diet. Moreover,

Osiris is said to have been the first to gather fruit from trees, to train the vine to poles, and to tread the grapes. Eager to communicate these beneficent discoveries to all mankind, he committed the whole government of Egypt to his wife, Isis, and travelled over the world, diffusing the blessings of civilisation and agriculture wherever he went.[96]

Budge points out that, in the Plutarch version, "during the absence of Osiris his own kingdom was administered by his wife Isis, who performed the duties committed to her charge with great wisdom and prudence." Frazer does not emphasize this aspect of the Isis story. But here he speaks of what happened after Osiris came back: "Loaded with wealth that had been showered upon him by grateful nations, he returned to Egypt, and, on account of the benefits he had conferred on mankind, he was unanimously hailed and worshiped as a deity."[97] Osiris worship might be explained in a less fanciful fashion.

The legend, up to this point, was obviously functioning as an explanatory myth to account for the Neolithic Revolution in the Middle East; it expressed the priority claim of the most venerated nation of antiquity. It should, of course, be taken with a grain of salt in the absence of archaeological verification. (The Hebrew version of these events, as given in the Old Testament, is that of a pastoralist people who considered agriculture the invention of the accursed Cain, who slew his brother Abel. Indeed, to the ancient pastoral Jews most of the elements of "civilization," including metallurgy, urban living, and musical instruments, were inventions of the accursed Cain's descendants. As an enslaved people in Egypt, the Hebrew people became "civilization's" victims, and their hostility to that mode of life found expression in the folklore about origins.)

Accounts of what happened after the triumphant return of Osiris from his civilizing mission abroad have been set out briefly by Budge, who suggests that the elements of tragedy were maturing while Osiris was away. This version would seem to have grown up during the period when the so-called Hyksos kings from Asia, whose favorite god was said to have been Set and who had an informal alliance with the Ethiopians against the Theban princes and priests who opposed them, were in power. (Later, the Theban priests and princes themselves became close allies of Ethiopia.) Isis was harassed by Set, who was both her half-brother and brother-in-law, a god in the Egyptian pantheon whom the Greeks made equivalent to their Typhon. He plotted, with the twenty-two heads of the Delta nomes (provincial leaders) and with Aso, queen of Ethiopia, to kill Osiris. Set's aim was to seize control of the kingdom and to take Isis for his wife, he being violently in love with her. (Set symbolized the desert to the Egyptians; Osiris the fertile Nile Valley. Set was usually portrayed as red and Osiris as black, when these geographical contrasts were meant.)

In the legend the Lower Egyptian and Ethiopian conspirators managed to kill Osiris and to conceal his body in an Asian nation, Phoenicia (present-day Lebanon), fronting the Mediterranean. Isis, with supernatural help, found the body, brought it home, and hid it in the Delta. Through charms given her by some of the gods, she was able to revitalize the corpse and to become pregnant by Osiris with the baby Horus. Her hostile brother, Set, then tried to kill Horus, but Isis was able, through divine instructions given her by a god, to save the baby. Set then found the body of Osiris and chopped it into many pieces. Isis and her sister, Nepthys, recovered all of the body pieces except one and reconstructed the body. The penis was never found, which explains why, in Osirian ceremony, the phallus played a prominent part either explicitly or as a conventionalized symbol. Isis eventually became transformed in the popular mind from the co-discoverer of agriculture in remote antiquity to the symbol of devotion and love of a wife for her husband, a healer, and a nurturing mother. Concurrently, Osiris became the symbol of life after death, of the possibility of a just reward for having lived a virtuous life.[98] Osiris and Isis, with these meanings, became objects of veneration throughout the Hellenistic world.

The story of the conspiracy fostered by Set—without the element of an Ethiopian queen's involvement—is included in versions of the Book of the Dead used during Old Kingdom times. It had cosmic significance and was not merely the account of an earthly king and culture bearer. The story of his death and revitalization, rather than his civilizing mission, became the central theme of the Osiris story. In fact, it became the focus for a pharaonic cult, with each ruler believing that if the proper rites were carried out, he too could become "an Osiris."

During the Middle Kingdom, the common people insisted upon being allowed to share in a religion that promised life after death, and the cult of Osiris was thus democratized. It spread throughout Egypt. Even temples consecrated to other powerful gods often had a chapel dedicated to Osiris. Inevitably, Osiris and Isis became the subjects of theological discussion among scribes and priests, and eventually all of the four theological systems—Theban, Memphite, Heliopolitan, and Hermiopolitan—agreed upon Osiris's mystical lineage even when they disagreed upon presumed details of his earthly existence or his relation to the solar cult. The priests of Re eventually assimilated

Osiris into the sun cult, at the opposite extreme from the fertility cult with which the masses associated him. But Osiris was always the popular god as opposed to whatever state deity may have been officially in vogue or whatever gods had priestly sponsorship. Isis acquired solar attributes, too, becoming the goddess associated with Sirius, or Sothis, whose appearance marked the first day of the solar year. This was consistent with her fertility symbolism, since the Nile flooding began with the appearance of Sothis, that is, Isis, on the horizon.[99]

An American author, Norma Loore Goodrich, has captured some of the spirit with which the ordinary Egyptians of the early periods must have told the story of Osiris and Isis, although the brother-sister aspect of the marriage may be a later, priestly accretion used to justify the prevalence of this kind of marriage in royal families obsessed with keeping their presumed special qualities within their lineages. Goodrich's highly romanticized account emphasizes a point that writers in antiquity did not deem it necessary to mention, but which is relevant to any discussion in our racist, color-conscious culture— that is, the skin-color of Osiris.

> *Long before the priests and even before the Pharaohs, the great dark King Osiris ruled in Africa.* He was a tall man and slender as all devout Egyptians longed to be so that their bodies might fit as lightly and easily as possible about their immortal soul, or ba. On his head he wore the lofty white crown of Upper Egypt with an ostrich feather on either side of it because these feathers are as light as the truth. A beautiful plaited beard fell from his chin as befitted a great and powerful ruler whose fertility made life swell even in the dry desert. . . . His naked body from ankle to wrists was beautifully decorated with crimson painted flowers. *Such was Osiris who ruled in Egypt, powerful and black, for black is the color of youth, as white is the color of old heads.* . . . Osiris had embraced his sister Isis before they were born, while both were tumbling in their mother's womb. When he had become a man and a king, he married her and took her from among all women as his queen. Together they ruled Egypt, making it a land of music and delight [italics added].[100]

During the late Roman Empire the worship of Isis spread widely from the Nile Valley, with shrines established in Spain, Italy, and Gaul. Although it was obvious (from the myth surrounding the cult and the location of her shrine at Philae, where the most Negroid part of Egypt and Ethiopia meet) that the goddess was not white, she was sometimes portrayed in statues as a Roman matron. She symbolized the ideal wife and mother, and she may have been the forerunner of the Christian iconography of Madonna and child (plate 3).[101] In Egypt and Ethiopia it was her role as the Mother Goddess who assured fertility to women, animals, and the earth that attracted simple people to Isis, and she and Hathor were often merged in the popular mind. While popular among both males and females in Egypt, Osiris never became as popular as Isis throughout the Roman Empire, where the Mithra cult from Asia Minor and Mesopotamia was more attractive to pagan males; and Osiris could not be assimilated into the emerging new religious symbol of the suffering and crucified Jesus Christ as Isis could be into the Virgin Mary symbology.

Christian monasteries and Muslim mosques have long since replaced chapels to Osiris and all the other gods in the Egyptian pantheon. However, one corner of a museum in Europe has re-created some of the mystery that once surrounded the veneration of Osiris. Here, in a French museum, is a Negroid image of Osiris, Judge of the Dead (plate 4). A prominent Egyptologist has written of it:

> All those who have walked through the rooms of the Louvre museum certainly recall the little chapel which has been placed there with the statue of the god Osiris: the god appears in his niche, skillfully lit by the side lamps. The visitor is impressed by the strange aspect of this wooden figure leaping from the shadow, crude and awkward but singularly fascinating. This is the way the god must have appeared when the priest set aside the doors of the naos [chamber where the image spent the night], a shape indistinct in the shadow, but shining with the brilliance of its jewelled eyes, its crown, its metallic decoration, and jewelry.[102]

THE BLACK PRESENCE IN THE EARLY DYNASTIES

The myths and legends of a black culture hero who lived during predynastic times symbolize the achievement of the tasks carried out during the Neolithic period of the predynastic era. Osiris and Isis were, first, fertility gods and symbols of struggles to unify the Nile Valley north of the first cataract. The head of Osiris was believed to be buried at Abydos near Thebes, an area sacred to the First Dynasty of pharaohs. The kings, as symbols of deities themselves, transformed the story of Osiris into a guarantee of their own immortality. This happened when a number of black pharaohs were in power.

By early dynastic times a class composed of priests and scribes had mastered enough knowledge of astronomy, mathematics, and engineering to predict and control the annual overflow of the Nile, and so provide for raising agricultural productivity to a level high enough to support a monarchy and court, a bureaucracy and army, as well as the temple communities of priests and retainers. Agriculture also provided sustenance for a large population of artisans and farmers, most of whom were tenants but none of whom were slaves. These farmers, in dynastic times, were conscripted for labor, when the Nile was not in flood, to work on large-scale projects for the pharaohs.[103] This practice began in predynastic times. Sometime between 3500 and 3000 B.C., agricultural productivity and Neolithic skill in tool and weapon-making began to support a stable, socially stratified society along the banks of the Nile between the first cataract and the point where the river now splits into several separate branches to form a delta.

As the archaeological data on predynastic Egypt reveal, and as inferences from legends suggest, the population of the Nile Valley all the way to the Delta was distinctly Negroid at the time when evidences of "civilization" first begin to appear.[104] But there existed also population pressure, from the Palestinian-Syrian sector to the northeast and from so-called Libya to the west, that resulted in extensive non-Negro settlement in the Delta area. The Nile was navigable up to the first cataract, and a busy maritime commerce brought European and Asian individuals deep into Nile Valley areas. It is likely that a gradient in skin-color appeared early in Nile Valley history whereby the proportion of very Negroid people in the population increased with distance traveled up the river.[105] However, miscegenation between people throughout the Upper and Lower kingdoms prevented the persistence of any absolute correlation between physical type and region, and kept social status from becoming associated with degree of "Negroidness." Sculpture in the round, bas-relief friezes, and colored paintings on walls and papyrus provide enough data for stating conclusively that some distinctly Negro pharaohs appeared in all of the dynasties and were numerous in a few. Portraits of others give the impression of a Negro ancestral strain. In addition to the kings, their wives, and members of their courts, religious functionaries and officials of the state show similar tendencies, as do other individuals in a wide variety of occupations.[106]

Since Egyptian portraiture displays a range in physical type from Caucasoid to Negroid, it is possible to make some generalizations about the status implications of "Negroidness." Not only were concubines often Negroid; there were also numerous Negro queens and Queen Mothers, some consorts of husbands less Negro than themselves. Some people of all racial groups are depicted as slaves, and despite the erroneous suggestion sometimes found in textbooks that most slaves in Egypt were Blacks from Nubia, there were periods when European and Asian prisoners of war far outnumbered Blacks among the slaves.[107] Slavery was not associated with blackness, nor low status with being Negro.

Since the skin-color of individuals is rarely mentioned in Egyptian written records, it is difficult to assess the extent to which considerations of color were involved in esthetic appraisals or in the evolution of somatic norm images from period to period. In the small amount of love poetry in existence (or that has been translated and published), the color of skin, hair, and eyes is virtually never mentioned. Inferences about attitudes drawn from reported behavior must be handled with extreme caution, such as the claim cited by Diop, taken from ancient Greek or Roman writings, that there was a flourishing market for any blonde women that Phoenician sailors could bring to Egypt for sale. Inferences made from paintings and sculptures depicting married couples are somewhat more trustworthy, but one must take care to find items that are personalized portraits, not representations treated according to certain conventions. For instance, when rendering those of relatively high status, it was customary to paint men a dark reddish-brown and women a lighter brown or yellowish color.[108] Assuming that Egyptian women were not actually lighter, on the whole, than the men, was this the expression of a wish that they were? The French Egyptologist Naville has maintained that this convention could express the ideal of wives who were not forced to work outdoors. Others saw in the custom a forerunner of the Greek practice and preference, by which bronzed men of outdoors were contrasted with the paleness of women, who were indoor people. (There are hints of similar attitudes toward lighter women among ancient Jews and contemporary East Indians.) In speculating about the meaning of color differences, care must be exercised not to read back into ancient Egypt conceptions and attitudes that are products of the racist societies prevalent during the past 500 years.

Arthur Weigall, in his *History of the Pharaohs*, emphasizes what he visualizes as a sharp cultural division between Lower and Upper Egypt; he insists that this division also reflected differences in race and inherited traits, and that a culturally advanced north, from late predynastic times on, resented domination by the more Negroid, culturally backward south, that is, Upper Egypt. Cyril Aldred, putting forward a more moderate, nonracist modern view, states of Lower Egypt that "in early days it seems to have been culturally more advanced than the rustic South; in historic times it maintained its lead as the center of the arts and crafts, probably attracting skilled workers from near and far." But "country cousins" are not tantamount to an inferior race. Aldred warns against overemphasizing regional differences:

> It would, however, be wrong to exaggerate the differences between the two regions. They shared a common language and the same material and spiritual culture. Certain fundamental religous concepts, such as that a divine power was imminent in certain men and animals, were accepted by both, even though the exact form of deity varied somewhat from place to place. The underlying unity of thought and feeling in all Egyptians is evident from the way the civilization of the whole land blossomed profusely as soon as the two parts were rejoined in vigour and purpose after periods of schism. Nevertheless there is a kind of antithesis between Upper and Lower Egypt, which the Egyptians themselves recognized by referring to their country as the Two Lands, an antithesis which particularly appealed to them since they saw the world as esentially a duality. While the North was the cultural leader, it was the South that provided the disciplined political direction. . . . We can detect, even in late Gerzean times, the emergence of a pattern that was to be repeated again and again in Egyptian history; it was the ambition of Southern princes that led them to extend their sway over larger tracts of the valley until they had created a unity out of the former anarchy, one kingdom out of a conglomeration of rival districts.[109]

Frankfort also emphasizes unity in the duality, stressing the point that the northerners did not resent southern conquest:

> We have shown elsewhere that the dualistic mould of the "Kingdom of Upper and Lower Egypt" satisfied the Egyptian mode of thought which conceived totality as an equilibrium of opposites. A meaningful symmetry was imposed upon the unified land, but it had no basis in fact, for Scorpion and Narmer conquered the north piecemeal, as far as we know. Nor is there any sign of resentment against the north. On the contrary, northerners were found among the highest in the land: two queens of the First Dynasty reveal a Delta origin by their names.[110]

Not all perspectives assert that at all times the north was the "cultural leader"; and if, as Weigall suggests, northerners harbored *racial* prejudice against southerners, it must have been a very complex cluster of attitudes, for southern conquerors of northern nomarchs and their people had additional assets to which northerners were forced to react other than the sheer weight of military power. All Egyptians shared the tradition that the holiest spots in Egypt were in the very Negroid south, from Abydos and Thebes up to the first cataract. The rulers there had high mystical status, and southerners were people who were believed to have close contact with "the ancestors" and were custodians of the earliest sources of mystical power, such as the shrine of Hathor (at Denderah), the Mother-Goddess who later was symbolized by a cow; and above all, the shrine of Hapi, god of the Nile, at the first cataract. During low Niles and floods, pharaohs traveled to the latter site to seek a change in the behavior of the river.[111] Northern political leaders pitted other gods against southern ancestral gods, some of whom, no doubt, were Asian in origin. The most powerful of these was the solar god, Re, whose priesthood at Heliopolis competed for power and prestige with priests at Memphis and Hermopolis. The problem of all Egyptian statesmen was how to unite the gods, as well as the people, of the two kingdoms—Re with Amon, Osiris with all—and to effect numerous other syncretisms.

Ambitious colleges of priests, as they vied for power, became political forces independent of both pharaohs and nomarchs. The priests of Amon at Thebes became patrons of the kings of Kush and were able to marshall military power from Upper Nubia at certain critical periods in the nation's life. In fact, they were a force for the reintegration of the nation upon several occasions when it had split apart. Throughout Egyptian history, there was, in the Nile Valley, a recognition that protection from invaders demanded national unity. When that unity was lost, Bedouins broke in from the eastern desert, Libyans struck from the western desert, and varied groups of Asiatics invaded from the north. Groups of Nehesi constantly threatened the southern frontier. In later dynasties the question was not whether union was desirable but whether kings from the north or the south would rule the united kingdom, and how much power local rulers would retain.

The first move toward political integration had probably come in late predynastic times when a southern prince, sometimes referred to as "Scorpion," moved north into the domains of the "Reed King," a local ruler near the northern border of Upper Egypt, and of the "Hornet King," in Lower Egypt. He placed his totem, the falcon or hawk, above them all. He then put on the White Crown (hedjet) of the Reed King and made it the symbol of southern royalty. The first pharaonic dynasty was also established by a southern king named Menes or Narmer. His victorious armies marched to the edge of the Delta around 3000 B.C. where they founded Memphis ("White-walled City"), the city that eventually became the northern military citadel as well as one of the more important religious and intellectual centers. Centuries later, Cairo was founded near the Memphis ruins. Narmer, whose totem symbol was the falcon or hawk, combined this with the Delta symbol of the cobra; and to the White Crown that he wore he added the Red Crown (deshret) of the Delta, thus forming the double crown, which thereafter symbolized the unity of Upper and Lower Egypt.[112]

The first two dynasties were characterized by 500 years of intermittent conflict between the pharaohs and local rulers of the Delta area, who stubbornly resisted the incorporation of Lower Egypt into a united kingdom, as well as by conflict between followers of the sun god, Re, and those of Osiris and other southern gods. Warfare, as well as compromise involving dynastic marriages and the adoption of matrilineal succession in the monarchical line, brought a substantial degree of unity between northerners and southerners. Thus the child of a northern queen could sit on the pharaonic throne. Religious and philosophical concepts were gradually merged. The king of the Two Lands organized the armies necessary to protect the entire Nile Valley below the first cataract, as well as immediately adjacent areas, from invaders so that ordinary peasants could live and work in peace, and arts and crafts and learning could flourish. The pharaohs provided protection against marauders from the deserts who would destroy the intricate systems of irrigation and flood control upon which life and prosperity in the valley depended. They also acted as protectors of the property of priests and feudal lords. The fifth king of the First Dynasty reported that he had to "hack up the Libyans" on the west; and the sixth that he had to "smite the Bedouins" in the east, who constituted a threat to the copper mines of Sinai. Occasional attacks from the Africans south of the first Nile cataract also had to be fought off, a case of "uncivilized" Blacks' being considered a menace by the "civilized" Blacks.

Throughout Dynasties One and Two, ethnic and regional wars were endemic, the conflicts often being symbolized in myths as religious struggles between Re, perhaps a solar god from Mesopotamia, and other deities, such as Osiris and Set. During the Second Dynasty, the Delta rulers revolted. Pharaoh Chennere marched his troops north from Thebes and defeated the rebels. Weigall, referring back to Narmer's unification, notes:

> This was the second time in Egyptian history that the armies of the south, under an Upper Egyptian king, had surged down upon the northern kingdom and had carried their ruler on to the great throne of the "Two Lands."[113]

Commenting on events that occurred later, Weigall makes his characteristic racial interpretation of all of these developments:

> The invasions of the north by the south, in fact, are regular occurrences throughout the history of Egypt; for the people of Lower Egypt were a more cultured and less warlike race than those of the upper country, the latter always having a slight strain of Nubian blood, which exhibited itself then, as it does now, in good fighting qualities against which the men of the north could not successfully contend.[114]

The events of the Third and Fourth dynasties indicate, however, that people with this "slight strain of Nubian blood" distinguished themselves in ways other than warfare. Weigall notes of Chennere that he laid the basis, during the Second Dynasty, for progressive public development:

> His reign, which had begun in such troubled times, ended in years of profound peace, all the factions being united. . . . These great wars of the Second Dynasty, in fact, had been the birth-pains of Egypt's greatness; and now in the peace of the Third Dynasty the nation was able to expand and develop with astonishing rapidity.[115]

OLD KINGDOM DYNASTIES

It was during the Early Dynastic Period (dynasties one and two) that the political framework for the Old Kingdom (dynasties three through six) was established. The first spectacular contributions to ancient civilization were made during the Old Kingdom, between 2750 B.C. and 2200 B.C. (See chart 3 for a summation of significant internal events and relations with Asians, Europeans, and Africans south of the first cataract during the Predynastic Period and the first twelve dynasties.)

Dynasties one and two, forming the Early Dynastic Period, had laid the basis for a great cultural efflorescence during dynasties three and four, which, with five and six, constitute the Old Kingdom. A system of writing that had existed since late predynastic times was improved. The priests devised a solar calendar and a mathematical system suited to Egypt's agricultural and engineering needs. Philosophical concepts were refined. So great was the interest in medicine that tradition spoke of several of the pharaohs as being themselves physicians. Although Delta cities and the capital at Memphis became a meeting point of Middle Eastern and African travelers, soldiers, merchants, and scholars, Egyptologists are agreed that the Egyptian innovations were independently developed. These contacts did result in the sharing of ideas, however, as well as in some miscegenation with Asians.[116]

An examination of sculptured portraits and paintings for the Early Dynastic Period and for dynasties three through six reveals a variety of physical types, but Negro and Negroid individuals predominate if North American standards of what constitutes a "Negro" are utilized. Moreover, a high proportion of them also meet anthropological criteria for being "Negro."[117] A sampling of portraits is presented in plates 5 through 9, which include likenesses of two members of the remarkable quartet of Negroid pharaohs of the Third and Fourth dynasties: Djoser (Zoser, Dzoser, Thoser) (plate 5); Cheops (Saoph, Kheu, Khufu); Chefren (Chephre, Khephre, Suph, Khufre); and Mycerinus (plate 7). (Chefren is the pharaoh whose visage the Sphinx reflects [see plates 1 and 2].) During the Third Dynasty and the two which followed, what some Egyptologists regard as an extreme centralization of government occurred, as well as the official deification of the pharaoh. A case can be made for these measures, given the need to maintain a high degree of solidarity for collective action on public projects, both civilian and military. At the same time these actions bore the seeds of inevitable disillusionment and conflict.

The one great Third Dynasty pharaoh who achieved distinction, Djoser, was indubitably Negro. Some of his portraits depict him with the so-called "convex" Negro profile, but a full frontal portrait in one of his statues, although noseless, reveals a distinct Negro appearance (plate 5). Of the five dynasty three kings, Djoser was the only one who gained any renown. This pharaoh was remembered for centuries in Egypt as a wise king who had the misfortune to rule during a low Nile, which brought on a severe famine. Tradition maintained that his skill in medicine was great. The historian Manetho, who lived during Hellenistic times, called Djoser a patron of literature and a physician of such eminence that he came to be identified with Asklepios, the Greek god of medicine.[118] Weigall, whose opinion of Upper Egyptians and Nubians was not high, has written that "the Pharaoh's greatness, as a matter of fact, seems to have been due to the labors of his minister, Imhotpe, the Imouthes of the Greeks, who was the shining light of the age."[119] Sometime after Manetho made the remark equating Asklepios and Djoser, Imhotep (Imhotpe, Imouthes) was not only given the credit that was apparently due him but became a god in the Greek pantheon.

Imhotep was already a demigod in the eyes of the Egyptian masses, when the Greeks deified him. Today, while he is honored by some Afro-American physicians as the "Father of Medicine," white scholars who write about him and laud him give no indication of his race. Imhotep "was revered by the ancient Egyptians as a philosopher, a proverb maker, a physician, a scribe, and an architect," according to Weigall.[120] Aldred compares Imhotep to a genius "of the order of a Newton or an Einstein." He notes that "his greatest memorial" is "the funerary monument that he erected for Djoser at Saqqara, to which the name of the Step Pyramid has been given."[121] Indeed, the principles were worked out there that made possible the building of the great pyramid at Gizeh during the Fourth Dynasty under Cheops.

Joel A. Rogers, in *World's Great Men of Color*, devotes a chapter to Imhotep with the subtitle "God of Medicine, Prince of Peace, and the First Christ." This somewhat extravagant eulogy presents no evidence, visual or otherwise, that this great Third Dynasty physician was Black, except in an explanation of his statement that "the child-Christ remained a starry-bejewelled blackamoor as the typical healer in Rome":

> A jewelled image of the child-Christ as a blackamoor is sacredly preserved at the headquarters of the Franciscan order, and true to its typical character as a symbolical likeness of Iusa, the healer, the little black figure is taken out in state with its regalia on to visit the sick and demonstrate the supposed healing power of this Egyptian Esculapius, thus Christianized.[122]

During the formative years of the Christian church, shrines to Imhotep were in existence throughout the Greco-Roman world and particularly at healing centers that bore his name. Rogers refers to the thousands of small statues from this period that reveal Greek, Roman, and Hellenized Egyptian conceptions of the deified Imhotep. Made of bronze, marble, basalt, and steatite in the Delta where Greek cultural influence became very strong, these were votive offerings in gratitude for cures with which Imhotep was credited in his role as a demigod. Greek or Hellenized Egyptian artists seldom portrayed Imhotep as Negroid; none depicted him as extremely Negroid. He was in the process of being transformed from an Egyptian of the Fourth Dynasty into Asklepios, the Greek god of medicine. Eventually the name of Imhotep was virtually forgotten, and the name of Asklepios, as the Father of Medicine, was passed on to Western Europe when the Roman soldiers and the church forced Mediterranean civilization upon the barbarians across the Pyrenees and the Alps, and in Britain.

The apotheosis of Imhotep was completed during the period of intermittent Persian domination of Egypt, 525 B.C. and 332 B.C., when he became a full-fledged deity with a temple on the island of Philae near the border with Ethiopia. A mural on the wall of the shrine portrays a very light brown god of medicine with Caucasoid features.[123] Even when portrayed on the walls of shrines in Meroë, Imhotep was not given pronounced Negro features. If there was a tendency to "whiten" Imhotep as Greeks and Persians established their dominance in Egypt, it is significant that, at an earlier stage, both Manetho and the Greeks claimed that Djoser, not Imhotep, was the great physician. This provides striking evidence of how little color prejudice per se was involved in these symbol system transformations, for the Greeks did not think of pharaonic Egyptians as "white," as comments by Herodotus make clear. When it was to the advantage of Christians, as they began to Christianize northern Africa, to assimilate Imhotep's image to that of the Christ child, they envisioned him as a Negro. Afro-American physicians, in making him a patron saint, are perhaps justified in choosing the black Imhotep tradition where there are two options, neither of which can be supported conclusively with pictorial or documentary evidence. In all likelihood, Imhotep was at least "nonwhite."

For students of race relations in ancient Egypt, as well as for black vindicationists, the Fourth Dynasty is the most relevant of the six Old Kingdom dynasties. It began about 2615 B.C. with a pharaoh named Sneferu (Snoferu)—"The Gladdener"—on the throne. This pharaoh was also called "Lord in Truth" and "Horus of the Golden City." He is best known for sending forty ships to Lebanon to secure cedar logs to be used in building boats and the great doors of his palace, and for a punitive expedition into the area between the first and second cataracts of the Nile using newly constructed warships. His stele boasts of the havoc wreaked on the Nehesi (or, as most books translate the word, "Negroes"). It claims that he came back with 7,000 prisoners and 200,000 cattle. Sneferu ordered the building of a defensive wall against the "barbarians" of the southland, but as subsequent history proved, it was to no avail, for "pacifying" Nubia remained high on the agenda of most pharaohs until the dynastic period ended.[124] When books and articles translate *Nehesi* as "Negroes," they pervert the probable contemporary meaning of Sneferu's action, as well as the record of it. For a dynasty with as many "Negroes" in it as the Fourth to have conceived of this as a racially motivated punitive action seems highly improbable.

Cheops was the most famous—and notorious—of the Fourth Dynasty pharaohs, because it was during his reign that the Great

Pyramid at Gizeh was built, and for centuries it was believed among the Egyptians that he was a cruel king who used Egyptian slave labor. A story was circulated in Hellenistic times that Cheops even made his daughters engage in prostitution to obtain the wealth needed to complete the pyramid. (He was said to have had one daughter who was blonde with red hair.) Modern Egyptologists consider this a libel perpetuated by unfriendly sectors of the priesthood and told to Herodotus, who spread the tale widely. They insist that the labor was performed by peasants when the Nile was not in flood, who may have considered the labor an honor as well as duty.[125] The statue of Cheops that appears most often does not reveal a person as Negroid as the Sphinx or the successor king, Mycerinus; but all of the individuals in this dynasty—including the more Caucasoid Hemon—could easily be considered members of the same "race" by Afro-Americans, who are familiar with such a range of color and features within their own extended families. Such a range is even more familiar to residents of Brazil, Cuba, or Puerto Rico. Sir Flinders Petrie states that the upper classes of the Pyramid Age, the Eighteenth Dynasty, and the Twenty-sixth Dynasty all had what he calls a "Sudany infusion." That is, according to North American definitions, they were "Black."[126]

The extent of miscegenation among Fourth Dynasty royalty is indicated by the so-called "reserve heads" now in the Boston Museum of Fine Arts. Two that are frequently compared are those of a prince and one of his wives. His head is considered Caucasian. She not only exhibits the alveolar prognathism so dear to anthropologists' hearts in defining the Negro type, but also gives the general impression of "Negroidness" that most Europeans and Americans are sensitized to (plate 8a and b). In this regard Aldred's remarks, written in 1949 describing this "Head of a Princess," are significant:

> The Americans who excavated it regard it as showing negroid characteristics; and although this view has been challenged, it is difficult to refute. A somewhat alien, un-Egyptian physiognomy is evident in several members of the royal family at this period.[127]

(One is struck by the suggestion, implicit in this 1949 statement, that it *should* be refuted if it could be. Writing about this same head almost thirty years later, Aldred no longer referred to the controversy or to "alien, un-Egyptian physiognomies" of Fourth Dynasty royalty.)

A bas-relief of Khufu-Kaf (another son of Cheops) and his wife shows features that suggest "Negroidness," whereas the statue of Hemon, Cheops's vizier and architect (and a relative, too), depict him as a Caucasian with pronounced Armenoid features. Bekt, an Old Kingdom sculptor whose statue is well known, appears considerably more Negro in facial configuration than Caucasoid. This refutes the suggestion sometimes made that the black pharaohs depended entirely on foreign Asian intellectuals and craftsmen during the Old Kingdom period. (Architect Nekhebu of the Fifth Dynasty was definitely Negro [plate 9].) The range of indigenous physical types even within single familes was very wide.[128]

One of the most celebrated pieces of Egyptian art comes from the Fourth Dynasty: the statue of Re-Hotep, high priest of Heliopolis and commander of the army, seated beside his wife Nofret. The "convention is followed in the skin-coloring with reddish brown for the man, and a creamy yellow for the woman." A European art critic is convinced that these are portraits and that they attempt to convey racial type as well as individuality. The features of the man suggest "Negroidness," as broadly defined. This is less true of his wife.[129] The portrait head of Ra-ded-ef, who followed Cheops, is Negroid, although of a different type from another presumably Negro head usually labeled "An Unknown King" (plate 6). Some statues of Mycerinus, last of the Fourth Dynasty kings, emphasize his "Negroidness"; some do not (plate 7). Any group of heads selected more or less at random from Fourth Dynasty sculpture would indicate a wide range of physical types that certainly included Negroid individuals at all social levels.[130]

There is a substantial measure of agreement among Egyptologists that the head of the Sphinx was intended as a portrait statue of Chefren, the pharaoh who succeeded Ra-ded-ef, and that Chefren was probably one of the latter's sons. An existing monumental statue of this pharaoh portrays him in profile as being less Negro than the Sphinx does, but a front view suggests "Negroidness."

While Weigall stresses the symbolic nature of the Sphinx, citing facts not widely known about that monumental piece of sculpture reputedly carved out of a rock *in situ*:

> Probably it was originally an actual representation of the Pharaoh Khafre [Chefren] in his aspect as an incarnation of the sun-god, and gradually it came to be regarded as the embodiment of the collective Pharaonic spirit, and hence at length a figure of the sun himself, of whom the Pharaohs were manifestations on earth, and from whom they derived their royalty. Originally the face, which is 14 feet wide across the cheeks, was painted with a pigment made of red ochre, the employment of which was established by ancient custom as the colour to be used for depicting the complexion of male Egyptians.[131]

The Sphinx was a symbol of all Old Kingdom pharaohs, not just Chefren. Placed as it was where the Delta ended and Upper Egypt began, it announced to all visitors that they were now entering the land of the Blacks. If this seems unbelievable today, it is because we now observe an Egyptian population made less Negroid by miscegenation over many centuries and by the Arab invasion after the eighth century A.D. While Weigall emphasized the Sphinx as a symbol of the sun, represented by the priests of Re in their shrine near Memphis, Aldred, in his book on the Old Kingdom, emphasizes an older level of mystical associations with the person of the pharaoh. These were psychologically so powerful that they brought prestige to the person of the Egyptian pharaoh throughout the then-known civilized world. The pharaoh objectified the belief that the rain chiefs of inner Africa, upon whom predynastic kingship in Egypt had been modeled, could control the rain. Aldred writes of these black rulers of the Old Kingdom:

> The Pharaoh exercised a profound influence over adjacent lands. At his accession and jubilees he received Magi-like gifts from foreign ambassadors who begged from him the gift of life that he was supposed to bestow upon their peoples. . . . The early dynastic monuments suggest that this relationship existed from the very first. . . . The size and importance of the king show that he was regarded as a god rather than the human agent of a god, and it is in this that Egypt presents us with a typically African solution to problems of government . . . for the Pharaoh is the classic example of the god incarnate as king. . . . A tangible god whose sole authority could produce results by the exercise of the divine attributes of "creative utterance," "understanding," and "justice" appealed particularly to the Egyptian psyche, and gave the nation confidence to overcome otherwise daunting obstacles.[132]

Not all Africanists would agree that this was a "typically African solution to the problems of government," but would concede its widespread presence in eastern Africa. In any event, in its Egyptian form it evoked the wrath of the Hebrew prophets as blasphemous presumptuousness. A creature was worshiped as a god. However, for many of the surrounding peoples this concept of the pharaoh's sacredness survived beyond the Old Kingdom, and the rulers themselves clung to the claim until the end of pharaonic Egypt, although by that time it had become tarnished in the eyes of some surrounding people by the ruthless imperialism that characterized the later dynasties.

John A. Wilson, of Chicago's Oriental Institute, has argued that during the period of the Middle Kingdom the mystique of Egypt's pharaoh in surrounding areas was still strong. He was "the god who brought fertility to Egypt. . . . He controlled the water which made Egypt and made her fertile"; *and* "as the pharaoh controlled the water of Egypt, the Nile, so also he was rainmaker for the foreign countries." Pleas came to him from other monarchs to bring the water, including rulers as far afield as the king of the Hittites. They called him *god*, but Wilson cites "utterances" demonstrating that "Pharaoh himself was a little more modest; he did not pose as the rainmaker for lands abroad but as the intermediary to the gods for water." Wilson concludes that he was considered "the master magician . . . who brought the abundant waters, and who gave the fertile crops." The scribes, the priests, and the government bureaucracy carried out the necessary human operations to produce, transport, store, and distribute the crop.

From the ranks of independent farmers paying taxes in kind and in precious metals came a middle class that displayed a degree of initiative impressive to Wilson. He emphasizes what he calls the "independent self-reliance of the Egyptian of the Pyramid Age," and that among the nobility and the priests and the scribes, "no servile dependency upon a god was necessary. . . . Man was generally accountable to the king, to the creator god, and to his own *ka*, but he was not humbly suppliant to a named god of the pantheon." Wilson speaks of the members of this cultivated Egyptian stratum as a "gay and lusty people." Neither Wilson nor Frankfort thinks of the system as unduly repressive, and the latter scholar says of the "institution of divine kingship" that "it was good, not evil; it gave a sense of security which the Asiatic contemporaries of the ancient Egyptians totally lacked. . . . Truth, Justice, were that by which the gods live, an essential element in the established order. Hence Pharaoh's rule was not tyranny nor his service slavery." This verdict was passed by a tolerant academic liberal. Yet this system "bore within itself the seed of its own destruction," as Marxian analysts would phrase it.[133]

Not only did the individualism that led to the emergence of a wealthy stratum generate hostilities toward the pharaoh and his bureaucracy among farmers and workmen who were not well-to-do but whose labor was used to build monuments and to ensure a good life for the nobility; it also weakened the prestige of the pharaoh. Wilson, who is not a Marxist, nevertheless analyzes the situation as they would:

> The real source of the collapse was a progressive decentralization. Rulers other than the dynastic pharaohs felt their individual capacity for independence and set up competitive government. . . . Now with the single central control dissipated, there was anarchy in the competing grabs for power, which went right down to the lowest strata of society.[134]

Wilson notes further that "the Old Kingdom of Egypt collapsed into turmoil heels over head," and Egyptologists have found documents in which scribes and priests pondered over the reasons for the dissolution of the Old Kingdom. Their highest ideals stressed *ma'at*—truth and justice—so "the Egyptians ascribed their woes in part to a dissolution of their own character, but also to the violent presence of Asiatics in the Egyptian Delta." It is this Egyptologist's considered judgment that

> it is doubtful whether the Asiatics came in as an invading and suppressing horde; it is much more likely that an inner breakdown of rule in Egypt permitted small groups of Asiatics to come in and settle but that these insignificant penetrations were result rather than cause of the breakdown.[135]

During the Fifth Dynasty, invasions came from the Syrians on the east and the Libyans on the west. A rock tablet in Sinai praises Rathure, the sixth king of the dynasty, as "the smiter of the Asiatics of all countries." This was to become a constantly repeated theme of pharaonic boasting, along with claims of "smiting" Nehesi. The oldest known version of the Pyramid Texts (one version of the Book of the Dead) comes from the tomb of the ninth king of the Sixth Dynasty, whose reign was generally one of peace. However, the third king of the Sixth Dynasty, Pepy I, raised a large army, including Nehesi from south of the border, and "hacked up the land of the Desert-dwellers." He also sent four more expeditions against the Bedouins and then one by sea into southern Palestine behind them. An oft-told story of the Sixth Dynasty involves the childish enthusiasm of Pepy II, when he was a small boy, over a dwarf (pygmy), brought back by an expedition to "the Land of Punt," "the land of the spirits." The pygmy was prized because he knew "the dances of the ancestors." Pepy I was reputed to have remained an active king well into his nineties.

The Old Kingdom withered away after Pepy's death because of a succession of weak dynasties.[136] After a period of 500 years, the Old Kingdom disintegrated. Although its pharaohs were venerated and its creative personalities highly respected within the other young civilized communities in the Fertile Crescent, which stretched from the northern border of Egypt through Mesopotamia, several groups of "barbarians"—Toynbee's "external proletarians"—constituted a constant danger.[137] In closest proximity to the Nile Valley were the desert peoples on both sides of it. Somewhat farther west, in the latitude of Lower Egypt, were the warlike "Libyans"; and eastward, toward the Red Sea, lived a number of "uncivilized" tribes, some of whom inhabited the Red Sea hills. Nehesi, a generic term meaning "southerners," referred to the "uncivilized" people in the valley itself and in the Nubian desert. These people often were referred to pejoratively, but not in terms of race or color. Wilson notes:

> The ancient Egyptian . . . was semi-urban and sophisticated of mind and felt foreigners to be rustic and uninitiated. . . . He made a distinction between "men" on the one hand, and Libyans or Asiatics or Africans [i.e., non-Egyptian Africans], on the other. The word "men" in that sense meant Egyptians; otherwise it meant "humans" in distinction to the gods, or "humans" in distinction to animals. In other words, the Egyptians were "people"; foreigners were not. . . . *However, the Egyptian isolationist or nationalist feeling was a matter of geography and of manners rather than of racial theory or dogmatic xenophobia. "The people" were those who lived in Egypt, without distinction of race or colour.* . . . Asiatics or Libyans or Negroes might be accepted Egyptians of high position when they had become acclimatized—might, indeed, rise to the highest position of all, that of the god-king who possessed the nation [italics added].[138]

Another American Egyptologist, Barbara Mertz, after commenting on the many racial strains in the Egyptian population, writes:

> Like the rest of us, the Egyptians were probably mongrels. . . . With such a heritage, racial discrimination, as such, was one error the ancient Egyptians never fell into. They discriminated . . . naturally, but not on the basis of skin color. Like the Greeks and others, the Egyptians called themselves "the people." Other men were not people; they were only barbarians.[139]

This was, of course, only ethnocentric hyperbole. Egyptians were fully aware of the humanity of other people. The role of the pharaoh as rainmaker for all nations was a symbolic expression of this empathy.

Although neither racial nor ethnic discrimination existed within the Old Kingdom, the society was elitist and class stratified, as were all other societies of antiquity with a settled community and a complex division of labor, but dependent primarily upon farmers. Such societies generated within themselves what the Marxists call the "contradictions" that V. Gordon Childe has analyzed for the civilizations of antiquity in *What Happened in History*. Toynbee, combining Marxist and non-Marxist terminology, popularized an explanation involving the rise of an "internal proletariat" within each of these ancient societies, which, in combination with attacks by "external proletariats" during recurrent "times of troubles," brought the civilizations down. He includes "Egyptiac" civilization in his analysis. Cheikh Anta Diop has made a neo-Marxist analysis of what he calls Egypt's "cycles." Wilson has argued that an almost inevitable conflict arose in the Old Kingdom because, on one hand, the society fostered individual initiative and, on the other, it tried to perpetuate an autocratic, highly centralized government focused on the cult of a deified leader. An incipient bourgeoisie, ready to give its allegiance to local political figures in the nomes, became a threat to national unity as symbolized by the pharaoh. Diop stresses another source of tension: the disparity between the rich and the poor. As he phrases it, "The sixth dynasty was to end with the first popular uprising in Egyptian history." A poverty-stricken unemployed mass lived in the cities and "the wretched of Memphis, capital and sanctuary of royalty, pillaged the city, robbing the rich and driving them into the streets. The movement soon spread to other cities."[140] A papyrus document from the period reads, "Luxury is now widespread but it is the poor who are affluent. He who had nothing possesses treasures, and the great flatter him." Out of the anarchy, numerous local centers of power emerged. The Old Kingdom was dead. (The end of the Middle Kingdom came with a similar crisis. Weigall, studying some papyri written during that period, commented that "the cause of the state of things seems to have been due to some sort of political upheaval curiously suggestive of Bolshevism as viewed by a member of the aristocratic party."[141] This was equally true at the end of the Old Kingdom, initiating what Diop calls the "cycles" in Egyptian history.)

After the chaotic end of the Old Kingdom, the first of what Egyptologists call "low" periods began—the First Intermediate—Dynasties Seven through Ten. Thus began a hundred years of decentralized authority and sporadic civil commotion. Since Egyptian history is not written from the perspective of the masses who pillaged Memphis, no attempt has ever been made to assess the possibility that the ordinary people might have been better off during the "low" periods that followed than under the closely knit regimes dominated by powerful pharaohs and their local representatives. Some modern Egyptologists may admire the functional utility of the god-king with a degree of sympathy not shared by those who were at the bottom of the social structure.

Toynbee uses his vast store of knowledge to establish a sequence of events in Egypt that he evaluates from a liberal democratic perspective with a pronounced Protestant Christian bias. Wilson draws lessons from the same body of human experience judging it against the values of the Enlightenment and a less explicit Judaeo-Christian scale of values. Diop combines a black vindicationist perspective with a Marxist view that leads him to ask why the protest pattern that began in the Sixth Dynasty never matured into a revolution later in Egyptian history but remained only "curiously suggestive of Bolshevism," as Weigall notes. The experience of the first thousand years of civilization in the Nile Valley viewed in comparison with similar periods in the Tigris-Euphrates, the Indus, and the Yangtze valleys and contrasted with the emergence many centuries later of civilization in Greece, would add a dimension of understanding to the problems of man in society that is usually omitted in college and university education in the humanities. The Greco-Roman and Hebrew sociopolitical paradigms are not the only ones relevant to our problems, but the Eurocentric focus of the academy makes it seem so.

THE MIDDLE KINGDOM'S BLACK DYNASTIES

Between the end of the Sixth Dynasty and the end of the Tenth, regional rulers fought several wars in an attempt to establish dominance in Egypt. A number of literary testimonies of the period speak of the internal turmoil and the near chaos that existed from time to time. Close to the end of this Intermediate Period a scribe wrote: "Offices are rifled and their census-lists are carried off. Officials are murdered, and their writings are taken away. All is in ruins. . . . Men have dared to rebel against the Crown. . . . A foreign tribe from abroad has come into Egypt." Then an obscure passage refers to a "divine Savior" who "shall bring coolness to that which is fevered. . . . He shall be the Shepherd of His People."[142] What actually happened was a military thrust northward from Thebes by Mentuhotep, who established the Eleventh Dynasty, the first of the Middle Kingdom. Some looked upon him as a "divine Savior"; others did not.

Groups of Asian nomads had begun to filter into the Nile Valley from the deserts to the north and east, while Nehesi constantly attacked the borders in the south. During the late Intermediate period the priests and princes in the southernmost nomes, taking seriously their role as custodians of the national shrines, marshaled the forces needed to expel foreign invaders and to unify Egypt under one ruler again. Mentuhotep, who marched his troops northward and accomplished this goal after the First Intermediate Period, emphasized the values that the Middle Kingdom professed to reestablish. He is supposed to have said to his son, in his old age, "There is no lie that has come forth from my mouth. . . . There was no violence done to anyone dwelling (even) in the desert."[143]

Wilson extols Middle Kingdom rulers for their devotion to ma'at, that is, justice, truth, and uprightness.

> There was a real emphasis on this *ma'at* in the Middle Kingdom in the sense of social justice, righteous dealing with one's fellow men. . . . We consider the Egyptian Middle Kingdom to have reached moral heights in its search for the good life.

He does, however, concede the point to potential critics that "this is a personal prejudice, in which we follow Professor Breasted."[144] Even the symbolism of the pharaoh's role was changed. The king was now "a herdsman who cherished his herds," and "even the sculptures of the time sought to bring out this emphasis on conscientious character and moved from a delineation of majesty and force to a portrayal of concern for obligations."[145]

At the same time, the pharaoh had to preserve the image of a shepherd who *protected* his herds as well as cherished them. Nevertheless, it is noteworthy, as evidence of a constant theme in Egyptian history, that Nebheptre Mentuhotep, the fourth king of the Eleventh Dynasty, who completed the task of establishing the authority of the princes and priests of Upper Egypt over all of the Two Lands, is honored with an inscription on his tomb emphasizing the violent way in which he established power over the Delta, by "smiting" Egyptians—his own recalcitrant people—as well as Libyans, Asiatics, and Nehesi.

Weigall, in discussing the rise to power of the first of the Mentuhotep kings, concludes:

> The people of Lower Egypt must have thought that the end of the world had come, and must have been terrified at the prospect of being ruled by a barbarian from the southern provinces. What was Thebes, they must have asked, but an unimportant little settlement hundreds of miles up the Nile? What was this conqueror, Mentuhotpe, but a dark-skinned descendant of a line of petty kings? Who were his nobles but an illiterate rabble of peasants and fighting men?[146]

There were no records of the Delta people calling the southerners *black* barbarians. Did they actually think of them as *"dark-skinned* descendants of petty kings," or is this twentieth-century imagination at work? The pictorial record of this period fascinated the archaeologist Karl Richard Lepsius when he saw frescoes of a black queen being waited upon by people colored brown, black, and yellow. Some of the records described enemies in the northwest as Teheniu, or "Yellows." No enemies to the south were described as "Blacks," no doubt because they were the same color as the pharaoh and his royal family. It is not at all clear that calling northern enemies "yellow people" had any other significance that as a descriptive label to distinguish them from most Egyptians. Nowhere are "Yellows" stereotyped on stelae or papyri, though "Asiatics" and "Libyans" are referred to sometimes as "vile." On the other hand, "Yellow" *could* have had pejorative overtones. The yellow people serving the black queen could be either prisoners of war or Egyptian nationals, for the Eleventh Dynasty artists may have conceived of the color range from yellow to black as being normal for Egypt (plates 10 and 11).[147]

Weigall sees some redeeming features in "Mentuhotpe," this king from the south, however, for

> [the new Pharaoh] had collected at Thebes some good artists and architects from the lower country; and presently we find that the miserable work which marked the earlier years of the dynasty has disappeared, and has given place to work of a high quality, evidently executed by artists and craftsmen trained in the schools of Lower Egypt which had very largely maintained the traditions of the Sixth Dynasty.[148]

Both Weigall and Aldred attribute most of what they deem to be an expression of good taste in art during the Eleventh Dynasty to influences from the north; but in discussing the achievements of the Twelfth Dynasty, whose pharaohs were also definitely Negroid, Aldred here does not specify any regional preeminence:

> The pharaohs of the Twelfth Dynasty promoted widespread economic development by irrigation works and land reclamation. . . . Trading posts were established in the Sudan, and mines and quarries were reopened in Sinai and Nubia. Fortifications were raised on the northern and southern frontiers to protect Egypt from the incursion of famine-stricken marauders. Trade was also reestablished with Byblos and the timber-bearing regions of the Lebanon.[149]

The strong faces of Sesostris III and Ammenemes II, who carried out such projects, could be those of modern Nigerian or Ugandan political leaders. Aldred is struck by the impression of power that their statues give, in contrast to the emphasis upon the "good shepherd" theme in some of the inscriptions.[150] These Eleventh and Twelfth Dynasty kings identified strongly with Osiris. The Osiride statue of Sesostris I, holding two *ankhs*, reveals his Negroidness as much as it emphasizes his sanctity (plate 12).

Although Weigall imagines the Delta dwellers as looking down with scorn on the Mentuhotep pharaohs from the south when they burst upon the scene, he discusses some aspects of life in the "barbarian" south that suggest all was not backwardness there, even judged by Delta standards. Yet even what northerners might have admired probably coexisted with some customs that were alien to them. Mentuhotep I had six wives, each of whom was also a priestess of the goddess Hathor, who, in one of her manifestations, was patron of women and motherhood. Their ties with Kush are emphasized here by Weigall:

> Eleventh Dynasty women evidently played an important part, as is perhaps to be expected in a family living so close to Ethiopian territory, where the queens were more important than the kings. The Pharaohs of this family are represented sometimes with their mothers, or mention them. . . . I cannot help feeling that with the rise of these southern rulers there comes a strong renewal of the matriarchal practice and the importance of women.[151]

One of the influential Theban women to whom Weigall referred is described on her tomb as "Royal Favourite, the Great Ancestress, eminent in ancestresses, Heiress of the South country, daughter of a King and Wife of a king." She placed her steward in charge "of the great collection (?) of her mother, learned in writing, eminent in the works of science in the great hall (library?) of the South." The steward states in his inscription that "I made extensions to the collection, enriching it with heaps of valuable matter, so that it was not wanting in anything within the scope of my knowledge of things." Weigall comments, "It is surprising to find that the queens of this period were learned women and patrons of the sciences."[152]

The tombs of Mentuhotep's six queen-priestesses have been carefully excavated by a group of American Egyptologists, and the names of five—Henhenit, Kemsit, Sadhe, Ashayet, and Mait—are well known to Nile Valley scholars. Scenes from the tomb of Kemsit portray her as black, distinct from the brown and yellow of other persons (see plates 10 and 11). Edouard Naville, who discovered the tomb, considers this not an artistic convention but rather a realistic portrayal: "She is black; it seems very likely she was a negress."[153] H. E. Winlock, former curator of the Egyptian collection in the Metropolitan Museum of Art and one of the directors of the excavation of the grave site, mentions both Kemsit and Ashayet when discussing some artifacts found in the tomb of Nefer-hotep, a bowman in the army during the Eleventh Dynasty:

These figures obviously represent negro slave girls from far up the Nile, jet black and wearing strange skirts covered with barbarous designs in gaudy colors, and many colored beads around their foreheads and necks. *Derry [the physician with the field party] had already noticed that the features of the tattooed dancing girl buried in the Neb-hepet-Re temple showed marked Nubian traits and that Nubian blood had probably flowed through the veins even of such ladies of the king's harem as Ashayet and Henhenit. Furthermore the pictures of Ashayet on her sarcophagus gave her a rich chocolate Nubian complexion, and her companion Kemsit was painted on hers an actual ebony black, just like these little figures* [italics added].[154]

Winlock goes on to conclude that "from above Aswan must have come many a girl in Neb-hepet-Re's palace and their dusky sisters have been beguiling Oriental potentates ever since."[155]

Winlock mentions, as the most recent case, "the little black-skinned concubine of the Kedive Ismail, whom Verdi and Mariette were commanded to take as their inspiration for the heroine of 'Aida.' "[156] It is obvious, of course, from the frescoes and from what both Weigall and Winlock have to say, that not all black women at pharaonic courts based in Thebes were either concubines or dancing girls, and that social class and degree of acculturation to Egyptian standards, not color, were the crucial indices of status. None of these matings between people on the two sides of the first cataract boundary were conceptualized as "interracial" or as instances of "miscegenation." Such offspring were within the range of color and features that made the southern Egyptians and Nubians a single people. Marriages with Asiatics and Europeans, sometimes arranged for political reasons, were apparently another matter.

Relations with people from "above Aswan," as Winlock phrases it, were not always peaceful during the period of the Middle Kingdom, despite the presence of Negroid pharaohs and of women like Kemsit and Ashayet as queens. During the Eleventh and Twelfth dynasties, what contemporary Nubian archaeologists call the "second-cataract forts" were built. These were enormous structures where Egyptian garrisons were quartered. Their principal function was to guard desert trade routes and Nile shipping points. A number of punitive actions kept raiding parties from coming close to Aswan and "screened" travelers between the second and first cataracts.

Senusret III, a Twelfth Dynasty pharaoh whose Negroidness is plainly evident in a number of statues, launched at least two campaigns against tribes south of the second cataract. A stele was erected to fix the boundary after the first campaign that indicates a desire for trade with a people who were to be prevented from moving northward as a group:

> Southern boundary, made in the year 8, under the majesty of the King of Upper and Lower Egypt, Khakaura Senusret III who is given life forever and ever; in order to prevent that any Negro should cross it, by water or by land, with a ship, or any herds of the Negroes; except a Negro who shall come to do trading in Iken, or with a commission. Every good thing shall be done with them, but without allowing a ship of the Negroes to pass by Heh, going downstream, forever.[157]

It is evident that Senusret is determined to keep invaders, marauders, or settlers out of that part of the Nile Valley south of Egypt over which he has established hegemony. Professor Walter B. Emery of the University of London, who has studied the forts, tombs, and burial mounds of the area in great detail, reminds us that

> The reference to Egypt's enemies as "Negroes" is misleading, for the people of Kush were not Negroes as we understand the term as applied to this racial group today. The Egyptians used the term "Negro" (nhsi) to designate all the dark-skinned peoples of the south, whatever their race.[158]

This warning is itself misleading, however, for the Egyptians did not use any term that should be translated as "Negro" at all! Many of the "people of the south" looked exactly like many of the Egyptians. *Nehesi was a geographical designation, not a label for a physical type.* Egyptians had no word equivalent to the narrow anthropological term "Negro" that Emery is using. Nor was it an ethnic term, for Egyptians spoke of many different "nations" in the area including "The Nine Nations of the Bow."

Senusret, like many other kings of Egypt, used Nehesi to refer to the "uncivilized" people south of the first cataract who did not differ from many civilized people of the Nile Valley in physical type. A second stele exults over the defeat of these "barbarians" who after eight years were still considered a threat to the outposts of Egyptian "civilization." The Budge translation rendered Nehesi as "Blacks," which Nehesi did not mean either. The stele reads:

> (1.) The Black listeneth to what falleth from the mouth, behold,
> (2.) he is answered when one maketh him to retreat. If any man attack him, he turneth his back to him in flight, and if any man retreat before him he will make an attack.
> (3.) [The Blacks] are not men of boldness, they are timid (or, weak), and have buttocks for hearts.

(4.) My Majesty hath seen them, and I exaggerate not. I made captives of their women, I carried off

(5.) their peasant labourers, I came to their wells, I slew their bulls, I destroyed their grain,

(6.) casting fire into it. I swear an oath by my father's life that I speak in truth, and that it is not

(7.) falsehood which cometh forth from my mouth.[159]

These pronouncements came from a black pharaoh assailing black enemies on Egypt's southern borders. Meanwhile, other enemies were weakening Egypt from within.

EGYPT'S "GREAT HUMILIATION"

Wilson here identifies a trend that culminated in the Middle Kingdom: "Egypt had been moving somewhat blindly along the road from theocratic autarchy toward democracy of a kind." But near the end of the Twelfth Dynasty,

> again the central government broke down; again there was competition for the rule by a number of small princelings. Probably a weakening of personal force and character in the central government unleashed the self-seeking individualism of local princes.[160]

Historian Harry A. Gailey emphasizes the materialism of the period, rather than the underlying spiritual values that Wilson maintains were menaced by "self-seeking individualism." He writes that this was "a time of great affluence, with the rich pharaohs and nobles demanding more luxury items such as ivory, gold, fine stones, and exotic woods." Expeditions were sent into Sinai and Nubia in an attempt to control sources of supply, resulting in hostile reactions among the native populations. "Such opulence . . . did not hide the weaknesses of the Middle Kingdom. The nobles still retained great power and the influence of the priesthood had been greatly expanded. . . . To insure against revolts a large standing army became necessary."[161] Soldiers from Libya formed an important part of that army.

The Afro-American historian Chancellor Williams insists that the pharaohs did not recognize the major danger, for although Mentuhotep II, "probably the greatest of Eleventh Dynasty kings," expelled many of the disloyal leaders of the Asian settlers, who had become numerous in the Delta, he did not dislodge the thousands of Asian settlers who were "the dominant people there." This point of view is shared, to some extent, by Aldred, who, in 1980, described the genesis of an Eleventh Dynasty "problem" as beginning much earlier:

During the First Intermediate Period, Asiatics, mostly Western Semites, had begun to infiltrate into the Delta, driven by famine and ethnic displacements in lands to their north and east. These newcomers sold themselves into slavery to exchange a penurious and uncertain existence for a modest livelihood, or offered themselves as cooks, brewers, seamstresses, vine dressers, and the like, in return for food and shelter. Many of them earned their manumission and assumed positions of importance and trust.[162]

Chancellor Williams considers them a "*white* fifth column" who were intent upon usurping Black Power in order to facilitate conquest of Egypt by subsequent invaders from Syria, Palestine, and Mesopotamia. Aldred, without reading racialist motivations into their minds, confirms the fact that some of the immigrants' leaders ruled parts of Egypt:

> The Egyptians referred to the tribal leaders of these Asiatics as *Hikau Khasut*, or "Princes of Foreign Uplands," a term which Manetho wrongly transcribed as *Hyk-sos*, and translated as "Shepherd kings." This name has since been applied, erroneously, but tenaciously, to the whole race of immigrant peoples, rather than to their rulers. During the Eleventh Dynasty the Egyptians built a string of fortresses on their northeastern frontier to regulate the entry of these incomers into the Delta; but in times of trouble and decline this control weakened, and the immigrations increased in volume and insolence. It is assumed that groups of Asiatics established themselves under their sheikhs in different localities in the Delta, until one of their number was sufficiently powerful and ambitious to unite them, seize Memphis and proclaim himself the ruler of Lower Egypt. Later, as the Thirteenth Dynasty at its centres in It-tawi and Thebes vanished in confusion, the Hyksos were recognized as a new family of pharaohs and formed the Fifteenth and Sixteenth of Manetho's list of dynasties.[163]

Josephus, without any convincing evidence, identified the Hyksos as the "Children of Israel" in *The Antiquities of the Jews*, written during the first Christian century.[164] Rudolph A. Windsor, writing in 1969 as an Afro-American Jew in *From Babylon to Timbuktu: A History of the Ancient Black Races, Including the Black Hebrews*, does his own myth building, arguing that the Hyksos invaders were Indo-European whites who befriended a group of fellow aliens, the Hebrews, Sons of Jacob, who were Black, elevating Joseph into a position of power. Windsor is correct, however, when he says that the Egyptians called the years of Hyksos rule the "Great Humiliation."[165]

Aldred has provided a convincing explanation for the weakening of Middle Kingdom leadership that supplements Toynbee's theory of

Egyptian "low periods," as well as the perspectives of Diop and Chancellor Williams. He cites an environmental factor:

> At the end of the Twelfth Dynasty, fluctuating climatic conditions seem to have returned to Egypt and were responsible for the wayward behaviour of the Nile. High floods, slow to fall and allow seed to be sown at the proper time, were as disastrous in their effects as feeble inundations. *The patent inability of the divine king to control the Nile may have been the chief reason for another slump in the prestige of kingship which is evident throughout the Thirteenth Dynasty* [italics added].[166]

The priests and princes of Thebes steadfastly refused to recognize the legitimacy of the Asiatic invaders who have been called Hyksos, even though the usurpers sought the prestige of an alliance with the South. They were rebuffed. Instead the Theban elites began to prepare a dynasty to replace them. But they also learned from them, adopting the use of bronze weapons and the horse and the war chariot. Amon, long revered as a creator, and as a fertility god assimilated to the god Min, now became a war god to whom priests and princes, the warriors and the king, prayed for victory. Historian W. H. McNeill of the University of Chicago believes the Hyksos succeeded partly because, after almost 1,400 years of "civilization," Egyptian rulers had never taken the measures necessary, through development of iron weapons and new military tactics, "to present effective opposition to a new and strange phenomenon in their historical experience: foreign invasion in force." Now such an invasion faced them from the northeast. As McNeill describes the situation:

> The Hyksos became a stench in Egyptian nostrils. The priests and nobles of Egypt, long accustomed to consider themselves vastly superior to all other peoples, found themselves subjected to despised Asiatic barbarians, who desecrated their temples and set their most cherished traditions at naught. This experience worked a fundamental change in the Egyptian mentality. Even after a new king had come from the south to liberate the Two Lands from the hated Hyksos, the Egyptians no longer felt secure behind their desert barriers. They therefore brought their long isolation from the rest of the world to an end, and for the next thousand years joined as an imperial state in the complex power struggles of the Middle East.[167]

Wilson sees the Hyksos invasion as the first step toward reversing a healthy trend in social evolution in dynastic Egypt, a trend he had charted from Middle Kingdom times:

Asiatic princes, whom we call the Hyksos, established themselves in armed camps within Egypt and dominated the land with a firmness which was repressive to the still flowering Egyptian spirit. For the first time Egypt as a whole suffered a setback in that philosophy which said: We are the centre and summit of the world; we are free to permit expansion of spirit to the individuals of our community. Now, for the first time, that community was aware of a serious threat from the outside world. Now, for the first time, that community had to draw together into a unity in order to meet and avert that threat.

Egypt did unite and throw out the "vagabonds," who had dared to rule the land in the "ignorance of Re." But the threat was not met by driving them out of Egypt; it was necessary to pursue them into Asia and to keep on pounding them so that they might never again threaten the land of the Nile. . . . That common sentiment for security welded the Egyptians into a self-conscious nation.

Wilson feels that the price paid for this success was too high. The priests who had been essential to keeping alive what he calls "a psychosis for security, a neuropathic awareness of danger," had invested heavily in an Egyptian victory. "The national gods commissioned the pharaoh to march forth and widen the land," and

for this they received an economic return. . . . The pharaoh erected buildings, established and endowed feasts, and presented land and serfs to the god who had given the victory. The previously modest temples in Egypt grew in physical size, in personnel, in land, and in total property, until they became the dominating factor in Egyptian political, social, and economic life. . . . After the Empire had had three hundred years of active life, the Egyptian temples owned one out of every five inhabitants of the nation and owned almost one-third of the cultivable land.[168]

The people they "owned" were prisoners of war and their descendants. Egyptians were not enslaved. Their relationship to the pharaoh and to local lords was closer to that between lords and serfs in feudal Europe than that between bond servants or slaves and their masters in the Middle East.

The kings who led the drive to "throw out the vagabonds" and to "widen the land" were black leaders from Upper Egypt acting in the name of Theban gods, and particularly in the name of Amon, "the hidden one." They trusted his priests, who professed to give messages from Amon through the oracle at Thebes. Negroid rulers of the Seventeenth and Eighteenth dynasties established the New Kingdom that came after the Hyksos rulers had been expelled. Wilson evaluates them from a liberal-democratic perspective that deplores their imperialism and its effect on Egypt and the Middle East. Viewed from a black perspective they have an entirely different significance. Without defending their acts that run counter to modern standards of humanity and personal behavior, these rulers could be considered of crucial importance in examining the Degler-Gergen proposition and some aspects of race-relations theory discussed in chapter 2. They also reveal that centuries before the beginning of the slave trade Blacks were playing important roles in the contemporary affairs of the Middle East.

The king who expelled the Hyksos was Black, and presumably the bulk of his army was from Kush (Ethiopia); the hated foe was "Asian." In terms of our contemporary patterns, we might expect this confrontation to have elicited pejorative skin-color comments from both sides. We do not find any such color designations in the literature, but contemptuous Egyptian comments about "Asiatics," "northern barbarians," and so on are numerous. Whether, in the minds of Egyptians, these epithets conjured up images of a hated or despised physical type we have no way of knowing. Whether, when enslaved barbarians were displayed in Egypt, they elicited barrages of pejorative comment that singled out their physical characteristics we do not know. Pictorial representations show all races and colors of men equally prostrate before the might of the pharaoh, or symbolically having their heads smashed in with his war club.[169] Paintings and bas-reliefs also show working people of all races and colors toiling side by side in farm labor.[170] Ethnic designations carry an emotional charge today that they did not necessarily carry in antiquity, and choice of words by translators may imply ancient attitudes that did not exist. Color may not have been associated with ethnicity.

The war against the Hyksos and subsequent battles with European and Asiatic invaders along Egypt's northern borders were contact situations likely to produce the generalized forms of racial prejudice, or some aspects of them, that appear in Blumer's paradigm (see chart 1). Diop and Williams both describe these conflicts and those that continued throughout pharaonic history as clashes between "races," but the former is on sounder ground than the latter when he suggests that the participants did not conceptualize them as such.[171]

Not only does a racialist interpretation of history not explain the events, but the actors in them do not reveal in written or pictorial records any evidence of skin-color prejudices or racist explanations of behavior. Although the actors in these ancient dramas may not have emphasized the fact that black warriors, frequently under black pharaohs, were locked in battle with Europeans and Asians for centuries in the Middle East, the race of the actors is of interest to modern vindicationist writers living in societies that have not accorded full equality or respect to African black people since the fifteenth century A.D. Vindicationists feel compelled to emphasize that early Egyptian history was *black* history, not that of some vaguely defined "Near Eastern" peoples. They are prepared to accept both the probable villainy of the foot soldiers and the greatness, in military terms, of a conquering pharaoh, because these attributes place Egypt on a level of full equality with the other members of an international state system. From the standpoint of internal Egyptian history, the Eighteenth Dynasty pharaohs—a group that would be considered "Black" by contemporary Anglo-American standards— were leaders of a national renaissance after what some Egyptologists call the "low years" under the "Great Humiliation" of Hyksos domination.

THE EIGHTEENTH DYNASTY: LEADERS OF A NATIONAL RENAISSANCE

Liberation and Empire Building

Egyptian chronicles refer to the 150-year period of Hyksos rule as the "era of national humiliation." This was the first time that conquering non-African aliens had worn the double crown and tried to influence the religious thought and practice of the Egyptians. However, the political and military leaders of the southernmost nomes clung stubbornly to their part of Upper Egypt, insisting that Thebes, not Memphis, was now the legitimate capital of the country. The priests of Amon became their spiritual advisers. An informal truce divided the nation. When the fourteenth Hyksos king broke the truce and tried to extend his rule by intrigue and arms into the Thebaid, Kamose, a Sudanese Negro who was functioning as king of Upper Egypt, began to organize for defense. When a Hyksos ruler, Apophis, began to urge Nubian princes between the first and second cataracts of the Nile to throw off Egyptian suzerainty and to attack the Thebaid from the rear while Hyksos troops made a frontal assault, Kamose decided to reject the Hyksos overtures and boldly to invade the northern part of Egypt. With an army composed of Nubian troops and some of the desert Nehesi, Kamose marched and sailed down the Nile around 1500 B.C., taking Memphis, and then penetrated the

Delta, where his troops besieged the Hyksos capital city.[172] But the task of completing the conquest of Lower Egypt fell to the brother of Kamose, Ahmose I, who succeeded him.

Ahmose and his queen, Nefertari, were eventually worshiped as founders of the "Glorious Eighteenth Dynasty." Lerone Bennett, an Afro-American historian, mentions that one Egyptologist called Nefertari "a Negress of great beauty, strong personality, and remarkable administrative ability." Sir Flinders Petrie referred to her as "the most venerated figure of Egyptian history."[173] Champollion found a frieze depicting Nefertari and her husband being worshiped and wrote that the coloring of her skin black meant she was an Ethiopian (see fig. 2). This tradition of strong women in high places in the Egyptian south extended back at least as far as the Eleventh Dynasty, as we have noted.

Ahmose pursued the Hyksos armies into Palestine but made no attempt to occupy the conquered lands. Instead, he rushed back to Egypt to put down some revolts on the home front and then continued on into Nubia, homeland of the queen, to quell disturbances there. Between the first cataract of the Nile and those areas south of the fourth cataract, where Kush, an Ethiopian kingdom, provided a framework for order, a number of so-called "barbarian" tribes were considered a threat to Egypt's southern border. These specific Nehesi groups having been subdued, Ahmose and Nefertari were able to leave a unified Egypt within secure and quiet borders to their successor, Amenhotep I, who, it will be noted, bore the god Amon's name (or Amen, Amun) as a part of his own.

Amenhotep I carried on a "pacification" campaign in the south, extending the frontier of Egypt into Wawat as far as the third cataract of the Nile and building fortifications against desert tribes on both sides of the river. He continued the policy begun by Ahmose of building up an Egyptian army from various ethnic groups in Wawat, or Lower Nubia. Some of these soldiers eventually became famous throughout the Middle East as archers, being known as the "Bowmen," or the "Eye Piercers." Other recruits from the eastern desert, the Madjoi, served on the armed Nile fleet, where they operated as assault troops when a landing was made during warfare.

In addition to pushing the Asiatics back across the border, pursuing them into the Middle East and extending Egypt's borders southward up the Nile, Ahmose made a punitive strike against the Libyans to the west. John Wilson considers the reign of Ahmose a turning point in Egyptian history because, for the first time, "that community was aware of a serious threat from the outside world." In his

FIGURE 2. AMENHOTEP I AND HIS WIFE, QUEEN-MOTHER NEFERTARI,
BEING VENERATED. Reprinted from Jean François Champollion,
Monuments de l'Égypte et de la Nubie, vol. 2 (Geneva:
Editions de Belles-Lettres, 1970–1971), plate CLXX.

view the reaction to the Asiatics was excessive, and "there was built up a psychosis for security, a neuropathic awareness of danger similar to that which characterized Europe in modern times." Wilson might have cited another modern parallel—French military triumphs under Napoleon over Prussia and Austria—to illustrate his point:

> That common sentiment for security welded the Egyptians into a self-conscious nation. It has been pointed out that only in this period of liberation do the Egyptians speak of the troops as "our army," instead of crediting the forces to the king. There was a patriotic fervor which put the country's interests before the interests of the individual.[174]

In preparing to protect themselves against future incursions from Asia, a decision was made to exploit the human and natural resources of Wawat and Kush, below the first cataract of the Nile, whose rulers were already considered only quasi-independent. The first act of Thutmose I, Amenhotep's son who succeeded him, was to extend Egyptian control of the Nile Valley up to the fourth cataract, near the capital and the burial grounds of Kushite kings. On a fertile plain adjoining the Nile, a striking hilly outcrop known as Jebel Barkal marked a spot sacred to the Nubians. It was now given to the priests of Amon, whose temple at Karnak was also greatly enlarged by the pharaoh. A partnership between the Eighteenth Dynasty pharaohs and Amon's priests was in the making.

With his rear secure and with the blessings of the priests, Thutmose I proceeded to invade Palestine and Syria, and so prepared the way for his successors to organize a string of vassal states from the Egyptian border to the Euphrates River. Egypt was now preparing to enter a contest with Assyria and Babylon for Middle Eastern hegemony. Wilson feels that this decision was a disaster, because it interrupted a slow development toward a more democratic and humane Egypt:

> The common desire for security need not have survived after the Egyptian Empire extended the military frontier of Egypt well into Asia and thus removed the peril from the immediate frontier. . . . However it was a restless age, and there were perils on the distant horizon which could be invoked to hold the community together, since unity was to the advantage of certain central powers. When the threat of the Hyksos had subsided, the threat of the Hittites appeared and endangered the Asiatic Empire of Egypt. Thereafter came the Sea People, the Libyans, and the Assyrians. A fear psychosis, once engendered, remained present.[175]

Egypt's priests—and especially the priests of Amon—were the powers to which Wilson referred when he pointed out that "after the Empire had had three hundred years of active life, the Egyptian temples owned one out of every five inhabitants of the nation and owned almost one-third of the cultivable land."[176] This concentration of land in the hands of the priests, along with people to work it, resulted from gifts of booty after victorious wars. The 20 percent of Egypt's population on temple lands consisted primarily of slaves—predominantly European and Asian—captured as prisoners of war. There were some Nubians but no Egyptians among the slaves. The early pharaohs of the Eighteenth Dynasty initiated the process of empire building and strengthening of the role of the priestly corporations in the national life. However, the tenth king of that dynasty, the well-known Amenhotep IV, rejected the god Amon, for whom he had been named, and became Akhen*aten* to symbolize his devotion to the *Aten*, symbol of the sun. He then tried to stop the process of concentrating power in the priesthood of Amon, but failed.

Under Thutmose II, who followed Thutmose I, some of the Nehesi revolted against the Egyptians. The rebellion was repressed with great severity. This was "black on black" military action in contrast to the empire building in the Middle East that Wilson deplores. He says little about the implications of Egypt's wars against her southern neighbors. Whether the Kushitic royal families were involved in this rebellion and received punishment is not clear from the records. A lull in the sequence of military operations came after the death of Thutmose II.

Hatshepsut, a half-sister, succeeded Thutmose II when he died, serving as regent for their young half-brother, who eventually became the pharaoh Thutmose III. The latter's mother was a Nubian concubine of Thutmose I. Hatshepsut, who claimed to be an actual daughter of the god Amon (although one of her titles was Chief *Spouse* of Amon), may have been greatly influenced by the priests. However, she avoided warlike measures that would further enrich the god's temples. Hatshepsut sent no punitive expeditions up the Nile and dispatched no warriors into Palestine and Syria. She fostered extensive commerce with neighboring peoples and sent expeditions down the Red Sea coast for purposes of both trade and exploration. A constant supply of tropical products, including precious ivory, as well as gold, flowed into Egypt from Nubia. Such items were used by Egypt for trade with Mediterranean and Mesopotamian lands. This period of peace was possible because Hatshepsut's predecessors had forced the rulers of most of the neighboring lands to become loyal vassals, but there was always the danger that either they or their successors would attempt to throw off Egyptian domination.

Modern Egyptologists credit Hatshepsut with encouraging extensive building. One observer has commented favorably on her tomb, praising "its brightness and its suavity; pretty shallowness and sunshine . . . full of finesse and laughter . . . like a delicate woman perfumed." She planned her buildings with her architect, Senmut, who, Joel A. Rogers notes, was "to all appearances a full-blooded Negro"; the name of her "Prince Chancellor" and "First Friend," Nehusi, marks him as a Nubian.[177] When Thutmose III, her ward, took the throne after Hatshepsut died, he embarked upon an aggressive expansionist policy sharply in contrast to that of his predecessor.

Thutmose III expanded the Egyptian empire widely in the Middle East while acquiring a reputation as a just ruler and a talented man at home. He may have been motivated by fear of an eventual attack, of which Wilson speaks, but it is just as reasonable to guess that he wanted to achieve some of the glory that his empire-building ancestors had acquired, as well as to reverse the "pacifism" of his half-sister. In any event, he had Hatshepsut's name chiseled from many monuments and made quite clear that he resented her reign as his regent. Joel A. Rogers includes profiles of both in *World's Great Men of Color*: she as "The Ablest Queen of Far Antiquity" and he as "The Napoleon of Far Antiquity."

In addition to the knowledge that the mother of Thutmose was a Sudanese concubine, vindicationist writers have used a statue in the British Museum to establish his reputation as a black pharaoh. A photograph of it appears on the cover of the American edition of Cheikh Anta Diop's *The African Origin of Civilization* (plate 13). Information provided in a recent letter to the author from the curator of Egyptian Antiquities at the British Museum is an example of the frustrations black scholars sometimes feel in trying to set the record straight. The curator states that after a century of labeling the statue Thutmose III the Museum is no longer sure that it is a statue of this pharaoh. Vindicationists can derive some comfort from the fact that the alternative attribution is to Amenophis III (Amenhotep III), father of the great pharaoh Amenhotep IV, or Akhenaten.

Thutmose began his career as an ordinary priest in the temple of Amon in Thebes and ended it after fifty-four years on the pharaonic throne, during which time his armies established Egyptian rule throughout the Middle East west of Assyria and Babylon. His armies may have actually invaded some areas claimed by those kingdoms. During his reign wealth poured into Egypt in the form of tribute and gifts from kings and princes who acknowledged him as either sovereign or protector. Implicit in this relationship was an obligation to protect them from raids by the forces of Assyria, which was emerging as a ruthless and cruel expansionist power anxious to extend its influence westward all the way to the Mediterranean.

It is noteworthy that James H. Breasted, who explicitly refers to Egyptian civilization as a creation of "The Great White Race" (capital letters are his), lauds Thutmose in extravagant terms:

> His character stands forth with more color and individuality than that of any other king of Early Egypt save Ikhnaton [i.e., Akhenaten or Amenhotep IV]. . . . We see the man of tireless energy . . . the man of versatility designing exquisite vases in a moment of leisure; the lynx-eyed administrator who launched his armies upon Asia with one hand and with the other crushed the extortionate tax-gatherer. . . . His reign marks an epoch not only in Egypt but in the whole east as we know it in his age. Never before in history had a single brain wielded the resources of so great a nation.[178]

Amenhotep II and Thutmose IV, who followed Thutmose III, in that order, both kept the Middle Eastern conquests intact and the tribute flowing in to enrich the domains of the priesthood of Thebes as well as secular supporters of the pharaohs. Amenhotep III, who followed Thutmose IV, vigorously quelled a number of insurrections in the Middle Eastern empire, but his greatest contribution to Egyptian empire building was the conquest of the Nile Valley down to the fifth cataract, using not only military means but also cultivating friendly relations with the Kushite kings, who became close allies. Their troops and Egyptian troops acting together kept the trade routes open in the valley itself and in the adjacent desert lands. Thereafter followed the remarkable episode in Eighteenth Dynasty history, the reign of Amenhotep III's son, Amenhotep IV, who renounced his patronymn and urged all Egyptians to worship Aten, the sun symbol, exclusively.

The Akhenaten Interlude

The October 8, 1973, issue of *Time* magazine carried an article describing "a stunning exhibit" presented by the Brooklyn Museum and the Detroit Institute of Arts, entitled "Akhenaten and Nefertiti: Art from the Age of the Sun King." It was mentioned that over 170 "masterpieces of the Amarna period (1378–1362 B.C.) from collections around the world were on display." Amenhotep IV was referred to in the article by the name—Akhenaten—he took after dropping

Amon's name from his title and denouncing the worship of all gods other than the Supreme Power, symbolized by the Aten, the sun. Of the fourteen kings of the Eighteenth Dynasty, only two have captured the imagination of the Western world: Akhenaten and a younger member of his line, Tutankhamen, who became the twelfth king in the dynasty.

Egyptologists were well aware, before World War I, of the story of the remarkable tenth king of the dynasty, who preferred peace to war and the propagation of new religious insights he had experienced to the exercise of pharaonic power. By World War II, the exploits of Thutmose III had been forgotten except by black vindicationist historians; in 1973 the effects of the religious and artistic revolution set in motion by another Eighteenth Dynasty pharaoh, Ahkenaten, were on display in Brooklyn, 3,000 years after his death.

No pharaoh has been praised so highly by white scholars as Akhenaten. James H. Breasted, the renowned pioneer American Egyptologist and Orientalist, lauds him as "history's first individual" and states that "the modern world has yet adequately to value or even acquaint itself with this man who, in an age so remote and conditions so remote, became the world's first idealist."[179] Sir Flinders Petrie, the pioneer among Britain's experts on Egypt, says of his intellectual contribution, "No such grand theology had ever before appeared in the world so far as we know."[180] Weigall calls him "the first Pharaoh to be a humanitarian. . . . He was the first man to preach simplicity, honesty, frankness, and sincerity, and he preached it from a throne." Weigall, who wrote an entire book about him, becomes almost lyrical in his praise:

> When the world reverberated with the noise of war he preached the first known doctrine of peace; when the glory of martial pomp swelled the hearts of his subjects he deliberately turned his back upon heroics. . . . He has given us an example three thousand years ago that might be followed at the present day.[181]

Others have presented Akhenaten as a tragic figure whose love of peace led to the neglect of the great imperial domain built up by his warlike predecessors and elicited the unremitting hostility of the vindictive priests of Amon at Thebes, whose booty from overseas conquests ceased under his rule.[182]

Sigmund Freud, who suggested that Moses acquired his monotheistic views from Akhenaten (and was perhaps himself an Egyptian), mingles admiration with criticism when he writes of the new religion Akhenaten espoused: "a strict monotheism, the first attempt of its kind in the history of the world, as far as we know; and religious intolerance, which was foreign to antiquity before this and for long after, was inevitably born with the belief in one God."[183]

A recent revisionist view of Akhenaten, which assesses him as an autocrat who was not at all the pacifist earlier admirers thought him to be, has grown up simultaneously with an objective appraisal of his life and work in an excellent book by Cyril Aldred.[184] Immanuel Velikovsky, psychoanalyst and student of folklore, in *Oedipus and Akhenaten*, downgrades the pharaoh to the status of an immoral and intellectually overrated Egyptian to whom Freud tried to attribute creative contributions that his own people, the Jews, had made.[185]

Both the Aldred and Velikovsky works include pictures of Akhenaten that depict the great pharaoh as indubitably Negro. Most of the white scholars who had previously lauded him used stylized representations that left his race unclear; and Breasted, by defining Egyptians as belonging to "The Great White Race" and treating Akhenaten as a member of it, revealed his own personal opinion on the matter. However, since the 1930s, those who read the works of Joel A. Rogers, the self-trained Jamaican historian, became familiar with evidence that Akhenaten was Black. Rogers included a chapter in his *World's Great Men of Color* entitled "Akhenaton: The First Messiah and Most Remarkable of the Pharaohs." Dr. Yosef ben-Jochannan, author of *Black Man's Religion* and a popular lecturer in university Black Studies programs, admires Akhenaten and considers him a precursor of Jesus Christ.[186] Chancellor Williams, Howard University professor and author of *The Destruction of Black Civilization*, speaks of Akhenaten as "more preacher than king, and the greatest single spiritual force to appear in the history of the Blacks." As Professor Williams sees it,

> his great religious reform movement aimed at a greater focus on the One and Only Almighty God, Creator of the Universe. . . . Such an unheard of stand by the leader of the nation meant revolution and certain rebellion by the powerful priesthoods all over the land. The new doctrine did not reach the masses. . . . After 17 years of heroic efforts . . . the old time religions still prevailed. Ikhnaten's [Akhenaten's] impact on the nation, however, was everlasting.[187]

In fact, his indirect impact on world intellectual history, rather than his impact on Egyptian religion, has been the enduring phenomenon. During the sixth year of his reign the young king and his wife moved from Thebes to a newly built city, Akhetaton or Tell el-Amarna. There a revolution in art styles occurred that his admirers and critics alike consider a highly significant event in art history. The Amarna emphasis on realistic portrayal of the royal family did not survive the Eighteenth Dynasty, but the productions of that period have become "art treasures."

The West African scholar Cheikh Anta Diop, in contrast to Afro-American Chancellor Williams, makes a singularly detached statement about this black pharaoh, stressing the point that Akhenaten sanctified the absolutism of the imperial dynasty with a universal religion that was made necessary by objective conditions. From the viewpoint of functional anthropologists, a belief in one God over all mankind was consistent with a government that professed to include all of mankind.[188] Wilson, like Chancellor Williams, makes an appraisal that combines sociocultural determinism with a recognition of Akhenaten's uniqueness as an innovative personality. He feels that an "irrepressible conflict" existed in Egyptian society between the priests of Re and the priests of Amon, and between both groups of priests and the pharaoh.

During the early years of the Eighteenth Dynasty a high degree of sophistication had developed among the upper social strata from extensive contact with their counterparts in other kingdoms and from the expansion of trade and contact between priests and scribes. That diplomatic correspondence during the reign of Akhenaten was carried out through a single medium of writing, cuneiform, is an index to the existence of a widespread "high culture." Sophistication bred a certain amount of skepticism and modes of thought approaching cultural relativism. Wilson, in analyzing Egyptian society of the time, notes:

> Certainly one admits that the tensions in Egypt were such that some violent crisis was inevitable, no matter who was pharaoh; but the peculiar trend of the crisis was very highly conditioned by the peculiar character of the pharaoh who came to the throne.

He refers to Akhenaten as an "iconoclast" and a "revolutionary." In the case of the great pharaoh,

> focus on the individual instead of the cultural process is justified because Akh-en-Aton was not an ordinary man, so that his high individuality in his position of power made him far more than a tool of the forces of his day; it is also justified because this pharaoh was the acknowledged leader of forces of the day.

But Wilson does not consider Akhenaten to be a person who had any lasting influence on Egyptian religion:

It must be emphasized that the Aton faith had no penetration below the level of the royal family as an effective religious expression; it was stated to be the exclusive faith of the god-king and his divine family, and the god-king welcomed and encouraged his subjects' worship of his divine being as the source of all the benefits which they might desire.

Wilson has no sympathy for the view that Judaism or Christianity have a monotheism similar to the religion of Akhenaten, for there were really two gods in the religion of the Sun King: "the Aton [sun] was concerned strictly with creating and maintaining life," but "ethics and religion derived from the pharaoh Akh-en-Aton." This dual-god concept was not at all alien to Egyptian thought so long as Aten worship did not make the worship of all other gods taboo. Wilson sees the weakness of the religious reform elsewhere:

> The self-centered nature of Akh-en-Aton's faith, the fact that only the royal family had a trained and reasoned loyalty to the Aton, and the fact that all of pharaoh's adherents were forced to give their entire devotion to him as a god-king explain why the new religion collapsed after Akh-en-Aton's death. . . . We cannot believe that they [the courtiers] cherished within their bosoms the teaching about a benevolent and sustaining sole god, the Aton, when all of their religious exercise was exhausted in worship of Akh-en-Aton. When that pharaoh died and the movement collapsed, they must have scrambled penitently back into the traditional faith, which they could understand and in which they were allowed wider devotion.[189]

Other black gods—Osiris and Isis—had never lost their popularity.

The older Egyptologists deemphasized evidence that Akhenaten was a Negro, or ignored that fact in writing for nonspecialist readers. Aldred belongs to a group with a new orientation. He reveals Akhenaten's race by his choice of illustrations for various publications. In several of these publications, prepared for the Brooklyn Museum, he provides evidence, wittingly or unwittingly, that should convince any doubters of Akhenaten's race. At one point in the catalog for a Brooklyn Museum exhibit, Aldred presents a photograph of a stone head excavated at Tel Amarna, which is now in the Egyptian collection of the University of London, under the title "Head of a Black Man" (plate 14). Aldred writes in his description that "it represents a black man with thick lips and prognathous jaw. This head unmistakably represents a man of one of the Nilotic tribes which the Egyptians subjugated during the New Kingdom." In another section of the same book, Aldred presents a bas-relief representation of Akhenaten that bears a striking resemblance to "Head of a Black Man" (plate 15). If one of these is Negro, the other surely must be also. He does not say so, but the evidence is there for perceptive readers.

In his description of the Akhenaten portrait, which most Africans would consider a familiar and acceptable somatic norm but which some Europeans would designate "typically Negro—ugly," Aldred points out "the distortions of the early style of Akhenaten's reign" and says they are "here shown in a manner that verges on caricature." He seems to be saying, in effect, that he does not believe that Akhenaten really could have looked that way. A slight Eurocentric esthetic bias is implicit in the choice of adjectives in his description:

> The narrow slanting eye, with the upper edge of the lid contoured, the long nose with slightly bulbous tip, the thick everted lips, the folds of flesh running from the nostrils toward the corners of the mouth, the elongated hanging jaw, the serpentine neck—these are all conventions characterizing portraits of the King in the early Amarna period.[190]

It is not clear why Aldred considers these traits "conventions" and not an example of "Truth—warts and all," on which Akhenaten insisted in the early Amarna period. Readers can decide for themselves whether or not the features of the king are any more "exaggerated" than those of the "Head of a Black Man," which is not defined as a caricature of the subject.

Nothing in any of Aldred's books about Egypt reveals racist orientations despite the obvious esthetic bias. Nevertheless, his book *Akhenaten* suggests that some of the pharaoh's anatomical features might have been the result of Fröhlich's disease. In particular, the discussion of Akhenaten's face gives the impression that Aldred sees abnormalities in it, although how much he would attribute to caricature by the sculptors and how much to the subject's actual traits seems not to be a matter settled in his own mind. Christiane Desroches-Noblecourt, another Egyptologist who is also certainly not a racist, commenting on this same representation of Ahkenaten, calls it a "symphony of degeneration." Her choice of words would suggest that it is not just the artistic style but also her own esthetic prejudices that make this portrait repulsive: "heavy features," "wide nostrils," "fleshy mouth."[191] These are all what are sometimes called "pronounced Negro features," and Desroches-Noblecourt, whose own antiracist credentials are beyond dispute, clearly does not favor that somatic norm image—regardless of whether it was a caricature of the pharaoh or whether he actually looked that way. Both Aldred and Desroches-Noblecourt seem to have esthetic biases against "pronounced Negro facial *features*," though they are not based on prejudice against black skin-color. Facial contours are the criteria for the esthetic rejection.

Numerous sculptured portraits of Akhenaten are available from several different periods, in both stylized and realistic form, some being finished pieces and some studio models. In one of Aldred's publications he has presented pictures of a broad sampling of this material. The profile in plate 14 might be compared with the bas-relief profile that both Aldred and Desroches-Noblecourt consider a caricature or a distortion. There is less of an "elongated hanging jaw," but the profile is essentially the same. Plate 16 presents a full-frontal view of a workshop model head. The "Negroidness" of the face is beyond dispute, and it would be more difficult to characterize it as "repulsive" by either Western or African norms than the profile that has excited so much pejorative comment. Yet even so enthusiastic an admirer of the pharaoh as the West Indian mulatto Joel A. Rogers, in a comment on a stylized representation that many Europeans would not find unattractive, made a remark that contains just a hint of his own European esthetic bias. Judged by prevailing standards, Akhenaten was not handsome, and Rogers notes that: "the jaw is exceedingly prognathous. His lips, as seen in profile, are so thick that they seem swollen." But in relation to the face as a whole, a purely esthetic appraisal might not dub the lips "swollen." Yet Rogers sees beauty of another kind in the face: "His bust in the Louvre shows a face of extraordinary sweetness, gentleness, and refinement."[192]

The lips shown in plate 17 are from a fragment of a statue made in a workshop known to have produced representations of Akhenaten. It is selected to emphasize his "Negroidness" from a number of pictures in Aldred's *Akhenaten and Nefertiti*, which presents numerous fragments of definitively Negro statues of the pharaoh. However, whether any of the representations are faithful, realistic portraits of Akhenaten it is impossible to know. Yet, whether in some of the portraits his features were exaggerated by the artists, distorted by Fröhlich's disease, or completely undistorted, there can be no doubt that the man lauded by the racist Egyptologist Breasted, as well as by the Jewish psychoanalyst Freud, was a Negro and he was not ashamed of that fact.

The Akhenaten interlude was of some importance in the subsequent history of Egypt, but it has much greater import for students of comparative religious history. It occupies a special place in the field of Black Studies. It also provides an important test case in examining evaluations that Egyptians placed on "Negroidness," and in studying reactions to those ancient evaluations by scholars who have inherited conceptions and attitudes about black people that make objectivity difficult to achieve. For the past two decades some Egyptologists have been in the process of making a break with the distortions and evasions of the past, the exhibition organized by the Brooklyn Museum and referred to here being a significant move in that direction. This is evident in a remark about Akhenaten's mother, reported in the *Time* magazine account of the opening ceremonies. It was stated that the exhibition included "a magnificent head in painted wood of the pharaoh's mother, Queen Tiye" (plate 18). Professor Bernard W. Bothmer, then the curator of the Brooklyn Museum, was said to have called her "a woman of color." In the American context this was, no doubt, a euphemism for "black woman" or "Negro woman." The article noted that a public display of this type had special significance for black schoolchildren, who were "flocking around all these pieces with obvious enthusiasm." The *Time* reporter recognized the meaning of these Eighteenth Dynasty sculptures to the children when he stated in ghetto argot that "one small statue of a 'Princess with Fruit' could be a funky black fox who just stepped off her I. Miller platforms."

American museums have not assigned a prominent place to either Akhenaten or his mother in their regular displays, although some of them have made Queen Nefertiti a familiar face to the American public through the presentation of replicas of the famous bust. Display advertising also has made use of the image of this attractive stylized head portraying Nefertiti as a graceful, lemon-colored woman with a swanlike neck and a softened variety of Caucasian features. By Western esthetic norms, she is beautiful, and it is assumed that the Egyptians thought she was too. This piece of art certainly merits the attention it has been given. However, insofar as museums are a part of our educational system as well as a recreational outlet for both adults and children, a case could be made for publicizing other members of the Akhenaten family as a contribution to our understanding of comparative race relations. Permanent educational exhibits at museums are not unknown. For instance, the Hall of Man in the Museum of Natural History in Chicago is a frank attempt to publicize concepts—the "unity of mankind" and the "brotherhood of man"—although in the arrangement and selection of some of its material it makes some varieties of man seem far less attractive than others.

An exhibit could be devised revealing the fact that Nefertiti was not the only type of woman who achieved prominence during the Eighteenth Dynasty, and that even if the somatic norm image she represents had been a favored one, lack of such color and features was not a barrier to upward mobility. One possible way to achieve such an educational goal would be to design an exhibit that would include at least four pieces of sculpture or pictorial representations: Queen Tiye, the Negro mother; her son, Pharaoh Akhenaten; his wife, Queen Nefertiti (who, incidentally, may not have been of Egyptian birth); and one of the daughters of Akhenaten and Nefertiti, and a granddaughter of Tiye (see plate 19a–d).

In considering such an assemblage of pieces, one must keep in mind the specific period of the pharaoh's reign during which each portrait was made. During the early years of Akhenaten's reign, conventional stylized art was in vogue. This was followed by the early Amarna period, which coincided with the ruler's adoption of revolutionary religious ideas. The concept of "Living in Truth," which he espoused, demanded highly realistic portraiture, including frank portrayals of aspects of the body that might strike some observers as ugly or that might deviate from whatever somatic norm image prevailed. The late Amarna period was more restrained. Aldred notes that the Amarna style also permitted considerable experimentation in posings and in portrayals of clothing. It also gave scope for individual sculptors to leave their imprint. Numerous examples are available in museums of representations of members of the royal family in all of these styles. Plate 19 represents a suggested educational grouping that emphasizes the "Negroidness" of Queen Tiye and one of her granddaughters, both done in a realistic style; at the same time it presents Akhenaten and Nefertiti in the familiar stylized forms.

It is important to note that the popular bust of Nefertiti is a stylization that underemphasizes her "Negroidness." Stylized portrayals from another period indicate Negroid facial features. In one case, however, these are not her own, but those of her husband placed on her body (plate 20). The workshops attached to the palaces at Amarna produced a number of heads of the queen, done in a realistic fashion, and these reveal a more Negroid Nefertiti than the well-known Berlin head portrays (plate 21). These portrayals might have less esthetic appeal to Caucasian tastes than the more conventional images of Nefertiti, but they would better serve "vindicationist" goals. In fact, in the most effective such presentation the stylized forms of both Akhenaten and his queen would be replaced by portraits from the early Amarna period, in which the attenuated Negroid features of the king that appear on monumental stylized pieces in the round are discarded in favor of the more Negroid features which the "Living in Truth" motto demanded.

The problem of trying to overcome deeply entrenched psychological resistance to facing the fact of the predominant Negroid strain in the Akhenaten family occurs not only with regard to the pharaoh but also in discussions about his mother, Queen Tiye, who, some insist, was not a Negro. Black scholars are certainly not prepared to have Queen Tiye declared "white" so long as the custom of denigrating black people still exists. To the charge that Blacks "make too much of the question," they respond, "Why have other scholars made it a matter of controversy among themselves? What was *their* hidden agenda?" On the basis of the famous wooden head in the Berlin Museum (plates 18 and 19a) Afro-American scholars have argued that Egyptologists, using some of their own criteria of craniometry, to be consistent, would have to call Queen Tiye "Negroid."

However, the controversy among anthropologists about Queen Tiye's race begins with argument about her parents. The mummies of her father, Yuya, and her mother, Thuya, have been found. The mother seems to have been a mulatto with Caucasoid hair but Negroid facial features; the father is described by Aldred as being "fairly tall for an Egyptian, a head of long wavy white hair, a large beaky nose and prominent lips." In further describing Yuya's face, he notes that "his unusual physiognomy, and the various spellings of his name, have induced some scholars to accredit him with a foreign origin." Of Queen Tiye's mother, Aldred writes that her appearance, "in contrast to that of her husband, was typically Egyptian, and she closely resembles the fellah women [rural Egyptian agricultural villagers]."[193] Because they both had estates in Upper Egypt, Christiane Desroches-Noblecourt speaks of the parents as "two provincial nobles of Nubian origin" who were "high ecclesiastical dignitaries" and prominent at the court of Amenhotep III. Their daughter, Tiye, became Amenhotep's queen and bore the son who became Akhenaten. She was his favorite wife and was a person of great influence at court.

Afro-American scholars find no problem in designating Tiye as "Negro" despite her having parents of the type described above. These scholars certainly have relatives or acquaintances in which a recombination of ancestral genes has produced a child considerably more Negroid in type than one or both of the parents. (Geneticists would easily concede this possibility if it were assumed that both parents carried some genes for Negro traits.) Some white Egyptologists—professional and amateur—do, however, find difficulty in classifying Queen Tiye as "Negro." Aldred, after describing the mummies of her parents, does not involve himself in the argument about Queen Tiye's physical type or race. Desroches-Noblecourt, on the other hand, in discussing the great power that Queen Tiye wielded, speaks of the "Nubian influence at the palace," which was increased because the court was "ruled by a queen almost certainly of their own race." Then, after citing the head in the Berlin Museum, she marshals more evidence:

> Her southern looks are even more pronounced in the portrait on a pendant (the *Menat* counter-poise) which was found during the excavations of her palace at Malkata, and another similar portrait found at Tell el Amarna. Finally there is little room for doubt left when one studies the small sardonyx tablet, now in the Metropolitan Museum, which depicts the queen as a female sphinx. The face clearly betrays her origins: it was recently compared with another image of her still to be seen at Sedeinga in Northern Sudan in the ruins of the temple dedicated to Tiye. Even the wigs of the royal ladies at Malkata as well as at Tell el Amarna were inspired by the short neat coiffures of the Nubians.[194]

A picture of a small, full-length statue (from the Metropolitan Museum collection) is presented in plate 22 that for many years was thought by some Egyptologists to be a youthful Queen Tiye. The woman wears a somewhat heavier and longer wig than the "short neat coiffure of the Nubians," although the texture of the hair is Nubian. The Metropolitan Museum of Art now accepts the position of its expert who first described the statuette as a "*Lady* Tiye," presumably not the Queen, but a member of the court circle who had the same name.

One American scholar, Barbara Mertz, although liberal in her views, expresses skepticism about Desroches-Noblecourt's argument that Queen Tiye was a Nubian Negro. She writes that "experts talk, expertly, about Negroid features on Ti's [Tiye's] portraits and the prominence of Nubians in the court hierarchy of the period and the popularity of the Nubian hair styles. These last are meaningless points, even if they are correct." She is scornful of those who make judgments from statuary, rejecting the very evidence that impresses others: "the description of the Berlin head as Negroid is highly subjective. The features do not show the characteristics defined as Negroid by physical anthropologists." In explaining why "the view that Queen Tiye was a Nubian is more popular in Egyptological circles than the blue-eyed version," Mertz imputes an unconscious bias to those who hold such a view:

> There is, in the Berlin Museum, a famous head which is usually identified as that of Queen Ti. It is a wonderful piece of work. . . . Because

it is so expert, so evocative, it makes a lasting impression. It is carved of black wood. I am sure that it would be doing the Egyptologists who make Ti a Nubian an injustice to claim that they think of her as black just because this great forceful face is black. However, I have a strong suspicion that such is the case.[195]

Aldred presents a profile of this head side by side with a Negroid profile gold mask of Tutankhamen and notes that "the strong family resemblance between them suggests a mother-son relationship." He proceeds to say, however, that the wooden head may be that of a daughter of Amenhotep III and Tiye, not of Tiye herself.[196] The uncertainty about the Metropolitan Museum statuette and the Berlin head may leave some doubt about how Negroid Queen Tiye's appearance actually was, but Aldred's juxtaposition of the photographs emphasizes the obvious. This *family* was Negroid, as was the entire Eighteenth Dynasty. The most highly respected contemporary Egyptologists admit that.

The Egyptian Penetration of Nubia

Desroches-Noblecourt takes it for granted that the Nubian ancestry Queen Tiye is presumed to have had means that she was "Black." Barbara Mertz disagrees. The attempt to "talk away" the blackness of Nubians perhaps reached an extreme in the case of a prominent American anthropologist, William Y. Adams. First, he clarifies a disputed point:

> There is no longer, today, any satisfactory reason for believing that the modern Nubians are a different people from the Nubians of antiquity or of any intervening period. On the contrary, I think everything points to their being the same people. That their numbers have been swelled by immigration, warlike as well as peaceful, from the north and from the south, goes without saying.

Then, referring specifically to their color, he states: "I have seldom referred to the Nubians as 'black,' not out of any racial sensitivity, but because they have only intermittently been 'black.'" Professor Adams goes on to develop a social-psychological definition of "blackness" paralleling that of Black Nationalists in the United States, who have to make room for fellow "Blacks" with blue eyes, blond hair, and Caucasoid features, while excluding "Oreos," who are "brown on the outside but have 'white minds.'" Adams continues, defining the term "intermittently" with amazing intellectual gyrations:

> By that I do not mean that their skin color and facial features have changed significantly in the historic period; I believe in fact that they

have remained pretty much the same since the earliest times. But race is largely in the eye of the beholder; it is more a matter of social ascription than of biology, and its defining characteristics have changed from age to age and from place to place. *To be technically accurate the Nubians are mostly of a chocolate-brown color; one could and can see them either as "black" or as "white" according to the prejudices of one's time and temperament.* There certainly have been periods when they have been subject to prejudice and oppression as a result of their dark skin color and when to call them "black" would be sociologically meaningful in today's terms. There have also been times when they were subject to the same attitude and treatment not because of their skin color but because they were unlettered barbarians, or because they were Christians surrounded by Moslems. There have been other times when the Nubians have joined with their northern neighbors in oppressing and exploiting the much darker peoples of inner Africa, and when it would be more sociologically meaningful to call them "white" [emphasis added].[197]

Because the Eighteenth Dynasty was one of those periods of imperialist expansion in Palestine as well as in Kush, the Egypto-Nubian coalition was presumably "Black" when it was attacking the Middle East but "white" when it was attacking the black barbarians to the south and west of Kush through Wawat!

Adams stresses the exploitative aspects of the Egyptian-Nubian relationship, insisting that, during the Eighteenth Dynasty, for all practical purposes, Nubia became colonized Egyptian territory and its people were Egyptian subjects. The evidence sustains his assessment that, having acquired this vast and lucrative domain—equal in size to Egypt itself and far exceeding in size the imperial domains in Asia—the pharaoh set out to govern and exploit it, and ultimately to Egyptianize it. The search for gold was a dominating concern. In the end these efforts succeeded beyond expectation, with an effect that was to be felt in Egypt for centuries to come. There was a tradition held by some Egyptians and Kushites alike that Egypt had originally been settled by people from the Kushitic area who went north as "civilizers." Now, even if this had once been true, the roles were reversed. Egypt was now "civilizing" people it considered "backward."

Egyptian cultural imperialism there certainly was—and it involved economic exploitation of Nubia as well—but there was no color discrimination involved. Some of the pharaohs were as dark or darker than any of their Nubian subjects, and a deliberate effort was made to bring Nubians into the ruling circles in Egypt—but as Egyptians. The Egyptian masses and Nubian masses were both exploited, although Egyptians were never enslaved. Some Nubians undoubtedly were enslaved, but slavery was not racial. European and Asian war captives predominated in Egypt and in Nubian gold mines as slaves.

Nefertari, the Black founding Queen Mother of the Eighteenth Dynasty, symbolized the ties between the Egyptians of the Thebaid and the people of Nubia (i.e., of Kush, which later came to be called Ethiopia). Indeed, during her time a temple to Amon was built near the fourth Nile cataract. The pharaoh's armies subsequently pushed into the heartland of the Kushite kingdom at Jebel Barkal. In addition to forming religious shrine cities and trading centers in Nubia with Egyptian settlers, the pharaoh's emissaries organized a flow of Nubians back to Egypt on a large scale. Dancing girls and concubines, agricultural workers, boatmen, and fishermen, along with high-status individuals, appear on the painted and sculptured walls of tombs and monuments coming to pledge allegiance and pay tribute. A viceroy of Nubia was appointed under Tutankhamen, and a beautiful painting was found well preserved on the wall of his tomb, showing Nubian princes bringing tribute to the pharaoh. They are depicted in a wide range of colors and features, wearing distinctive national clothing (plate 23). They are accompanied by individuals whose clothing and hair styles mark them off as being of a different stratum and whose roles in the frescoes define them as servants if not slaves (figs. 3 and 4). Some Egyptologists think "uncivilized" ethnic groups from south of Nubia were raided by the princes to secure slaves for the tribute.

A new institution was created to establish bonds between the pharaoh's court and a group of selected individuals from Nubia. It was called the Kap, and Desroches-Noblecourt describes it as a "military organization, probably set up within the palace precincts, at any rate during the New Empire, to educate the sons of Nubian princes brought to the metropolis (Thebes) after the Pharaoh's punitive expeditions." Nubian prisoners of war may have been working in the fields, but it was a different story for these upper-class Nubians:

> Although under strict discipline, these "sons of rebels" were treated with great consideration, sharing the education of the pharaoh's own sons, and later, imbued with the most harmonious culture of high antiquity, [were] allowed to place their experience at the disposal of their native country.

The priests of Amon at Karnak and Thebes, and the pharaohs whom they supported, as well as the rival priesthood of Aten who supported Akhenaten, played for big stakes during the Eighteenth Dynasty: control of the entire civilized world and the pools of barbarian

FIGURE 3. Nubian Slaves and Their Families Being Counted by an Official: Eighteenth Dynasty. Reprinted from Nott and Gliddon, *Types of Mankind* (1855).

FIGURE 4. Drummers and Dancers from Wawat and Kush: Eighteenth Dynasty. Reprinted from Nott and Gliddon, *Types of Mankind* (1855).

slave labor on its fringes. The geographical position of Egypt dictated a foreign policy in which the "barbarians" to the south were at first exploited in order to mobilize power for an attempted conquest of the Syrian-Palestinian and Mesopotamian "civilizations." Gold, soldiers, and masses of laborers were collected in the south, and Nubia-Kush-Ethiopia was Egyptianized culturally in the process.

However, the ruling families of Kush eventually made a bid for acceptance as equal partners. During the Eighteenth Dynasty they influenced Egypt through Nubian queens and concubines and the strategically placed "Children of Kap," many of whom indeed "spent their entire lives in the palace and tutored the children of the king whose academic and military education they had shared." Desroches-Noblecourt states that they were

> invaluable to the rulers of the XVIIIth Dynasty, although they never abandoned their ties with their mother-country nor with one another. . . . Most of them became assistants to the Viceroy of Nubia, but others chose careers in the Pharaonic armies, and as childhood companions of the royal princes often remained attached to their persons at court.[198]

They helped to prepare their own country for becoming a host to Egyptian refugees when Asian and European invaders moved into the Nile Valley from the north, and for using the Kingdom of Kush as a base for recapturing power in the Egyptian homeland. During the Twenty-Fifth Dynasty, Kush and Egypt were merged and an Ethiopian or Kushitic Dynasty of Pharaohs sat on the throne.

"Civilization" from north of the first cataract of the Nile had been constantly interpenetrating the lands of the Nehesi to the south (where much of Egypt's core culture had originated), carried by priests, soldiers, and Nile sailors even before the Eighteenth Dynasty. A complex acculturational process went on within Egypt on one hand and in Kush on the other. Trade, military conquest, and contact between working people, spread customs in both directions. (One Egyptologist refers, for instance, to the Nubian wig as an item of fashion during the Eighteenth Dynasty that diffused northward.) The acculturation process was highly accelerated during this dynasty, when it was deliberately fostered.

The priests of Amon cultivated the goodwill of the Napatan rulers in Kush, who eventually took the opportunity to loosen their ties with Egyptian *political* authority when it was usurped by outsiders. Simultaneously they strengthened their relations with the *religious* authorities of Upper Egypt. Thus the Eighteenth Dynasty, allied with

Theban priests, laid the foundation for an independent kingdom of Kush. These Nubian rulers threw off Egyptian suzerainty after the "Glorious Eighteenth" collapsed, but they did not break their ties with the Theban princes and the priesthood of Amon.

The Social Impact of the Eighteenth Dynasty

During the twelfth or thirteenth year of Akhenaten's reign, some tragedy occurred within the royal family that seems to have resulted in hostility between Queen Tiye and Nefertiti, and perhaps in a rift between the royal couple. Then, for four years, the pharaoh and his younger brother occupied the throne together. With Akhenaten's death, this brother, Smenkhare, became the eleventh ruler of the Eighteenth Dynasty. His reign was very brief, being followed by that of another young king, Tutankhamen. It was during his reign that the restoration to power of the priests of Amon began. It is possible that Queen Tiye was a factor in the reversal of her son's reforms. Ay, who followed Tutankhamen, began to destroy as much of the visible evidence of Akhenaten's rule as he could, with special attention being given to completely effacing the symbolism of Aten worship.[199]

No kings of the "Glorious Eighteenth," including Akhenaten, who was concerned with theological, philosophical, and artistic reforms, attempted to make any alterations in the social system. Whether under a pharaoh who tried to introduce the worship of one god, or under the priests of Amon, "Egypt was faced with social conflicts of great scope," as Diop phrases it. The causes of these problems were "excesses of bureaucratic agents, the crushing weight of taxation, and the poverty of the people." When there was no integrating force of a strong, respected pharaoh after the death of Akhenaten, internal conflict sharpened. The head of the army, Horemheb, with the sanction of the priests of Amon, had himself proclaimed pharaoh after Ay and became the last of the kings of the Eighteenth Dynasty. He was remembered as one who "decided to espouse social justice." He "enacted a series of laws intended to protect the weak and improve their living conditions. These laws were designed to punish government employees, soldiers, and judges guilt of theft or fraud against little people."[200] But the dynasties that followed Horemheb emphasized foreign conquest, not social reform.

THE RAMESSIDE AGE AND THE DECLINE OF THE EMPIRE

With Horemheb's death the Eighteenth Dynasty came to an end. His vizier, or prime minister, an army colleague, became the pharaoh known to history as Rameses I. He was the first king of the Rames-side Age, which covered a period of 235 years and included two dy-nasties of thirteen kings and one queen. Rameses I immediately marched his troops into Palestine and Syria in a reassertion of the Egyptian power that had waned after Akhenaten became pharaoh and neglected his alliances. Seti I and Rameses II completed the restora-tion of Egyptian political influence in these areas. They also strength-ened the Egyptian grip on Nile River fortresses in Wawat and Kush. Thus the traditional boundaries of the empire were restored. Wealth began to flow into Egypt once more over Nubian trade routes as trib-ute from conquered areas. Egypt's dominant role in the Middle East seemed secure.

During the sixty-seven years of his reign, Rameses II not only brought military renown to Egypt once again; he also renovated monuments to gods other than Re, which had been defaced during the period of the Akhenaten reforms. He lavished attention upon the tem-ples of Amon in Thebes and at Jebel Barkal, in Nubia, but he was also careful not to neglect the temples of other gods. He was particularly solicitous about shrines to favorite Delta deities, since the loyalty of that area was essential to successful ventures in the Palestinian-Syrian territories. Next to Tutankhamen and Akhenaten, Rameses is the pharaoh most highly publicized in modern times, in part because of the widespread belief—probably erroneous—that he was the wicked pharaoh who enslaved the Jewish people. Most recently the UNESCO-sponsored salvage operation of the Abu Simmel temple near the Egyptian-Sudanese border focused attention upon Rameses II as the builder of that massive structure upon which his likeness is sculptured in several places in monumental style, displaying, in some cases, a degree of "Negroidness" lacking in many other representa-tions of this same pharaoh. The variation may be due to differences between treatment in certain kinds of stone and painting.

When Seti I and Rameses II fought to consolidate Egyptian power in the areas bordering the eastern Mediterranean Sea, they involved the Nile Valley kingdoms in a struggle for control of the entire "civi-lized world" west of India and China. It was a world whose elites shared in an international "high culture," with cuneiform writing used for diplomatic correspondence, and with a cosmology, mythol-ogy, and pantheon made up of many common elements despite local variations. The folk cultures throughout this area, which were numerous, displayed ethnic and tribal differences. The Egyptian Em-pire, as first established by the pre-Akhenaten pharaohs of the Eigh-teenth Dynasty, had included the areas to the north of Egypt that appear on today's maps as Palestine, Lebanon, and Israel, and to the south as the Republic of Sudan. The empire had been formed by forcing the rulers of several kingdoms, among them Tyre, Sidon, Damascus, and others with names less familiar, to accept Egyptian military garrisons on their soil and to pay regular tribute.[201] In return they were offered protection from other potential invaders, such as the Hittites, Arab tribes, Assyrians, Babylonians, and numerous "sea peoples." Vassal rulers were quick to complain when Egypt did not give the military protection they expected—even against local rival kingdoms—or did not supply gold in barter arrangements or in the form of gifts.[202]

By the ninth century B.C. Egypt had become an integral part of the system of states that had evolved as "civilized" communities emerged in the Nile Valley and Mesopotamia in the post-Neolithic era. A portion of the agricultural surplus in each was expended upon feeding troops involved in the process of empire building. A rudimentary code of international relations developed. By the time the Eighteenth Dynasty collapsed, this system of states included Egypt, Babylon, Elam, and the Hittite kingdom as the dominant expanding units. Later, Assyria would bid for dominance and Kush, Israel, and Judea would play important roles, along with a number of Arabian, Syrian, and Mesopotamian kingdoms that formed shifting alliances in an attempt to avoid paying tribute to one or another of the "Great Powers" (see map 4).

The larger states competed with each other for control of the entire area from the Mediterranean Sea to the Persian Gulf, as well as the Nile Valley. These ancient imperialists were ruthless, unleashing their mercenary armies against each other in an orgy of looting, burning, and raping. When a victory had been achieved, tribute was exacted from the conquered peoples in the form of precious metals and gems, slaves, and valuable commodities, including rare woods and metallurgical and ceramic products, foodstuffs, and brewed or fermented beverages. Wives, concubines, and eunuchs were required for the households of the mighty, and often an exchange of these between monarchs sealed the peace, as did dynastic marriages. The "civilized" states conquered, enslaved, and exploited the "barbarians" on the fringes of the empires, often reviling them for their "barbarism" but, nevertheless, recruiting mercenary soldiers from among them and taking hostages whom they "civilized" and sent back as proconsuls. Such relations between Egypt and Nubia have been described in this chapter as one example of this process, in which, as late as the eighth century B.C., neither Rome nor the Greek city-states yet participated.

While individual Greek city-states established colonies on Mediterranean islands and in Asia Minor, they were not organized for imperial conquest.

Although each state within this world system retained its distinctive ethos, the process of cultural borrowing went on continuously
and miscegenation took place on a vast scale. The marauding soldiers
were major contributors to the gene flow. The spread of Egyptian culture, along with genes for Negro physical traits, was one consequence
of the constant invasion of the states along the eastern Mediterranean
seaboard. Assyria and Babylon deported and resettled tens of thousands of people from this area, and from Egypt as well, thus modify-
ing both the cultures and genetic composition of Mesopotamia.[203]
Some of these ancient ethnic groups have disappeared; others are involved in contemporary nationalistic struggles in the Middle East that
have an ethnic origin.

One ethnic group, whose descendants are now known as the Jewish people, has been scattered throughout the world; but it has kept
its identity through distinctive family and communal beliefs and
rituals grounded in the monotheistic Hebrew religion out of which
both Christianity and Islam developed. Because of the close relations
of the Jewish people with Egypt and other parts of Africa for over
1,500 years, their early history is of special relevance to a study of the
Black Experience in antiquity. From the period of the Nineteenth
Egyptian Dynasty until the first century of Roman rule in the Middle East, the leaders of the Jewish people tried to build and maintain
a nation in a very vulnerable position at the western tip of the Fertile Crescent, close to the border of Egypt. They occupied an area that
both the Mesopotamian powers and the Egyptian rulers considered essential to their respective imperial aspirations, and that the latter
deemed vital for the defense of the Nile Valley against invasion. The
Jews were thus constantly subjected to military attacks. When Rome
decided to destroy the refractory, although truncated, Jewish state in
A.D. 70, the great diaspora to the west was precipitated. During the
previous thousand years a series of disasters had resulted in the destruction of a portion of the nation and the carrying off of tens of thousands of Jews into the Mesopotamian diaspora.

The intellectual and spiritual leaders of the Jewish people interpreted these disasters as punishment by their god, Jehovah, for sins
that included lack of concern for the weak by the powerful and injustice to the poor by the wealthy, as well as periodic deviations from
the rigid monotheism their god had prescribed for his "Chosen People." By 500 B.C. several civilizations had produced lawgivers, sages,

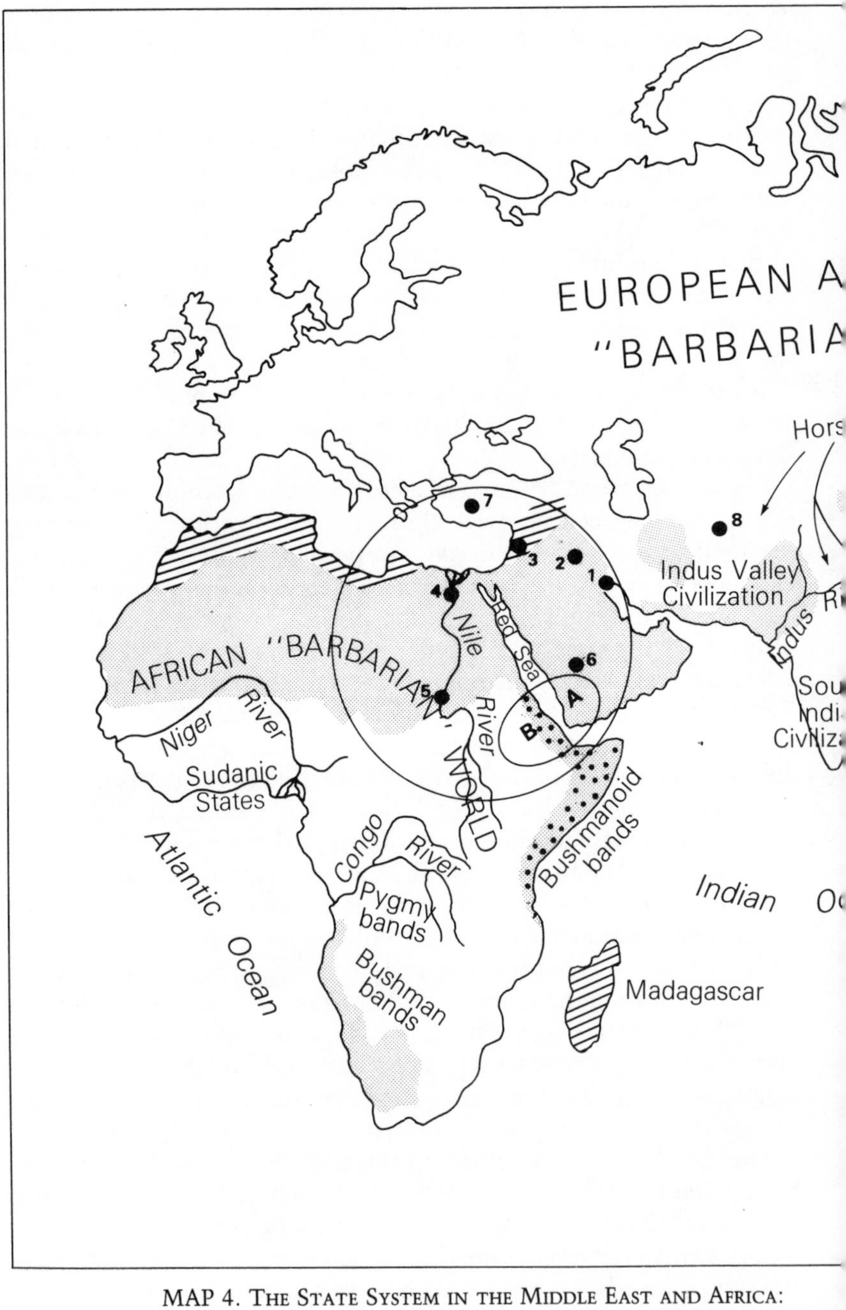

MAP 4. THE STATE SYSTEM IN THE MIDDLE EAST AND AFRICA:
NINTH CENTURY B.C. Cartography based on a concept by the author.

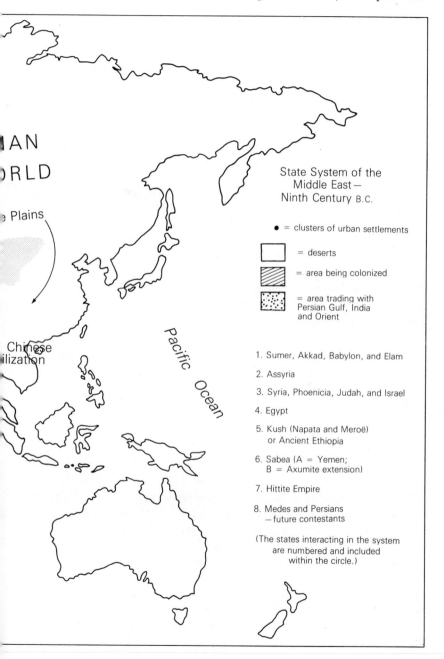

IAN
RLD

Plains

Chinese
ilization

Pacific Ocean

State System of the Middle East — Ninth Century B.C.

● = clusters of urban settlements

☐ = deserts

▨ = area being colonized

▦ = area trading with Persian Gulf, India and Orient

1. Sumer, Akkad, Babylon, and Elam

2. Assyria

3. Syria, Phoenicia, Judah, and Israel

4. Egypt

5. Kush (Napata and Meroë) or Ancient Ethiopia

6. Sabea (A = Yemen; B = Axumite extension)

7. Hittite Empire

8. Medes and Persians — future contestants

(The states interacting in the system are numbered and included within the circle.)

and teachers who taught compassion and justice for the powerless and poor within the nation. None, however, except the Jews had ever linked the survival of the nation with the implementation of these teachings. No others had ever dared to suggest that eventually justice would prevail everywhere and that the warfare that plagued the earth would cease. From the eighth through the sixth centuries B.C., prophets in Judah and Israel proclaimed the coming of some future age when "men would beat their swords into ploughshares and their spears into pruning hooks" and would make war no more. Scholars agree that prolonged residence in Egypt contributed toward the elaboration of Judaic ethical concepts and perhaps their monotheism as well. However, it was their travail as a nation—to which Egypt contributed—that evoked the great insights and visions of the prophets that had universal as well as ethnic significance.

The Jews, as a people, do not appear in either mythic history or actual history until the time of Egypt's Second Intermediate Period. Then sometime between the founding of the Eighteenth Dynasty and the end of the Twenty-fifth, they enter recorded history as the descendants of one of several wandering Semitic-speaking pastoral groups on the margins of the Fertile Crescent.[204] This group had come to Egypt during a famine to seek food, but its members were later enslaved. They left Egypt, in what is usually referred to as the Exodus, sometime during the Ramesside age. After wandering in the Sinai wilderness for some years, they fought their way across the Jordan River and into Canaan.[205] This was a highly urbanized western portion of the Fertile Crescent, but it had enough arable land around the "walled cities" and the "fenced cities" to support additional agricultural settlers. The newcomers claimed that a large part of this "Land of Canaan" had been promised to them by Jehovah before the famine forced their ancestors to enter Egypt in search of food.[206] Through victorious battle against some of the Canaanites, and by the negotiation of strategic alliances with others, the newcomers were able to carve out a small kingdom best known in later years for legends about its third king, Solomon, the son of David. After a brief period of acceptance as a state of some importance by other Middle Eastern kingdoms and by Egypt, the Hebrew nation fell apart into two kingdoms—Israel in the north and Judah in the south.[207] These two states, being located at the crossroads between Southeast Asia and Egypt, and at the vortex of the conflict that swirled continuously as empires fought for dominance, were battered and eventually broken.

The Mesopotamian powers were determined to control the entire eastern seaboard of the Mediterranean in order to have unhampered access to the sea and to the wealth of the Nile Valley. The Egyptian and Ethiopian rulers were equally determined to push these empire builders back into Mesopotamia, and they thought of Israel, Judah, Syria, and the Canaanite kingdoms as states that must constitute the spearheads in a thrust against Assyria and Babylon. From the time of the first Assyrian moves into Syria during the Twenty-first Dynasty, Egyptian pharaohs, priests, local rulers, and merchants made the containment of Assyria the cornerstone of their foreign policy. This meant that they would have to attempt to regain the hegemony north of Egypt that the early Eighteenth Dynasty pharaohs had once had. The effort to do so had actually begun earlier.

Wilson considers the ethos of the Ramesside period one in which "actions based on a fear psychosis" evoked by the Hyksos invasions gave way to "a crusade, the acceptance of a 'manifest' destiny to extend one culture in domination over another."[208] This was especially true in relations with Kush. But there were more materialistic reasons, too, for this "crusade." The priests of Egypt had a vested interest in the Ramesside conquests, because as a reward for their blessings, the conquering pharaohs showered booty upon them in the form of captured wealth and slave manpower. As Wilson summarizes it: "The previously modest temples in Egypt grew in physical size, in personnel, in land, and in total property, until they became the dominating factor in Egyptian political, social and economic life."[209] The priests of Amon at Thebes became the most powerful of all.

During the reign of Rameses XI, a military man named Heri-hor took the title "First Prophet of Amon" and, supported by the army and the clergy, forced the pharaoh to share power with him. The rulers of Kush supported this coup. Then, as Egyptologist Sauneron phrases it, "progressively the official sovereign seems to disappear" and "hardly any more is said of Rameses. . . . The Ramesside monarchy has evacuated, replaced for awhile by the clergy of Amon."[210] Cheikh Anta Diop chooses not to stress this influence of the black south during the reign of Rameses XI but emphasizes, rather, events in the Delta. Here were settled "branded white slaves" taken by the first four Ramesside rulers in the victories won against the "sea peoples," the Asians, and the Libyans. They, and their descendants manumitted from slavery, had accumulated considerable wealth and power. Diop states that "their freed descendants, from the time of Psammetichus on, were to seal Egypt's doom." If this is accepted simply as fact, without imputing any ideologies of "white supremacy," and if "doom" means simply falling under foreign domination, the Diop interpretation seems to be substantiated by other sources.[211]

Egypt became increasingly "whitened" by Libyans, Greeks, Persians, and Romans.

The first large contingent of such slaves was captured by Mernepthah, the successor to Rameses II, who had to fight off massive attacks of seaborne invaders from Mediterranean islands and their allies who were attacking eastward from Libya. Some of the people who later became organized politically as the Phoenicians may have been among them. Mernepthah defeated the invaders and then carried the battle into the land of the Canaanites and the Israelites (he is the first Egyptian ruler to call them by that name), and to Tyre, Sidon, and Syria. His stele exults over the destruction he caused:

> Tekenu is laid waste. Khatti is pacified. Canaan is pillaged. Ascalon is despoiled. Gezer is captured. Yenoam is annihilated. *Israel is made desolate and no longer has any crops.* Kaharu has become like a widow without any support against Egypt. All the countries are unified and pacified [italics added].[212]

After Mernepthah, the next fourteen rulers, when faced with invasions, preferred to relinquish control of lands north of Egypt and to concentrate upon the defense of the Delta. To this end, a fleet for executing coastal raids was constructed. Four massive coalitions of northern people attacked Egypt during a period of 120 years, and all these assaults were successfully resisted. Four times troops had to be brought up from the black South in Egypt and from Nubia to win these victories. Rameses III destroyed the enemy fleet of the fourth coalition in 1191 B.C., following which he established the practice of conscripting one Egyptian out of ten, along with auxiliaries recruited from among prisoners of war, to help defend the country. Referring to the enemy coalition that challenged but was defeated by Rameses III, Diop notes:

> The most formidable coalition ever witnessed during Antiquity was formed against the Egyptians. It comprised the whole group of white-skinned peoples who had been unstable since the first migrations in the thirteenth century. . . . *Yet this was not a racial conflict in the modern sense.* To be sure the two hostile groups were fully conscious of their ethnic and racial differences, but it was much more a question of the great movement of disinherited peoples of the north toward richer and more advanced countries [italics added].[213]

Diop sees two countertrends operating to weaken Egypt as a result of these repeated conflicts: an immense strengthening of the centralized state, allied with the priests of Amon, which became increasingly oppressive; and, on the other hand, "feudalization," the tendency of individual princes in the Delta nomes to ignore the interests of the entire Egyptian nation and to maximize their profits from trade with the Mediterranean countries. One index to the severity of these stresses and strains was a series of strikes near the end of the Twentieth Dynasty, the most dramatic of which occurred among the workers who took care of the burial grounds of the kings in the Thebaid. They marched on Thebes and presented their demands for greater supplies of food. When the high priest of Amon interceded for them, their demands were met. Meanwhile, undisciplined workers were breaking into tombs and stealing valuable grave goods.[214] The end of the Twentieth Dynasty marked the end of the Ramesside Age and the New Kingdom. Thus commenced the beginning of another one of the recurrent "low periods" in Egyptian history.

During the 140 years of the Twenty-first Dynasty, which followed the Ramesside Age, seven so-called "Tanite" kings ruled from the Delta city of Tanis with the support of Europeans and Asians whose ancestors were former prisoners of war. The basic constituency of these kings was an old Delta population that had always been involved in a contest with the south for control over a unified Kingdom of the Two Lands. However, the Tanite kings were content to claim sovereignty over a weakened South without attempting to invade it.

Meanwhile, the kings of Kush, well aware of the military weakness of the Tanite dynasty, took advantage of Egypt's internal division to assert complete independence. While accepting the spiritual hegemony of Amon's priests at Thebes and Jebel Barkal, they refused any longer to take orders from any Egyptian viceroy. Thus the kingdom that the Greeks would eventually call Ethiopia first asserted its full sovereignty during this Twenty-first Egyptian Dynasty. It apparently had two capitals: one at Napata, the old headquarters of the Kushite kings who had first accepted the overlordship of Egypt; and a newer capital at Meroë, near the sixth Nile cataract.

While the priests of Amon and the local princes of Upper Egypt were preventing the Delta dynasty of Tanite kings from exercising effective control over them, and the kingdom of Kush was completing the process of asserting its independence, another group of fourteen princes (bearing Libyan names) took power at Tanis as the Twenty-second Dynasty—the "Libyan" kings—a process that had begun during the late Ramesside age. Simultaneously, at Thebes, what Manetho called the Twenty-third Dynasty ruled over the southern portion of Egypt. An informal understanding prevailed by which the priests of Thebes gave limited recognition to the Tanite rulers so long as they kept their military forces out of the south and did not try to tax southerners.

The Twenty-second Dynasty, unable to exert any influence in southern Egypt or Nubia, began to pursue an active policy in the lands north of the Egyptian border that had once been under Egyptian dominance. The best-known Tanite pharaoh, Shoshonk, tried to use the recently established Jewish nation, whose king was Solomon, as a fulcrum for political leverage. He opened up an epoch of intervention in Hebrew state affairs that was to have significant but tragic consequences. And he has been accused of generating antagonisms that lasted for centuries. But, from his perspective, the actions may have been considered necessary for Nile Valley defense.

There are a number of legends about the period of Solomon's reign involving the relations of his kingdom with other parts of Africa than Egypt. For example, the late Haile Selassie of the East African highland kingdom of Abyssinia (Ethiopia) was known as "King of Kings, Conquering Lion of Judah, Elect of God and Heir to the Throne of Solomon and the Queen of Sheba." The emperor carefully fostered the ancient legend that the queen returned from her famous journey to Jerusalem pregnant and bore a son, Menelik, who eventually went back to Solomon's kingdom and carried away the Ark of the Covenant from the land of his father. The Ark presumably remained somewhere in the Ethiopian highlands, the land of his mother. This Abyssinian version of the queen's visit locates her homeland in East Africa. Josephus called her the "Queen of the South" and located her kingdom in the upper Nile kingdom of Ethiopia, whereas some Muslim accounts place the Queen of Sheba's realm in Yemen. (Origin myths compounded the confusion.) No version except the Abyssinian one includes the story of the birth of an illegitimate son who returned to Solomon's kingdom and ran away with the Ark. Immanuel Velikovsky developed an elaborate argument in *Ages in Chaos* in an attempt to prove that the Queen of Sheba was Hatshepsut, the Egyptian Eighteenth Dynasty queen.

In any case, Solomon had his legendary trials and tribulations as well as his triumphs. A rebel leader named Jeroboam tried to stir up a revolt in one of Solomon's provinces and was forced to flee into exile. He found refuge in Egypt, where Pharaoh Shoshonk (the biblical Shishak) welcomed him and gave him the sister of one of his wives for his own wife. Nevertheless, Shoshonk managed also to retain friendly relations with Solomon, to whom he gave one of his own daughters for a wife for whom, according to the Old Testament, Solo-

PLATES

PLATE 1. Sphinx: Early 1800s. Reprinted from Vivant Denon, *Travels in Upper and Lower Egypt* (Arno Press, [1803] 1963).

PLATE 2. Sᴘʜɪɴx: Eᴀʀʟʏ 1970s. Courtesy Cyril Aldred.

PLATE 3. Isis Suckling Horus. Courtesy Runoko Rashidi.

PLATE 4. Osiris as Judge of the Dead. Courtesy Musée du Louvre, Paris.

PLATE 5. A THIRD DYNASTY KING: DJOSER. Photograph by Victor Boswell.
Courtesy the National Geographic Society and the
Egyptian National Museum, Cairo.

PLATE 6. Unknown King of Third Dynasty.
Courtesy Brooklyn Museum.

PLATE 7. FOURTH DYNASTY KING: MYCERINUS.
Courtesy Museum of Fine Arts, Boston.

a.

b.

PLATE 8. FOURTH DYNASTY PRINCESS: A WIFE OF CHEOPS'S SON.
Courtesy Museum of Fine Arts, Boston.
a. PROFILE
b. FRONTAL VIEW

PLATE 9. Fifth Dynasty Architect: Nekhebu.
Courtesy Museum of Fine Arts, Boston.

PLATE 10. PRINCESS KEMSIT AND MALE SERVANT. Courtesy Committee of the Egypt Exploration Society, London.

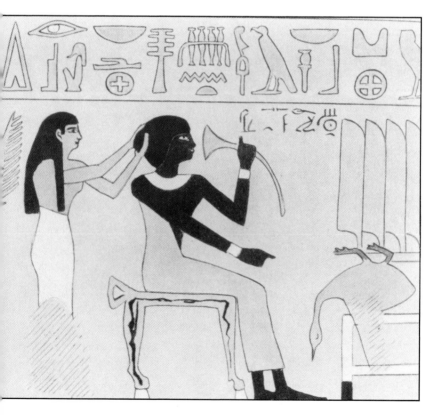

PLATE 11. PRINCESS KEMSIT AND FEMALE SERVANT. Courtesy Committee of the Egypt Exploration Society, London.

PLATE 12. Sᴇsᴏsᴛʀɪs I Dᴇᴘɪᴄᴛᴇᴅ ᴀs Osɪʀɪs.
Courtesy American Research Center in Egypt, Inc.

PLATE 13. An Eighteenth Dynasty Pharaoh: Thutmose II or
Amenhotep III. Reproduced by courtesy of the
Trustees of the British Museum.

PLATE 14.
HEAD OF A BLACK MAN. UC. 009. Courtesy Petrie Museum,
University College, London.

PLATE 15. AKHENATEN: EARLY AMARNA SCULPTURE.
Courtesy Ägyptisches Museum, Berlin (West).

PLATE 16. AKHENATEN: LATE AMARNA SCULPTURE.
Courtesy Ägyptisches Museum, Berlin (West).

PLATE 17. Akhenaten: Fragment from a Late Amarna Sculpture.
Courtesy the Metropolitan Museum of Art, New York.

PLATE 18. QUEEN TIYE: THE BERLIN HEAD.
Courtesy Ägyptisches Museum, Berlin (West).

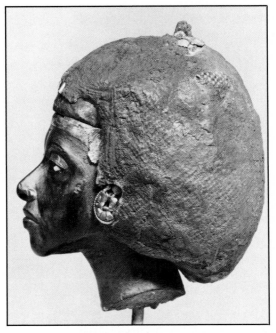

a.

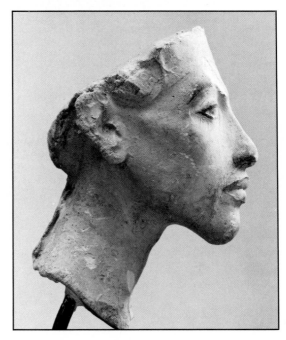

b.

PLATE 19. THREE GENERATIONS OF THE EIGHTEENTH DYNASTY
a. QUEEN TIYE. Courtesy Ägyptisches Museum, Berlin (West).
b. AKHENATEN. Courtesy Ägyptisches Museum, Berlin (West).
c. NEFERTITI. Courtesy Ägyptisches Museum, Berlin (West).
d. PRINCESS MERYT-ATEN, DAUGHTER OF AKHENATEN AND NEFERTITI.
Courtesy Metropolitan Museum of Art, New York.

PLATE 20. Nefertiti Worshiping the Aten. Courtesy Brooklyn Museum.

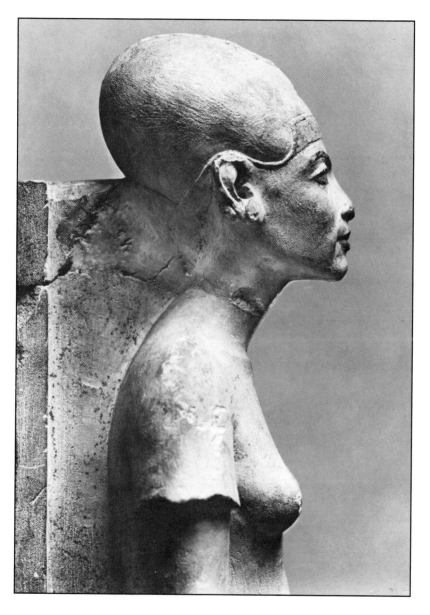

PLATE 21. NEFERTITI: UNFINISHED SCULPTURE.
Courtesy Egyptian National Museum, Cairo.

PLATE 22. Lady Tiye: Metropolitan Museum Statuette
Courtesy the Metropolitan Museum of Art, New York.

PLATE 23. YOUNG NUBIAN PRINCES BRINGING TRIBUTE:
EIGHTEENTH DYNASTY. Courtesy Committee of the
Egypt Exploration Society, London.

PLATE 24. HEAD OF TAHARKA FOUND AT NAPATA. Courtesy
Sudan National Museum and Ny Carlsberg Glyptotek, Denmark.

PLATE 25. NUBIAN BRINGING TRIBUTE TO ASSYRIAN COURT.
Courtesy Metropolitan Museum of Art, New York.

PLATE 26. TAHARKA: PORTRAYED AS A SPHINX.
Reproduced by courtesy of the Trustees of the British Museum.

PLATE 27. MEROITIC QUEEN SLAYING ENEMIES. Reprinted, by permission, from Wenig, ed. *Africa in Antiquity*, vol. 2 (1978). Courtesy the Sudan National Museum, Khartoum and Prestel Verlag, Munich.

PLATE 28. Queen Aminitore of Meroë Worshiping Amon.
Reprinted, by permission, from Wenig, ed. *Africa in Antiquity*,
vol. 2 (1978). Courtesy the Sudan National Museum, Khartoum and
Prestel Verlag, Munich.

PLATE 29. QUEEN AMINITORE OF MEROË BEING VENERATED.
Reprinted, by permission, from Wenig, ed. *Africa in Antiquity*,
vol. 2 (1978). Courtesy the Sudan National Museum, Khartoum
and Prestel Verlag, Munich.

PLATE 30. KUSHITE KING: NAPATAN PERIOD.
Reprinted, by permission, from Wenig, ed. *Africa in Antiquity*,
vol. 2 (1978). Courtesy the Sudan National Museum, Khartoum and
Prestel Verlag, Munich.

PLATE 31. NIGERIAN WOMAN: NOK PERIOD. Photograph by Herbert List.
Reprinted, by permission, from Fagg, *Nigerian Images*.
Copyright © 1963 by Praeger.

mon built a special palace. She was one of the monarch's many foreign wives for whom he did favors. These foreign wives, however, were defined by the religious leaders as the root cause of the nation's disasters. They were accused of leading Solomon astray by persuading him to erect shrines to false gods within the kingdom. Jehovah, being a "jealous god," punished the nation for Solomon's lapses by letting the kingdom fall apart. When Solomon died there was widespread dissatisfaction with his son, Rehoboam, who succeeded him. Ten of the twelve tribes that formed the Hebrew confederation seceded and those in the North formed the kingdom of Israel with its capital in Samaria, not Jerusalem. The two remaining tribes in the South, Benjamin and Judah, remained loyal to Rehoboam and formed the kingdom of Judah with its capital at Jerusalem. This southern kingdom shared a border with Egypt.

The official southern version of the dissolution of Solomon's kingdom, as presented in the Old Testament, like other less biased versions, speaks of Egyptian connivance with Jeroboam as a factor in the dividing of the kingdom. Jeroboam returned home from exile in Egypt and became king of Israel, the northern kingdom, with Shoshonk's active support. Later the Egyptian pharaoh devastated the southern kingdom and carried off the treasures from the temple in Jerusalem as part of the booty.

Legends about Shoshonk abound—and not all of them are confined to antiquity. Professor Willis Huggins, a black vindicationist, describes Shoshonk's exploits and proudly presents him as a "Libyan Black Pharaoh." Velikovsky, in one of his characteristic bold reconstructions of ancient history, insists that Shoshonk (or Shishak, as he prefers to call him) was really the great black empire builder Thutmose III, of the Eighteenth Dynasty; but he does not refer to him in terms of race or color. Joel A. Rogers, reflecting upon what he regards as ancient Jewish antagonisms to black people, is certain that the shock of Shoshonk's raid on the temple left a residue of antiblack feeling that became embedded in Hebrew tradition.

While Shoshonk was preoccupied with exploiting the tensions between Israel and Judah and despoiling the latter kingdom, the kings of Kush in the vicinity of Napata cultivated close relations with the priests of Thebes and the princes of Upper Egypt and strengthened their own armies. Among the stories of dubious validity that give comfort to black vindicationist writers is the statement by the eminent historian Rostovtzeff that Shoshonk himself was a Nubian! Older legends speak of groups of tribesmen from the northern kingdom of Israel who came to Kush riding their camels and, finding prosperous cities, settled there. Others became bandits. A few had encounters with people who, they said, were cannibals. The "disturbance" in the Hebrew lands seems to have had some indirect effects on Kush, whereas Shoshonk exploited it to benefit Egypt.[215]

Whatever the truth may be about Shoshonk deliberately conspiring with Jeroboam to split the Hebrew kingdom, the fact remains that Israel and Judah became embroiled in bitter warfare with each other for many years, despite pleas from influential leaders on both sides to end the fratricidal strife. Assyria, of course, took advantage of the disunity to further its own imperial aims. It is possible that Shoshonk and the Delta princes decided to support Israel, the northern kingdom, because of their desire to see a buffer state close to the path of Assyria, which was expanding in the direction of Syria just north of Israel. It would have been sound preventive action to stop the Assyrian thrust before it turned southward and began to knife through Syria, then Israel, and eventually Judah, adjacent to Egypt.

In 876 B.C., Ashur-nasirpal did march southward from the upper reaches of the Euphrates River, and the boasting in his chronicles did not bode well for the future of Israel, Syria, Judah, Egypt, and the other lands south of what is now Lebanon:

> Then I approached the slopes of Lebanon. To the great sea of Akharri [i.e., the Mediterranean] I ascended. In the great sea I purified my weapons and offered sacrifices to the gods. Tribute of the kings on the shores of the sea, of Tyre, Sidon, Byblos, Makhallata, Maiça, Kaiça, Akharri, and Aramada [Arvad] in the midst of the sea, silver, gold, lead, copper, copper vessels, variegated and linen garments . . . I received in tribute. They embraced my feet.[216]

Having extracted pledges from the rulers of these lands that they would send the commodities on to Mesopotamia regularly that their conqueror demanded, Ashur-nasirpal left small garrisons in these areas. He then led his dreaded formations of foot soldiers, his chariots, and his cavalry back to Mesopotamia, not yet attacking Syria, with its capital in Damascus. All the tribute payers, as well as the peoples not yet conquered, were sure the Assyrians would return. But twenty-two years elapsed before the Assyrians came back to harass the western lands.

After Shalmaneser I, who followed Ashur-nasirpal, had put down rebellions and civil wars in the heart of the Assyrian Empire in Mesopotamia, he took the armies westward once more. Any disturbance along the Mediterranean seaboard and in its immediate hinterland was a threat to the stability of the empire. And there were good reasons for expecting that a disturbance might come. For two decades the kingdoms and organized tribes had been negotiating a pact for joint defense if the Assyrians returned. It was rumored that sentiment was running strong for defying Assyria by refusing to pay the assigned tribute. Shalmaneser was taking no chances.

Ahab, king of Israel; Benhadad, king of Damascus; and Irkhuleni, king of Hamath, formed an alliance to resist the Assyrians and had persuaded the kings of nine other peoples to contribute troops. When Assyria attacked, over a five-year period this coalition managed to repel them three times. Then, in 842 B.C., despite serious internal upheavals in Israel and Damascus, the alliance was forced to come together to fight off another assault. This time, near the end of the struggle, Israel, Tyre, and Sidon broke the united front by agreeing to pay tribute if the Assyrians would stop fighting them. Damascus refused to make any such agreement. However, the Assyrians considered their punitive action a victory since the unity of the rebels was broken and some had agreed to pay tribute. Nevertheless, the Assyrians decided to make a show of force by marching through Judah, with whom they had not been at war, in order to reach the Egyptian border and thus to give the pharaoh a symbolic warning not to interfere in the area that Assyria had just "pacified." Shalmaneser's forces then marched back to Mesopotamia.

As soon as the Assyrians had withdrawn, the king of Damascus used his troops to attack those members of the alliance who had broken the unified front by agreeing to pay tribute to the enemy. The Assyrians rushed back to deliver a crushing blow to the forces of the king of Damascus. Now, with a quick shift of sides, the rulers of Israel, Tyre, and Sidon welcomed their former enemy as a "deliverer from the oppression of the king of Damascus"! Their renewed assurances of an intention to pay the tribute secured the withdrawal of the Assyrians once more.

The pharaohs were apprehensive over these repeated Assyrian incursions into areas that had once been firmly within their sphere of influence, when they were not actually part of the Egyptian Empire. They reasoned that if these territories became part of the Assyrian Empire, they could constitute the staging ground for an invasion of the Nile Valley. Thus the pharaohs exerted every possible effort to urge the Syrian and Jewish kingdoms to reconstitute the defensive alliance, and to plan for an eventual war of resistance that would force Assyria to relinquish its control over them.

Over the next seventy-five years, the kingdoms of Damascus and Israel entered into alliance once again. A number of Philistine cities joined with them. They collectively threatened the reluctant king-dom of Judah, Egypt's neighbor, if it did not join. A glimpse of the politics of this period can be gained from a reading of the Old Testa-ment. The prophet Isaiah advised the kings of Judah not to join an anti-Assyrian alliance but to maintain a position of absolute neutral-ity. King Ahaz ignored him and took a drastic partisan step. He ac-tually *invited* the Assyrians to invade Judah in order to protect his kingdom from Israel, Damascus, and the other members of the north-ern coalition! The Assyrians responded by using enough force, first, to decimate the Philistines who were enemies of Judah, and then to overrun most of Israel, installing Hoshea as king in the section of the country Assyria did not occupy directly. They then devasted the king-dom of Damascus, after which they pursued the queen of Arabia and her soldiers into the desert in an attempt to punish her for not hav-ing paid the tribute assigned to her in the past. The Assyrians were now firmly in control of all the territory between the northern borders of Egypt and the southern borders of the Hittite Empire at the head-waters of the Euphrates River north of Syria. Judah had facilitated the Assyrian conquest of Israel.

Goodspeed, an Old Testament scholar with some pro-Assyrian leanings, notes that, during the eighteen years of his rule, by taking the strong measures just described, Tilgath-Pileser III "succeeded in raising Assyria from a condition of degenerate impotence to be the first power of the ancient world, with an extent of territory and an ef-ficiency of operation never before attained."[217] Egypt, in contrast, was divided and militarily weak. It watched this Assyrian triumph without intervening, but the Delta kings saw this vast empire as a threat to the entire Nile Valley. The rulers at Thebes were fearful, too. And so were the kings of Kush.

Finally, the Saite pharaoh of the Delta, despite Egypt's military weakness, offered assistance to Hoshea, the king of Israel, if he would refuse to pay the tribute to Shalmanesar IV, Tilgath-Pileser's succes-sor. With dynastic disputes taking place in Mesopotamia and restless-ness among eastern conquered areas, the pharaoh seemed to visualize the possibility of a successful organized resistance against Assyria. The armies of Israel held out for two years against the Assyrian troops sent to collect the tribute. Then, in 722 B.C., a powerful ruler, Sargon II, came to the throne and decided that the rebellion in Israel must be stamped out. He sent troops to take the besieged capital city of Samaria. *For reasons that no historians explain, the pharaoh did not send the troops that had been promised to Israel should that kingdom need them.* Samaria fell. Sargon's official annals report that he ordered 27,290 inhabitants of the kingdom of Israel deported to Mesopotamia and other parts of the Assyrian empire between 722 and 715 B.C. Sargon proceeded to settle members of other ethnic groups where the kingdom of Israel had once existed.[218]

Thus the oft-referred to "Ten Lost Tribes of Israel" came into existence, while Israel itself disappeared from history as a nation to become the subject of speculation, folklore, and legend. The Mormons believe some of the Israelites found their way to North America and became the ancestors of American Indian tribes. The Anglo-Israelites believe that at least some of them came to the British Isles. Some Afro-Americans are convinced that the Falashas in the highlands of Ethiopia, the "Black Jews," are descended from the "Lost Tribes." Jewish folklore reports that some of the Jews carried away into the Mesopotamian diaspora eventually found their way to the "Land of Kush"—presumably in eastern Africa—and there fought against the black inhabitants, in some cases taking their land, in others simply raiding farming communities as camel nomads and horsemen.[219] Most of the deportees from Israel stayed in the Tigris-Euphrates Valley, forming persisting diaspora communities that, over the years, became prosperous. It was within such communities that a group of intellectuals developed the Babylonian Talmud, which eventually influenced the fate of black people in a manner described in a forthcoming chapter of this work.

The wiping out of the kingdom of Israel by the Assyrians had some effects that were of substantial importance in the development of philosophical and religious thought over the subsequent centuries. The intellectual leaders of both Judah and Israel—the Prophets—raised what was, for them and their people, a crucial question: "Why, if we were God's chosen people, did he allow this national disaster to happen?" In their search for an answer they left a legacy of lofty ideas about the relationship between social ethics and national survival and about what it means to be a "chosen people," a body of ideas that profoundly affected Judaism, Christianity, and Islam. On a more mundane level, historians in search of proximate causes rather than theological explanations of the disaster that fell upon Israel mention the role of Judah in urging the Assyrians to break up the Damascus-Israel alliance and the failure of Egypt to give the promised military assistance. The constant urging by Egypt that an alliance be formed to confront Assyria must be evaluated, also, as a possible factor in provoking Assyria's forceful response. With Israel gone, Egyptian statecraft put some effort into urging its northern neighbor, Judah, to resume close ties with Egypt and to disengage from its tribute-paying relationship to Assyria. But a more realistic perspective seemed to be the formation of some sort of alliance with states north of Syria to resist Assyrian expansion there. For any aggressive policy in Judah, Israel, and Syria, however, a united Egypt and at least a neutral Kush were necessary. Neither the Twenty-first nor the Twenty-second Dynasty met these conditions so necessary for organizing effective resistance to an expanding Assyria.

During the same year that Sargon broke the siege of Samaria and Egypt failed to send the promised military relief to Israel, Bocchoris, a prince of Tanis in the Delta, assumed power in a dynastic dispute and formed the Twenty-third Egyptian Dynasty. The South, however, did not consider him a legitimate pharaoh. During his brief fifteen years in power, Bocchoris succeeded in infuriating Sargon. Goodspeed has explained why:

> Shut off from the south by his Ethiopian rivals he looked to the north for the extension of his power, and naturally began to interfere in the affairs of Syria, whither, both by reason of immemorial Egyptian claims to suzerainty and in view of commercial interests his hopes were directed. His representatives began to appear at the courts of the vassal kings, and made large promises of Egyptian aid to those who would throw off the Assyrian yoke. Already representations of this sort had induced Hoshea to refuse the tribute, though in his case rebellion had been disastrous. Now a new conspiracy was formed.[220]

Bocchoris had some success in stimulating the organization of a new anti-Assyrian coalition, and just two years after the destruction of the kingdom of Israel, Sargon had to rush troops westward again to put down what he perceived as a conspiracy against him—this one having been encouraged by Bocchoris. First, he defeated the ruler of a small kingdom north of Syria, capturing him and having him skinned, or "flayed," alive as an example to any other rulers who might be planning rebellion. Then he turned his attention to a group of Arabian princes who were supporting the revived anti-Assyrian alliance, defeating them and forcing them to resume the tribute they had stopped paying. He did not attack Judah or threaten Egypt on this occasion, however.

The plotting of Bocchoris and his promises of Egyptian troops, if needed, ceased abruptly in 715 B.C. when serious internal troubles confronted him. While Sargon's troops were rampaging through the Arabian principalities dangerously close to Egypt's northeastern border, conditions in the Delta became almost chaotic. Rivalries between competing princes and landholders made unified support of an expedition outside of Egypt's borders virtually impossible and a successful defense against invasion problematical. The priests and nobles at Thebes had been watching this situation in the Delta, and they now gave their blessing to a military expedition led by the Kushite king, Shabaka, to invade the Delta and "restore order." Shabaka marched into Egypt and won control of both the upper and lower regions. From the Delta, where he established his capital, he instituted what an Italian scholar, Salvatore Cherubini, has called "a guardianship invited by the prayers of a long suffering country." Assessing Shabaka's twenty-one years in power he writes that it was viewed by his subjects as "one of the happiest in Egyptian history."[221] Black Power, as represented by an Ethiopian ruler and Ethiopian troops, was now extended to the Mediterranean coast. The foundations for it had been laid some decades earlier.

THE RISE AND FALL OF THE ETHIOPIAN (TWENTY-FIFTH) DYNASTY

Shabaka was the third Ethiopian king during the Twenty-fourth (Tanite) Dynasty to march into Egypt, and second among the five who constituted the Twenty-fifth Dynasty. The first was Kashta, who came in about 700 B.C.:

> Precisely how it was that a Kushite king, called Kashta, came to decide that Kush was strong enough not merely to make itself independent of Egypt, but actually to conquer its former masters is not known. He invaded and conquered Egypt, and ruled over that country as far north as Thebes, the capital of Upper Egypt. This happened about 700 B.C., and not very long afterwards Kashta's son, Piankhy, completed the conquest of Egypt, and so became ruler of a land which stretched from the shores of the Mediterranean to the borders of modern Ethiopia—almost a quarter of the African continent.

This is archaeologist Margaret Shinnie's brief account of a momentous shift in Egyptian history. Surprisingly, neither Diop nor Chancellor Williams mentions Kashta, but the Kushite king's son, Piankhy, is given some praise and Shabaka is lauded as the founder of the Twenty-fifth Dynasty.[222]

Piankhy, the second Ethiopian king to enter Egypt with his army, was motivated, in part, by what he perceived as a threat to his own borders—a renewed miliatry action in southern Egypt by the Delta kings. It is usually assumed that he also had his eye on the pharaonic throne and on restoring the glories of the days of Thutmose III and

Amenhotep II, the empire builders. In any event, he took his armies all the way to Memphis. This was Piankhy, brother of Shabaka the first king in the Twenty-fifth Dynasty, who would bring seventy years of "Black Power" to Egypt in the sense that pharaonic authority was in the hands of Ethiopians rather than the "Libyan kings" whose Negro ancestry was much more attenuated.

Piankhy the Pious

Weigall, in *Personalities of Antiquity*, a book written for popular consumption, includes a general article on Egyptians, whom he calls "the kindest race of the ancient world," and several on specific Egyptian individuals. Among those profiled is Thutmose III, of whom he gives a vivid description, at the age of thirty-seven, winning the Battle of Armageddon, where, in addition to 2,200 horses and 924 chariots, the Egyptians captured "nearly every prince in Syria." He praises Thutmose for pardoning his foes and reinstating them "on condition that each should send his son or other heir to Egypt to be educated."[223] (But this policy was not an innovation, it having been initiated in the Eighteenth Dynasty. Weigall also included a chapter that bore the offensive title "The Exploits of a Nigger King." There was no doubt in this British Egyptologist's mind about Piankhy's "blackness," and the circumstances surrounding his decision to write the chapter have Pan-African implications. Weigall states that he was led to reread what he calls "the grandiloquent and deeply religious annals left by King Piankhi . . . the most famous of the nigger Kings," after a long conversation with an Afro-American professor who had visited him to discuss his interest in "the buried relics of the ancient glories of his dusky forefathers." Most of the chapters in Weigall's *Personalities* have a sarcastic tone and are full of snide comments about his subjects; but this one, despite its offensive title, conveys a favorable impression of the king. It also suggests why Weigall would say: "My visitor was probably right in his belief that it takes a negro to understand a negro."[224] Weigall may have had difficulties in doing so, but his sources, Herodotus, Diodorus, and Strabo, did not. They made the name Piankhy a symbol for laudable monarchical piety throughout the classical world. Frank Snowden remarks, in *Blacks in Antiquity*, that Piankhy won a reputation for being "scrupulously attentive to religious ritual, respectful of the temples and gods of Egypt, unwilling to deal with conquered princes who were ceremonially unclean, chivalrous in battle and moderate in relations with the vanquished."[225]

Piankhy's insistence upon correct ritual behavior by himself and his close associates was apparent when he sent the first contingent of troops from his capital in Ethiopia to Egypt. According to Weigall, he instructed them: "When you arrive in Thebes, baptize yourselves in the sacred river, put on clean clothes and unstring your bows. . . . Sprinkle yourselves with holy water at His altars [i.e., Amon's] and bow to the ground before Him, saying, 'Show us the way that we may fight in the shadow of thy sword.'" When the city of Memphis had been taken and his army had crossed the Nile to the city sacred to Re, the sun god, Piankhy "washed in the holy pool, bathed his black face in the sacred stream, said his prayers on the holy hill, performed the customary ceremonies in the temple, worshipped at the sacred pyramidion, and finally went into the Holy of Holies, and came out saying that he had seen God face to face." Piankhy grieved over the starving horses who had not had sufficient food during the siege and made arrangements for their care.

Weigall notes that while Piankhy's army besieged Hermopolis, another city of religious importance, a delegation of women led by the local ruler's wife came to the camp of the Ethiopian pharaoh and, "throwing themselves on the ground before Piankhy's black women-folk," begged for mercy for the city. An armistice was arranged and the enemy king was pardoned for resisting the army that came from Thebes. Piankhy was self-confident in his acts of magnanimity. His victory stele opens with boastful but pious words: "Listen to what I did—I who am a celestially born king, the living image of the sun god, destined to rule from birth." At one temple a characteristically Nubian note was struck when the choir sang, "Happy is the mother that bore you. She is a cow and she has borne a bull." Coming from an area where the cow-headed goddess Hathor was venerated, the compliment had a double meaning. His earthly mother traveled from Ethiopia to Memphis to see the double crown placed upon the head of her son.[226]

Piankhy possessed a temperament that combined elements of self-serving arrogance and fanatical piety with generosity. Out of that mixture Piankhy legends were made. Joel A. Rogers devotes a chapter to him in *World's Great Men of Color*, with the subtitle "King of Ethiopia and Conqueror of Egypt." Rogers chooses to stress his role as a conqueror, with a dramatic excerpt from the victory stele detailing how, as the emissary of Amon, Piankhy strode into the Holy of Holies of the temple of Re at Heliopolis, and the priests "threw themselves upon their bellies before his majesty saying 'To abide, to endure without perishing. O Horus, Beloved of Heliopolis.'" In this way, as Rogers interprets it, "Piankhi symbolized the mastery of

Egypt. Ethiopia had become mistress of the then known world!!'' Piankhy did not omit one important aspect of any such conquest from his victory stele—loot. He wrote, for all of Ethiopia to read, or have read to it, that his ships sailed south "laden with silver, gold, copper, clothing, and everything of the Northland"; and then, with unintended irony, "having gained domination of the North . . . Thou art unto eternity, thy might endureth, O Ruler, beloved of Egypt." Not everyone in the Delta perceived him in that benign fashion.[227] However, Egyptologist Budge adds a note of justification: "Nubia had enriched Egypt greatly with her gold and silver, and now Nubia was receiving back a little of her own."[228]

Shabaka's Foreign Policy

Piakhy's piety, like Akhenaten's religious zeal, inhibited him from initiating an active empire-building policy or continuing the intrigues of the Twenty-fourth Dynasty rulers in Israel. However, the Ethiopian pharaohs who followed him considered an aggressive intervention in Syria and Palestine necessary to prevent an Assyrian invasion. It was the fate of this dynasty to bear the brunt of the Assyrian attack when the rulers of that empire decided to end all possibilities of future support from Egypt for rebellion in Judah, Damascus, Tyre, Sidon, and Arabia. Had the kings who followed Piankhy decided to abandon all ideas of continuing the historic policy of intervention in the affairs of their neighbors to the north, an attack on Egypt by the Assyrians might have been averted. With threats in the east of revolt against that power by Elam and Babylon and of invasion by the Medes and Persians, a firm decision to defend Egypt's borders but not to intervene outside of them might have led the Assyrian ruler to abandon whatever plans he had for conquering the Nile Valley. There was an increasing need for Assyrian troops to contain rebellion on the eastern front, yet there was no certainty that Assyria was prepared to halt its imperialist expansion at Egypt's borders after it had decimated Syria, Israel, Judah, and the tribes and city-states of Canaan. Whatever the possible wisdom might have been of withdrawing from Middle Eastern intrigues, Shabaka, who succeeded his brother Piankhy to the pharaonic throne, had no intention of following such a policy.

After transferring his administrative capital from Napata in Ethiopia to Memphis in Egypt, Shabaka moved his armies on into the stronghold of Delta disaffection and made Sais his capital. Although Cherubini, as noted above, claims that Shabaka's reign was viewed as "one of the happiest in Egyptian memory," he had used terror in establishing it. When he captured Bocchoris, the last Saite pharaoh,

Shabaka had him burned alive and installed Bocchoris's son Necho as his viceroy in the Delta. His dynasty would later regret this act. At the same time, Shabaka placed an Ethiopian prince in charge of the city of Thebes and had him invested as a "fourth prophet of Amon."[229] When Shabaka finally felt secure at home, he adopted the same foreign policy Bocchoris had been pursuing—active interference in the political affairs of the states north of Egypt. But he concentrated on Palestine, rather than upon the kingdom of Damascus and other Syrian kingdoms, and the states near the upper reaches of the Euphrates River.

Goodspeed, writing of Shabaka from a pro-Assyrian perspective, notes:

> He did not wait long before undertaking the same measures as the Saite king had to extend Egyptian influence in Asia. His agents began their work at all the vassal courts in Palestine. In Judah, Edom, Moab, and the Philistine cities, Egyptian sympathizers were found everywhere. Proposals were made for a league between these states. In Judah the chief opponent of this policy was the prophet Isaiah.[230]

Sargon's troops immediately squelched an attempted revolt in Judah, no Egyptian/Ethiopian troops having been dispatched to aid the Jewish rebels. Sargon made no attempt to invade Egypt but took his troops back to Mesopotamia to punish the Babylonians, who, recently incorporated into the Assyrian Empire, had revolted.

While Assyria was busy coping with the Babylonian problem, Judah, although held in vassal status by Assyria, prospered under King Hezekiah and was not interfered with. But the king decided to join with the Egyptians, the Bedouin Arabs, Tyre, and several Palestinian states in throwing off Assyrian suzerainty. When he became aware of the plot, Sennacharib, who had replaced Sargon as the ruler of Assyria and had completed the job of subduing the Babylonians, sent a punitive expedition westward. Shabataka, who had taken the Egyptian/Ethiopian throne when his uncle, Shabaka, died, honored that ruler's pledge to Judah and dispatched troops to help resist Sennacharib.

Taharka Confronts Assyria

Shabataka placed the expeditionary force to aid Hezekiah of Judah in charge of Taharka, a younger member of his family (the Tirhakah of 2 Kings 19:9; see plate 24). They fought as allies of Judah but their joint efforts could not defeat the Assyrian army. Sennacharib boasted in his official chronicle: "But as for Hezekiah of Judah, who had not submitted to my yoke, forty-six of his strong walled cities and the smaller cities round about them without number . . . I besieged and captured." He then claimed to have marched off to Assyria 200,150 people and "horses, mules, asses, camels, cattle, and sheep, without number." And of the king he said, "Hezekiah himself I shut up like a caged bird in Jerusalem."[231] After moving southward and spreading devastation throughout Judah, Sennacharib returned to continue the siege of Jerusalem. According to the Old Testament story, Ethiopian troops under the leadership of Taharka again marched against the Assyrians, who withdrew from Jerusalem, apparently because a pestilence struck Sennacharib's forces and not because of a defeat in the field by Taharka.[232] But the military alliance of Egypt and Judah, put into effect by Shabataka, brought a future pharaoh on the scene— Taharka. He had proved himself in battle.

Taharka became king of Egypt at about the same time that Esahardon was taking power in Assyria after the death of Sennacharib. For more than twenty years after the fall of Jerusalem in 701 B.C. and the defeat of the joint Jewish–Ethiopian/Egyptian military operations, there had been no trouble among Assyria's vassal states in the west. Then when the king of Sidon withheld tribute in about 678 B.C., Esahardon beheaded him and destroyed his city on the Mediterranean coast. A list of kings specifies those who contributed toward the building of a new city, to be named after Esahardon. The name of Manasseh, king of Judah, is on the list. Goodspeed, commenting on this expedition, notes:

> Esarhaddon's activities in the west, however, contemplated something more than the restraining of uneasy vassals or the conquest of rebellious states. Egypt was his goal. . . . He regarded Egypt as "an old and inveterate foe."[233]

What Goodspeed calls "the interference of Egypt with Syria and Palestine" had been "offensive and persistent," and had continued under "the vigorous and enterprising Taharqa."[234] Esahardon was determined to end it.

In 674 B.C., fifteen years after Taharka became pharaoh, Esahardon sent the Assyrian army across the border into Egypt.[235] Taharka's troops drove them out. Four years later Esahardon struck again, this time with the necessary force. He erected a stele boasting that after a fifteen-day march his troops took Memphis in half a day:

> I besieged, I conquered, I tore down, I destroyed. I burned with fire, and the wife of his palace, his palace women, Usahahuru, his own son, and the rest of his sons and daughters, his property and possessions, his

horses, his oxen, his sheep without number, I carried away as spoil to Assyria. I tore up the root of Cush [Ethiopia] from Egypt. . . . I placed on them the tribute and taxes of my lordship.[236]

The Assyrians had been familiar with Ethiopians coming to Nineveh to trade and to bring gifts (see plate 25). Now they came as humiliated prisoners of war. But Esahardon did not capture Taharka, who slipped away from Memphis southward to Thebes.

Diop, in reference to this defeat, comments that "Taharqa intervened in Asia in an effort to regain Egypt's international prestige," but was "betrayed a second time by alien chiefs of the Delta." Diop considers the Libyans, as well as the descendants of Asian and European prisoners of war who were now influential in the Delta, to have been a fifth column interested in helping the rulers of foreign countries to detach the Delta from Egypt.[237] In any event, twenty Delta-city rulers agreed to accept positions under Necho of Sais, who was appointed Assyria's "king" of the Delta. Esahardon proclaimed himself "King of the Kings of Egypt" and ordered the princes of Thebes to pay tribute to him, as Necho and the Delta princes were preparing to do. That Necho collaborated in this fashion with Assyria is not surprising. Shabaka had burned his father, Bocchoris, alive. Memories of Taharka's draconian act of carrying off to Thebes the wives and harems of the conquered Delta lords were still fresh.

Necho bestowed Assyrian names on his capital city and on himself as he made his peace with the conquering power. Meanwhile, the princes of Thebes defiantly refused to pay the tribute that Assyria had imposed. Taharka moved his refreshed and reinforced army back down the Nile, stormed the city of Memphis, and took it back from the Assyrians. Esahardon was now dead, but his successor, Ashurbanipal, decided that Taharka must be driven out of Memphis, because of its proximity to the Assyrian "protectorate" in the Delta. The first skirmish on the border was inconclusive. Then additional Assyrian troops marched down from Syria, crossed the border at another spot, and delivered a crushing blow to Taharka's troops. He immediately withdrew again to Upper Egypt, there to regroup in preparation for another attempt to evict the Assyrians from northern Egypt. Goodspeed contributes an interesting observation on this contest of wits and wills between Taharka and the Assyrians:

> The Ethiopian king was already in Memphis and his troops met the Assyrians somewhere between that city and the border. The battle went against Taharqa who retired to the vicinity of Thebes. Whether the Assyrians pursued him thither, as one of the several somewhat contradictory inscriptions states, is doubtful. With good reason it has been held

that the Assyrians were content to renew their sway over lower Egypt only, restoring the vassal princes to their cities under oath of fidelity to Assyria, and did not attempt to advance farther up the river.[238]

The Twenty-fifth Dynasty of black pharaohs was fated to receive the full force of Assyrian determination to attack the Nile Valley. It seems obvious that the Delta leaders at this juncture preferred to live as provincial rulers carrying out Assyrian orders than as provincial rulers carrying out the orders of Amon's representative, enforced by an army based in Memphis. Had Taharka been content to let the Assyrians rule the Delta through the Libyans, Europeans, and Asians, and to have thus permitted it to secede from Egypt, it is possible that he could have consolidated a single unified Ethiopian kingdom stretching from Memphis to Meroë, covering most of Egypt and the Nile Valley to the sixth cataract. But it would have been a landlocked kingdom, its egress to the Mediterranean controlled by Assyria. Yet its territory would have been exempted from invasion or the payment of tribute. Assyria was having trouble on its eastern border and might not have wished to invest men and resources in trying to conquer Egypt south of the Delta. Eventually Ethiopia did become such a landlocked nation, but without *any* territory below the first cataract of the Nile. Taharka and the priesthood of Amon were in no mood to consider such a compromise with the Assyrians. Taharka's son had been carried off to Nineveh and humiliated, and this was a score that had to be settled, too.

While the Assyrians were installing puppet governors in the Delta and collecting a huge indemnity in gold and art objects, slaves, and other forms of wealth, Taharka was assembling an army in Upper Egypt from his base at Thebes. It is highly significant that if the Delta rulers held antagonisms toward the Twenty-fifth Dynasty rulers they diminished as soon as the marauding Assyrian troops had stripped the Delta of its wealth and the envoys had returned to Nineveh. Having had enough of the Assyrians the Delta rulers now sent emissaries to Taharka imploring him to assist them in preventing their part of Egypt from being completely absorbed into the Assyrian Empire. The governors of Tanis, Sais, and Per-Sept, who had been appointed by the Assyrians, now began to correspond with Taharka, putting forward a plan whereby the Ethiopian king's army could wipe out the Assyrian garrison forces left in Egypt and then organize the defense of all of Egypt against another invasion.

This proposal must have appealed to Taharka since there was a deeply entrenched tradition, extending back to the days of the Hyksos, of forces from the black south expelling invaders from

"Egypt's sacred soil." However, before any action of this sort could be organized, Ashur-banipal discovered the plot and rushed Assyrian forces back into the Delta. They slaughtered many soldiers in the Egyptian army and captured the governors of Sais and Per-Sept. Some of Taharka's replies to the letters from Delta rulers had been intercepted by the Assyrians, so Ashur-banipal had decided to strike first. The governors of Sais and Per-Sept were sent to Nineveh. The latter was killed but the other was pardoned and sent back to Egypt to continue ruling under Assyrian auspices. When Taharka saw the disastrous outcome, he took his troops out of Egypt and brought them back to the Kushite capital of Napata, where he died two years later, perhaps murdered.[239] Taharka became a legendary figure, along with Piankhy, in Kushite history—and for some of the same reasons (see plate 26). A summary by Budge of data from a stele Taharka set up in Tanis to commemorate his coronation indicates:

> He went from Nubia to Lower Egypt when he was twenty years of age in the train of a king, who was probably Shabaka, and there he was settled, presumably by this king, on a farm. He worked on the farm for some years, taking as his share the grain, whilst the king seems to have taken the cattle. It is probable that Shabaka employed him on one or more of his campaigns against the Assyrians, but, be this as it may, a time came when Amen [or Amon] made him king, although he was only a younger son. [Apparently the stele does not speak of the Jerusalem episode.] Taharqa then thought of his mother, whom he had not seen since he was twenty years of age—now he must have been at that time between forty and fifty, for he began to reign about B.C. 690—and sent a messenger to her at Napata, bidding her to come to the north to witness his coronation. She came, and saw her son with the double crown of the South and North on his head, and she rejoiced over him as Isis rejoiced when she saw her son Horus seated on the throne of his father Osiris. Taharqa's affection for his mother is a touching trait in his character, and is another illustration of the love and regard of Sudani children for their mothers which has always been one of their best characteristics.[240]

The End of "Black Power" in Middle East Politics

Shabataka's son, Tanutamun (or Tanwetamani), succeeded Taharka. He may not have intended to challenge Assyrian power in Palestine and Syria, but he was determined to dislodge those rulers in the Delta who accepted Assyrian overlordship on a part of Egyptian soil. He attacked a coalition of the Delta city rulers who depended for their defense upon soldiers the Assyrians had left to garrison the Delta. Tanutamun killed the son of Bocchoris, Necho I,

Assyria's most loyal ally, who was nominally the ruler of Egypt on their behalf. The Ethiopian ruler then released all of the other princes who were being held as prisoners and restored them to their former posts, but under his rule instead of under that of the Assyrians. All pledged their loyalty except one, Psammetichus, the son of Necho, who fled to the capital city of Nineveh in Assyria, where he remained until the Twenty-fifth Dynasty had been defeated. He then returned and eventually became pharaoh of all of Egypt.

Assyria had suspected the Delta rulers who swore allegiance to Tanutamun of supporting him in his ambition to expel Assyria from the western portion of the Fertile Crescent as well as from Egypt. From the Assyrian point of view, not only would this be a turnabout in alliances but it would also be tantamount to treason. Ashur-banipal decided to deliver a crushing blow. He attacked the Egyptian Delta with all the savagery once used by the early Assyrian conquerors whose actions have given that empire such an odious reputation. The "traitors" of the Delta were not only defeated militarily but their leaders were beaten and hanged. Then they were flayed, their skin being peeled off for preservation as trophies of the victory. The Delta cities were burned to the ground and many of the inhabitants were rounded up and deported to Mesopotamia. But Ashur-banipal knew that the center of resistance to Assyria was in the south, not in the Delta. He ordered his troops to march and sail up the Nile, and to storm and sack Thebes, citadel of Amon, the Egyptian war god, and a great international shrine city known as "Hundred-gated Thebes." It must be destroyed if Nineveh was to be the most important city in the world. Here was the spiritual citadel of Tanutamun's Egyptian/Ethiopian empire. The troops did their job thoroughly.

Thebes, in Upper Egypt, had always been the spiritual center of Kush, although the political capital prior to the merging of Egypt and Ethiopia in the Twenty-fifth Dynasty was at Napata in Kush itself. Chancellor Williams describes Thebes in its heyday as both a spiritual and military center:

> As the City of Amon, the King of the Gods, and of his wife, the great goddess, Mut, the temples and monuments to them alone had to be on a massive scale. There was also the war god of Thebes, the source of power of the mightiest armies, the proudest and most fearless warriors. From this center of empire alone 20,000 war chariots could be put into the field. . . . Many of the temples were what we could call colleges, as the different fields of study were temple-centered. Here scholars from foreign lands came to study, and from here religious ideas and architectural designs spread abroad.[241]

Cheikh Anta Diop, commenting on the triumph of the Assyrians, considers the destruction of Thebes a turning point in the history of Kush as well as of Egypt:

> Tanutamon escaped to Napata. The fall of the most venerable city of all Antiquity aroused deep emotion in the world of that time and marked the end of the Nubian Sudanese or Twenty-fifth Ethiopian Dynasty. The date also marked the decline of Black political supremacy in Antiquity and in history.[242]

Thus both Chancellor Williams and Diop consider the fall of Thebes a turning point in black history—and it was. Williams comments further:

> Being the center of black power [Thebes] was a main object of destruction by non-African invaders. . . . *But we have to remind ourselves constantly, racism as we know it today was practically nonexistent.* . . . No one believed that the conquered people were actually, that is, innately, inferior to the conquerors. Neither did the relatively backward Asian whites who invaded Egypt consider themselves superior to the Black builders of the civilizations they found there [italics added].[243]

Nevertheless, Assyrian rulers, parvenus vis-à-vis both Egypt and Babylon, humiliated the black rulers when they were able to capture them; and they pictured their foes, symbolically, as humiliated when they could not get their hands on them. The conquered black kings were treated like others who suffered a similar fate. One of Sargon's stelae portrayed Taharka with a ring in his nose being led along with Baal, king of Sidon. Sometimes captive kings were portrayed as beasts with rings in their noses crouching at the feet of the Assyrian ruler. (However, plate 25, which depicts in ivory the figure of an African bringing tribute to the court of Nineveh from Egypt, is comparable to figures of tribute bearers from other ethnic groups.)

The Hebrew prophets saw the destruction of Thebes as having cosmic significance, but not as the destruction of *Black* Power. To them it represented a resounding victory of Jehovah over the citadel of false gods, over Thebes (or No), the Unholy City, as contrasted with the Holy City, Jerusalem. The pharaoh who was considered a god on earth, Amon-Re incarnate, had fallen. The corrupting influence of Min, Amon in his manifestation of virility and fertility, had felt the punitive power of Jehovah in his stronghold. The prophets rejoiced at the downfall of Amon-Min.

The black pharaoh led his armies back to Kush after the fall of

Thebes, although he and his descendants, from their capital in Napata at the fourth Nile cataract, still claimed to be the legitimate wearers of the Double Crown, to be Kings of Upper and Lower Egypt and Lords of the Two Lands. But after seventy years they were now forced to make such claims from outside the borders of Egypt.

Weigall characterized the Twenty-fifth Dynasty as the "amazing epoch of nigger domination." Older Egyptologists felt that the dynasty must, of necessity, be classified as equivalent to a "low" period because it was Black. It is significant that Cyril Aldred, in 1980, gave a quite different assessment of the Ethiopian pharaohs in "The Kushite Period—Dynasty XXV," in his book *Egyptian Art*:

> They brought order and stability to a divided realm. A deep veneration for tradition was inherent in their religious outlook, and research was undertaken into ancient and sacred literature. . . . Under these new patrons, the pharaohs themselves, the Divine Consorts of Amun, and their officials, a great surge of activity is apparent in the arts.[244]

The withdrawal of the black kings to Ethiopia marked the end of a cultural epoch in Egypt as well as the establishment of a new international order in which Greece and Persia would play dominant roles. The end of the Twenty-fifth Ethiopian Dynasty in Egypt did not, of course, mean the end of Ethiopian history—only a redirection, geographically and culturally. The Kushite kings eventually established a capital near the sixth cataract of the Nile, and the kingdom of Meroë preserved a distinctive ethos while Egyptian culture was being "Hellenized."

THE HELLENIZING PROCESS IN EGYPT

After the fall of Memphis, the Assyrians sent Necho, the son of Bocchoris, home from Nineveh to be installed as the ruler of Egypt. His effective power, however, was confined to the Delta. An Assyrian garrison was left to supervise his actions and to maintain order. All of the influential political leaders and merchants of the twenty-two Delta nomes accepted this arrangement. After Necho's death his son, Psammetichus (known to history as Psammetichus I), came to power and began to extend his control over Upper Egypt as well as the Delta. He let it be known that he did not intend to remain a puppet ruler for Assyria. But it was also clear that he did not intend to place his fate in the hands of the Ethiopians if they made another bid for power in Egypt in cooperation with the priests of Amon and the princes of Thebes. Thus Psammetichus formed a military alliance with the king of Lydia in Asia Minor, an act that marked a decisive break with the past. Instead of bringing up masses of Ethiopian troops from Nubia to make up the backbone of his army, he employed battle-hardened Carian and Ionian mercenaries from Asia Minor.²⁴⁵ This may have been a case of making the best of a bad situation since recruiting black mercenaries from a region where the hostile Kushite kings were in control may not have been feasible. On the other hand, there may have been a deliberate decision to use soldiers with a fighting style that had been tested in wars against the Assyrians. Egypt might have to face another invasion. The historian W. H. McNeill has pointed out that the military advantage in facing the Assyrians lay with troops who had been trained in disciplined close-order infantry fighting, a style perfected by the Assyrians. Primary reliance on horse-drawn chariots with infantry as supporting and mopping-up forces, a technique in which Egyptians and Ethiopians excelled, was no longer as useful as it had been from the Eighteenth Dynasty through the days of Rameses II.²⁴⁶

The Psammetichi Who Opened the Door

Assyria was still having problems in the east even though Thebes had been destroyed. Babylon revolted against its northern neighbor, who bore the same relation to it as Ethiopia/Kush did to Egypt during the Twenty-fifth Dynasty—that is, a once-colonized people rising up against the country of the former colonizer, and establishing rule over it. The kingdom of Elam and the Bedouins of northern Arabia became allies of Babylon when it prepared to deliver the final blow to Assyria. Psammetichus took advantage of the difficulties his overlord was having on the eastern front and ordered his army of Carian and Lydian mercenaries to expel the Assyrian garrisons from Egypt. They did so easily. The Twenty-fifth Dynasty rulers were never so fortunate as to have such a situation in which the bulk of the Assyrian forces were so involved elsewhere that a large-scale punitive strike against the Egyptians was impossible. This time the Assyrian rulers needed all their troops to defend the heartland of the empire.

After the Assyrians had been expelled, and with the support of the Delta nomarchs, the priests proclaimed Psammetichus pharaoh, and thus the Twenty-sixth Dynasty was established. Although his capital was at Sais in the Delta, Psammetichus claimed to be the ruler of all of Egypt, of both parts of the Two Lands. The Kushite rulers, from their capital in Ethiopia, made the same claim. The priests in Thebes made an uneasy peace with Psammetichus, and with the two Twenty-sixth Dynasty rulers who followed him. Aldred notes:

The princes of Sais, who as vassals of Assyria had rallied Lower Egypt against their Kushite rivals, went on to become the pharaohs of an independent and prosperous Egypt, which they ruled as powerful merchant princes, having command of a large *corps d'elite* of Carian, Ionian, and Lydian mercenaries, and control of a strong fleet. They neutralized the influence of Thebes as the capital of Upper Egypt, by having their daughters adopted as Consorts of Amun, and they gradually replaced the old officials in the government of the South with their own nominees.

Under the rule of Psammetichus II the names of the Kushite pharaohs were excised from the monuments; but Aldred points out that "even before this, however, the Saites had shown their execration of all things Kushite by stressing carefully their own Lower Egyptian character."[247]

There is some evidence to suggest that this animosity toward Kushite rulers and stress on Delta superiority could hardly have been conceptualized as racial prejudice symbolized by differences in somatic norm. One Oxford University Egyptologist, Professor F. Llewellyn Griffith, notes "It has been conjectured that the family of the Psammetichi was of Libyan origin; on the other hand some would recognize Negro features in a portrait of Psammetichus I which might connect him with Ethiopian rulers." A bust of Amasis, greatest of the three Saite kings, has pronounced Negroid features. These rulers brought the Delta deliverance from Theban power but not from the presence of what Weigall called "nigger kings." There may not be inconsistency in these two attempts to characterize the pharaohs of the Twenty-sixth "Libyan" Dynasty, for the term "Libyan" was used in antiquity as a tribal or ethnic term, and some writers referred to two kinds of Libyans, "black" and "yellow."[248]

Whatever their attitudes toward race, color, and somatic norm images may have been—or their own physiognomy—the three Psammetichi rulers decided to orient Egyptian life, political and cultural, away from close relations with Ethiopia and toward close relationships with new commercial and military elites emerging in the Mediterranean. Previous Egyptian rulers had permitted Greeks to visit Egypt but had barred them from settling permanently. This may have been the result of apprehensions aroused by watching the continuous expansion of Greek power and influence throughout the Mediterranean world by the establishment of colonies. In a reversal of traditional Egyptian policy, Psammetichus I invited the Greeks to establish a city near Sais, Naucratis, which became an important commercial center. Aldred feels that certain art styles of the Greeks show the influence of the Egyptians from the time of this settlement, since sculptors from Archaic Greece "doubtless were now exploring the monuments of Egypt from their base at Naukratis."[249]

Snowden presents representations of Negroes in the art of Naucratis and concludes that Greeks first had contact with Blacks in some numbers in that city. Some of the paintings on vases at Naucratis seem to symbolize changed relations between Greeks and Egyptians. There had been an old legend about Busiris, an Egyptian king, who sacrificed to Zeus any "red men," that is, presumably, Greeks, who landed on his shores—to bring good luck, according to one account. In these paintings Heracles, the Athenian hero, is depicted defeating Busiris and his Ethiopian troops. The message is clear: under Psammetichus I the old Egyptian anti-Greek attitude is dead. In fact, an era of close military and cultural cooperation would now follow the commercial cooperation. While Assyria and Babylon were declining in power, a new threat loomed in the east: Persia. Egypt and the Greek city-states became allies in the successful attempt to prevent the Persian rulers from making any permanent gains in either place. Naucratis became the first point of entry for scores of Greek philosophers and historians, who, following the merchants and the soldiers, began the massive transfer of ancient knowledge and wisdom from Africa to the Greco-Roman world that became an enduring legacy to Western civilization.[250]

Having opened the door to Greek merchants Psammetichus I was ready to cooperate with Greek city-states in developing their trade in North Africa and the Mediterranean islands, but he first wished to reestablish the historic Egyptian presence in Palestine and Syria, and to seize the maritime trade of Phoenicia that bordered these two areas. One way to achieve this goal was to work out some arrangement with the now-weakened Assyria that would result in that empire relinquishing control of, or any claim to, these areas.

Assyria was attempting to reconquer territory in the west held by Babylon while new powers, the Medes and Persians, were attacking her empire in the northeast. If he offered to strike at Assyria's old foe while she fought the newcomers to the state system, Psammetichus expected a free hand in Judea and Syria. As the negotiations were proceeding, to the surprise of Psammetichus, the Medes and Persians sacked Nineveh, the capital of Assyria, in 612 B.C.—just forty-nine years after the Assyrians had sacked Thebes. Egypt's new ally in the east had suffered a serious reverse.

Psammetichus's son, Necho II, who succeeded him, continued the policy of offering aid to the Assyrians against Babylon. When the

Babylonians attacked the Assyrians, Necho II immediately marched his troops into the Hebrew lands and defeated Josiah, king of Judah, on the plains of Megiddo (Armageddon), where Thutmose III had once won a great victory. He made certain that his own nominee, Johoi-kam, was placed on the throne of Judah, and then he proceeded on to Syria to join the Assyrian garrison there and to prepare for contact with the Babylonian foe at some point farther north.

Fighting side by side, the Egyptians and the Assyrians clashed with the Babylonians in 605 B.C. on the banks of the Euphrates River at Carchemish. They were defeated, and the king of Judah abandoned his Egyptian ally and rushed to pay obeisance to the king of Babylon. This battle is sometimes referred to as a "turning point" in world history, because the Babylonians defeated the dominant military force in the then-known world, the Assyrian army. Egypt was on the side of the loser. If it were to retain its influence in Judah and regain power elsewhere, it would have to adopt new strategies. Sporadic military victories on a small scale after Carchemish were ineffective and the results of minor victories short-lived. George Goodspeed, writing of this period for a popular audience interested in biblical history, notes:

> In general, Egypt was the troublesome factor in this region. . . . After Necho's conclusive defeat at Karkhamish [i.e., Carchemish], he did not, however, make a new attempt in force upon Palestine (2 Kings XXIV, 7), but preferred to use intrigue to induce the communities there to rebel.[251]

When Nebuchadnezzar, king of Babylon, became aware of Necho II's attempt to stir up new rebellions, he rushed his troops to the king-dom of Judah and deported over 9,000 of its leading citizens, includ-ing the monarch. He then installed a new king, Zedekiah, who pledged his loyalty to Babylon. Immediately, some of the Jews in the Babylonian diaspora began to conspire with those who had remained in Judah, hoping that they might combine their forces in an effort to shake off Babylonian rule in the homeland at some propitious mo-ment. Pharaoh Apries (the biblical Hophra), who had succeeded Psammetichus II, openly supported the rebels. Nebuchadnezzar once more sent his troops against a rebellious Judah and besieged Jerusa-lem for a year and a half. This time, the Egyptian army was able to force the Babylonians into a temporary retreat from the walls of Jerusalem, as in Taharka's day. The obligation to Judah had been met. But the Babylonians returned. In 587 B.C. the people of Jerusalem felt they could hold out no longer. The Babylonian captivity imposed by Nebuchadnezzar this time meant that thousands of additional inhabitants of Judah were forced into exile in the Mesopotamian diaspora.[252] This is known as "the second Babylonian captivity."

Although Apries had made some effort to aid his Jewish allies, he had not involved Egypt in an all-out war with Babylon. After the defeat of Judah and the setting up of a Babylonian puppet government, Apries turned his attention to another part of what the Jews called "the Land of Canaan." He sent his fleet to occupy the port of Sidon, stronghold of the Phoenicians (in what is now called Lebanon). An Egyptian fleet fighting successfully in Mediterranean waters was something new, and from Apries's point of view, something to be proud of. It was one of the results of cooperation with the Greeks. Meanwhile, his Greek allies invaded and occupied Cyrene, the territory just west of Egypt in North Africa.

Apries used his army to aid the Greeks in subduing his African neighbors. At this point, the Egyptians in his army mutinied, presumably because Apries had sent them, and not the Greek and Carian mercenaries, to put down some African rebels. The rebellious troops proceeded to install an army officer from southern Egypt as their king, whose name, Ahmose, suggests that he was either a Nubian or was identified in some way with the Theban circles out of which his namesake, Ahmose I, who founded the Eighteenth Dynasty, had come.

Ahmose II continued to employ Greek mercenaries and, indeed, married a Greek princess, although he remained a symbol of Egyptian national independence. Herodotus, writing about Ahmose under his Greek name, Amasis, presents a vivid portrait of this pharaoh as a "shrewd, convivial, soldier-king," during whose reign Egypt was very prosperous. The Roman historian Diodorus, on the other hand, speaks of his "harshness, injustice, and arrogance." Neither historian knew him.[253] Both were at the mercy of their sources. Herodotus visited Egypt during the reign of Xerxes, the Persian leader under whom there was an Egyptian revolt. Conceivably his Egyptian informants glorified the reign of one of their own kings before their nation fell into Persian hands.

Ahmose remained on the throne for forty-four years (569–526 B.C.). During this period he kept Egypt free from foreign military adventure until near the end of his reign, when the expanding Persian Empire excited apprehension throughout the Middle East. A league was formed to resist the Persians, composed of Egypt, Sparta from mainland Greece, Lydia (Egypt's wealthy ally in Asia Minor), and Babylon, the kingdom most immediately threatened. Ahmose did not invade Judah, in part because it was in Babylon's sphere of influence and Babylon was now an ally; and in part because the last serious battles Egypt had been involved in occurred when the father of Ahmose, Apries (Hophra), gave aid to King Zedekiah in Jerusalem just before the final catastrophe that led to the Babylonian captivity. Babylon had attacked Egypt in reprisal. From then on, Egypt accepted the status quo in Judah.

The Greek "Penetration" under the Persians and the Ptolemies

In 546 B.C., twenty-three years after Ahmose was enthroned, Cyrus the Great, king of the Persians, annexed all of western Asia Minor. Lydia, one of the members of the defensive league, had now been incorporated into the Persian Empire. The king of Kush, still calling himself "Lord of the Two Lands" (even though he lived in Ethiopia, not in Egypt), could view these events in Asia Minor with a certain degree of aloof detachment. Ahmose, pharaoh of Egypt, could not afford such disinterest, since one of his Greek allies was under attack in Ionia, as was the friendly king of Lydia, from whose land many soldiers in the Egyptian army came. Whether or not the Ethiopian king knew the full significance of these events—or cared about them if he knew—actions were set in motion that would profoundly affect the history of Western civilization. The contest between Persia and the Greek states was brewing. Meanwhile, in 539 B.C., Babylon, now an ally of Egypt against Persia, fell to the armies of Cyrus (later named "the Great"). One of his first acts was to give the exiled Jews permission to return to Judea. As area after area fell to Persian armies, Cyrus exhibited a high degree of humanity and respect for other cultures and religions.[254] In 525 B.C., the year after Ahmose died, the troops of Cambyses, who had succeeded to the Persian throne when Cyrus died, marched into Egypt. This conqueror was less humane and tolerant than Cyrus had been.

The Persians had been assisted by some individual Greeks and Arabs in their invasion of Egypt, so they very quickly took Upper Egypt as well as the Delta. Psammetichus III was treated with leniency until he was suspected of planning a revolt. Then he was executed. During his three years in Egypt, Cambyses sought legitimacy by worshiping the gods of the previous Saite dynasty, but Herodotus reports that he was a capricious and cruel ruler. He led his forces in an attack on Ethiopia but, after occupying a part of lower Nubia near the Egyptian border, was forced to retreat, and the king of Kush rebuked him for "coveting the lands of other people."[255] The episode became legendary.

The Persians ruled in Egypt for 121 years, forming what Manetho called the Twenty-seventh Dynasty. Throughout this period the Egyptians and Greeks were constantly at war with the Persians, and for a brief five-year period a native Twenty-eighth Dynasty took power, after which the Persians returned for another fifty-six years. Persian rule ended in 332 B.C. when Alexander the Great, a Macedonian Greek, captured the Delta and was greeted as a liberator. The priests of Memphis made him a pharaoh, and the myth spread widely that he was the son of the last native pharaoh by a Macedonian mother and thus an incarnation of Amon. Alexander is said to have believed in his Egyptian divine paternity.

After Alexander's death, one of his generals, Seleucis, took over the Persian Empire, and another general, Ptolemy, assumed control of Egypt and made Alexandria, a recently established city on the Mediterranean seaboard, his capital. It eventually became the wealthiest and most renowned city in the civilized world and the center from which Hellenistic culture diffused widely. Ptolemy and Seleucis became embroiled in warfare over Palestine and Syria when Ptolemy I (Sotere) moved to establish his rule in these lands that most Egyptian rulers since the Eighteenth Dynasty had considered at least within their sphere of influence, if they had not annexed them outright. The Seleucids and the Egyptian pharaohs fought for possession of these territories from 367 B.C., when Ptolemy I came to power, until 34 B.C., when Cleopatra, last of the line, was presented with Judea, Phoenicia, Cyprus, Crete, Cyrene, and Arabia by her lover, the victorious Roman general Marc Antony. With Cleopatra's death, Egypt became a Roman province, but the culture of the upper classes remained Hellenistic, that is, Greek as modified by ideas and customs borrowed from many sources. After the fall of the Roman Empire, Egyptian Islamic rulers, with their capital at Cairo, resumed the struggle for dominance in Palestine and Syria. (Eventually Turkish rulers incorporated both into the Ottoman Empire, along with Egypt.)[256]

The struggle of the thirteen Ptolemy rulers over a 333-year period to prevent the Seleucids from establishing their dominion over Judea, Syria, and Phoenicia, the African province of Cyrene (now Libya), west of Egypt, and to establish a foothold in Greece itself after taking Cyprus and Crete required an enormous expenditure of funds for hiring mercenaries, building a large fleet of war vessels, providing pensions to retired soldiers, and supporting an administrative bureaucracy in conquered lands as well as in Egypt. The financing was secured by heavy taxation of the Egyptian rural population, including levies in kind on agricultural products, and by intensified exploitation of the gold mines of Nubia and control of trade between the Mediterranean and southern Arabia and the Persian Gulf. Deep-seated disaffection among the people toward the rulers and the landowning classes occurred with an intensity never before seen in Egypt, except in certain "low periods." Class conflict became the rule under the Ptolemies.

The scholarly consensus is that, despite considerable miscegenation (for example, Cleopatra's father seems to have been part Negro), the ruling family and the wealthy class whose interests it served remained predominantly of Greek ancestry. The ordinary Egyptians considered the members of this upper stratum to be oppressive foreigners and did not tolerate the exploitation of Egypt by them without resistance. The most common response was a traditional Egyptian form of passive resistance in which workers on state plantations and private farms would run away to the domains of the priesthoods, requesting asylum. They would remain in these privileged sanctuaries, which the troops of the Ptolemies respected. Occasionally, however, instead of passive resistance, violent outbursts occurred. The two most dramatic episodes that have been recorded took place following wars in Judea and Syria in which drafted Egyptian soldiers had been used. This practice had been instituted in an attempt to give the ordinary people a "stake" in the Ptolemies' wars, to make the wars national struggles rather than "private" struggles of the Ptolemy dynasty fought with mercenaries. The unintended consequences, however, were the heightening of nationalist objections to foreign rulers and the provision of military training for potential insurrectionaries.[257]

In both of the major rebellions there was evidence of intervention on behalf of the rebels by Ethiopians who, collaborating with Theban princes and priests, tried to turn economic and social discontent into a fight to restore indigenous Egyptian rule, that is, to overthrow the Ptolemies. Thus the black presence in the South, as in the past, was evident in attempts to expel foreign rulers from Egyptian soil. The Ptolemies put down these revolts ruthlessly, and in the course of doing so made punitive strikes into Ethiopia. The protests were in part expressions of disapproval of the process of Hellenization that began under Ptolemy I and involved the organization of the entire economy for the benefit of a small upper class composed mainly of Greeks; the co-opting of a few Egyptians who were admitted into full upper-class status; the setting of standards for the intellectual life of the nation by the predominantly non-Egyptian group of scholars at the museum and library in Alexandria and the transfer of manuscript collections from the Houses of Learning in temples to Alexandria; and the attempted "whitening" of Ethiopian and Egyptian color values and religious symbols by syncretization with Greek deities. To understand this last process as well as the role that southern Egypt and Ethiopia played in the resistance to Greek control of Egyptian economic and intellectual life it is necessary to examine, in some detail, the role of color symbolism in pre-Ptolemaic Egypt.

Color Coding in Egypt before Hellenization

The process of Hellenization under the Ptolemies and the Romans was regarded by the masses of Egyptians as an aspect of foreign military conquest and exploitation, even after considerable miscegenation had taken place with Greeks and Romans at upper-status levels. The privileged few among the Egyptians adopted Greek intellectual and religious concepts and practices through a process of reinterpretation and syncretism. For them a cosmopolitan world view—not an Egyptian world view—became a prime value. This was not true of most Egyptians, however. Aldred reminds us that, as Hellenization proceeded under the Psammetichi and the Persians,

> in the face of this foreign domination, the Egyptians more than ever turned to the virtues they had learnt in recent centuries of cultivating their past, resisting their conquerors with a xenophobic zeal and rising against them under native princes whenever an opportunity presented itself. In the sphere of art, the antiquarian return to the great styles of the past was pursued with fervor.[258]

When the Ptolemies added aggressive economic exploitation to the cultural imperialism that had elicited this type of response several times in the past, the Egyptian "return to the roots" was intensified. It was most pronounced in Upper Egypt, in the Thebaid, close to Ethiopia. To identify with a remote Egyptian past was to identify with a *black* past—the past of the Old Kingdom, the Eighteenth Dynasty, and the Twenty-fifth. A return to the past in the form of glorifying it and paying homage to ancient personalities, myths, and customs (what anthropologists call a *nativistic* movement) meant, in Egypt, a focusing of attention upon the Old Kingdom, the period of the pyramid builders, the Sphinx, and the Book of the Dead, as well as upon the Eighteenth Dynasty and the Twenty-fifth Dynasty. As we have demonstrated, these were dynasties in which a number of very Negroid pharaohs played prominent roles.

The nativistic movement elevated Ahmose and Nefertari, Amenhotep III and Queen Tiye, to the position of worshiped deities, and Imhotep was venerated as the God of Medicine. Aldred notes that Pharaoh Nectanebo, of the last native dynasty to rule before the Ptolemies seized power, had begun to erect a large temple at Edfu in the Thebaid. This became a major shrine during conquest by the Persians when "back to the roots" was a widespread theme. In the case of this pharaoh and others of his dynasty, Aldred notes a "bulbous modeling of the chin, lips, and nose tip," which gave "a peculiar character to the facial appearance." As in the case of Akhenaten, what Aldred sees as "peculiar" others might define as "Negroid." This Egyptologist notes, too, that during this period of struggle against the Persians the art was reminiscent of the Eighteenth Dynasty and the Old Kingdom.[259] The art of styles favored by the upper classes shifted toward Greek models under the Ptolemies, but it is not likely that this had much influence upon the farmers of the Nile Valley who were viewing the old monuments around them as they went about their daily labors. The new models were those of the Delta and of Greek cities established in the valley.

As Persian, Greek, and Roman rulers entrenched themselves in the cities, the somatic norm image of the upper strata came to differ markedly from that of Nectanebo and the earlier pharaonic dynasties. The art of the Ptolemy period portrays predominantly Caucasoid types, and, as Imhotep was transformed into Asklepios, and Isis worship spread, statuettes and paintings of both reflect a "whitening" process.[260] It is also possible that esthetic values among many people underwent a Hellenizing process that resulted in a more Caucasoid norm of beauty than had prevailed in the past. Even Joel A. Rogers did not claim that Cleopatra, last of the Ptolemy rulers, was a very Negroid beauty.[261] What effect these changes had upon the somatic norm images of ordinary people we do not know, but elite norms and values certainly changed.

Despite the tendency of some worshipers to prefer a Caucasoid image of Isis, Osiris, or Imhotep, blackness was not completely downgraded among either ordinary Egyptians or the elites, and may even have been accepted by foreign conquering elites with some positive connotations in the domains of magic and religion. All of the religions of the Mediterranean and the Middle East had symbols and rituals to ensure fertility among plants, animals, and human beings. In Old

Kingdom times, as we mentioned, the pharaoh himself was widely regarded throughout the Middle East as such a symbol. (Alexander the Great had himself declared a pharaoh and believed he was a son of Amon.)

A striking example of the equivalence in Egypt between fertility and blackness occurs in the representation of an important god of the Thebaid who was venerated from remote antiquity in Upper Egypt and Lower Nubia (Wawat). This was Min, who, according to one source, was portrayed as "an ithyphallic bearded man, usually a statue with legs close together in the Archaic fashion, painted black."[262] (Ithyphallic refers to a representation with an erect penis.) One ithyphallic representation from a tomb in Upper Egypt was reproduced in 1979 in the inaugural issue of an Afro-American publication, the *Journal of African Civilizations* (fig. 5). During late dynastic times Min was worshiped in the Delta as well as in Upper Egypt, and his annual festival was very popular. No records exist that make it possible to estimate the extent to which these festivals focused upon the symbolism of fertility in contrast to the eroticism of some Greek and Roman festivals in which dancers sometimes cavorted about with large artificial phalluses or in which orgiastic behavior was an essential aspect of the event. (Rafael Patai, in *Man and Temple*, notes, too, that at times it was difficult to prevent what was called "light-headedness" in the temple precincts in Jerusalem during the Succoth festival.) There was nothing unusual about overt sexual symbolism being displayed in the religious iconography, and in some of the rituals, of Egypt. To what extent it was erotic, as in some Indian temple art, is not clear.

Min was not the only black deity worshiped in pharaonic Egypt. Amon, with his great temples at Thebes and Jebel Barkal during the New Kingdom, has been called "god of the national resistance" by the French Egyptologist Sauneron. He was portrayed as black or dark blue and often as ithyphallic, having assimilated to himself, as time went on, the characteristics of Min.[263] *During the Eighteenth Dynasty, sexual power and military power thus coalesced into a single potent male symbol which remained strong throughout Egypt until the end of the Ramesside period.* Amon and his wife, Mut, were worshiped, and Queen Hatshepsut claimed to be Amon's daughter by divine conception. The royalty of Kush and Meroë claimed special relations with Amon through his priests, whose oracles they consulted about affairs of state.[264] The prestige of Amon is attested to by Alexander the Great's consultation of the oracle for personal prophecies immediately after his conquest of the Egyptian Delta. Sauneron

FIGURE 5. THE GOD MIN IN ITHYPHALLIC FORM.
Courtesy Ivan van Sertima.

notes that there were some periods during the New Kingdom and the age of the Rameses kings when

> the clergy of Amon was richer and more powerful than the king himself. . . . The god patronizes the sovereign, assures the triumph of his dynasty, extends his victories to the limits of the known world, but the king, in exchange, splits with the god. . . . To enrich the god, to overwhelm with gifts, to increase the temples in his name and spread his glory, this was the effect of a legitimate filial attitude—of a well understood interest.[265]

Despite their role during periods of warfare and empire building, neither the fertility cult of Min nor the war cult of Amon, with which it was eventually fused, ever generated such horrors as the sacrificial burning of children, actions for which the prophets of Judah denounced several of their own kings. Such actions as the sacrifice of babies to the goddess Tanit and the god Baal Moloch, or similar holocausts, took place on a massive scale in the North African Phoenician city of Carthage. Yet, as we have noted, a sensitive black pharaoh of the Eighteenth Dynasty, Akhenaten, considered the Theban priesthood oppressive. He tried to dethrone and demystify Amon, "the hidden one," whose symbol of the ram exemplified both power and sexuality, and to substitute the symbol of Aten, the sun disc, symbolizing one god presiding benignly over all mankind. But Akhenaten failed in his attempt to break the power of the priests of Amon. They endured and became the spiritual and temporal advisers to the Ramesside kings. When that dynasty passed away, these priests presided over the "compromise" with northern Egyptian gods that kept Amon-Re powerful enough to exert some influence until the coming of the Romans, when their powerlessness was evident in the face of legions commanded by the god-king Augustus Caesar. Egypt had no more black god-kings.

The political advisers of Ptolemy I must have informed the pharaoh of the role that nationalistic movements based in Upper Egypt had played in the past in mobilizing the nation against rule from the Delta. He and his successor must have known, too, of the immense power that the priests of Amon had wielded. Both the Ramesside kings and the Delta dynasties had tried to secure the sanction of Amon's priesthood, and actually to have members of their families included in it. However, the Ptolemies of the earlier part of their 300 years of rule were so obviously foreigners that, as Macedonian-Greeks, they could not establish claims of fictional ancestry in the south of Egypt at the shrines in Edfu and Abydos. Even after miscegenation had made the later Ptolemies part Egyptian, none claimed to be a living embodiment of Re or to be guided by omens of Amon, although Ptolemy VII (Eugertes II) did support those who clung to traditional Egyptian gods while demonstrating his own preference for secular Greek learning. As previously mentioned, Egyptians took advantage of crises precipitated by foreign wars to stage rebellions, and these were supported by both the Theban priesthood and the kings of Kush. The Ptolemies mainly relied upon their armies to keep order rather than attempting to woo the Egyptian priesthood to their side with lavish gifts.

As a subsidiary means of social control the Ptolemies created a syncretistic civic religion that included both Greek and Egyptian gods and used some of the ritual and ceremonies that Egyptians treasured from the past. The god was named Serapis, and an imposing Serapeum was built in Alexandria as his shrine. Within it was the statue of a Greek male, representing Zeus, standing with a scepter in his hand (in contrast to the phallic representations of either Min or Amon). The figure had a basket on his head, and the dog Cerebus lay at his feet. The man, Serapis, was proclaimed as the Hellenic equivalent to "a much revered and highly popular beast divinity, the dead Apis [a mummified bull in a shrine near the Delta] assimilated to Osiris." Thus, to Egyptians, Serapis was expected to evoke emotions associated with the worship of Apis and Osiris. Provision was also made for the worship of Horus and Isis in the Serapeum and in its replicas throughout the Hellenistic world. Serapis became much more popular outside of Egypt than in the land where the Serapeum was established. Despite elaborate public rituals under the patronage of the Ptolemies, ordinary Egyptians remained unimpressed by a god that was not only syncretistic but also synthetic.[266]

However, Serapis and some of the old Delta gods did become the favorite deities of the Hellenized upper strata in Alexandria and the cities of the Delta. Meanwhile, the priests of Amon retained a center of power at Thebes. But with Egypt's military power serving the wishes of foreigners, Egyptian faith in their war god diminished. The main source of strength for Amon shifted to the independent kingdom of Kush, with its capital first at Napata and later at Meroë where rebellion could be plotted. In Egypt itself, however, which suffered from economic exploitation by the Ptolemies and the wealthy stratum in whose interests they ruled, gods other than Amon, a symbol of successful military might, became popular. Osiris and Isis became the beloved deities of the Egyptian masses, and Imhotep became the highly venerated god of medicine. It is significant, too, that while the cult of Serapis and the Oriental cult of Mithra had a widespread appeal for men throughout the Roman Empire, the cult of Isis became attractive to women of all classes from Italy to India. These religious preferences have relevance to our inquiry about the meaning of blackness within Egypt.

Diop has reminded us that no matter what changes religious syncretisms, as a special form of acculturation, brought to Egypt, in the beginning, in the early stages of Egyptian history, both Isis and Osiris were conceived of in Upper Egypt as black deities. Discussing an analysis of linguistic data carried out by his colleague Sossou Nsougann, Diop reported, in the 1981 UNESCO article previously mentioned, that this was not a unique situation—that "black or negro is the divine epithet invariably used for the chief beneficent gods of Egypt, whereas all the malevolent spirits are qualified as *desret* (red)." Diop and Nsougann present a number of hieroglyphics that contain the symbol for *Black* (fig. 6) and state that one of them, when used with a qualifier, applied to the goddess Hathor, to the gods Apis and Thoth, and to several other deities. The outstanding black deities, however, according to Diop, were Osiris and Isis.[267]

FIGURE 6.
Hieroglyphic Symbol
for *Black*.

Some Egyptologists state that it was only when Osiris was being thought of in his role as Judge of the Dead, after the Old Kingdom period, that he was portrayed as black; that he was portrayed as green when conceived of as the god of fertility (as was Hapi, god of the Nile, whose most sacred animal, nevertheless, was a black bull). Budge noted that "The Mnevis Bull at Heliopolis is, like Osiris, black in colour." He states that some priests specifically referred to Osiris as black.[268] Black being the color of the resin used in embalming, it was also closely associated with death, and statues of the dead were sometimes painted in this color. In these cases, and that of Osiris as well, *Black* did not signify gloom and disaster but, rather, the prelude to resurrection, a necessary stage in the movement from this life to the next.[269]

Not all Egyptologists agree with Diop in his assessment of the extent to which "blackness" was correlated with beneficent states and positive values in ancient Egypt. However, discrepancies between his interpretations and theirs can usually be explained by taking two factors into account: (1) the polysemic nature of associations with the colors *Black* and *White* in Egypt and (2) differences in color symbolism employed at different periods in history and in different regions of the Nile Valley, as well as among different strata of the population. *Diop's concern is with the earliest periods of Egyptian history and with Upper Egypt, especially the Thebaid.*

The theology and mythology of Upper Egypt was dominant during the Old Kingdom, and positive associations with ''blackness'' were the rule. In later periods, when influences from the Delta and surrounding cultures became important, the pantheon became polychromatic. *Where black gods remained, the color may have lost ethnic and racial implications and assumed only abstract symbolic significance.* Under the impact of Greek, Persian, and Roman conquerors, not only new gods but also new systems of meaning associated with various colors were introduced. Some of these meanings became part of the so-called Hermetic system of knowledge that was in vogue during Roman times.[270] The extent to which color connotations carried over from the abstract level or from associations with specific gods and goddesses to attitudes toward the color of people is difficult to assess. We have discussed the political situations that set the context in which acculturation took place. We shall here examine briefly what the meaning of ''blackness'' seemed to be in the basic Egyptian symbol system before a massive penetration by values from other social systems began—that is, before Hellenizing and ''whitening'' took place.

Anthropologist Victor Turner has suggested that the symbolism of *Black* should be considered in relation to meanings attached to other colors, especially to *Red* and *White*.[271] In this regard, the significance of *White* to the early conquerors from the black south is of some interest. ''Spiritual whiteness'' existed side by side with ''spiritual blackness,'' and both colors were positive in some contexts and negative in others. The white crown was the symbol of the black south; the red crown of a perhaps somewhat lighter-skinned north. The conquerors from the south called the capital city, which they established on the border of the north, Memphis, or ''White Walls.'' Frankfort states that *White* was the color of Nekhbet, the protectress of Upper Egypt and the King's House. Why this was her color we do not know. Budge says that when these same people painted Osiris *White*, it signified mourning for death.[272] It hardly meant that in the case of Memphis or Nekhbet. Another interesting case is that of the white bull that was consecrated to the black god Min during the New Kingdom.[273] The priests never explained what these *Black/White* contrasts meant to the Greeks and Romans who inquired about the ''mysteries.'' It is probable that *White*, in these cases, usually signified what Frank Snowden calls ''spiritual whiteness,'' always meaning purity.[274] If so, it does not seem to have been placed in Manichaean contrast to ''blackness,'' symbolizing impurity, sin, or evil. In fact, as in the case of Min and his bull, *Black* and *White* seem to have complementary sacred meanings of a positive sort, and *Red* carried some, but not all, of the negative meaning. After all, one of pharaoh's two crowns was *Red*.

Black was sometimes contrasted with *Red* in such a way as to elicit unfavorable emotional associations with the latter. Thus *Red* was the color of Set, who murdered the favorite god of the South, Osiris. But in some areas where Set was an honored god, favorable associations were attached to both red Set and black Osiris.[275] Some students of symbolism have a strong suspicion that since *Red* also referred to the desert, the Osiris versus Set myth may have been a metaphor for the encroachment of the desert on the fertile Nile black soil in some areas of the valley.[276] In any event, Egyptians feared and disliked the desert, which they referred to as *Red*. But *Red* was also applied to people in a negative sense, meaning "aliens," perhaps originally desert nomads who attacked Nile Valley people. Egyptologist Budge reports a belief held during Greco-Roman times that red-colored oxen were once sacrificed by Egyptians to secure an abundant harvest, and that if "red-colored people" landed by accident on Egyptian shores, these aliens would be considered an especially potent sacrifice to the gods for bringing rain.[277] This same theme of sacrificing "red foreigners" appears in the story of Busiris, previously referred to, and this story provided a theme for the painters of Grecian vases. One version of this story implies fear and hate of foreigners; the other emphasizes only the magical-mystical significance of red-skinned foreigners. The paradox in these stories is that the preferred color used by the Egyptians for depicting Egyptian males was also red—a dark red. Thus there are subtleties in the usage of the term and the color that offer a challenge to students of semiotics.

Red is a good color choice for examining the proposition that the meanings attached to specific colors varied according to whether the referent was the skin of a human being or the color of some sacred animal or a god. There were other referents, too. In Egypt, according to Birren, the color *Red* was "the most significant of colors," and he presents evidence of a preference for *Red* in the making of amulets from precious stones. But *Red* was also "the supreme symbol of man."[278] It was the standard color, in varied shades, during all periods of history for portraying Egyptian males in fresco paintings and statues, and it certainly assumed ethnic significance when contrasting Egyptian males with males of neighboring peoples. But since we know that many of the males actually were not *Red*, the question of the precise symbolic significance of the color has to be explained contextually. We have mentioned that Weigall considers *Red* symbolic of the sun when it was used to color the face of the Sphinx. If this is so, it was probably interchangeable with *Yellow* in other contexts that symbolized both the sun and gold, or wealth. The tomb of Tutankhamen was resplendent with gold, including his death mask. Thus the painting *Red* of gods and high-status figures may, on the one hand, have a material referent such as gold; on the other hand, it may have an esoteric mystical significance.

Red as a male attribute was more easily used in an idealized pictorial expression than as an actual guide to the choice of friends and associates, husbands for daughters, or in recruiting soldiers and bureaucrats, for the number of men who actually approximated the color *Red* in skin-color must have been small indeed. Calling an Egyptian male *Red* must have been similar to calling an Afro-American male *Black*. It has been suggested that the convention of painting Egyptian males *Red* and the women *Yellow*, or lemon-colored, may have had the same connotations that it did among the Greeks, where darkness of skin-color signified virility, and lightness the qualities associated with the sheltered existence characteristic of women.

Color symbolism would have been included in the "Mysteries" conveyed to those Greeks who were accepted as learners in the Houses of Life attached to the temples. Such esoteric knowledge found its way into the body of Western knowledge in two ways. Philosophers incorporated some of it into their own systems, amplifying, expanding, rejecting, but not mentioning sources. The best-known case of a Greek who used this system for a wide spectrum of learning was Pythagoras.[279] The other manner of transmission was through the so-called "Hermetic" books, the secret writings that eventually became part of alchemical lore in Europe and of various cult groups such as the Rosicrucians. Some codings became connected with astrology and alchemy, and *Black* had a special mystical significance. For instance, *Black* was Saturn's color, and when applied to people it indicated high intelligence and wisdom but a slow, unenthusiastic manner.

Birren, when discussing Egypt in *The Story of Color*, states explicitly that the "Mysteries" that arose in connection with colleges of priests associated specific colors with certain deities, ideas, and moods. He notes that the priests "carefully studied the cosmos and chose colors to symbolize its great enigmas," but he does not consider the fact that colleges of priests at Thebes, Memphis, Heliopolis, and Hermopolis developed competing theologies and cosmological views.[280] It is probable that there was some variation in the use of color symbolism among them, and that each variant changed from time to time over the long span of Egyptian history. "Blackness" was more likely to have had enduringly high salience at Thebes than at Heliopolis, close to the Delta. It is likely that change in color connotations took place more frequently and easily where self-conscious intellectuals, in colleges of priests, discussed these matters and developed philosophical arguments than among the ordinary people who handed down folk traditions from generation to generation. In Ptolemaic times, for instance, Isis and Osiris may have "remained Black" among the masses long after the Hellenized upper class began to think of them as being closer to a Mediterranean Caucasoid norm image. On the other hand, the ordinary people of the North may also have developed different mental images of Osiris and Isis because of differences in color affect rooted in conceptions of theology and cosmology different from those held in Upper Egypt.

Diop's major thesis is that early Egyptians, predynastic and Old Kingdom, were Black and Negroid. In his 1981 UNESCO article, after arguing that the glyph for *Black*, when associated with the Egyptian glyph for a person, indicates a "black person," he notes that long after the average skin-color had been lightened by centuries of miscegenation, the hieroglyph designating "black person" was still used. He is here suggesting a usage similar to that which designates many Afro-Americans "black" who are very light in skin-color. Egyptologists are still disputing the precise referent for this hieroglyph. Diop might have advanced the hypothesis that as the color of the people shifted toward a lighter average, the meaning of the symbol tended to take on another referent—for example, the black *soil* instead of black *people*—and that it came to mean "those who live on the black land," even though at first it meant "black people."[281] In any event, there is no doubt that throughout its long history, Egyptian culture invested "blackness" with positive affect and with religious and magical significance. Therein lies the important significance of the hieroglyphic for students of attitudes toward "blackness."

Jules Taylor, formerly a staff member of the Brooklyn Museum, writing in the inaugural volume of the *Journal of African Civilizations* in 1979, claims that the positive affect of "blackness" was not confined to the religious and magical domains. He comments that "Egyptian iconography includes a tradition of representations which assign black complexion to particular gods and royal persons." After giving a number of examples, including several pharaohs, Osiris, and Min, he points out that some scholars insist that the positive affect associated with this "spiritual blackness" did not imply a similar attitude toward the dark skin-color of ordinary people. It is Taylor's view, on the other hand, that "the attempt to disassociate the 'black-ness' of cosmic and divine fertility from the 'Blackness' of African ethnicity must be challenged."[282] In making the challenge, however, the fact of a progressive "whitening" process that took place after the fall of the Eighteenth Dynasty cannot be ignored, and Diop takes this into account in his vindicationist writings. What he insists upon, however, is a recognition that "blackness" was not *devalued* in Egyptian *antiquity*.

The conquest of Egypt by "white" military and political elites gave prestige to a somatic norm image at the opposite pole from "Negro." Paradoxically, however, resistance to Persian, Greek, and Roman domination gave renewed prestige to early "Negro" rulers, and to contemporary Egyptian rulers who, because of centuries of miscegenation, represented many shades of "black." While somatic differences between the ruler and the ruled after the Ramesside Age were highly visible and must have assumed some social salience, it is impossible to document this process until late Roman and early Christian times. Even then the traditional dichotomy between "civilized" versus "barbarian" still prevailed; but, at the level of abstract color coding, new modes of thinking were penetrating northern Egypt and were being carried over into social relations to a limited extent. "Black" had never meant "barbarian" or "uncivilized" among either Greeks or Egyptians.

Sociocultural Context and Color Evaluations

As Chancellor Williams quite correctly emphasizes, the destruction of Black Power in Egypt by the Assyrians and the withdrawal of the kings of Kush back to Ethiopia had nothing to do with the fact that the victors were "White" and the Egyptian/Ethiopian foes were "Black."[283] Esthetic prejudices or pejorative stereotypes that did not find expression in the records handed down to us may have existed, but one fact is clear: in the great conflicts of the ancient world, race was irrelevant in the choice of foes and allies and in the meting out of punishment and rewards by victors. It is noteworthy, too, that a tradition celebrating Piankhy's piety and his compassion as a victorious conqueror were handed down by Egyptian priests to the classical and Hellenistic worlds, not comments about his color. Judah's kings were concerned about the ability of an Ethiopian/Egyptian coalition to help them resist Babylon and Assyria, not about the color of the potential allies. When the Hebrew prophets rejoiced at the destruction of Thebes, the city of heathen gods that tried to "seduce" Judah and defy Jehovah, it was not because the devotees of those gods were

Black. It was because they were wicked. These color-free judgments seem strange to people living in modern racist societies and are therefore sometimes even questioned as facts.

After the withdrawal of the rulers of Kush from the contests for power in the eastern Mediterranean and the Middle East, three social and intellectual currents affected cognitive and emotional reactions to the colors *Black* and *White* and the attitudes, stereotypes, and behavior affecting black people. One of these currents was the process of Hellenization that began in Egypt under the Psammetichi, reached its peak during the reign of the Ptolemies, and affected the new religion, Christianity, that emerged during the period of Roman imperial rule. Another social current was the Christian crusade against paganism that reached its peak in Africa during the sixth century A.D. when Justinian used military force to destroy old Egyptian shrines. Finally, after the seventh century A.D. the Islamization of northern and eastern Africa began with the invasion of Egypt by Arabs. Some of the apparent contradictions relating to race and color that accompanied the operation of these intellectual, political, and social currents can be understood only by observing them in specific sociological and ecological contexts.

Three geographical areas in which *Black/White* relations underwent continuous redefinition were: (1) Egypt, where for centuries the process of miscegenation had been shifting the somatic norm away from the early Negroid form, but where evidences of black political and cultural leadership in the past could not be ignored and a predominantly Negroid population, the Egyptian Nubians, persisted in Upper Egypt; (2) the black diaspora in cities on both sides of the Mediterranean as well as in parts of Mesopotamia, Syria, Palestine, and Arabia, where an early black presence became greatly augmented under Islam, and in Greece, Crete, and Cyprus (during some periods), where Blacks were a minority and were continuously being absorbed into the majority population through miscegenation; (3) "Ethiopia," broadly conceived as Africa south of the Saharan, Libyan, and Egyptian deserts, where tribal organization was the rule but where statebuilding by black elites was proceeding rapidly during the early Christian period in Egypt and North Africa. Egypt has been discussed, and the diaspora cases will be examined in the second volume of this work. One part of Ethiopia, Meroë, is examined briefly in the concluding pages of this chapter. The existence of an independent state in Ethiopia after the Twenty-fifth Dynasty lost its power in Egypt was a primary factor in preventing "blackness" from becoming a synonym for *slave* or a symbol for innate inferiority.

THE CHANGING IMAGES OF ETHIOPIA AND ETHIOPIANS

From Mythological Ethiopia to the Kingdom of Meroë

Classicist Frank Snowden is convinced that contact with black men functioning as soldiers during the Persian wars constituted the first relationship that people from the Greek city-states had with any substantial number of Africans who were not Egyptians.[284] Greeks had been using the term "Ethiopian," or "people with burnt faces," in reference to non-Egyptian dark-skinned people for several centuries. A map of the make-believe world of Greek mythology would contain numerous legendary places where Ethiopians lived, stretching from the Atlantic Ocean, where the Hesperides were and the Ethiopians close to the setting of the sun resided, eastward to Elam, near the mouth of the Tigris and Euphrates rivers. Somewhere in Ethiopia was the place where Perseus rescued Andromeda from the sea monster, but its location was never clearly designated; nor was the homeland of the "blameless Ethiopians" specified, where the gods went occasionally to banquet, according to Homer.[285]

After the sixth century B.C., the Greeks gradually narrowed the use of the term "Ethiopian" to apply only to people living on the continent of Africa outside of Egypt. Thus Memnon, who brought 10,000 black troops to fight at the battle of Troy, was originally said to have come from Mesopotamia—from Susa in Elam. However, by the time of Amenhotep III, father of Akhenaten, it was widely believed that he and his soldiers had come from the Nile Valley, and two monumental columns were erected at Thebes by this pharaoh in his honor.[286] There were traditions among the Jewish people that one of the sons of Noah, named Cush, had settled somewhere in Africa and that he had descendants in Mesopotamia and Arabia as well. By the time of the Twenty-fifth Dynasty, the Egyptians were using the term "Kush" (Cush) to apply to the kingdom that had grown up near the third cataract of the Nile.[287] They expanded it to include the kingdoms of Napata and Meroë. The Greeks translated the word Kush as "Ethiopia." Kush ceased to be a vague place in Homeric mythology and became a kingdom with its capital on the Nile. The Greeks used the skin-color of the dominant ethnic groups south of the first Nile cataract in naming the area. By contrast, a cultural-geographical term was used for the area between the Mediterranean and the first cataract. They called it "Aigyptos," the Greek form of a word used by the people who lived there to designate their land as "House of the god Ptah."

Ethiopia during the Ptolemaic Period

During the reign of the Ptolemies, the land that the Greeks called "Ethiopia" became a focal point of interest for several different groups. The priests, in their search for Egypt's "roots" that began under the Psammetichi, included the kingdom of Kush as well as some other areas as part of the mythological "God's Land," or "Land of the Spirits," from which Egyptians from time immemorial believed their religious rites and ceremonies—and perhaps ancestors—had originally come. Some priests even taught that Egypt began as a "colony" established by Ethiopians. The precise geographical extent of "God's Land" was not clear, but the upper Nile Valley was certainly a part of it.

Another influential circle in Ptolemaic Egypt was composed of historians and geographers of several nationalities. Associated with the museum in Alexandria, they were interested in extending and correcting the work of Herodotus, who had visited Egypt during the time of the Persians and interviewed priests, travelers, and any other people who claimed to know the history and contemporary conditions of the African areas south, west, and east of Egypt. Herodotus had divided the inhabitants into Eastern Ethiopians and Western Ethiopians, and because the color and features of some peoples in Mesopotamia and India resembled those of the Africans he defined a group that he called Asiatic Ethiopians. Herodotus also classified the Africans into "red" and "black" Ethiopians, and into those with straight hair and those whose hair was kinky. To these many tribes and peoples he applied the basic Greek division between "civilized" and "uncivilized" peoples. Among the "civilized" Ethiopians, he deemed the inhabitants of the city of Meroë most worthy of comment. Later classical scholars supplied additional details, most of them fanciful, about the "uncivilized" Ethiopians, whom they had never seen. They also recorded the beliefs of priests who said that the Ethiopians had taught mankind the proper way to worship the gods, and that Egypt had passed on to Greece the Ethiopian gods, who were renamed, and the rituals, which eventually took on new forms. "Ethiopian" gradually became a term that meant "black Africans" only. Their physical traits were frequently discussed, but seldom in a pejorative fashion.

The Ptolemaic kings were also interested in Ethiopia. But in addition to the scholarly concerns that some of them had, there were important economic and political motives involved. They sent expeditions deep into Africa in quest of ivory and other trade goods, including ostrich feathers and precious stones. Elephants were always in demand for public spectacles and as troop carriers during wars. And, as in the past, Nubia supplied most of Egypt's gold. Some of the products were obtained by trade and some were seized by force, as were people who were used as slaves and soldiers. The southern frontier of Egypt was inevitably a disturbed frontier despite the existence of a seventy-five-mile-long condominium along the Nile south of the first cataract, which Egypt and Meroë administered jointly as land dedicated to Isis. This area was known as the Dodekaschoenos (or twelve schoenoi [a unit of land measurement]).[288]

An old pattern of Nubian resistance to Egyptian encroachment flared up occasionally. This made Ethiopians popular with the Egyptian masses, but a foe to be fought by the monarchs. The fifth Ptolemy is reported to have sent 500 horsemen recruited in Greece to attack what were not too precisely referred to as "the Ethiopians." Snowden writes:

> In some of the Egyptian rebellions which plagued the later Ptolemies, especially in Upper Egypt, Ethiopians played a role. An important factor inspiring their revolts, it has been suggested, was the maintenance of a continued Pharaonic tradition in the region south of Egypt which, unlike Egypt, had not been subjugated by the Greek conquerors. The existence of an old tradition and an independent Nubia, just beyond their southern frontier, was a source of hope to nationalists who remembered legends of Egyptians who had taken refuge in Ethiopia and had returned to recover what had been lost.[289]

But Meroë, the capital of the leading kingdom of Kush, was not "just beyond their southern frontier." Herodotus, who never made the journey to Meroë, reported, as a result of his inquiries, that it took two months to get there.[290] Yet, as the Ptolemies knew, the kings in Meroë claimed all of the territory up to the Egyptian border, even if they did cooperate in administering the Dodekaschoenos.

The interest of the Ptolemaic kings in securing information about Kush was neither detached nor sentimental. For them, knowledge had an intelligence function related to the ever-present possibility of armed conflict. Despite their objective of controlling the mines and trade routes through the Meroitic kingdom by force if necessary, Snowden suggests that the Ptolemies reversed the policy of the Psammetichi and resumed the earlier practice of using Ethiopian soldiers in the Egyptian army. It is not clear whether these were recruited with the approval of the rulers, or whether they were secured from among the desert tribes and disloyal Nile Valley subjects of Meroë, or whether they were simply slaves from inner Africa. In any event, Snowden, referring to the Middle and late Meroitic periods when the Ptolemies and Romans were dominating Egypt, comments on the reappearance of Blacks in a role in which they had often appeared in the past: "Ethiopians and Mauri fought in the great imperial armies on all fronts and far from their homelands in the same manner as black soldiers of colonial countries formed a part of later European armies."[291]

Greeks living in Naucratis and the people of varied nations and races in Alexandria were in contact with individuals from the kingdom of Meroë and other parts of Ethiopia who were in these cities in a variety of roles. Sculptors, painters, and ceramicists have left a fascinating record of their presence, but how the ordinary people reacted to them we have no way of knowing.[292] We do know that one of the traditional black deities—Isis—was venerated by Egyptians, Kushites, and Greeks alike. Anthropologist Adams reminds his readers:

> In the Isis cult of Roman and Meroitic Nubia we have to recognize the beginnings of one of history's most important ideological transformations. Within the microcosm of the Nile lands, the worship of Isis became the first truly international and supra-national religion. . . . Philae became a holy city and a place of pilgrimage alike for all classes and nationalities: Greeks, Romans, Egyptians, Meroites, and desert nomads. No wonder then that the temporal influence of the priestly oligarchs of Isis came to resemble that of the Vatican in later times. . . . The worship of the age-old fertility goddess of Egypt anticipated the role which was to be played by Christianity and Islam on the larger stage of the Middle Ages.[293]

As the worship of Isis spread outside of Egypt, a tendency to "whiten" her became apparent in the European lands. One favorite form for depicting her was as a Roman matron; another was as a Caucasoid woman holding a baby. But her connection with the shrine on the border between Ethiopia and Egypt was not forgotten, and Snowden presents pictorial evidence of Negroid idiom in some of her places of worship in Italy. It is no mystery that the Byzantine emperor Justinian, at the beginning of his attempt to stamp out the last vestiges of paganism, sent his soldiers first, in A.D. 540, to the island of Philae to close down the temple of Isis. The troops took the statues from the shrine to Constantinople, and the temple of Isis was reconsecrated as the church of St. Stephen.

During the 650 years between 300 B.C. and A.D. 350, the Greeks, Romans, Egyptians, and people of the Middle East considered the kingdom of Meroë to be the most "civilized" portion of the vast African area they called Ethiopia. In fact, the term "Ethiopia" was often used as a synonym for the kingdom of Meroë. The Meroitic period of Ethiopian history had been preceded by the Napatan period (750 B.C.–300 B.C.), when the capital was at Napata, near the fourth cataract of the Nile, and from which the Twenty-fifty Dynasty came. Before that, Ethiopia had been a land of myth and legend, except for the Nile Valley between the first cataract and the third, which was well known to the Egyptians, but not to other people. The Napatan and Meroitic kingdoms can be viewed in relation to Egypt somewhat as Macedonia is in relation to Greece. The latter received a "civilizing" impulse from Athens, and then Alexander emerged on the international scene much as the Twenty-fifth Dynasty had done. Macedonians were considered relatively "uncivilized" Greeks vis-à-vis Athenians and Corinthians, just as the Kushites were relatively "uncivilized" Blacks vis-à-vis Egyptians.

The sculptured figures of high-status Negroes found in Alexandria, Naucratis, and Rome are testimony to the acceptance of some Blacks as competent persons and social equals, in contrast to "wild" Ethiopian tribes such as the Blemmyes and numerous others described by classical writers.[294] But "wild" people were being described by Tacitus and others as inhabitants of Europe, too. The Scythians had a particularly bad reputation. The kingdom of Meroë was accepted as a black civilization that had evolved from a more rude and crude past, just as Roman and Greek civilization had. "Civilized" people were close enough to their own "less civilized" pasts to be tolerant of customs among others, such as human sacrifice and infanticide, that they had abandoned but whose memories still existed among them in myth and legend. Their philosophers had begun to ridicule deities among whom adultery, incest, and murder were common activities, but there was little of what we now call superstition that any "sophisticated" people then felt constrained to apologize for tolerating.

The detached cultural relativism of the ruling strata and religious and intellectual elites of the ancient world was first abandoned when the prophets of Judah and Israel began to measure nations against ethical norms that they believed had absolute validity, and to apply the same judgment to all nations that had been passed upon Babylon when conquered by the Persians—including their own, "Thou hast been weighed in the balances and found wanting." A cosmic purging process was envisioned that would eventually "redeem" some nations. After the fifth century B.C., Greek philosophers of the Platonic tradition elaborated norms of the Good, the True, and the Beautiful, and the Stoics concentrated upon defining an ethic that would characterize the good man. Meroë, like Athens and Rome, would fall short according to these norms. It is likely, although it cannot be proved, that Greek criticism would have given Meroë a lower rating in esthetics than in the domain of social ethics. In any event, direct evaluations of Ethiopians were seldom made except in terms of comparative soldierly virtue and comparative piety. This is true of Ethiopians of the Meroitic period as well as those in the mythological past. Ethiopian soldiers were considered superb archers, and their rulers had a reputation for devotion to the gods.

By the time the Greeks assumed the initiative in organizing resistance to Persian control of the eastern end of the Mediterranean, the Kushite kings had moved their capital to Meroë from Napata, where the Twenty-fifth Dynasty had won a reputation for piety and wisdom. They did not participate in the great struggles when Greek and Egyptian fleets fought the Persians by sea and the Carian and Greek soldiers bore the brunt of the fighting on land. (However, individual Ethiopian soldiers fought as mercenaries on both sides.) They won respect for their resistance when Cambyses threatened to invade Ethiopia and his troops met disaster; and, later, for their defeat of Oroödontes on their border with Egypt. The Ptolemies had a healthy respect for the fighting prowess of the Ethiopians as well as for the difficulties of terrain and climate involved in invading their territory. They rested content with keeping open the roads to the gold mines and to the Red Sea, and did not try to incorporate Ethiopia into Egypt. Nor did the Romans make any serious attempt to make a province of it. They depended, rather, upon stirring up desert tribes within the kingdom's boundaries to weaken the control of the king at Meroë. The kings and queens of Ethiopia confronted the power of Rome with the same air of assurance that characterized the Berber kings of North Africa before and during the Punic wars. Rome did not care to invest resources in an attempted tropical African conquest while fighting on the northern borders against the tribes in Europe and trying to pacify Arabia and Palestine. Nero sent an expedition far up the Nile between A.D. 50 and 68, but it seems to have been a joint exploring and trading expedition, not a Roman invasion. There are also accounts of exploring and trading expeditions into sub-Saharan areas west of the Nile.[295]

The Kingdom of Meroë and Its Culture

The kings and queens of Meroë were able to defend a large area south of Egypt against aggression, carry on diplomatic relations with

Egypt and Rome, and administer jointly with them the temporal domain of Isis in the Dodekaschoenos during a period of vigorous Roman expansion and war with the Ptolemies and with the Seleucid rulers, and of each of them with the other. The kings of Kush had deliberately withdrawn from these struggles and concentrated on preserving sovereignty within their own boundaries, while occasionally giving aid to the people of Egypt when they made a move to throw off foreign domination. Protected by the Nile cataracts and the deserts, the kings and queens of Kush were able to achieve a high degree of stability despite the ethnic heterogeneity of the Ethiopian population. One scholar has observed that "for over a thousand years, first at Napata and then at Meroe, there flourished a strongly original civilization which, beneath an Egyptian-style veneer fairly constantly maintained, remained profoundly African."[296] Some critics of this culture consider it also profoundly conservative as compared with the more "adventurous" Mediterranean and Mesopotamian cultures. Margaret Shinnie has commented on the extent to which cultural borrowing was highly selective over this long span of years, stating that "Kushites took and used what they found attractive and useful from the civilizations with which they came into contact, yet their own character was never submerged."[297] After the fourth century A.D., however, it became transformed, a matter to be discussed subsequently. In its most highly developed form, in the late Meroitic phase, Kushitic culture had its own form of writing, Meroitic cursive script (not yet satisfactorily deciphered), and distinctive religious concepts and rituals, as well as unique forms of social organization.

Up to the end of the Twenty-fifth Egyptian Dynasty, when Napata, not Meroë, was the seat of the royal family and the great shrine of Amon was close by, the rulers of Kush conceded a higher value to Egyptian culture than to their own (no doubt considering it a more advanced variety of their own). Much of the energy of the Kushite royal family went into a struggle to play what it considered its proper influential role in a common Egyptian/Ethiopian civilization. It was evident that, historically, the labor of the Ethiopian people, the gold from their mines, the exertions of their soldiers, and the efforts of intellectuals whose roots, if not their place of birth, had been in Nubia, contributed to the development of the civilization north of the Nile's first cataract. Facts of geography—river cataracts, increasing dessication, and lack of flood plains between the first and fourth cataracts—had separated the Egyptian and northern Ethiopian populations over a long span of time. Yet, from the period of the pre-dynastic A-Culture on, the development of a Nile Valley civilization had been a joint endeavor that utilized the most desirable part of the northern valley. The pharaohs of the Twenty-fifth Dynasty reclaimed their heritage in a heroic fashion. Then, after a brief seventy years of power, for reasons that they never made explicit but that appear to be a conscious recognition that they were in a "no win" situation, the black kings withdrew from the competitive empire-building contest of the Middle East. During the era of the Psammetichi, in a region far removed from the conflicts in that area that consumed so much of Egypt's wealth and energy, the kings and queens of Kush developed their flourishing kingdom at Meroë.

The Kushite royal family, whose origins seem to have been in the vicinity of the third Nile cataract, eventually established its capital at Meroë in the fertile triangle formed by the confluence of the Blue Nile and the Atbara River. Apparently an industrious population was already settled there, growing durra (a variety of sorghum) for subsistence and cultivating cotton on a large scale for making cloth and for trade. Weaving became a thriving industry. Pottery of high quality had been exported from the area since predynastic times. Living in symbiotic relationship with the cultivators were pastoralists who kept large herds of cattle on the pasture lands provided by the flood plains formed by both rivers. While Psammetichi, Ptolemies, and Romans were dominating Egypt, Meroë developed into that prosperous African kingdom of which Rostovtzeff gave the first clear, coherent, although brief, account in 1927, and to which full scholarly treatment is given in UNESCO's 1981 *General History of Africa*.[298]

How the Kushite dynasty established its power at Meroë is not known; by the time of the Egyptian Ptolemies, it was receiving taxes paid in kind or personal service and was presumably thought of as an effective force that protected important trade routes, grazing lands, and farms from desert marauders. Until Meroitic script is deciphered, recorded traditions of origin, if any, cannot be known. Myths abounded, from the time of the Ptolemies, that assigned considerable antiquity to a kingdom of Meroë, but these are Greek, Hebrew, Egyptian, and Roman accounts and are of doubtful authenticity. Recent research may confirm the legends.[299]

The extensive building of temples and tombs embellished with gold, and the presence of gold objects in graves, indicates the existence, during Ptolemaic times, of mining on a large scale under the control of the Meroitic authorities, as well as the existence of skilled goldsmiths. However, the relative scarcity of iron objects in archaeological sites has led some scholars to doubt the still widely held view that Meroë was also the center of an important iron-smelting industry. Great slag heaps nearby led the British archaeologist Sayce to refer to it as "the Birmingham of Africa," but the slag heaps have not been excavated or the contents analyzed. Some skeptics doubt that they were connected with the working of iron at all. Although the burden of proof has been shifted to those who support the concept of an African Iron Age originating in Meroë, that older theory should not be rejected forthwith since so little careful archaeological excavation, analysis, and interpretation of Meroitic culture has been done compared with efforts expended in Egypt and in the Nile Valley between the first and fourth cataracts. Furthermore, new evidence is now appearing, such as a bellows recently discovered near Meroë, that strengthens the argument of those who believe a center of iron smelting existed there. In any event, as Chancellor Williams points out (censoriously, it might be noted), iron was never utilized during the Napatan period for the making of arms to match those of the Assyrian foe, although it may have been used later for weapons that carried conquering armies from Meroë southward and westward in Africa.[300]

A substantial middle class composed of traders, craftsmen, and minor officials existed when Meroë's civilization was at its height. Some observers feel that slaves were used in the building and maintenance of temples, these being individuals captured as prisoners in wars against weak tribal peoples in the south and west, and against the desert raiders who occasionally attacked the valley. However, it is the conclusion of the Sorbonne Egyptologist Jean Leclant that slavery "developed very slowly and never constituted the main base of production. . . . In inscriptions a greater number of women than men is always mentioned, which indicates that domestic slavery was the prevailing form." In Egypt the bulk of the slaves after the Eighteenth Dynasty were European and Asian prisoners of war; in the kingdom of Meroë they were "uncivilized" Blacks. There was no demographic basis for the emergence of *racial slavery*, since nonblacks were so few. The records indicate that a few slaves were exported to Egypt along with other tropical goods, and it is presumed that these were secured from outside the boundaries of the kingdom.[301]

Culturally, Meroë was not part of the Mediterranean and Middle Eastern world from which it was separated by vast, sparsely inhabited territories south of the first cataract of the Nile and by all of Egypt. Despite centuries of contact with Egyptian elites, the Kushite royal families preserved their own distinctive ethos. It was this, no doubt, that Chancellor Williams had in mind when he referred to a potential high development of black civilization that never had a chance to flower because it was repeatedly overwhelmed by invasions from Egypt and Arabia—a *second* black civilization, since Williams considers Egypt a black civilization. A study of the distinctive qualities of the Meroitic civilization is an exercise in "what might have been" if its institutions could have been refined rather than supplanted.

That the Meroitic political system stressed the divinity of the monarch, as in the Egyptian system, can be stated only as probable; but for over 500 years the system gave cohesion to a multiethnic society with widely varying levels of social complexity. From the scant data available it seems as though internal disorders of the type that were cyclical in Egypt did not occur in the Napatan or Meroitic kingdoms. The major crises seem to have come from invasions by ethnic groups breaking in upon the valley from the deserts and from the loss of a trade monopoly between Egypt and the East.[302]

Commenting on the way in which the king was chosen, and emphasizing the fact that there is some evidence that "the right to the throne might depend even more on claims through the maternal line than on royal paternity," one scholar notes that "some of these traits have close parallels among kingdoms and chiefdoms in various parts of Africa."[303] Leclant mentions that "the entourages of Kushites frequently included the mothers, wives, sisters, and female cousins." Pharaohs Piankhy and Taharka exemplified this custom among the kings of the Twenty-fifth Egyptian Dynasty. Egyptologists have considered this a distinctively Ethiopian cultural trait in these two cases. A. A. Hakem, an Egyptian Africanist, summarizing the available Nubian data for the 1981 UNESCO volume, has noted:

> The exact role played by royal ladies in the earlier periods is not quite clear but there are many indications that they occupied prominent positions and important offices in the realm. During the Kushite rule over Egypt the office of the chief priestess (*Dewat Neter*) to god Amun in Thebes was held by the daughter of the king and gave her great economic and political influence. Even after the loss of Egypt, and consequently of this office, royal ladies continued to hold prominent positions coupled with considerable power among the temple priesthood of Amun at Napata and elsewhere.[304]

The Queen Mother, known as the "Mistress of Kush," adopted the wife of her son, thus entrenching her influence (did Queen Tiye have such a relationship with Nefertiti?); and after the reign of King Nastasen (335 B.C.–310 B.C., that is, about the time Alexander the Great entered Egypt), an increase in the power of Queen Mothers can be deduced from a study of religious scenes on Meroitic temple walls. Hakem continues:

> In the later period these queens—either mothers or wives—started to assume political power and proclaim themselves sovereign, even adopt-

ing the royal title Son of Re, Lord of the Two Lands (*sa Re, neb Tawy*) or Son of Re and King (*se Re, nswbit*). Many of them became famous, and in Graeco-Roman times Meroe was known to have been ruled by a line of *Candaces, Kandake,* or queens regnant.[305]

Some of these influential women ruled as sole sovereigns; in other cases they were co-rulers in what Hakem calls "an interesting development":

> This was the close association of the first wife of the king and, perhaps, their eldest son on many of the important monuments. This suggests some degree of co-regency since the wife who survived her husband often became the reigning candace.[306]

There were persistent traditions in the Hellenic world that both Alexander the Great and Augustus Caesar met with Candaces to discuss problems relating to a border between Egypt and Ethiopia. The Ethiopian queens are depicted as wise and shrewd and, in some of the legends, are said to have been beautiful.

Reviewing the institution of the monarchy as a whole, Hakem writes:

> This kingship system which developed in Kush had some advantages over a rigid system of strict direct succession since it eliminated the danger of an unsuitable successor, whether a minor or an unpopular personality. The injection of new blood into the royal family was assured by the system of adoption. The various checks and controls inherent in this system, the prominence given to the queen-mother and the insistence on rightful descent ensured the rule of the same royal family. All this may have contributed to the continuity and stability enjoyed by Napata and Meroe for such long centuries.[307]

There has been a tendency among some European and American scholars to either dismiss Meroitic culture as an inferior "bastardized" imitation or reflection of Egyptian culture, or else to admit its worth while insisting that the Kushite kings couldn't have been Black. The Afro-American scholar Snowden has suggested some cautionary guidelines in appraising Meroitic culture:

> There was a remarkable lack of bias in the classical commentaries. The Greeks expressed no astonishment that Ethiopians, a people whom they at times described as black or dark and as having several so-called Negroid physical traits, had conquered Egypt or had constructed great temples. Westerners, it has been pointed out, have traditionally regarded the civilization of the Napatan and Meroitic periods as Egypt "running downhill to an inglorious and too long protracted conclusion." No such view existed among the Greeks and the Romans. The

Ethiopia of this period, according to one modern view, when considered from the perspective of African history, was ancient Egypt moving closer to black Africa at a time when a portion of black Africa possessed a capacity, greater than ever before in its history, of experiencing influences from an urban civilization.[308]

The Somatic Norm in Meroë

What kind of people were these kings and queens of Kush? One of the older Egyptologists, Petrie, has referred to the Twenty-fifth Egyptian Dynasty as "Libyan-Negro." Oliver and Fage state that "throughout its long period as an Egyptian colony, and also during the first two or three centuries of its independent existence, Kush, like Egypt, was basically a country of white Caucasians. . . . The new capital was at Meroe. . . . The Kushite dynasty henceforward ruled over a mixed population of Caucasians and Negroes, with the Negroes no doubt predominating."[309] In both cases the reader is left with some ambiguity about the actual appearance of the royal families of Kush. However, all of the available evidence indicates that these Kushites would fit neatly within the North American definition of "Negro" and would include Latin American "Negro" and "mulatto" types as well. The excellent photographs published by the Brooklyn Museum in 1978 in *Africa in Antiquity: The Arts of Ancient Nubia and the Sudan* leave no doubt about how the kings and queens of both the Napata and the Meroitic period looked. And the portrayals and inscriptions on stelae give us some clues as to their attitudes toward themselves. Many of the males, self-confident in their aggressive masculinity, were usually depicted by the artists in a style that Brooklyn Museum curator Bothmer calls "brutal realism." Nevertheless, there are also some portraits in a "softer" mode.[310]

Where statues of the kings and a few other males were painted or where bas-reliefs were colored, the conventional Egyptian reddish brown was usually used, although in most cases the features are what some physical anthropologists call "True Negro." Only one sculptured head had been found that was painted black, and the significance of this exception is not clear. A break with Egyptian practices is evident, however, in the use of this same reddish brown for coloring men and women, the Egyptian convention of a lighter color for the latter not being used. Obviously the red is a convention for the actual dark-brown skin-color of both sexes.[311]

Despite centuries of close contact between ruling Kushite families at Napata with Egyptians, the Kushites developed a female somatic norm image of desirable body proportions that differed from that of

the Egyptians of any period after the Old Kingdom. Archaeologist
Shinnie once observed, "The Kushites' own wall carvings on their
temples showed their queens as plump rounded ladies, and quite
different from the very slender ladies portrayed by the Egyptians."[312]
Another scholar, Steffen Wenig, subsequently modified the generalization to say that "the amplitude of queens" is characteristic of *late*
Meroitic sculpture in contrast to the figures of goddesses, who are
"always slender." Shinnie's observation should be further modified
to take account of the fact that many less slender ladies appear in
Egyptian Old Kingdom sculpture. Time as well as place is a factor in
producing differences in esthetic norms. The generalizations of both
scholars must be treated with caution, also, because they ignore context. For instance, a queen depicted as slaying enemies on a pylon of
the Apedemek temple has "amplitude" (plate 27). However, Queen
Aminitore, when portrayed worshiping the Egyptian god Amon,
resembles the slender Egyptian type (plate 28). But when this same
queen is portrayed on one wall of the temple dedicated to the Meroitic
lion-god Apedemek, she has greater "amplitude" than the queen
depicted on the pylon (plate 29). These representations suggest that
the context of action, and perhaps even age in the life cycle, may have
determined how an artist portrayed a Meroitic female sovereign. Furthermore, such representations may not be trustworthy guides at all
as to how queens and princesses actually looked.[313] In a general way,
however, it seems accurate to conclude that Meroë's somatic norm
image for the ideal *queenly* woman, after the Twenty-fifth Dynasty,
differed from that of both the Greeks and the Egyptians. On the other
hand, some of the corpulent portrayals of the queens may be stylized
representations symbolizing maternity and fertility, intended neither
as realistic portraits of queens nor as the somatic norm image of
women in the royal families. What is significant is that the Meroitic
queens had no objections to being represented as obese.

Some experts on Meroitic art are convinced that a "typical"
woman can be defined. After discussing one trait, a student writes,
"Meroitic characteristics are also clearly expressed in the rendition
of obese females with pendulous breasts."[314] That this was not a trait
that Kushite artists associated only with the royal family in Meroë
or with a specific age group in the population is suggested by some
small statues of females found in tombs in northern Kush (that is,
Lower Nubia close to Egypt), so-called *ba* statues that are supposed
to represent actual persons. The report on these specific objects states
that "the female figures always have pendulous breasts rendered in
high relief."[315] Because they are ba statues, the commentator has
ruled out the possibility of this being a kind of stylization used to

represent fertility, which often occurs in West African wood carving by exaggeration of the breasts. In some other Meroitic and West African art, steatopygy may have the same meaning. In discussing these features of Meroitic art that can easily lead to stereotypes of the population, an examination of some of the paintings and drawings which illustrate the Brooklyn Museum's *Africa in Antiquity*, vol. 2, ed. Steffen Wenig, might be relevant. They suggest that both class and ethnic factors, reflecting degree of "civilization," may have resulted in a heterogeneous population in Kush, with breasts and hair styles being criteria of social status.[316]

Instances could be cited of other features of sculpture and bas-relief that are distinctively Meroitic. For instance, Egyptians produced images of a pharaoh being suckled by Isis, as Horus was. A Meroitic bas-relief shows the goddess suckling a queen, a Candace, not a king. One striking portrait dated between A.D. 50 and A.D. 62 shows King Amanitenmemide being protected by a winged goddess. Both king and goddess are very Negroid, with the latter wearing a disk and horns characteristic of both Hathor and Isis.[317]

There may be differences in the treatment of sexuality also in sculpture, painting, and drawing. Erotic phallism, as distinct from the fertility symbolism in the representation of Min in figure 5, does not appear in Egyptian art (although it may have been present in some of the mass religious ceremonies), and the one case found in Meroë may not be indigenous. Archaeologists were surprised to find what appears to be a piece of erotic graffiti drawn on the walls of a temple to Apedemek near Meroë. It exhibits a degree of explicitness about sexual relations that, according to classical Greek and Roman esthetic canons, should be handled more subtly, unless satyrs were being depicted. A woman with that "amplitude" of which the art critics speak stands with her legs spread wide, ready to receive a large penis held in the hand of a man who is apparently kissing her. Both are shielded from prying eyes by a large piece of fabric they, together, are managing to hold behind them.[318] Travelers, traders, and soldiers passed through Meroë from many lands, including Ptolemaic Egypt, Rome, India, Persia, and parts of East Africa and Arabia. The graffiti may be from an alien hand "profaning" Apedemek's temple. The discussion that follows assumes, however, that it is the work of some talented Meroite who did not happen to be employed in producing art for either the priesthood or the court.

Although esthetic norms of both classical and Egyptian art are breached, this is not a drawing that would have elicited moral strictures from the Greco-Roman world. From Judaeo-Christian perspectives, however, such a public display in a temple was evidence of a kind of "depravity" that demanded a missionary crusade to eradicate it. (Similarly, the English would eventually recoil from erotic Hindu temple art.) It was only less reprehensible to them than a picture of Min, because it was not blasphemous in the sense of depicting an ithyphallic god. Eventually Christianity prevailed in Meroë, and while this bit of graffiti was not defaced, it was apparently ignored. What the ordinary people thought about any of the old images or the new ones that came with Christianity is a kind of data archaeology cannot retrieve. The graffiti may have represented the impact, at a somewhat crude artistic level, of the eroticism associated with Alexandrine Hellenistic court styles, which combined both Greek and Roman elements. This appears in Meroë at a more sophisticated level in the case of a structure built in either the second or third century A.D. and which contained a modified Roman bath. A group of sculptured male and female forms surrounded the bath, and these have been characterized as "derivative of Alexandrine art."[319]

Apparently the males who frequented these baths found acceptable a statue that combined Meroitic preferences in female beauty with Greek esthetic norms. It was a statue of a naked woman, with features less Negroid than the Meroitic somatic norm, erected by the pool and painted reddish brown, not yellow or very light brown, as it would have been according to Egyptian conventions. It has been noted that "the figure's hips are strongly emphasized in accord with the Meroitic ideal of beauty."[320] Another striking statue at the bath, said to have "a characteristic Meroitic fullness to the female form," is also painted reddish brown. The Brooklyn Museum catalog mentions that "this naked girl, dubbed the Venus of Meroë by the excavator is, perhaps, copied from a figure of Aphrodite." The major differences can be inferred from the description: "The cheeks are plump and fleshy and the lips protruding. . . . The breasts are heavy and the thighs are powerfully built."[321] The piece of sculpture was obviously an imitation of a Mediterranean statue, but this "Venus" was Negro, not Caucasian.

As the sculpture surrounding the bath indicates, Meroë did not exist in total isolation from the Mediterranean civilizations. King Ergamenes, who lived during the reign of Ptolemy VI, probably received a Greek education in Alexandria. He displayed a degree of rational skepticism about the oracle of Amon that led him to defy it in some unspecified way. For doing so the priests ordered him to commit suicide. He not only refused but had the priests executed, according to an account given by Strabo. However, rejection of domination by the priests of Amon did not mean rejection of everything Egyptian. Ergamenes administered the shrine of Isis jointly with the Ptolemies, but also gave some aid to rebels fighting against them. After this brief period of rule by a king with an interest in the Hellenistic world, a tendency to emphasize local Meroitic gods seems to have become dominant. Some scholars also detect the influence of East Indian cultures, but there are no equivalents of Hindu erotic temple sculpture or of Tantric rites that merge sexuality and worship.

Transformations in Meroitic Society

By the beginning of the Christian Era, according to Snowden, thousands of black people were living in the Mediterranean and Middle Eastern diaspora. There were considerably more in Egypt, where some were native. Most black people, however, were scattered unevenly through the vast spaces of the African continent below the Saharan, Libyan, and Egyptian deserts, on the savannah lands north of the equatorial rain forests and in the eastern highlands north of the equator. They were just beginning to move into the southern African areas sparsely inhabited by the Pygmies and Bushmanoid hunters of the steppes. No Roman legions had ever marched into the sub-Saharan lands determined to impose "civilization" upon them as they were doing in Britain and among the Gauls and Franks and Goths in Europe.

Throughout the continent south and west of Egypt, hundreds of tribal societies had been developing for centuries, some pastoral, some agricultural, each with an ethos of its own. Evolving in isolation from the Mediterranean littoral and the Nile Valley, all were structured around solidarities of kin organized into families, lineages, and clans, and bound together by religious systems in which veneration of ancestral spirits played a prominent part. Cosmology and iconography, as well as myth and ritual, were influenced by the complex of climate and fauna and flora in specific areas; but anthropologist Jacques Maquet presents a convincing case, in his book *Africanity*, for enough similarities of social structure, basic unifying values, and esthetic principles to justify those who, like Leopold Senghor, define a distinctive African quality that they call *Négritude*.[322] Cheikh Anta Diop has stated the salient characteristics of what he designates "Negro-African" cultures and argues convincingly that they formed the substratum of Egyptian civilization in antiquity.[323] The Afro-American historian Chancellor Williams accepts the ancient division into "civilized" and "uncivilized" Ethiopians, deplores the customs of the latter, and theorizes that their "degeneration" resulted from harassment by invading whites who drove successive waves of Blacks from the Nile Valley.[324] Egypt and Ethiopia, for him, represent the acme of black achievement. Anthropologists are inclined to avoid judgments as they apply the principle of cultural relativism in evaluating these societies. Vindicationists, however, must be sensitive to critics and detractors. They cannot react with the detachment of anthropologists.

All of the societies of Africa south of the deserts, being insulated from the pressures of the empire builders in the Mediterranean and North Africa, preserved some customs that antedated the development of "civilization" in the Nile Valley. Some south of Egypt in the valley preserved customs from as late as the early period of the Psammetichi that may have once existed in Egypt. Thus, while the Egyptians buried statuettes (*shawbati*) with a corpse to symbolize servants, or members of families of kings, who would be needed in the afterlife, the sacrifice of actual human beings took place at the death of some Kushite kings.[325] The rulers at Meroë, from whose line the Twenty-fifth Dynasty came, had abandoned such practices by Ptolemaic times. They had adopted many Egyptian customs, but some customs that still prevail in inner Africa, such as facial scarification, were not abandoned. Scarification carries overtones of "savagery" to Westerners—to an extent that facial painting and tattooing have never excited. By Old Kingdom times Egyptians had dropped this aspect of a common Nile Valley culture along with human sacrifice at the death of prominent people. However, one Kushite king portrayed on a bas-relief from late Roman times had three facial scars that were probably ethnic symbols (plate 30). Other kings had scars such as these or scars across the forehead similar to those of the contemporary Nuer and Dinka peoples of the upper Nile region.[326] These Ethiopian monarchs were not ashamed to display their scarifications. It is significant that thousands of miles to the west, in what is now Nigeria, the people who developed the Nok culture, so well known for its art, also accepted scarification as a normal part of their culture. A small, attractive terra-cotta sculpture of a woman, in which facial scars have been rendered according to a deliberate canon of a black esthetic, would not necessarily have struck a Grecian sculptor as unattractive, though far from his esthetic norm (plate 31).

Revolutionary transformation in Kushite society began in the sixth century A.D., when a campaign to Christianize the northern part of the kingdom of Meroë was successful. Whole clusters of custom and habit defined as "pagan" disappeared, and the kingdom of Nobatia emerged. Makuria became the second Christian kingdom and Alwa the third (see map 4). Architecture and art reflected this process.[327] A period of stabilization and reintegration took place but had less than three centuries of growth before the strains imposed upon Ethiopia by the conquest of Egypt in the eighth century A.D. began to be felt. However, Islamization was a slow, prolonged process that finally resulted in the obliteration of most of the evidences of the Christian culture, except slave raiding among "pagans" in the areas southwest of the Nile, in Darfur and Kordofan and the Nuba Hills, as well as among the people in the riverrain south of the Bahr el Ghazal. The slave trade flourished under both Christianity and Islam to an extent that it never had in the pagan kingdoms of Napata and Meroë.[328] The dissolution of the kingdom of Meroë was a gradual process that began during the period of the late Roman Empire and was completed by the end of the sixth century A.D.

The Dissolution of the Meroitic Kingdom

Its geographical isolation from the troop movements in the Mediterranean and the Middle East, as well as the stability of its political system, permitted the kingdom of Meroë to avoid conquest by the Egyptians, Greeks, Persians, and Romans. These factors could not assure its existence after the sixth century A.D., however, and, indeed, it has been customary to assign an even earlier date to the "fall" of Meroë: A.D. 320, the year in which armies from the kingdom of Axum in the African highlands to the east attacked the capital. This date focuses attention upon an important fact, namely, that although Meroë was able to avoid disastrous confrontation with the armies in North Africa, a menacing kingdom with military power—Axum—was growing up between its eastern borders and the Red Sea. It was ruled by an Africanized Semitic-speaking dynasty originally from Yemen in Arabia. Axum had raided Meroë's lands several times before A.D. 320, when a combination of factors led to a gradual economic and cultural decline that weakened the kingdom. The details of this process, about which there is now considerable consensus among historians, archaeologists, and anthropologists involved in Nubian studies, have been succinctly described by Jean Leclant. However, writing in the *General History of Africa*, he reminds us that we actually know very little about the last centuries of Meroë as compared with some other areas of the world at the time. It is Leclant's opinion that Meroë did not have sufficiently trained defensive troops to beat off the attacks of "wilder" peoples—the Nuba from the west and the Blemmyes from the east.[329] The blows of the Nuba probably weighed more heavily than those of Axum in the disintegration of the Meroitic kingdom.

The Nuba were a warlike ethnic group that seems to have been encouraged by the Romans to move into the area between Aswan at the first cataract and Dongala at the fourth cataract to offset attacks from the warlike Blemmyes, who were harassing both Egypt and the Lower Nubia province of the kingdom of Kush. This area eventually broke away and formed the independent kingdom of Nuba, or Nobatae, and its language, Nubian, gradually replaced the Meroitic language there. It was then absorbed by another breakaway province that formed the kingdom of Makuria, the province in which the old Kushitic capital of Napata was located, near Dongola. Meroë itself became part of another kingdom, Alwa, with its capital at Soba, near the confluence of the Blue Nile and the White Nile (see maps 3 and 4).

Virtually nothing is known of the internal tensions that seem to have been weakening the social structure of the Meroë kingdom prior to the military attacks by Axum. While it is tempting to speculate about a possible internal proletariat dissatisfied with the inequities of a class-stratified society, we can actually document some conflict between pastoralists and agriculturalists that seems to have had an ethnic as well as an economic basis. Anthropologist Adams is inclined to feel that a general malaise occurred within ruling circles and the rather extensive mercantile middle class when prosperity declined as a result of the shift of trade away from the Meroë–Egypt routes and toward caravan trails closer to the Red Sea, under the control of Axum.[330] Rostovtzeff before Adams, as well as Leclant and Hakem since, have all stressed basic economic factors intertwined with Roman Empire politics as the key to the decline of Meroë.

The kingdom of Meroë controlled a network of trade routes between the Red Sea and Egypt, and its own craftsmen augmented the stream of commodities flowing northward from India, Persia, and Arabia. Hakem, professor of history at the University of Khartoum, now located where the city of Meroë once stood, wrote recently:

> At the beginning of the first century before our era, the main route was transferred from the Nile axis to the Red Sea. This diminished the volume of goods directly exported from Meroe since many could be obtained in northern Ethiopia where Aksum had just started to rise. The last centuries of the Meroitic Kingdom coincided with the crisis of the Roman empire which led at first to a sharp decline and later to a quasi-total interruption of trade relations between Meroe and Egypt. Many towns in Lower Nubia dependent on this trade were ruined. Moreover, neither Rome nor Meroe were at this time able to defend the trade routes against the raids of nomadic Blemmyes and Nobades.[331]

The Axumite reports of their invasions speak of them as expeditions against "black" and "red" marauders who, they claimed, were disturbing the peace in the lowlands. They mention nothing of their own attack on the capital city of Meroë. Axum left no occupying forces, a fact that seems to indicate that its objective was attained by merely disrupting trade routes running parallel to the Nile.

In view of an ongoing argument among Africanists about the impact of Meroë on other parts of Africa, Leclant's remarks are apposite:

> Some authorities have theorized that the Kushite royal family fled westward and settled at Darfur where there would seem to be traces of the survival of the Meroitic traditions. In any event explorations in these regions and in the southern Sudan should afford us a better understanding of how Egyptian influences were transmitted towards inner Africa through the intermediary of Meroe. The glory of Kush is quite surely reflected in certain legends of Central and West Africa. The Sao have legends of the bringing of knowledge by men from the east. Knowledge of techniques spread; certain peoples cast bronze by the "cire perdue" method, as in the Kushite kingdom; but above all, and of vital importance it would seem to be thanks to Meroe that the working of iron spread over the African continent.[332]

Basil Davidson, in a section entitled "The Mystery of Meroe" in his *Lost Cities of Africa*, argues persuasively for an Iron Age that transformed central and southern Africa and had its genesis in the diffusion of peoples and techniques out of Meroë.[333] Leclant seems to accept this view. Military conquest was one means of diffusion.

Map 5 indicates the extent of monarchical political organization superimposed upon lineage and clan structures in Africa when Europeans first began to explore the continent in the fifteenth century. The contrast with state building in America at the same time is striking. Most Africanists attribute the highly developed state of African political evolution primarily to the early domestication of plants and animals and the food-producing revolution that had provided a broad base for the multilinear evolution of complex political institutions. But some feel that migration and diffusion from the Nile Valley account for the specific patterns.[334] Leclant presents a conclusion more relevant to vindicationist scholarly interests than are arguments about the precise details of "cultural penetration" when he remarks, "Whatever the importance of this penetration of Meroitic influences through the rest of Africa, the role of Kush should never be underestimated."[335]

The Adoption of Christianity

The kingdom of Axum absorbed a number of ethnic groups to form a nation that became known as Abyssinia. Sometime after the disappearance of the kingdom of Meroë, the expanded Axum kingdom assumed the name Ethiopia.[336] Both this new Ethiopia and the old

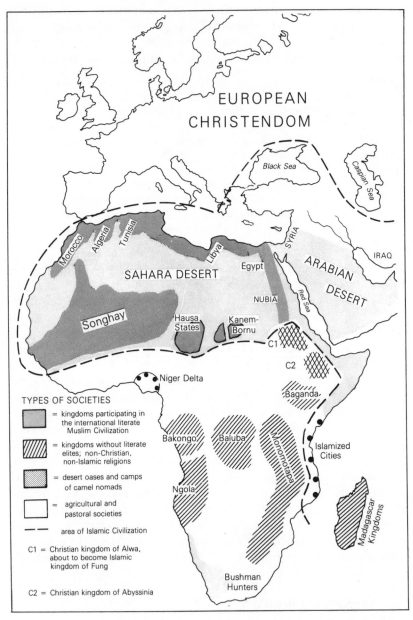

MAP 5. Extent of Urbanization and Political States in Africa and the
Americas: Fifteenth and Sixteenth Centuries a.d. Cartography
based on a concept by the author.

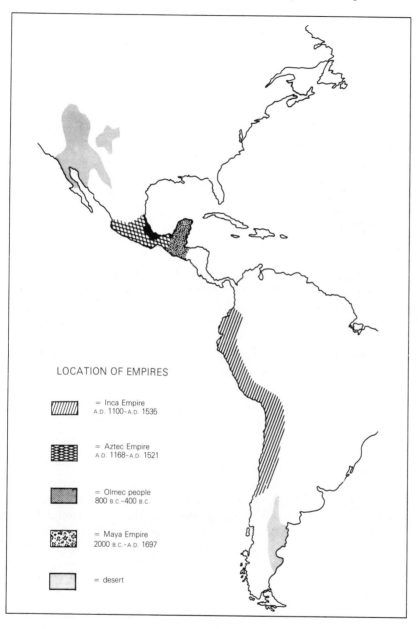

LOCATION OF EMPIRES

= Inca Empire
A.D. 1100–A.D. 1535

= Aztec Empire
A.D. 1168–A.D. 1521

= Olmec people
800 B.C.–400 B.C.

= Maya Empire
2000 B.C.–A.D. 1697

= desert

Ethiopia became symbols of black sovereignty to nationalist-minded eighteenth- and nineteenth-century Blacks throughout the world. When Afro-American and South African leaders quoted the psalm, *"Princes shall come out of Egypt and Ethiopia shall soon stretch forth her hand unto God,"* multiple layers of meaning were present. Implicit in the slogan was a vision of what they called "the redemption of Africa," a concept that in its secular import meant eventual release from domination by European colonial powers and, perhaps, the restoration of the glories of ancient Egypt and Ethiopia. Insofar as Ethiopia was a metaphor for "black men everywhere," it meant the disappearance of slavery and racial discrimination. For Black Zionists it meant a return to "the Motherland," an ingathering of the exiles. For all devout Christians it meant that the entire continent would eventually be converted to Christianity.

About 1,400 years before the ambivalent exiles in the Americas began to interpret the psalm and the phrase about "redeeming" Africa to mean the spread of Christianity, the church fathers in Alexandria, Constantinople, Carthage, and Antioch in Syria were using the same prophecy to refer to the evangelization of Africa. They were applying the term "Ethiopia" very specifically then to the Nile kingdoms south of Egypt, that country having already become Christian by the end of the sixth century A.D. The land between the first cataract and the sixth, with the exception of the portion dedicated to Isis, was claimed by the royal family of Meroë until a few centuries before Christian evangelism began. However, because of internal problems combined with attacks from the east and west by desert tribes, Kush fragmented into three parts during the fourth and fifth centuries A.D.: Nobatae, or Nubia, in the north; Alwa in the far south; and Makuria in between. Nubia was Christianized first.

The enthusiasm of the missionaries was reinforced by a New Testament story that convinced them that one of the apostles had introduced Christianity into Ethiopia soon after the crucifixion of Jesus Christ. (The same story was cited centuries later by Afro-American vindicationists to stress Ethiopia's high estate in antiquity.) The compilers of chapter 8 of the Acts of the Apostles did not know that *Candace* was a general term for "queen," but such ignorance did not affect their use of the legend:

26. And the angel of the Lord spake unto Philip, saying, Arise and go toward the south unto the way that goeth down from Jerusalem unto Gaza, which is desert.

27. And he arose and went: and behold, a man of Ethiopia, an eunuch of great authority under Candace queen of the Ethiopians, who had

the charge of all her treasure, and had come to Jerusalem for to worship,

28. Was returning and sitting in his chariot read Esaias the prophet.

According to the story, Philip, after convincing the eunuch that the prophecies in Isaiah referred to Jesus Christ, converted and baptized him. Then "the eunuch saw him no more and went on his way rejoicing." As Snowden points out, the early church fathers interpreted the story at several levels of allegorical symbolism, and most of them thought it held the promise that the Ethiopians, "remotest of men," as Herodotus had called them, would eventually be converted.[337] Sometime within the first three Christian centuries, a work of fiction, *An Ethiopian Romance*, was published, in which the king of Meroë emerges as a man with a streak of natural piety and ethical insight that made him an unusually attractive prospect for conversion, a man in the mold of Piankhy. Some critics think a churchman wrote the romance to make this point; others believe that a Greek gymnosophist wanted to emphasize the equality of all men.[338] From a black perspective, in contrast to a Christian or a humanitarian one, it is significant that both the biblical story and *An Ethiopian Romance* take black kings and queens and court officials seriously as normal participants in the life of the epoch. Neither the compilers of the New Testament nor the author of the romance seemed to feel that their readers would find anything incongruous in discussing black pagan royalty in the same manner that other people of similar status would have been discussed.

When the conversion of the kings of the shattered Meroitic kingdom began, it was only one incident in the complex maneuvering of Middle Eastern church politics. The people of Kush became the objects of a special kind of cultural imperialism that carried with it important implications for the future of race relations. Professor Bruce Trigger stresses the international politics in which Kush was a pawn, beginning with the fate of Lower Nubia, the northern portion of the kingdom between the first cataract and the fourth:

> Early in the sixth century, Byzantium [i.e., Constantinople] concluded a military and trade alliance with the Kingdom of Axum which had been Christian since the fourth century [the century during which it invaded Meroë]. Already in A.D. 524, the Byzantines had promised to provide Blemmye and Nobadae recruits to support the Axumite invasion of Yemen. It therefore seemed desirable to the Byzantines to convert the Nubian kingdoms in order to confirm their friendship and support. It was Byzantine policy to convert pagan peoples living beyond

the borders of the empire as a means of promoting imperial security. The final closing of the Temple of Isis at Philae about A.D. 540 was accepted by the Nubians without incident.[339]

Professor Adams is not only impressed with Nubia's "acceptance without incident" but also by the speed with which Christianity spread. He does not feel that the people experienced it subjectively as a foreign imposition:

> When the new faith was formally introduced by missionaries in the middle of the sixth century, it seems to have been rapidly accepted by rulers and subjects alike from Aswan to the junction of the Niles. Although both the motives and the success of the early evangelists may be attributed partly to political considerations, *in a larger sense the rapid spread of Christianity south of Aswan probably reflects the Nubians' desire to rejoin the civilized world.* The advent of Christianity wrought an ideological transformation in Nubia unparalleled since the introduction of civilization itself . . . a needed replacement for the obsolete traditions of the pharaohs [italics added].[340]

Adams is here interpreting Nubian history from a Western Christian perspective in which the conversion to Christianity is Nubia's gain. Professor Chancellor Williams, himself also a product of Western Christian culture, views the political maneuvering from a black perspective: White people with power deliberately manipulated black people who had less power, and in the process the Blacks lost the ability to read and write in their own language (Meroitic) and may have undergone a type of psychological reorientation that made them less confident of their own abilities on earth while reassuring themselves that they were precious in the sight of God—a white god.[341] Nubia, or Nobatae, in the north was said to have embraced the new faith in A.D. 543, when the leading people adopted the Monophysite brand of Christianity that Egyptian and Syrian churchmen espoused. Makuria was converted to the rival Orthodox fold of the Bishop of Constantinople in A.D. 570. Alwa was last, its rulers becoming Orthodox in A.D. 580. Trigger suggests that the rulers in each area were trying to forge advantageous alliances with different groups within the Byzantine Empire. Their attacks on each other were often vicious; those on pagans were merciless.

The isolation from Middle East political affairs was forced upon Kushite kings by the fall of Thebes; their isolation from Hellenizing cultural influences came partly from geography but was partly by choice. Now, in the sixth century A.D., as Adams phrases it, "they were joining the civilized world again" by embracing a world religion backed up by Roman military power. While pagan Rome was persecuting the Christians, and emperors like Caligula and Nero were simultaneously indulging in dissolute displays of decadence and monstrous acts of sadistic cruelty while serving as patrons of learning, the Meroitic rulers were relatively "civilized," even if by modern standards their "world" was less sophisticated than either the Roman or Hellenistic world. True, their queens are depicted at the gruesome task of spearing captives in the stylized pharaonic fashion. But did the women of the Meroitic royal family know that while the missionaries were trying to wean them away from such practices the Bishop of Alexandria was lending his sanction to the murder of a brilliant female scholar (415 B.C.)? The victim, Hypatia, taught Platonic philosophy in Alexandria and was admired even by some prominent Christians. Cyril, Bishop of Alexandria, considered her a bad influence. He is reported to have given his explicit sanction to a mob led by clergymen that assaulted her one evening, dragged her through the streets, and murdered her in a church after torturing her.[342] Perhaps the rulers of Meroë did not know how fanatical Christians treated some recalcitrant "pagans," or heretics. Even if they knew, perhaps they did not care. The Christian Blacks learned quickly how to justify enslaving "pagan Blacks." What could the rulers of Meroë hope to gain by participating in the ecclesiastical politics of Egypt and the Middle East, especially since, as Chancellor Williams points out, what Adams calls their "reentry into civilization" was at the price of accepting asymmetrical relations within the hierarchy? There is some evidence that this was done to gain allies in their own secular factional struggles.[343]

Chancellor Williams describes the interplay between local politics and international affairs, and in doing so observes, with evident disapproval:

> White administration and control of African Christianity was assured by establishing the head of the Church in Lower Egypt (the Patriarch of Alexandria) with power to appoint all bishops in Africa. The bishops appointed were always white or near white until token appointments of Blacks to lesser posts, such as deacons, had to be made following protests by Black church leaders, supported by their kings.[344]

Although objectively the discrimination was along a line of color, it was experienced primarily by the churchmen and rulers on both sides as a struggle for power between different national groups and between

competing theological doctrines, as well as for control of the institutions of education and propaganda in a pagan land that had valuable natural resources and controlled a trade route to Christian lands
bordering the Red Sea. Whether or not the actors in the drama ever
conceptualized the struggle as a color conflict we do not know.[345]
Alexandria won out over Constantinople in the conflict over which
type of Christianity was to prevail in Makuria and Alwa, but in Chancellor Williams's assessment of the situation:

> "White" Egyptian control over the churches reflected the same poli-
> cies that were to follow through the centuries into our own times: No
> church sponsored theological schools for the training of African clergy.
> By thus preventing educational opportunities, they could always main-
> tain that the Blacks were simply "not qualified" for this or that high
> post. . . . *There were no situations, however, in which some Blacks did
> not override all obstacles and become bishops* [italics added].[346]

The last sentence punctuates the crucial contrast between race relations during this period in the history of Christianity in Africa and the
situation that prevailed for centuries after the modern missionary
movement in Africa began during the fifteenth and sixteenth centuries A.D. No such concessions were made by either Catholics or Prot-
estants until the nationalistic upsurge among Africans after World
War II forced changes in the Western Christian approach to Africans.

Chancellor Williams wrote about the Nubian church before he had
an opportunity to see the colorful murals found on the walls of the
Bishop's Cathedral in the town of Faras near the second cataract.
These were discovered by a Polish expedition working with the UN-
ESCO salvage project in conjunction with the building of the Nile
high dam near Aswan. Pictures of the murals are now available in all
of their colorful splendor in several sources, the most accessible being the Brooklyn Museum publication *Africa in Antiquity*, 2 vols.
(1978). It is unlikely that Chancellor Williams would be satisfied by
either the murals or the comments about them. One cathedral mural
portrays a dark-brown bishop with two protective hands laid on his
shoulders, those of a white St. Peter. There are those who will prefer
the symbolism of another photograph, mentioned earlier, in *Africa in
Antiquity*, a pagan Negro king of Kush standing proudly while a
Negroid Isis throws her protective wings around him. The writer of
the caption to the plates depicting the bishop was sensitive to some
of these black concerns, stating of Bishop Marianos: "As we see from
his brown skin, this dignitary was certainly a Nubian." Elsewhere a
comment is made about Bishop Petros: "That the bishop was a dark-

skinned African is clear not only from this painting but from his remains."[347] Adams makes these observations: "The dominance of Coptic influence in the Nubian paintings is obvious. . . . Even so, the mural art of Nubia is not simply a faithful imitation of the contemporary Christian art of Egypt; it betrays also influences from Palestine, Syria, and Byzantium." A feature of that art would excite cynical remarks from Afro-American black nationalists, however. The white symbols of religious power and holiness that they would resent do not seem as important to Adams as the Coptic artists' inclusion of Nubians in the paintings: "A purely local and realistic touch is added by the portrayal of native rulers and bishops with dark features in contrast to the white faces of the Holy Family, saints, archangels, and nearly all the other figures depicted."[348]

In the Christian iconography of Axum, realism gave way to active African imagination, which turned many biblical figures brown, though not Christ or the Virgin Mary. There is no way of knowing whether the Nubians invested the whiteness of the religious figures with any symbolic significance of superior purity or simply considered the use of this color as an attempt by the artist to portray the way biblical personalities probably looked as contrasted with Ethiopians. Whatever the subjective reactions, the fact remains that Christianity introduced a "whitening" process that had reached Egypt earlier through Hellenization.

The Christianized culture of Axum produced a substantial body of literary and historical material in the language of the Amharic ruling class. Until Meroitic script has been deciphered, the question of whether some comparable material exists for Meroë cannot be answered. None seems to have been preserved in other vernaculars, such as Nubian, nor in Greek or Coptic. Neither Adams, who considers the Christianization of Ethiopia as "rejoining the civilized world," nor Chancellor Williams, who considers it a case of racist brainwashing, has commented on the extent to which the churches of Nubia, Makuria, and Alwa produced individuals who made contributions to the international Christian culture of the Middle East. It was too late for any to have played a part in the great debates that took place before the evangelization of Ethiopia, that is, the ecumenical councils of Nicea (A.D. 325), Constantinople (381), Ephesus (431), and Chalcedon (451). Research on the role of Ethiopian Christians, if any, at the councils of Constantinople in A.D. 553 and 680 is necessary in order to determine whether the leaders of the new black churches preferred to concentrate on local pastoral duties and to let theology remain the affair of Middle Eastern and Mediterranean

Christians, arguing in a Hellenistic manner over abstruse theological questions. Both the questions and the behavior were alien to the
ethos of the elites of Meroë—and of Egypt, for that matter. It was the
Alexandrine church, operating in the Greek tradition, not the Coptic monasteries, that did the hairsplitting. Nevertheless, an examination of council records and Eastern church literature—theological,
devotional, liturgical, and historical—including the Syriac (Nestorian)
for evidences of black input, if any, would be relevant to the theme
of this book. It is hoped that eventually this will be done.

HELLENIZATION, CHRISTIANIZATION, AND THE
BLACK SELF-IMAGE

The Hellenizing process never affected the Meroitic kingdom to
more than a superficial extent except during the reign of Ergamenes
(Arkamani), whose rule was coterminous with that of Ptolemy V.
The Candaces who came later, those impressive female sovereigns,
seem to have set Meroë on a course away from one that had Alexandria as its model, and even away from the Egyptian pharaonic model.
When Meroitic culture did finally succumb to outside cultural influences, it was to Middle Eastern and Egyptian Christianity rather
than to Greek or Roman paganism or to Hellenistic syncretisms. The
dominant centers of early Christianity—Antioch in Syria, Constantinople, Carthage, and Alexandria—were successful in replacing the
syncretic gods of northern Egypt and the black gods of Upper Egypt
with Christian myth, ritual, and iconography by A.D. 500. They also
replaced the cult of Amon and the lion god, Apedemek, in Meroë; Isis
in Nubia; and various other local gods in Ethiopia by A.D. 600. The
process of Christianization involved both evangelization by missionaries and military action. In sharp contrast to Hellenization, it affected the culture of the masses of the people as profoundly as that
of the elites.

Negroid Egyptians continued to make up a substantial proportion
of the population in Upper Egypt after the Hellenizing process had begun under the Psammetichi, but this area gradually lost its religious
significance. Ptolemy IX destroyed Thebes between 88 and 80 B.C. because it was a center of political disaffection, and the priests of Amon
thereafter had to depend upon kings in Ethiopia for asylum. Darius
of the Persians closed down temples and persecuted and killed Egyptian priests, but his action only drove the faith underground and made
the priests popular heroes. His successors relented, and the later
Ptolemies tried to make political accommodations to Egyptian

religion while co-opting the priests to support their rule. They had very limited success. During the sixth century A.D., after Christianity had developed strong roots among the Egyptians, the Roman emperor Justinian used the imperial troops to demolish the major pagan temples, including the great shrine of Isis at Philae. Coptic Christianity gave the final blow to the power of the old black gods in Egypt when the Virgin Mary replaced Isis and the Christ Child took the role of Horus.

While black gods were being denuded of their symbolic value as holy, beneficent beings, after a period of being co-opted and "whitened" by the pagan Greeks and Romans, the invaders still considered "black magic" to be a malevolent power associated with Egyptians and Ethiopians who refused to become Christians or were only partially Christianized. As the process of "whitening" took place, with respect to deities there is no firm evidence to indicate that the devaluation of "blackness" in the religious domain was accompanied by an esthetic devaluation of *Black*—that it was defined as an ugly color of skin, that dark skin-color indicated a cognitive deficit, or that a Negroid facial configuration was repulsive. There seems to be some evidence, however, that "Negroidness" had implications of *low social status* in some parts of the Greco-Roman world; but this is not the same thing as an implication of moral or intellectual inferiority or lack of ability. We have no way of knowing what stereotypes the lighter-colored masses of Middle and Lower Egypt held about the more Negroid part of their national population or their Ethiopian neighbors, until the tenth century A.D. when some Arab scholars stated that the populace's resentment against cruel Nubian soldiers was sometimes expressed in pejorative racial epithets.[349] Nor do we know whether the darker portion of the Egyptian population expressed any resentment toward lighter Egyptians and toward the Greek and Roman oppressors with remarks about *their* skin-color. The silence of the historical documents is not, of course, a conclusive statement about the presence or absence of color consciousness and color prejudice. Indirect evidence of an archaeological or onomastic type suggests, however, that if racial prejudice was present it was not institutionalized as racism.

Where pronounced difference in skin-color distinguishes the conquerors from the conquered a potential exists for the institutionalization of the asymmetrical social relations into systems of color caste or into class systems in which skin-color is an important variable in limiting or facilitating upward social mobility. This potential does not necessarily realize itself. As noted in chapter 2, Hoetink has suggested, also, that when a differential in power is associated with a difference in physical traits, the somatic norm image of the dominant group tends to become the desired somatic norm for those dominated. They will tend to devalue their own self-image.

There is no evidence that skin-color assumed a status-conferral function in Egypt before the reign of the Ptolemies, but it seems likely that it took on such connotations during that period and in the period of Roman rule that followed. Meroitic Ethiopia, however, was outside the area where a color line marked off those who ruled from those who were being ruled, and it was not until the advent of Christianity and Islam that the religious personalities held up for admiration and veneration differed markedly in skin-color and features from the worshipers. Although dark skin-color and "Negroidness" may have been evaluated negatively in making judgments about beauty or acceptability of a woman in marriage in Greco-Roman antiquity, there is no clear evidence that this was so in either Egypt or Ethiopia; and if it was, such evaluations would not necessarily have affected the status of the individual in other domains. If such esthetic evaluations were being made, it is difficult to detect them, since they were obviously ignored in mate selection by prominent people (as, for example, during the Eighteenth Dynasty in Egypt, or in the case of the Ethiopian Candaces).

Pictorial evidence from the Fourth, Twelfth, Eighteenth, and Twenty-fifth dynasties, as presented in this book, indicates clearly that "Negroidness" was no barrier to participation at the highest political and social levels in Egyptian society. Nevertheless, some passages in the written record suggest the presence of a mild skin-color prejudice in some circles or, alternatively, a corruption in the texts that reflects editing by someone later who did have such prejudices. Such passages, although rare, should not be ignored. One cycle of stories, "King Cheops and the Magicians," is extant on a papyrus that was inscribed during the Hyksos period before the Eighteenth Dynasty, when Asians were in power. Included is a legend about the mother of the first three kings of the Fifth Dynasty. She gives birth to a first child with the aid of Isis and Nephthys, "whose limbs were of gold." When another child was about to be born, Isis is reputed to have said, "Do not be dark (kkw) in her womb in this your name of Keku." The meaning is difficult to interpret. It could be a statement of a preference for a lighter child, or it could be, as one scholar suggests, a pun on King Keku's name, whose meaning is obscure.[350]

A manuscript is in existence that most Egyptologists think was written during the reign of Amenhotep III, husband of Queen Tiye, black mother of Akhenaten. Yet it contains a passage that seems to imply a preference for light skin-color. Amenemope advises his son to avoid the "hot-tempered" type of man who

> sets families to argue
> He goes before all the winds like clouds,
> He darkens his color in the sun
> . . .
> His lips are sweet but his tongue is bitter.

Is this a metaphorical derogatory use of dark skin-color? The color is accepted as sacred in another passage in which Amenemope invokes

> The seer of the Mother God,
> The inspector of the black cattle of the terrace of Min,
> Who protects Min in his chapel?[351]

Akhenaten, of this same period, in his famous "Hymn to the Aten," reveals a consciousness of anatomical difference but makes no esthetic or moral judgment:

> you have set every man in his place, . . .
> Tongues are separate in speech,
> and their characters as well;
> their skins are different,
> for you have differentiated the foreigners.[352]

Could there be a hint of a belief in inborn ethnic differences in this hymn, even though no invidious distinctions are necessarily involved?

Among fifty-nine love songs of the New Kingdom presented in a comprehensive anthology by Professor William Kelly Simpson, only three references to skin-color occur. In one of the "Songs of the City of Memphis," the lover refers to the beauty of "The Golden Goddess," which a footnote explains is Hathor, patron goddess of women, often depicted as Negroid.[353] In the "Cairo Love Songs" the lover wishes he were his beloved's "Negro maid" so "the skin of all her limbs would be revealed to me," but the question arises as to precisely what Egyptian word has been translated as "Negro."[354] In the "Chester Beatty Love Songs" there are extensive descriptions of a man and a woman in love in which the man refers to her arms as "finer than gold." The woman states that she identifies with the "Golden Goddess of womankind [Hathor]" and mentions that her lover "brings a blush to my skin."[355] That only a few such references appear in the entire anthology seems significant, but these few suggest a female somatic norm image, at least in some circles, closer to light brown than dark brown. But what of Queen Nefertari and Queen Tiye? Were they admired for their status but considered less than attractive physically?

There are also some puzzling unresolved questions connected with the process of "whitening" during Hellenistic and Roman times that may be examined by considering several cases. The data are sparse, and generalizations derived from what we have must be as tentative as they are tenuous. The cases, from both pre-Christian and Christian written sources, stimulate reflection upon the question: How serious are the consequences to the personalities of black people in societies where skin-color prejudice exists, or where the derogation of "blackness" as a value exists, but where institutionalized racism is not present? Such societies exist today as in the past—in Latin America and the Middle East, for example.

The Candace in the biblical story about the apostle Philip was a familiar personality throughout Christendom by the end of the fourth century A.D., when a serious effort to convert the Ethiopians was about to begin. Another Candace was known to a more limited circle of people, those who could read Greek and Latin manuscripts. An apparent contradiction in tales told about that Candace is relevant to our inquiry. This story appears in Latin in a collection of legends known as *Pseudo-Callisthenes*, from the third century A.D. It told of Alexander the Great, visiting one of the Candaces in her palace in Meroë in the fourth century B.C. He found her to be "of wondrous beauty," but she was reported to have said of her people during the conversation: "We are whiter and brighter in our souls than the whitest of you."[356] This statement is similar in its apologetic tone to that in the poem written 1600 years after *Pseudo-Callisthenes* by the American slave girl, Phillis Wheatley.

The Candace story presents what seems like a paradox: a proud woman of high status apologizing for her dark skin-color to a man she considers her equal, and even though the man is said to consider her to be of "wondrous beauty." The context of Phillis Wheatley pleading for respect even though her color is "the sign of Cain" is completely different. She is an ambivalent exile, sold into slavery and befriended by a white Christian family, existing in a cultural milieu that considers *Black* a sign of evil whether in the abstract or in human skin-color. There is no room in her culture for a strong statement of self-assertion that would challenge what the Other considers a flaw. The Candace, on the other hand, is rooted in her own culture and could, perhaps, accept the abstract Manichean distinction between spiritual "whiteness" and "blackness" without ever thinking that a carry-over to the skin-color of people was implied. The implication of the story, too, is that Alexander drew a distinction between "blackness" as a metaphor for evil and the esthetic implications of heavy melanization.

Apparently the compilers of *Pseudo-Callisthenes* expected any educated Blacks who read this story to believe that a famous queen of a race like themselves, ruler of a well-known and respected black kingdom in Ethiopia, once downgraded her own body image. Would such readers believe this had actually happened? If so, did they think of her remark as part of a diplomatic exchange that probably revealed little of her true feeling about the matter, or as a deeply internalized low estimate of her body because it was dark? Some of the readers of *Pseudo-Callisthenes* may have been aware of another body of literature among the Jews that would have led them to believe that esthetic devaluation of dark skin-color may have existed long before Alexander's conquest of Egypt, even though Alexander reportedly regarded the Candace as beautiful.

The Hebrew sacred writings were in existence in Greek translation when *Pseudo-Callisthenes* was compiled. They contain an account of an episode in which "blackness" entered into an esthetic judgment with status-conferral implications. In the "Song of Solomon" a peasant girl speaks to other girls with whom she is presumably competing for the attention of the king. She says, "I am black *and* beautiful (Greek translation), or "I am black *but* beautiful" (Latin Vulgate translation). In either version she is apologizing for her skin-color and goes on to explain that the sun has darkened her and that she works in the vineyards.[357] The significant point for our discussion is that this self-image has not inhibited her from competing with the other girls for the king's favor. It has not paralyzed her with self-doubt. She considers her darkness a handicap, but not an insurmountable one, and she insists that even though she is dark she is beautiful. It is not clear whether darkness of skin in this passage is considered a racial trait or a consequence of her outdoor work as a peasant, but it does have status-conferring implications that the girl refuses to invest with any esthetic significance.

The apology in the "Song of Solomon," the somewhat defiant statement of the Candace to Alexander, and Phillis Wheatley's statement about the color of Cain are all expressions of the undesirability of dark skin-color. But the social context in each case is different, and the impact upon the personalities of the women therefore was probably different. The Ethiopian woman had the security of not being an outsider and of being at the top of the social pyramid within her own group. Both of the other women were of lowly status. But Phillis Wheatley's position as an African slave in Puritan Massachusetts makes it almost inconceivable that she would aspire to an open love relationship with any prominent white male in that British colony. It is inconceivable, too, that those males could empathize with—or perhaps even understand—the nuances of such a story as that of the Candace and Alexander, or that of the peasant girl and Solomon, about whom they read in their Bibles.

The two cases cited from antiquity might be compared with two stories told by Josephus, the Jewish historian, who wrote around A.D. 90, before Christian values and symbols had become prevalent within the Roman Empire, but at the time when the "Song of Solomon" would undoubtedly have been known to many of his readers, both Jewish and Christian. One of the Josephus stories tells of how Moses, as a young man, being a protégé of the pharaoh's daughter, was given the task of leading an Egyptian army against the capital of the Ethiopian king. When he arrived at the gates of the Kushite capital, he saw the king's daughter standing on the wall and fell in love with her. She admired him and persuaded her father to make peace. She married Moses, and the kingdoms of Egypt and Ethiopia were thus united.[358] This story was written at a time when the word "Ethiopian" was being used to apply exclusively to black Africans and when the kingdom of Meroë had relatively high status.

The other story tells of a visit by "the Queen of Egypt and Ethiopia" to King Solomon.[359] This is the biblical Queen of Sheba, and Josephus locates her kingdom in the Nile Valley. There was no thought in the mind of Josephus that the "blackness" of such women made them unattractive to men of high status, and the custom of speaking of "white souls in black bodies" seems to have not yet been in vogue among either the Jews or the Greeks, from whom he had secured his education. (The English translator of Josephus, centuries later, felt impelled to insert a footnote stating that Josephus must have made a mistake in locating the kingdom of the queen in the Nile Valley. The translator was living in a sociocultural context that made the idea of a black queen visiting Solomon and being praised in this fashion unthinkable.)[360]

Something seems spurious about the story of Alexander and the Candace if it is compared with the story of Phillis Wheatley, with which this chapter began. Wheatley's reaction to being Black seems believable, and this is partly because we are sure she actually wrote the poem. In the case of the Candace, however, we are dealing with a story being told over 600 years after the event allegedly occurred. Since we know from other sources that church fathers had by that time begun to refer to "white souls in black bodies," it is possible that Christian words were being put into a pagan queen's mouth, and that *Pseudo-Callisthenes* reveals more about the thinking on such matters by Christians of the third century A.D. than about how Alexander and the Candace thought in the fourth century B.C. Of some significance, too, is the fact that stories about more recent Candaces were prevalent at the time and one of them refers to Amanirenas, who led her troops against the armies of Augustus Caesar and sent her envoys to negotiate an agreement with his general, Petronius, that preserved the independence of Meroë for several centuries. One tradition held that she was "one eyed and ugly," but brave! Heliodorus's *Ethiopian Romance* appeared during the fifth century A.D., and one of the heroines is a black queen who had a very light-skinned child. It seems that there was a lively interest in tales about Ethiopian royalty in these early Christian years, and that color consciousness was close to the surface when Greeks, Romans, and western Asians were discussing Ethiopians. The reasons for this interest are complicated, and some of them will be discussed in the second volume of this work.

It is not difficult to understand why Christian converts in Ethiopia might have accepted a "mystique of whiteness" in the realm of the supernatural beings who displaced their old gods. Nor is there any mystery as to why individuals in Egypt who were anxious to advance their careers might have adopted, along with other values, the somatic norm image of the Greeks and the Romans, who monopolized economic and military power. It is also understandable why, in areas as remote from one another in time and space as Hellenistic Egypt and the twentieth-century United States, resistance movements would reverse the values imposed by white ruling groups and develop cults that emphasized the mystique of their own culture, as black people had originated, cherished, and developed it.[361]

However interesting the modern phenomena of race and culture contact may be, the crucial cases in examining the Degler-Gergen propositions come from ancient Egypt and Ethiopia and, where data are available, from relatively untouched African settings where contacts with the image-defining Other wielding great military and economic power had not yet made "contrast conceptions" operative and where black people were not yet constantly measuring the worth of their body images against those of white bodies—or yellow, brown, or red bodies, for that matter (or, when they were doing so, made these comparisons from positions of cultural and military dominance, as in the Eighteenth and Twenty-fifth Egyptian dynasties).

That dominance ended as we have noted when the Psammetichi

began to collaborate with rulers of some of the Greek city-states. Eventually, as Egypt was drawn into the political and cultural system of the far-flung Hellenistic world (with Meroë retaining its independence from it) myths developed to legitimate the Hellenizing of Egyptian intellectual and political life. The key myth involved Alexander of Macedon. This youthful soldier, who won for himself history's verdict Alexander the *Great*, encouraged the spread of the story that his real father was not Philip, king of Macedonia, but was rather the great Theban war-god, Amon, who, in the guise of a human being, had seduced his mother. When Alexander's conquering armies entered Egypt, the priests at Memphis proclaimed him a pharaoh, and the oracle of Amon predicted success in the future for his armies.

After his death in Persia, Alexander's body was brought to Egypt for burial. The cultural center of the Hellenistic world bore his name, Alexandria. Along with his body came a story that symbolizes the drastic effect of the Hellenizing process on Egypt, at first through its scholars and the Ptolemy dynasty and later, indirectly, through Christianity, which was, in some aspects, itself a product of the Hellenizing process. For black vindicationist writers, the story has the import of a parable with meanings perhaps not imputed to it at all when it was told among Egyptians, or when Plutarch's readers became acquainted with it.

At a banquet in Persia, when Alexander was celebrating his victories and he, like all his soldiers, had been drinking to excess, he made some remarks that one of his closest associates considered a slur upon the honor of the Macedonians in the ranks. This was Clitus the Black, an old family retainer and a brave soldier, whose mother had been a nursemaid to Alexander. This assimilated black Macedonian upbraided Alexander who, in return, accused Clitus of "giving Macedonian cowardice the name of misfortune." There had been considerable discontent in the ranks over what many considered Alexander's vanity and his enthusiastic adoption of Persian customs. Feeling ran particularly deep among Macedonians who felt he had forgotten his roots. Now Clitus the Black spoke for them all by pointing to an episode that proved his own bravery in the face of Alexander's charge that other soldiers were more courageous:

> This cowardice as you are pleased to term it saved the life of a son of the gods when in flight from Spithridates' sword; it is by the expense of Macedonian blood, and by these wounds that you are now raised to such a height as to be able to disown your father Philip, and call yourself the son of Amon.[362]

Alexander was furious. Before the evening was over he had plunged a spear into the body of Clitus the Black and killed him. When Alexander became sober he not only wept bitterly but even contemplated suicide. He fell into a great depression. But the fit of remorse disappeared as quickly as the fit of murderous anger had flared up. Clitus the Black had been murdered by the Macedonian Greek whose life he had once saved and to whose career he had contributed much. This is a parable fraught with paradox, for the black man that Alexander killed was already Hellenized, and was criticizing a Macedonian for trying to establish a claim to "blackness"!

This chapter has argued that prior to the massive Hellenic impact there had been no generalized skin-color prejudice in Egypt; nor had there been discrimination against the Negroid physical type in the esthetic and status-allocating domain in pharaonic Egypt. In Ethiopia these phenomena were not apparent until after the fall of Meroë in the fourth century A.D. It has been suggested further that Blacks, in their relations with Israel and Judah, do not seem to have experienced color prejudice. Some evidence is presented to suggest that, in addition to the possibility of color prejudice existing as a result of Greek and Roman imperialist rule in Egypt, Christianity may have introduced color prejudice into Kush after the fall of Meroë. It was then reinforced after the coming of Islam in the seventh century A.D. Since both religions have their roots in Hebrew religious traditions, these will be examined in the second volume of this work, with reference to conceptions and attitudes about skin-color and the *Black/White* contrast. The question of when and where extreme derogation of "Negroidness" first appeared receives special attention. Because the Greco-Roman tradition, as well as Judaic ideas, became a part of the Christian inheritance, these too will be examined in volume 2.

Bibliographic Essay

The reexamination of Egyptology from a black perspective, initiated by the Afro-American scholar Dr. W.E.B. Du Bois in 1915, in several chapters of his book *The Negro*, eventually became a Pan-African enterprise that reached its culmination in a book-length publication—*The African Origin of Civilization: Myth or Reality*—by Dr. Cheikh Anta Diop, a West African scholar, almost sixty years later. Diop's book resulted from the condensation, within a single volume, of material he published during thirty years of research. Much of it had appeared under the imprint of *Présence Africaine*, the journal of the Paris-based, French-speaking Pan-Africanists, who were the counterparts of the London intellectuals who had formed the International African Service Bureau and the Pan-African Federation, to which such men as Kwame Nkrumah, George Padmore, and Du Bois belonged. An Afro-American professor of French who was close to the *Présence Africaine* group, Dr. Mercer Cook of Howard University, collaborated with Cheikh Anta Diop in the selection and translation of materials for a one-volume work in English. During this period Diop was on the staff of IFAN (Institut Fondamental de l'Afrique Noire) and the University in Dakar, Senegal. In 1966, three years after Du Bois's death in Ghana at the age of ninety-five, Du Bois and the forty-three-year-old Diop were honored at the First World Festival of Negro Arts as the two writers "who had exerted the greatest influence on Negro thought in the twentieth century."

In 1970, four years before *The African Origin of Civilization* appeared, Oxford University Press republished Du Bois's *The Negro*. It was fifty-five years old then, and had been superseded in 1941 by Du Bois's updated work on Egypt contained in *Black Folk Then and Now*. Yet *The Negro* was more than a "period piece," as George A. Shepperson, professor of African history at the University of Edinburgh, made clear in his perceptive and sympathetic, but also critical, introductory essay. Du Bois opened up issues that have remained alive. His role in this respect has been discussed in the preface as well as in chapter 3 of this volume. One of these issues concerns the use and misuse of the terms "Negro" and "Black," and the significance of these verbal symbols to vindicationist scholars. As we have noted previously, this issue has been at the center of Diop's controversies with other Egyptologists.

Four years after the republication of *The Negro*, and during the same year that *The African Origin of Civilization* appeared, a conference under UNESCO auspices met to address the question "How black was ancient Egypt?" one issue raised by Du Bois and insistently brought forward by Diop during the fifties and sixties. From January 28 through February 3, 1974, the scholars met in Cairo to discuss "the peopling of ancient Egypt," with the International Scientific Committee of UNESCO as sponsor. Diop had thus secured an opportunity to lay before the world's most eminent Egyptologists the results of his own research and his criticisms of the research of others. The proceedings have been published in the General History of Africa Series, Studies and Documents, no. 1 (Paris: UNESCO, 1978). The papers and discussions are summarized in G. Mokhtar, ed., *General History of Africa*, vol. 2 (Berkeley: University of California Press, 1981), pp. 58–78. This volume, in which the summary appeared, was published twenty years after the writing of a history of Africa by African scholars was proposed at an international conference of Africanists meeting at the University of Ghana under the sponsorship of President Kwame Nkrumah. Du Bois had recently come to Ghana at the age of 91 to edit the *Encyclopedia Africana*, and died there two years later. Many Pan-Africanists consider both the symposium and the *General History* as a triumph, after over sixty years, of Du Bois's pioneering idea that African history be reexamined from a black perspective.

Increased interest in African history in general and in Nile Valley history in particular accompanied the upsurge of African nationalism and Afro-American protest after World War II. One result of these political events was the proliferation of African Studies programs during the fifties in Europe and the United States, and the founding of the *Journal of African History* in 1960. Another by-product was the emergence of a critical mass of black scholars in Africa, the Caribbean, and the United States with an interest in this area of research and writing. The birth of the Black Studies movement in the United States after 1965 accelerated the trend, already under way, to reexamine black history from a black perspective in order to correct, supplement, and, in the hopeful view of some, supplant the dominant Eurocentric perspective. A reassessment of Egypt was high on the agenda.

One of the most important events in the development of research and publication from the perspective of Pan-African scholarship was the founding in 1978 of the *Journal of African Civilizations* in the United States by a group of Afro-American and Afro-Caribbean scholars, some of whom were affiliated with Black Studies programs (variously called Afro-American, African-American, Africana, or Pan-African Studies). The *Journal of Negro History* had been in existence since 1916; the *Journal of Black Studies* had been founded in 1969; and *The Black Scholar* was started soon thereafter. However, the *Journal of African Civilizations* encouraged ventures into territory that individuals devoted to a more conventional type of historiography (among them Du Bois, Carter G. Woodson, and Frank Snowden) had avoided, and it gave legitimacy to schools of anthropology with which an older generation of black anthropologists felt uncomfortable.

The guiding hand behind the launching of the *Journal of African*

Civilizations was Professor Ivan van Sertima, a Guyanese scholar teaching at Rutgers University in the United States. An anthropologist with an interest in literature as well as social science, van Sertima had demonstrated, in his treatment of a highly controversial subject—the possibility of a pre-Columbian African impact upon the Americas—that diffusionist anthropology, folklore, and historical materials could be synthesized in such a way as to present a convincing case, with high probability that such contact occurred. There is little to which his peers in "the academy" could object in his book *They Came Before Columbus.* There have been contributors to the *Journal of African Civilizations,* however, who have used folklore and mythology, along with esoteric types of linguistic analysis, in ways that raise questions about the scholarly character of their intellectual operations. (Of course, epistemological questions may be fundamental to the disagreements about the use of such material.)

Although the *Journal of African Civilizations* had carried individual articles from time to time that were relevant to a review of Egyptology from a black perspective, volume 4, number 2, the November 1982 issue, presented a section, slightly under a hundred pages in length, devoted to the theme "Egyptian History Revised." The first article is a reprint of Cheikh Anta Diop's chapter entitled "Origin of the Ancient Egyptians," from volume 2 of the UNESCO *General History of Africa,* referred to frequently in this chapter. Editor Ivan van Sertima expresses his ire, in an editorial in this issue, at the Egyptian editor of the UNESCO volume, who, in granting permission for use of the chapter, insisted that his assessment of objections to it raised by others be retained as a part of the republished chapter. Fitting in closely with Diop's discussion of "blackness" in early Egypt is an article on the Eighteenth Dynasty under the title "Black Rulers of the Golden Age," by an Afro-American lawyer, Legrand Clegg II, who also teaches in an African-American Studies program in California and has become a specialist on Egyptian history. Thoroughly documented and presented with bold but critical insight, the article is a definitive treatment of a subject dealt with in a portion of this chapter. Phaon Goldman, who sometimes writes under the name Tarharka, presents an article entitled "The Nubian Renaissance," based upon thorough research.

The view that well-organized kingdoms existed south of Egypt, in what the Greeks later called Ethiopia, for several generations before the first pharaonic dynasties in Egypt receives decisive support in an important article by a University of Chicago specialist, Bruce Williams, under the title "The Lost Pharaohs of Nubia." It had previously appeared in *Archaeology* 33, 5 (1980), but would have escaped the attention of the black reading public to which the *Journal of African Civilizations* makes a special appeal.

The articles discussed so far all deal with Nile Valley history by means of "orthodox" approaches to archaeology and historiography. Two articles, however, are in a different tradition in that they accept the findings of philologists who believe that folklore has validity as history, as well as diffusionist anthropologists with very active imaginations. Charles S. Finch, M.D., contributes an article on the life and works of Gerald Massey, entitled "Kamite Origins." The significance of Massey will be discussed briefly later. John G. Jackson writes on the theme "Egypt and Christianity," a subject about which he has mobilized a vast amount of fact and speculation, not always presented in such a way as to satisfy academic critics.

The editors of the *Journal of African Civilizations*, without foundation support or subsidy, have been able to keep alive a publication outlet for people sharing a similar universe of discourse and a passion for reviewing history from a black perspective. Individuals with varying degrees of mastery of the literature on the Nile Valley are able to make vindicationist contributions in this field, while others concentrate on other facets of the Black Experience. They have been able to extend the circle of awareness and knowledge, too.

Thus, during September 1984, the *Journal of African Civilizations*, in collaboration with the Bennu Study Group of Atlanta, Georgia (named for an Egyptian mystical bird), and the Human Values Program of the Morehouse School of Medicine of Atlanta University, convened a Nile Valley Conference in Atlanta. Discussion themes were entitled "Nile Valley as a Cradle of Civilization"; "Nile Valley: A Dynastic Overview"; "Nile Valley as Mother of Western Civilization"; "Nile Valley Background of Judaeo-Christian-Islamic Heritage"; and "Nile Valley Presence in Ancient America and Asia."

The sponsors attempted to bring Cheikh Anta Diop to the United States from West Africa to deliver the keynote address, and to arrange a number of speaking engagements for him before he returned to Senegal. They were disappointed when at the last moment he did not come. Publicity for the conference referred to Diop as "the world's leading Nile Valley cultural historian." With Dr. Diop's death in early 1986, the *Journal of African Civilizations* group has become the major source for the dissemination of his point of view, and for encouraging black participation in the field of Egyptology. Diop's career remains their model.

That interest in Nile Valley history is not confined to the *Journal of African Civilizations'* staff and its contributors and the small Bennu Study Group, was demonstrated by the fact that, quite independently of the preparations being made for the Nile Valley Conference, an Afro-American economist was publishing an article entitled "The Egyptian Ethnicity Controversy and the Sociology of Knowledge" in another journal at the same time (*Journal of Black Studies* 14, 3 [March 1984]: 295–325). The author, Frank Martin, commented that "a very special mention must go to the pioneering efforts by the brilliant scholar from Senegal, Cheikh Anta Diop. . . . Besides having the technical preparation and an excellent liberal arts education, his being African puts him in the advantageous position of being able to grasp and understand readily certain aspects of Ancient Egyptian society, which was African to the core" (p. 297).

In April 1984, some months before the Nile Valley Conference in Atlanta, the *Journal of African Civilizations* published a special issue entitled "Black Women in Antiquity" (6, 1) that emphasized Nile Valley female rulers and consorts of Nubian kings and Egyptian pharaohs. Runoko Rashidi presented a thoroughly researched, although admittedly speculative, discussion of the Egyptian goddesses Isis, Neith, and Hathor, stressing their influence on Middle Eastern and European religious beliefs, practices, and symbolism. Poetess Sonia Sanchez contributed an article on Nefertiti, the title of which calls her a "Queen With a Sacred Mission." Sanchez writes, as a poet, that Nefertiti had "a face of beauty and intellect," that it was also "a face of destiny," and that she was "perhaps the most admired woman of her day." Being Akhenaten's "Divine female partner," she "did what she could to maintain the dominance of Ma'at (truth, justice, and righteousness) and Aton. She played the game well but she lost." Sonia Sanchez's intuitive reaction is in sharp contrast to Rashidi's scholarly article. "Egypt's Isis: The Original Black Madonna" is also somewhat short on facts, and the professor of English who wrote the article leaned almost entirely on Budge's *Osiris and the Egyptian Resurrection*, 1973, to support her view that "Isis had a profound influence upon major concepts of the Virgin Mary." Another professor of English who had taught for three years in Egypt (1961–1964), Virginia Spottswood Simon, relied too much upon her imagination in writing "Tiye: Nubian Queen of Egypt." She visualizes Tiye as persuading her husband, Amenhotep III, to abandon the use of force in Nubia and to "embark upon his ambitious program of Nubian pacification as a way of saving her people from a gradual decimation." Out of his love for her, the pharaoh instituted a progressive political program. Tiye is referred to as "healthy, intelligent and strong-minded as well as beautiful," and she "passed her full dark Africoid looks down to her children." But the author is on sound, less romantic ground when she states that "the very fleshy lips and jutting jaw of her elder son, Akhenaten, have elicited every explanation except the obvious." The scholarly worth of the articles in this issue varies, as in other issues of the *Journal of African Civilizations*, but the editor's insistence upon lists of references makes it possible for readers to search the sources and make their own judgments if they wish to.

Both Diop and Clegg cite some standard Egyptologists with approval, the latter utilizing works of Cyril Aldred and Christiane Desroches-Noblecourt, who have been referred to in this chapter. When Dr. Du Bois wrote *The Negro* in 1915, he pointed out that Egyptologists had a tendency to ignore the role of Negroes in the development of Egyptian civilization. At the same time he recognized the need for using the factual information—as distinct from their interpretations of it—that they had gathered. He mentioned Breasted, Petrie, Budge, Newberry, and Garstang as authors of "the standard books on Egypt" that he had consulted. He criticized them, however, on the grounds that "they mention the Negro but incidentally and often slightingly." That Du Bois did not mention French and German Egyptologists could mean either that he did not consult them and evaluate their racial attitudes (which is unlikely) or that he felt the Home University Series readers for whom the book was written would be interested only in the sources written in English. This omission is paralleled by Diop's tendency to use very few non-French sources. This is a weakness in both books.

When Du Bois wrote *The Negro*, Egyptology as a discipline was based, as it still is, in museums and in a few of the larger European and American universities. It was only a hundred years old at the time. At its birth, two competing interpretations of the rise of Egyptian civilization battled for adherents. One accepted the ancient classical view that "Egypt was a colony of Ethiopia" and was therefore greatly influenced by so-called "Negro Africa"; the other maintained that Egyptian civilization could not possibly have been a product of African Blacks and must have been introduced from either Arabia or Mesopotamia. This latter position, although honestly believed by some nonracist scholars, became one cornerstone of nineteenth-century racist thought.

Except for some Egyptian scholars and Diop, few people of color have been involved in either the retrieval or interpretation of data about ancient Egypt. In becoming the first African specialist on Egypt from outside of that country, Cheikh Anta Diop utilized the works of European Egyptologists and succeeded in demonstrating that some of them had been less Eurocentric than others. However, their work tended to be ignored and discounted by their extremely Eurocentric and sometimes racist colleagues who came to dominate the field. Diop skillfully used the work of some of these neglected Egyptologists to support an Afrocentric postion.

Within the Afro-American group that has cohered around the *Journal of African Civilizations* since 1978 are individuals who went beyond Diop in the mobilization of allies among nonblack scholars. He mentions the value of the work of a few German, Italian, and British Egyptologists, in addition to his basic French sources. The Afro-American scholars have also given legitimacy to a group of British anthropologists and folklorists whom more cautious black scholars, including Diop, have sedulously avoided. (Diop used folklore in a cautious way, except when accepting certain biblical and Arabian traditions as facts.) Afro-American scholars, even those who were vigorous vindicationists, had, on the whole, exercised similar caution prior to World War II.

During the same year that Du Bois published *The Negro*, another Harvard-trained historian, Dr. Carter G. Woodson, founded the Association for the Study of Negro Life and History, which the next year began to publish the *Journal of Negro History*, followed by a number of books. The historians who grouped themselves around Woodson concentrated on Afro-American studies and were anxious to win the approval of their teachers and peers as "sound scholars." Dr. John Hope Franklin, who eventually became chairman of the Department of History at the University of Chicago, was a product of this tradition, as, in one sense, too, is Dr. Frank Snowden, who wrote *Blacks in Antiquity*. Interest in Egypt was, for them, peripheral; but they utilized the same sources Du Bois did.

Somewhat outside of the academic tradition of Woodson and Du Bois was Dr. Willis N. Huggins, who, during the thirties, as a member of the Department for Social Studies of the New York City high schools, published *An Introduction to African Civilizations*, with the collaboration of an industrious, imaginative, self-educated scholar, previously referred to, John G. Jackson. It was a book that included a plea for support of Ethiopia in its struggle against the Italians, along with excellent bibliographies and pedagogical hints for teachers. Among the chapters were those entitled "Early Egypt," "African Elements in Aegean Civilization," and "Ancient Egypt, Ethiopia, Libya and Nubia." The bibliography indicates familiarity with all of the current standard sources in Egyptology as well as many that mainstream scholars would deem unorthodox.

Huggins felt, in 1937, that "an increasing number of white historians and writers are becoming fairer in dealing with data pertaining to Africans," and that some were actively seeking curriculum revision, but that "most of the white writers are still too timid to enter the lists and help make the proper adjustments." He hoped that his little volume would be useful as a textbook for supplementary reading. On the whole, the book was well researched and temperate in tone, but it was marred by some carelessness in the checking of historical facts and by a tendency to claim too much and to classify some high-status figures in antiquity as Negroes for whom there was neither certain evidence nor enough credible data to assure a high degree of probability. Nevertheless, the Huggins book was the first after Du Bois's *The Negro* to attempt a comprehensive integration of all the available knowledge about Egypt and Ethiopia into a single coherent narrative written from a black perspective. Huggins went further than this. He discussed, in detail, the impact of what he called the Egyptian/Ethiopian Empire on the Hebrew kingdoms, and thus pioneered in one approach that *Black Folk Here and There* seeks to emphasize. The Huggins book should be read as a historic document; it is no longer useful as a textbook and contains too many inaccuracies to be accepted as standard history. Nevertheless, the book played an important part in the consciousness-raising process among young black people during the late Depression years and during the early days of World War II. His collaborator, John Jackson, later wrote a book that was widely used in Black Studies courses during the seventies: *Introduction to African Civilizations* (Secaucus, N.J.: Citadel Press, 1970).

More influential than either Du Bois or Huggins in educating black Americans about some of the details of ancient Egypt was a remarkable, self-trained historian-anthropologist from Jamaica, Joel A. Rogers, who spent most of his adult years in New York. Even Du Bois wrote of Rogers's first book, *From Man to Superman*, that it was one that a person should "buy and read and recommend to his friends." Rogers's *100 Amazing Facts about the Negro with Complete Proof: A Short Cut to the World History of the Negro*, published in 1957 after three decades of research in museums and libraries in Europe and the Americas, contains references to Isis, Osiris, and Akhenaten, as well as to Cheops, Piankhy, and the line of Kushite kings. As in his three-volume *Sex and Race* and his one-volume *Nature Knows No Color Line*, Rogers amassed precise documentation for "facts" based upon written sources and photographs, which, in his judgment (or speculation) defined certain individuals as "Negroes." Formally trained scholars, because of what they consider his recklessness in drawing conclusions from photographs, have tended to ignore the scrupulous care that Rogers exercised in his documentation, some of which did not sustain his point, but which, as an honest investigator, he included. (For instance, his references on Hannibal, the African popes, and Cleopatra were far from conclusive.) His most important contribution to our study of the Nile Valley cultures is in the profiles given in *World's Great Men of Color*, from which we have quoted in this chapter. Employed with caution, as we have tried to do, the use of photographs to establish Negro identity is a legitimate research tool. Rogers was not always cautious. The more conservative schoolteachers preferred the pictures and books distributed by Dr. Carter G. Woodson's Association for the Study of Negro Life and History in connection with Negro History Week; but very few of these dealt with the ancient Nile Valley.

After Du Bois's two books, *The Negro* (1915) and *Black Folk Then and Now* (1941), and the contribution of Huggins and Jackson (1937), no black scholars presented integrated narrative treatment of Nile Valley history until the 1960s, when ben-Jochannan's *Black Man of the Nile* appeared (1969). Meanwhile, the professional Egyptologists were providing additional grist for the vindicationists' mills. It was available when they were ready to utilize it. For instance, the Edwin Smith Surgical Papyrus was published by the University of Chicago in two volumes in 1930, edited by J. H. Breasted, Sr., of the Oriental Institute. By 1928, Budge had published *A History of Ethiopia, Nubia, and Abyssinia According to the Hieroglyphic Inscriptions of Egypt and Nubia, and the Ethiopian Chronicles*. By 1949, Aldred was publishing numerous photographs of ancient Egyptian statues and bas reliefs (see plate 2). Tomes about tombs were piling up, and the *Journal of Egyptian Archaeology, Kush*, and *Revue de Egyptologie* were replete with raw data waiting to be assimilated, analyzed, and interpreted. One of the first post–World War II Afro-American scholars to use the older sources in Nile Valley studies was Dr. Chancellor Williams, professor of history at Howard University, Washington, D.C., Egypt and Ethiopia were included among other African societies in his important contribution to vindicationist research. The Black Consciousness movement in the United States and the anti-colonial movements in Africa, as they gained momentum during the 1960s, resulted in some scholars, among them, Chancellor Williams, turning to an examination of the mass of available source material on the Nile Valley.

Williams's book was one tangible scholarly result of the passion and energy released by the black youth movement in the United States. The author dedicated his book "*to the black youth of the nineteen sixties for beginning the second great emancipation—the liberation of our minds and thus changing the course of history."* The *Destruction of Black Civilization: Great Issues of a Race from 4500 B.C. to 2000 A.D.*, published in paperback by the Third World Press of Chicago (1974), is one of the most widely used books in Black Studies classes and study groups both at schools and in communities.

Another Howard University professor, the late Dr. William Leo Hansberry, prepared Chancellor Williams for the vindicationist role. As Williams phrases it, "Standing alone and isolated in the field for over thirty-five years, William Leo Hansberry was the teacher who introduced me to the systematic study of African history and, of equal importance, to the ancient documentary sources." Another devoted student rescued him from obscurity, Dr. Joseph E. Harris, who edited *Pillars in Ethiopian History: The William Leo Hansberry African History Notebook*, published by the Howard University Press (vol. 1, 1974; vol. 2, 1977). If Chancellor Williams's inspiration came from this black scholar, much of his detailed information, of necessity, came from others, and it is significant that Williams did not quarrel with the older generation of Egyptologists, as Du Bois did, but simply noted that "Petrie headed a line of investigators and writers without whose works the world would be intellectually poorer— Breasted, Budge, Arkell, Africanus, Baikie, Boas, Delafosse, Garstang, Griffith, Nims, and others. The illustrious role [*sic*] is long" (*Destruction of Black Civilization*, p. 385). He omits Weigall, whose work I use, and unlike Du Bois, does not name Reisner. His restrained treatment of the white scholars is significant because the youth to whom he dedicated his book often gave short shrift to *all* white scholars!

Chancellor Williams, like Du Bois, was interested in the history of the entire African continent, not just the Nile Valley; but both felt that an understanding of that area was crucial to an understanding of the entire Black Experience. They felt, too, that any analysis of the rise and fall of Black Power in the Nile Valley must come to terms with the long, tragic story (one that has not yet ended) involving powerlessness and ambivalence about identity. Chancellor Williams shows the same thorough grasp of the history of Egypt and the upper Nile Valley (Nubia, Kush, or Ethiopia) that Du Bois displayed. However, unlike Du Bois, Williams writes from a very explicit Black Nationalist perspective in his chapters entitled "The Black World at the Crossroads" and "Organizing a Race for Action."

Du Bois always espoused a nonchauvinist variety of black solidarity that did not shut the door to close cooperation with friendly white people and that, as far as the United States was concerned, favored cultural assimilation to American liberal, middle-class norms and values. Chancellor Williams reports on his own extensive fieldwork in Africa, which led him to discern a unique "African way of governing." This, he feels, is something Afro-Americans, as well as Africans, should cherish and develop. He expresses impatience with those who, he believes, have allowed miscegenation and assimilationist values to weaken black solidarity, and his book not only describes and analyzes but criticizes, exhorts, and puts forward a plan of action. Egypt and Ethiopia are studied for the lessons they teach about "organizing a race for action."

Differences between the theories of social action held by Chancellor Williams and W.E.B. Du Bois are related to the general social and political philosophies to which each adhered. When Du Bois wrote *The Negro*, he had been for five years on the executive board of the recently organized National Association for the Advancement of Colored People, an organization in which white liberals and moderate socialists were working in coalition with relatively well-educated Blacks of all political persuasions. Also, from the mid-thirties on, Du Bois supported interracial groups of the "popular front" type that sponsored programs advocating civil rights for minorities and world peace. He and Paul Robeson organized a Council on African Affairs. Intellectually, Du Bois was attempting to combine and reconcile Marxist theory with a very attenuated variety of Black Nationalism—as were a number of other Afro-American and West Indian scholars. Although he was a Pan-African leader, Du Bois never proposed, as Chancellor Williams has, the adaptation of African cultural values and practices to Afro-American institutional life.

In explaining invidious discrimination against people of color, Du Bois increasingly came to adopt an orthodox Marxist position, namely, that economic exploitation was at the basis of anti-Negro attitudes and behavior, and that for significant change capitalism would have to be replaced. Chancellor Williams, in *The Destruction of Black Civilization*, interprets events and trends in African history almost entirely in terms of a conscious and deliberate White Racism, and effective responses to it as requiring black solidarity. This results in his reading modern racial attitudes back into ancient Nile Valley history, although he himself occasionally warns against doing so. Du Bois used ancient Egypt to extol the virtues of assimilation and amalgamation; Chancellor Williams uses the same data to emphasize what he believes to be the evil, antiblack consequences of both, then and now. Both men interpret Nile Valley history from a black perspective, but from different ideological positions. Students of black intellectual history cannot afford to ignore the work of either scholar.

Communicating with black people, not changing the minds of white people, is the primary objective of Chancellor Williams, as it was of the Black Studies movement, in relation to which he conceived of himself as something of an elder statesman. Du Bois and Diop, on the other hand, sought a much wider circle of readers. Both of them remained close to conventional historiography in research methods and style of presentation. Both were trying to meet their peers on the common ground of proficiency in their academic disciplines. Both were also trying to reach a widespread liberal-left public as well as black readers.

Chancellor Williams and Du Bois, in dealing with Egypt, were handicapped by lack of training in the field of Egyptology. To their valuable, but necessarily limited, treatment of the subject, Diop added, during the seventies, *The African Origin of Civilization*, which has become the standard work of reference on ancient Egypt in Black Studies programs. Diop interpreted the data in such a way as to demonstrate convincingly that Egyptian artists, priests, and political leaders accepted a wide range of physical types as Egyptian, and that only racist scholarship gives credence to the view that early Egyptians were not "Negroes" in the broadest sense of that term.

The African Origin of Civilization included a group of specific criticisms of Diop's work made by a French archaeologist, along with the West African scholar's replies. Diop's general thesis has been defended in this chapter, but even sympathetic readers will have minor criticisms of this erudite work. For instance, Diop takes disconcerting leaps into the dark with lexical comparisons that carry more weight than they should in demonstrating certain points. He sometimes accepts mythology (especially biblical) and African and Arabian oral tradition as having more substantial truth than can be proven. He lets his own esthetic biases obtrude and reads them back into history when he suggests that Negro women have always been dissatisfied with the kind of hair they have! But, on the whole, this book is both a work of sound scholarship and a tour de force in vindicationist writing. *The African Origin of Civilization* cannot be brushed aside because of minor flaws or the occasional idiosyncrasies of the author. The works of Chancellor Williams and of Cheikh Anta Diop are examples of two contrasting black perspectives, both of which are critical of conventional Nile Valley research. Du Bois and Diop are both neo-Marxists; Chancellor Williams is a Black Nationalist. Diop is also much closer to Du Bois than to Chancellor Williams in the breadth and profundity of his scholarship.

Diop, more highly trained in Egyptology than either Du Bois or Chancellor Williams, attempts, as they do, to explain the gradual "whitening" of Egyptian culture and to account for conflicts with European and Asian invaders. However, in *African Origin*, he rejects the kind of racial interpretation of history that Chancellor Williams presents in *The Destruction of Black Civilization*, but offers a less orthodox Marxist interpretation than Du Bois does in his later works. Diop's last book (available only in French as recently as 1983), *Civilisation ou barbarie: anthropologie sans complaisance* (published by Présence Africaine, Paris, 1981), contains a chapter entitled "Race and Social Classes," which stresses the interaction between ethnic group, race, and economic class as one important type of intergroup relations and source of social change. *Ethnicity is presented as a more basic factor than either race or class in premodern society, but color is not discussed as a symbol of either race or ethnicity.* For instance, the Watutsi/Wahutu conflict in Ruanda is discussed as a case of ethnic conflict, with both groups being Black. Class conflicts based on ethnicity among the Spartans are discussed. Here both groups are white.

What Marx calls the "Asiatic mode of production" Diop would rename the "African state model," since Egypt was the first and most distinctive case. It is Diop's contention that Marx's Eurocentric preoccupation with industrial societies and the role of the Western working class is a weakness when historical materialism is applied to African societies. He develops an elaborate theory of revolutions to explain events in Asia and Africa that did not follow Marxian predictive schemes, and he cites the "Osirian, or proletarian, revolution" in Egypt at the end of the Sixth Dynasty as the first in a type that has since recurred throughout history.

Professor Leonard Jeffries of the City University of New York, in analyzing this important work (*Journal of African Civilizations* 4, 2 [November 1982]: 125–135), states that Diop "makes a major contribution by providing an Afro-Centric critique and enlargement of Marxist and revolutionary theory." Indeed, Jeffries considers the book "an extraordinary intellectual achievement" and concludes of Diop's role that this is "another outstanding contribution to the intellectual process of rethinking and rewriting African and world history which he helped to initiate many years ago." Jeffries was completing a translation of *Civilisation ou barbarie* which, when available to the broad circle of American English-speaking Africanists and teachers and students in the field of Black Studies, would further enhance the already well-established reputation of Diop as a vindicationist scholar. His command of the sources in archaeology, anthropology, and history is unrivaled.

The basic concepts utilized in Diop's last book are ones that have always informed his work: "ancient Egypt was an African civilization," and "ethnology and linguistics show the essential unity of all African cultures." Jeffries notes that in this book Diop devotes a section to emphasizing the theme that "universal knowledge runs from the Nile Valley toward the rest of the world and in particular toward Greece which serves as an intermediary." The one book available that elaborates this theme will here find additional scholarly support: George G. M. James's *Stolen Legacy* (San Francisco: Julian Richardson, 1976). Diop uses this knowledge not only to remind the West of its intellectual "roots" but also, and of greater significance to him, to reassure Africans that when they borrow from so-called "mainstream" culture, they are only taking back to rework for themselves something that was originally their own.

Diop makes very sparing use of mythology and folklore; but some students of the Black Experience lean heavily upon this type of material, at which others look askance. The interpretations that some British writers have made of folklore are so arcane as to discourage all but those with an overpowering "will to believe." For instance, only devotees of mystical literature will be able to assimilate the contents of Gerald Massey's *A Book of the Beginnings: An Attempt to Recover and Reconstitute Lost Origins of the Myths and Mysteries, Types and Symbols, Religion and Language, with Egypt for the Mouthpiece and Africa as the Birthplace* (2 vols., first published in 1881 in England; reprinted by University Books, 1974). During the same year, Samuel Weiser, of New York, reprinted Massey's *The Natural Genesis: Or Second Part of a Book of the Beginnings* (2 vols., first published in 1883). Massey also wrote *Ancient Egypt, the Light of the World: A Work of Reclamation and Reconstitution in Twelve Books*, which was originally published in 1907 and was reprinted in 1973 by Samuel Weiser.

Godfrey Higgins's *Anacalypsis, an Attempt to Draw Aside the Veil of the Saitic Isis; or an Inquiry into the Origin of Languages, Nations, and Religions*, is somewhat less abstruse but no less disconcerting to orthodox scholars because of its dependence upon intuition for interpretations and its intricate idiosyncratic use of linguistic analysis. Most of Higgins's folklore cannot be accepted as fact, but he presents enough acceptable data to make a convincing case for "blackness" having had high symbolic value in the religions of antiquity (see, for example, pp. 137–138 of vol. 1 of the 1883 edition of *Anacalypsis*). The prestige of this work rose in some circles during the 1960s, when it was reprinted in 1965 by University Books, Hyde Park, New York.

The work of these arcane defenders of "blackness" merits critical scrutiny because of its rediscovery by scholars and students active in the Black Studies movement. Modern conventional scholars generally ignore this genre except to ridicule it or to assign it a respectable role only in the study of English and European intellectual history. Some vindicationists use it in their search for data that archaeology cannot furnish. It merits serious critical attention by scholars using modern semiotic analysis. It cannot bear scrutiny using the canons of historiography or ethnography.

The work of Higgins and Massey has, perhaps, received its widest dissemination through its incorporation into two chapters of John G. Jackson's *Introduction to African Civilizations*. Even though the author uses citations and quotations judiciously, the work lends an aura of reliability to these sources that academy scholars will not accept. "Ethiopia and the Origin of Civilization" and "Egypt and the Evolution of Civilization" are chapters that treat folklore as fact in the absence of reliable history. A scholarly introduction to the book (and an endorsement of it) by Professor John Henrik Clarke fails to hoist a warning flag. (In his own work, Clarke, who has been widely trusted as an adviser by editors and publishers, emphasizes classical Greek and Roman sources, as well as archaeology, rather than folklore.) The Jackson book also gives credibility to a group of ethnologists of the early twentieth century who are outside of modern mainstream anthropology—the so-called "extreme diffusionists."

About the same time that Du Bois was writing *Black Folk Then and Now* (1937–1939) in an attempt to update his book *The Negro*, using quite conventional methods of historiography and sociology, Jackson, who had collaborated with Willis Huggins, published *Christianity Before Christ* (1938), *Ethiopia and the Origin of Civilization* (1939), and *Pagan Origins of the Christ Myth* (1941). Huggins is identified by his Ph.D.; Jackson, only by the words, "Member, Rationalist Press Association, London, England." Jackson's work, unlike that of Du Bois, Frank Snowden, or John Henrik Clarke, reflects the influence of the British diffusionist school of anthropology in its most extreme form, as well as the ideas of the small group of late-nineteenth- and early-twentieth-century British antiquarians and self-trained historians mentioned above, who emphasized the profound impact of Egypt upon the Middle East, the Mediterranean, and later the entire world. Alchemy, astrology, Rosicrucianism, and Freemasonry were considered the modern inheritors of some of ancient Egypt's wisdom. They all, quite correctly, brought to the fore the indebtedness of Greek secular thinkers and Jewish religious thinkers to

Egyptian learning. Some of them, however, invested "blackness" with the same mystical significance that ancient Egyptians did, and used this intuitive understanding as a tool for interpretation.

While Higgins's *Anacalypsis* and Massey's *Book of the Beginnings* form a prominent part of the chapters on Egypt and Ethiopia in Jackson's *Introduction to African Civilizations*, some of the more arcane interpretations of ancient Egypt have been given even wider currency by Professor Yosef ben-Jochannan, to whom the issue of the *Journal of African Civilizations* that has a special section on Egypt is dedicated. "Dr. Ben," as he is fondly called by hundreds of black students who have attended his lectures or taken his classes, has mastered the factual minutiae of Nile Valley history as well as the intricate details of the religious beliefs and observances of ancient Egypt, what the Greeks called "the Mysteries." He has studied the various texts of the Book of the Dead and has mastered the works of the standard Egyptologists. His knowledge of Middle Eastern history is impressive, and he is acquainted with the Koran, the Talmud, and various translations of the Bible. He is also acquainted with a great deal of the esoteric European literature mentioned above. Despite the fact that he does not have the formal training in Egyptology that Diop was able to secure, the *Journal of African Civilizations* dedicated volume 4, number 2 (November 1982), to both men.

Ben-Jochannan uses all of his considerable knowledge for launching a fusillade of devastating verbal attacks upon what he considers a conspiracy among white Jews and Christians to deny the contributions of black pioneers to the founding of these religions, as well as upon Muslim arrogance toward black pagans. (He states that he himself is an Ethiopian of the Jewish faith.) His most widely used books are *The Black Man of the Nile* (1969); *The Black Man of the Nile and His Family* (1974); *African Origins of the Major Western Religions* (1971); *The Black Man's Religion* (1972, 1974); and *Africa: Mother of Western Civilization* (1972). His most original work is *The Black Man's Religion: Excerpts and Comments from the Holy Black Bible* (1970). All of his books are published by his own company, Alekebu-Lan Books Association of New York.

Despite occasional carelessness in checking facts and idiosyncrasies that will annoy some readers, ben-Jochannan's books display keen analytical skill. One serious factual error in his work is the charge that East European rabbis, not Mesopotamian Jews, originated the Talmudic story that Noah's curse on Ham turned him black. (See chapter 4 in the forthcoming volume of this book for a correction of this error.) But his interpretation of the meaning and function of that

legend among Europeans after the sixteenth century is both perceptive and plausible. Ben-Jochannan's books challenge the reader to exercise alert vigilance to distinguish between fact, statements with a
high degree of probability, and assertions based merely on a will to
believe. His books are informative and deserve reading if for no other
reason than to enjoy his superb polemical style so characteristic of the
Black Consciousness movement of the sixties and early seventies.
Ben-Jochannan has dismissed in advance any such partial acceptance
of his views by fellow Blacks with eloquent words of scorn and contempt. Du Bois always hoped to educate his white readers as well as
to inspire his black ones. Ben-Jochannan is concerned only with what
he considers the "debrainwashing" of Blacks, and his main target has
been students involved in Black Studies programs. For a succinct
reliable historical account by one of the younger scholars see Runoko
Rashidi's *Kushite Case Studies* (privately printed and distributed,
4140 Buckingham Road #D, Los Angeles, CA 90008).

Reference has been made to a pre–World War II group of British anthropologists who unwittingly reinforced black vindicationist arguments about the importance of Egypt as a civilizing agent. It should
be noted, however, that their message did not lend the same strong
reinforcement to those who claimed that Egyptians were Black as did
the work of the folklorists. These anthropologists are known as the
"extreme diffusionists" by students of anthropological theory.
Although their position appealed to the few black intellectuals of the
time who knew of their work, within less than five years after World
War I this influential school in British anthropology that had been
almost obsessed with Egypt suffered a serious loss of academic respectability. Its "conjectural history" was assailed as "pseudohistory" by
the British functionalists. Nevertheless, there was a market in the
United States for some of this school's highly romantic books. In
1923 E. P. Dutton published W. J. Perry's *The Children of the Sun*,
which described the alleged wanderings of dynastic Egyptians over the
whole world, serving as the civilizers of mankind, spreading their religious ideas and symbols, their pyramids and burial customs, to Asia,
Latin America, and remote corners of the globe. That same year
Harper and Brothers published Grafton Elliott Smith's *The Ancient
Egyptians and the Origin of Civilization*. Both of these anthropologists agreed with Breasted that the Egyptians were not Negroes and
were inclined to view them as a brown-skinned variety of Breasted's
"Great White Race." Some black vindicationists welcomed the
migration theory while rejecting the anti-Negro bias.

There was another Englishman, however, who was more useful to black vindicationists than the diffusionist anthropologists. This was the physician and antiquarian Albert Churchward, who insisted, in his *Origin and Evolution of the Human Race* (London: Allen and Unwin, 1921), that the original global culture bearers, although African, were not dynastic Egyptians. He instead postulated several migration waves. First came the "less highly evolved" reddish African Pygmies; later came the dark brown Nilotic Negroes from whom dynastic Egyptians evolved. Millennia before the appearance of the second group, certain basic concepts and customs from Africa spread everywhere. Churchward was already well known for his *Signs and Symbols of Primordial Man* and his *Origin and Evolution of Free Masonry* when this book was published. He warned against confusing the Nilotic Negroes with the "True Negroes" of West Africa, arguing that the former were more like the Masai of East Africa in physique and culture. "True Negroes," from whom Blacks in the Americas were descended, he considered degraded, retarded, and caught in an evolutionary blind alley. Again, only some of a potential ally's theory could be accepted by vindicationists. (Jackson, in his *Introduction to African Civilization*, was willing to ignore Higgins's and Churchward's dislike for "Negroidness" and to play up their respect for non-Negroid "blackness.")

This preoccupation with proving that culture bearers from Egypt were not "True Negroes" did not necessarily involve denial that they were Black, but it did reveal esthetic biases against "Negroidness" and it associated Negroes with a lower stage of evolution. (This was similar to Higgins's views, as stated in *Anacalypsis*, that the original, unprepossessing black men in India evolved into a "fine Cristna [or Krishna] type of black" who developed civilization. These black men became the objects of worship throughout the Middle East as they carried civilization into Mesopotamia and Egypt.)

The black scholars of the 1920s ignored the extreme diffusionists. Not only were there no black Egyptologists at the time but there were also no black anthropologists. The historians, sociologists, and economists were too absorbed in fighting racial discrimination, organizing Pan-African congresses (1921, 1923, 1927), reacting to Garvey's Universal Negro Improvement Association, and participating in the Harlem Renaissance in literature and art to devote any time to mastering the details about Egypt necessary for criticizing the diffusionists' racial theories or for speculating about origins.

During the sixties and seventies, however, a number of Afro-American literary figures chose to ignore the anti-Negro biases of the diffusionists and to accept their argument regarding a worldwide spread of Egyptian culture. They blended their findings with those of the group of nineteenth-century English mystics who were trying to establish the priority of *black* Egyptians as civilizing agents in both Africa and Asia. Books by the British diffusionists Higgins and Massey, as well as Churchward, have been regularly appearing on reading lists for the past decade in some of the newly organized Black Studies programs and in the bibliographies of books written by vindicationists. *In my opinion they should be read as "period pieces" and assessed critically in the light of modern anthropological fact and theory. They also constitute a baseline for the study of changing thought styles about "blackness."* I consider them of minimal value in establishing a baseline of factual data about the Black Experience, unless we wish to accord the same value to intuition in developing a black epistemology as we give to the proof and verification required in standard historiography.

The retrieval and interpretation of facts about Nile Valley history has always been considered crucial in carrying out the tasks assumed by vindicationist scholars. Despite their flaws, ranging from inadvertent but disconcerting omissions to flagrant, offensive, racist statements, the works of European and American Egyptologists and Africanists concerned with Nubia have been indispensable in the acquisition of factual data. Du Bois, Diop, Chancellor Williams, and the editors of the *Journal of African Civilizations* explicitly mention the usefulness of the work of these scholars. Critical analysis is necessary, however, whenever these nonblack scholars attempt to discuss the significance of their material. It is then that biases obtrude.

Among the older Egyptologists I have found Weigall one of the most "offensive" yet most valuable for securing important factual data. Among modern Egyptologists, I have found Cyril Aldred to be highly perceptive and appreciative of Egyptian cultures, as Adams is of Nubia. That I have been critical of both does not imply any lack of esteem for them as scholars, nor imply that I consider them hostile to black vindicationist goals. In attitude they stand in sharp contrast to Weigall.

Chapter 3 has drawn from these sources, too, but in it I have chosen to use only materials relevant to a discussion of race and color. Readers will no doubt want to place that discussion within a broader social context, or even to enjoy the literature on Egypt and Ethiopia for its own sake. A voluminous amount of literature exists that discusses many facets of ancient Egypt. A smaller amount is available on Kush (ancient Ethiopia), usually located in card catalogs under such designations as "Nubia," "Meroë," "Ethiopia,"

"Sudan," or listed in the footnotes and bibliographies of articles in the journal *Kush*.

Much of the material on Egypt and Ethiopia is uninteresting, or even unintelligible, except to specialists in anthropology, archaeology, or ancient history. Fortunately, popularizers and interpreters are available among the specialists. Reference has been made to *The Making of Egypt*, by Sir Flinders Petrie, in addressing the issues of this chapter; but he is also the author of an interesting, readable book free of archaeologists' jargon, *Social Life in Ancient Egypt* (1923, 1932). The most attractive, accurate, and reasonably objective recent book designed for a popular audience (despite its author's assertion that Queen Tiye was not Black) is *Temples, Tombs, and Hieroglyphics: A Popular History of Ancient Egypt*, by Barbara Mertz, whose *Red Land, Black Land: Daily Life in Ancient Egypt* has been referred to in chapter 3. An excellent work to accompany the Mertz books is a volume to which she has contributed one of the eight essays that accompany an attractive selection of photographs: *Ancient Egypt: Discovering Its Splendors*, published in 1978 by the National Geographic Society, Washington, D.C. This work also includes an essay by William Kelly Simpson, whose Yale University Press paperback, *The Literature of Ancient Egypt: An Anthology of Stories, Instructions, and Poetry* (1977), provides additional insight into the ethos of a people whose written works have not been widely disseminated. Wilson and Frankfort, who are cited in the endnotes and quoted frequently in this chapter, drew upon this type of material, most of which has been translated from previous documents. In 1980 the Grove Press released a paperback edition of *The Priests of Ancient Egypt* by Serge Sauneron, a French Egyptologist who participated in the Cairo conference with Cheikh Anta Diop. It includes a number of quotations from rare sources as part of a nontechnical narrative accompanied by numerous illustrations.

Writing twenty-five years after the publication of *The Negro* (1915), Du Bois in *Black Folk Then and Now* made an assessment of Nile Valley studies. All scholars, Black and White, had been dependent for their data upon classical Greek and Roman references to Egypt and Ethiopia, biblical accounts, the few Arabic sources that were available through translation into English or a European language, and the constantly increasing mass of records resulting from archaeological expeditions to the Nile Valley. Du Bois noted the significant fact that there had been some increase in the attention given to the role of Negroes in Egyptian history but little change in the tone of the comments about them.

Since World War II, treatment of data about black people in Nile Valley history has become less offensive. Still, however, no Blacks other than a few Egyptians have been included in the collective enterprise of opening the tombs, deciphering the hieroglyphics, and participating in the debate about the race of specific fossils and mummies. Subtle institutional racism still exists in the field of Nile Valley studies, although individual Egyptologists and Nubianists exhibit far less racial prejudice than in the past.

The best of the modern Egyptologists are not guilty of perpetuating the overt racism that formerly pervaded the field, exemplified, for instance, by that dominating figure among American Orientalists, James H. Breasted, Sr., who always insisted that Egyptian civilization was originated by what he repeatedly referred to (always with the capital letters) as "The Great White Race" (see, for example, his widely used textbook *The Conquest of Civilization* [1926]). Today, the early Egyptians are usually thought of simply as "brown-skinned Caucasians" or "Euro-Africans" or "Hamites" who very early began to absorb Negro genes. They are seldom called "Negroes" by "mainstream" Egyptologists.

Cyril Aldred, in his booklet *Egypt to the End of the Old Kingdom*, has emphasized the point of view of one of the English pioneers, E.A.W. Budge, when he stresses the Nubian (that is, ancient Ethiopian) roots of pharaonic Egyptian culture. Like most modern Egyptologists, Aldred avoids discussion of the race of the pharaohs and their families. However, in making photographs widely accessible in his books he provides very useful material that can be used by those writing from a black perspective. Aldred, like all Egyptologists with an interest in art and art styles, describes facial features using an art critic's terminology and discusses at great length the esthetics and craftsmanship of the several representations of specific individuals. This is of little interest to vindicationist scholars. However, the photographs, if not the text, of his *Akhenaten, Pharaoh of Egypt: A New Study* (1968) document the Negroid physical features of Akhenaten and his family, as do the illustrations in *Akhenaten and Nefertiti* (1973). Both the text and the illustrations do so, too, in Christiane Desroches-Noblecourt's *Tutankhamen: Life and Death of a Pharaoh* (1963). Serious students, regardless of their race, will appreciate the enthusiasm and the scholarly devotion that have gone into the production of these books. Black readers, however, are likely to reject some of Aldred's theorizing about Akhenaten, even while appreciating his integration of the factual data into a coherent narrative and his selection of photographs. The esthetic biases of Desroches-Noblecourt are compensated for by the progressive features of her work that have been mentioned in chapter 3. One of Aldred's recent volumes, in its selection of photographs, including a Negroid Queen Tiye that he uses to illustrate her "imperious royal dignity," not only has unusual esthetic appeal but also much of value for students of the Black Experience.

During the 1974 UNESCO symposium on the theme "The Peopling of Ancient Egypt," as well as in his *African Origin of Civilization*, Diop, like Du Bois, pleaded for the use of consistent criteria in defining a "Negro" both in Egypt and in North America, the United Kingdom, and most of Europe. Readers may wish to judge for themselves how "Negro" Egypt is if viewed in this fashion. Enough illustrations of Egyptians from all periods are available to make this a rewarding exercise. The following publications will be especially useful in such a survey:

(1) Vagn Poulsen, *Egyptian Art* (Greenwich, Conn.: New York Graphic Society, 1968)

(2) Kazimierz Michalowski, *Art of Ancient Egypt* (New York: Harry N. Abrams, n.d.)

(3) Walther Wolf, *Die Welt der Ägypter* (Stuttgart: Gustav Kilpper Verlag, 1958)

(4) Walther Wolf, *The Origins of Western Art*, part 1 (New York: Universe Books, 1971)

(5) Cyril Aldred, *Egyptian Art in the Days of the Pharaohs* (New York: Oxford University Press, 1980)

(6) Cyril Aldred, *Akhenaten and Nefertiti* (New York: Viking Press, 1973)

(7) Ernesto Scamuzzi, *Egyptian Art in the Egyptian Museum of Turin* (New York: Harry N. Abrams, 1965)

Some of the most reliable clues to racial type are found in sculpture associated with burials—when human images were placed in tombs, where, according to Professor H. S. Smith, they were "needed to be as true and life-like an image . . . as possible." (See Smith's introduction to Anthea Page, *Egyptian Sculpture: Archaic to Saite, from the Petrie Collection* [London: University College Press, 1959]). These *shawtawbi* images must be distinguished from other types of grave images, however. For instance, the striking coal-black images of Tutankhamen at the door to the inner shrine, where his sarcophagus was found, represent *conventionalized* blackening to symbolize death. They should not be used to speculate about King Tut's color.

Readers interested in examining the claim that the Egyptian population was similar to the modern Afro-American population in degree of "Negroidness" and wide range of physical types might wish to replicate (or refine) my crude study of the Petrie collection sculpture in the Page volume. Of the 109 photographs where the head was intact and was relatively undamaged, I judged 28 to have pronounced Negro characteristics, if anthropological criteria were used, and another 50 as likely to be classified as "Negro" by an observer from the United States. Only 31, or about 28 percent, would be classified as "white" by contemporary Americans. It is significant that very few of the statues in the Petrie collection were of servants or slaves. A similar incidence of "Negroidness" is apparent in the photographs in James H. Breasted, Jr., *Egyptian Servant Statues* (1948), although a slightly higher proportion may be non-Negro. (This is by the son of the pioneer Egyptologist who bore the same name. See also "He who tends his crop will eat it" and "I made vineyards without limit" in the splendid display of illustrations in *Ancient Egypt: Discovering Its Splendors* [National Geographic Society, 1978].)

The following plates in Ernesto Scamuzzi, *Egyptian Art in the Egyptian Museum of Turin* (New York: Harry N. Abrams, 1965), are relevant to this discussion: plate 13, "Statuette of Nude Female Figure" (an attractive Negroid girl, Sixth Dynasty); plate 18, "Head of Statue of the Monarch, Ibu" (Negroid features, red coloring, Twelfth Dynasty); plate 23, "Head from Statue of the God Osiris" (Negroid features, red coloring, wearing the white crown of the Thebaid, Eighteenth Dynasty); plate 57, "Rameses II at Abu Simmel" (Negroid, but note says this statue is probably a "fake"); plate 93, "A Priest of Memphis" (very Negroid, Twenty-fifth Ethiopian Dynasty); plate 100, "Head of a Priest" (quite Negroid, end of fourth century, B.C.); plate 110, "A Ptolemaic Queen" (very Negroid); plate 112, "Male Head" (quite Negroid, first century B.C.); plate 95, "Noble of the Said Dynasty" (Negroid).

Objections have sometimes been raised to claims made by Joel A. Rogers that statues of Buddhas and some Cambodian rulers in antiquity were Negroid, even though their facial features and hair resemble those of individuals so defined in Africa. Such problems do not arise in dealing with Egyptians of that type, who are obviously either from the area immediately south of Egypt or have resulted from miscegenation with Negroes from inner Africa. The Asian examples might conceivably have other explanations. Assessment of "Negroidness" from Egyptian sculpture is not a comparable case.

NOTES

PREFACE

1. Rejection of "Negro" as an acceptable ethnic designation by Afro-American scholars did not occur until after the rise of the Black Consciousness movement during the 1960s. The term is used routinely today, as in the past, in anthropological discussions of basic population stocks (i.e., Caucasian, Negro, Mongolian).

INTRODUCTION

1. Karl Mannheim, *Ideology and Utopia: An Introduction to the Sociology of Knowledge* (New York: Harcourt, Brace and Co., 1936), pp. 244, 246.
2. E. E. Evans-Pritchard, *Social Anthropology and Other Essays* (New York: The Free Press, 1962), p. 152.
3. Sidney W. Mintz, "History and Anthropology: A Brief Reprise," in Stanley L. Engerman and Eugene D. Genovese, eds., *Race and Slavery in the Western Hemisphere: Quantitative Studies*, pp. 477–494; quotation from p. 479.

CHAPTER 1

1. For an excerpt from Jefferson's *Notes on the State of Virginia*, see "Thomas Jefferson Condemns Slavery but Asserts Racial Differences," in *A Documentary History of Slavery in North America*, ed. Willie Lee Rose (New York: Oxford University Press, 1976), pp. 68–75.
2. Ibid., p. 74.
3. Ibid.
4. Ibid., p. 72.
5. For a detailed, documented examination of Jefferson's views on black people and American Indians, slavery and manumission, as well as the future of American society, see Winthrop Jordan, *White Over Black: American Attitudes Toward the Negro, 1550–1812* (Baltimore: Pelican, 1969), pp. 429–481. The quoted material is from p. 436.
6. In letters written between 1809 and 1814, Jefferson seemed to be resolving his doubt in favor of an environmentalist interpretation of the "backwardness" of Negroes in the United States. Anthropologist Ashley Montagu is convinced that he "several times repudiated his earlier opinions." Historian Winthrop Jordan, however, after a careful study of all of the available documentary evidence, is not convinced. In fact, he says, "one looks in vain for indications of a happily receptive scientific mind patiently awaiting appropriate evidence." Jefferson was clearly a prisoner of his prejudices. See Ashley Montagu, *The Idea of Race* (Lincoln: University of Nebraska Press, 1965), p. 11; see also Jordan, *White Over Black*, p. 454 and pp. 448–457.
7. Rose, *Documentary History*, p. 70. The idealization of the white physical type was not unusual in the late eighteenth and early nineteenth centuries. For instance,

Sir William Lawrence "believed firmly in white superiority," and in his 1819 *Lectures on Physiology, Zoology, and the Natural History of Man* "had to find grounds for his beliefs in qualities that were not scientifically measurable. He found one criterion in esthetics—that is, in self-admiration of his own physical type." One of his contemporaries believed that " 'Negro features' were the result of a 'low state of civilization' and would 'improve' as the Africans became more 'civilized'." Philip D. Curtin, *The Image of Africa: British Ideas and Action, 1780–1850*, vol. 1 (Madison: University of Wisconsin Press, 1964), pp. 231–232; 238.

8. "George Tucker Criticizes Jefferson's Views of Racial Differences," in Rose, *Documentary History*, pp. 76–77. That Tucker did not challenge the truth of what he called the "obscene" orangutan story cited by Jefferson may mean that he was not sure it was false. Between 1774 and 1792 James Burnet (Lord Monboddo), in his six-volume work, *Of the Origin and Progress of Language*, contended that apes could speak and that orangutans copulated with human females. The eminent Comte de Buffon, in his *Natural History*, claimed that orangutans were "equally ardent for women as for their own females." These were respected scientists of the time. Edward Long, in his *History of Jamaica* (1774), included orangutans as one of three human species. His ideas on race and on Blacks received considerable circulation in 1783 through the *Columbia Magazine* of New York. Jefferson and Tucker, as well as other well-educated Americans, may have been exposed to the orangutan story through this medium if they had not read Buffon and Burnet directly. A significant point is that many of these well-educated individuals were unaware that there were no orangutans in Africa. Not all literate Europeans believed in the story. For instance, the French scientist Cuvier is reported to have chided a friend in 1790 for being so credulous as to believe the story about copulation between orangutans and human females, calling it a tale spread by "some stupid voyagers." However, those who believed the story could never feel sure that any specific black person was not part ape! See Jordan, *White Over Black*, chapter VI-2, "Negroes, Apes, and Beasts," pp. 228–233.

9. Rose, *Documentary History*, p. 77.

10. See Jordan, *White Over Black*, pp. 78–79, for a summary of such legislation with citation of examples. The Maryland law of 1664 reveals some very practical reasons for planter concern, "forasmuch as divers freeborne English women forgettfull of their free Condition and to the disgrace of our Nation doe intermarry with Negro slaves by which also divers suites may arise touching the Issue of such women and a great damage doth befall the Masters of such Negroes." When the law was tightened up twenty years later, moralistic appraisals were more pronounced, the marriages of white women to Negroes being described as "always to the Satisfaction of theire Lascivious and Lustful desires, and to the disgrace not only of the English butt also of many other Christian Nations."

In Puritan Massachusetts punishment for lewdness, fornication, and lasciviousness fell with equal severity upon Blacks and whites for sexual relations within and across racial lines until early in the eighteenth century. Then laws began to appear similar to those in southern plantation areas, but for quite different reasons. In explaining the 1705 law in Massachusetts, entitled "An Act for the Better Preventing of a Spurious and Mixt Issue," one careful study notes a growing revulsion against the few Blacks in the population as an aspect of a mood of serious introspection that gripped the colony: "The new Negro policies were responses to three social concerns: a widespread anathema for the slave trade, a pervasive uneasiness about the colony's economic future, and a growing anxiety about the

Negro's behavior." Guilt, not aristocratic pride and a desire to clarify the question of ownership rights in slave women's progeny, motivated the Massachusetts legislators. Robert C. Twombly and Robert H. Moore, "Black Puritan: The Negro in Seventeenth-Century Massachusetts," in *Blacks in White America Before 1865: Issues and Interpretations*, ed. Robert V. Haynes (New York: David McKay, 1972).

11. Jefferson's political opponents charged him with keeping a "Congo harem" in which "a lass so luscious ne'er was seen as Monticellean Sally." Jefferson refused to answer the allegations, but some of his descendants named two of his close kinsmen instead of Jefferson as the fathers of Sally Hemings's children. Then, for a century biographers ignored the matter. Meanwhile, Sally Hemings's children gave occasional interviews to black historians, thus keeping alive their family tradition of descent from Thomas Jefferson. In 1968 Professor Winthrop Jordan, in his *White Over Black*, broke the taboo among white historians with chapters entitled "Jefferson: Passionate Realities" and "Jefferson: White Women and Black," both sympathetic but honest examinations of this moralistic Founding Father's seemingly inconsistent attitude toward miscegenation. Jordan left open the question of whether or not Jefferson had sexual relations with his female slave, but an impassioned defense of Jefferson's honor and morality against what he called vile charges of miscegenation appeared in 1969 as a part of Thomas Fleming's *The Man from Monticello: An Intimate Life of Thomas Jefferson* (New York: William Morrow), pp. 280–281. Five years later Fawn M. Brodie published an impressive biographical work, *Thomas Jefferson: An Intimate History* (New York: Norton). Examining all of the available documentary evidence, direct and circumstantial, she concluded that not only was there an affair between Jefferson and Sally but that it was "a serious passion" and not a case of "scandalous debauchery," as contemporary gossip implied and as modern Black Nationalist critics of Jefferson charge. Two years later, Page Smith's *Jefferson: A Revealing Biography* (New York: McGraw-Hill) appeared and explicitly endorsed Brodie's conclusion, including her psychoanalytic interpretations of Jefferson's love for Sally. In 1980 an Afro-American woman, Barbara Chase-Riboud, published a novel, *Sally Hemings* (New York: Avon Books), using the Brodie and Smith interpretations as the basis for a plot. The following year a distinguished southern journalist, Virginius Dabney, attempted to defend the honor of the Sage of Monticello with *The Jefferson Scandals* (New York: Dodd, Mead, 1981). He argued that the entire story was concocted by one of Jefferson's political enemies. Dabney succeeded in demonstrating that political opponents exploited the story, but he did not succeed in the impossible task of proving it to be untrue. It is equally impossible to prove that it is true. At the moment, however, circumstantial evidence and the testimony of Sally Hemings's descendants are a bit more convincing than the denials of Jefferson's relatives and defenders, with their lack of alternative hypotheses to counter the circumstantial evidence.

12. The fact that some Afro-Americans were accepting derogatory esthetic stereotypes as late as the 1930s is revealed by a study made in the southern states by the Fisk University Social Science Research Center. Interviews with Afro-American teenagers and men and women in their early twenties elicited very negative responses toward "blackness." Some of the reactions involved rejection of a black body image because of social status connotations, but others were esthetic: "Black is ugly"; "Black isn't like flesh"; "Black looks dirty"; "Black people can't use makeup"; "Black is too black." Nicknames were mentioned that ridiculed dark skin-color: Midnight, Snow, Blue Gums, Shadow, Dusty, Shine (Gunnar Myrdal,

An American Dilemma, vol. 2 [New York: Harper and Brothers, 1944], p. 1382). For a study made of adults in a northern city during the same period, see "Dark-skin Women," in W. Lloyd Warner, Buford H. Junker, and Walter A. Adams, *Color and Human Nature* (New York: Harper & Row, 1969), pp. 83–128. Despite the striking revolution in evaluation of "Negroidness" during the 1960s in the United States, very little research has been carried out on the effect of new self-images on dating and marriage choices. A significant beginning, however, appears in J. Hraba and G. Grant, "Black Is Beautiful: A Reexamination of Racial References and Iden-tification," *Journal of Personality Psychology* 16 (1970): 398–402. An inventory of relevant research on changing self-images appears in Vivian Verdell Gordon, *The Self-Concept of Black Americans* (Washington, D.C.: University Press of America, 1977). For an informed opinion by a black sociologist on the extent and significance of the changes, note C. Eric Lincoln, "Color and Group Identity in the United States," *Daedalus* 2 (1967): 527–541. H. Hoetink's *Caribbean Race Relations: Two Variants* (New York: Oxford University Press, 1971) is both factual and specula-tive in discussing situations in Latin America where no black value-revolution has occurred.

13. Carleton S. Coon, *The Races of Europe* (New York: Macmillan, 1939), p. 456.
14. Rose, *Documentary History*, p. 78.
15. Jordan, *White Over Black*, p. 143.
16. Curtin, *Image of Africa*, vol. 1, p. 29.
17. Montagu, *Idea of Race*, p. 10. The frankness with which highly respected figures of British society at the turn of the century expressed the concept of White Supremacy is sometimes startling. For example, one prominent scholar wrote: "It is a false view of human solidarity, a weak humanitarianism, not a true human-ism, which regrets that a capable and stalwart race of white men should replace a darkskinned tribe which can neither utilize its land for the full benefit of mankind nor contribute its quota to the common stock of human knowledge." These are the words of Karl Pearson, inventor of the Pearsonian Coefficient, in *The Gram-mar of Science* (London: J. M. Dent, 1892), p. 310. For American cases, see the chapters entitled "The Vanishing Negro: Darwinism and the Conflict of the Races" and "Accommodationist Racism and the Progressive Mentality," in George M. Fredrickson, *The Black Image in the White Mind: The Debate on Afro-American Character and Destiny, 1817–1914* (New York: Harper & Row, 1971). Some in-teresting and informative remarks on the subject appear in Sir Alan Burns, *Colour Prejudice* (Westport, Conn.: Negro Universities Press, 1971), chapter 9, "Physi-cal Repulsion Between the Races."
18. Joel Kovel, *White Racism: A Psychohistory* (New York: Pantheon Books, 1970). See also Arthur de Gobineau, *The Inequality of Human Races*, trans. Adrian Col-lins (New York: Putnam's, 1915); Houston S. Chamberlain, *The Foundations of the Nineteenth Century*, trans. John Lees, 2 vols. (New York: John Lane, 1910; reproduced in 1968 by Fertig, New York); Lothrop Stoddard, *The Rising Tide of Color Against White World Supremacy* (New York: Scribner's, 1920); and Madi-son Grant, *Passing of the Great Race, or the Racial Basis of European History* (New York: Scribner's, 1916; reproduced in 1970 by Arno, New York).
19. Lothrop Stoddard, *Racial Realities in Europe* (New York: Scribner's, 1924), pp. 120–121.
20. Frederick L. Schuman, *The Nazi Dictatorship* (New York: Knopf, 1935), p. 115.
21. Ibid., p. 383.

22. A. O. Lovejoy, *The Great Chain of Being: A Study of the History of an Idea* (Cambridge, Mass.: Harvard University Press, 1936); see also "The Negro Bound by the Chain of Being," in Jordan, *White Over Black*, pp. 482–511.

23. Jordan, *White Over Black*, "The Hierarchies of Men," "Confusion, Order and Hierarchy," and "Negroes, Apes and Beasts," pp. 491–496, 216–217, 228–233.

24. For a vivid description of the way in which stereotyped conceptions of Africans and people of African descent in Europe and the Americas developed, see the following chapters in Curtin, *Image of Africa*, vol. 1: "Towns and Elephants," "Barbarism: Its Physical Causes," and "Barbarism: Its Moral Causes"; vol. 2: "The Racists and Their Opponents" and "Language, Culture, and History." On the acceptance of some of the stereotypes by black people and their integration into favorable concepts of "soul" and "*Négritude*," see the discussion of "romantic racialism" in Fredrickson, *Black Image*, pp. 97–109, 327–328. For a thoughtful discussion of a desirable vindicationist strategy in using the *Négritude* concept, note Cheikh Anta Diop, *The African Origin of Civilization: Myth or Reality* (New York: Lawrence Hill, 1974), pp. 24–26.

25. Curtin, *Image of Africa*, vol. 1, pp. 38–39.

26. The term *negro* did not appear in written English until 1555, when it was borrowed from the Portuguese. See Winthrop Jordan, *White Over Black*, p. 61; and Robert Froman, *Racism* (New York: Dell, 1970), p. 66.

27. Curtin, *Image of Africa*, vol. 1, p. 38. For an alternative view of how the hierarchy was formed, see Jordan, *White Over Black*, pp. 217–228.

28. Ibid., pp. 366–369.

29. Quoted in Curtin, ibid., p. 231. For a scholarly evaluation of the role of Cuvier in the development of racism, see "Georges Cuvier and the Preservation of Savage Skulls," in George W. Stocking, Jr., *Race, Culture, and Evolution: Essays in the History of Anthropology* (New York: Free Press, 1968), pp. 29–41. For statements by contemporary nonracist anthropologists, see Ashley Montagu, *Statement on Race* (New York: Henry Schuman, 1951); and Jean Hiernaux, "The Concept of Race and the Taxonomy of Mankind," in *The Concept of Race*, ed. Ashley Montagu (Toronto: Collier-Macmillan, 1964).

30. Curtin, *Image of Africa*, p. 47. Montagu in *Idea of Race*, pp. 36–41, mentions Blumenbach, Herder, Buffon, Rousseau, Alexander von Humboldt, and Wilhelm von Humboldt to illustrate his point that "eighteenth-century scientific students of the variety of mankind were to a man all on the side of equality." This did not necessarily mean, however, that they were free from color prejudice involving esthetic bias and doubt about intellectual capabilities. Insistence on equality of rights for the individual was not incompatible with the idea that Blacks as a group were biologically inferior and physically repulsive. For an illustrative case involving an Episcopalian bishop, see Burns, *Colour Prejudice*, p. 110. The bishop prayed continuously for a better attitude!

31. "*The* Negro," in quotation marks, is used in this book to indicate the stereotyped caricature of sub-Saharan Africans that was prevalent from the fifteenth century onward. It seldom accorded with the actual appearance or behavior of the majority of the people so described. From the end of the Civil War until the 1960s, the word *Negro*, spelled with a capital *N*, was accepted without objection by Afro-Americans in the United States. In the 1960s it came to be rejected as a symbol of slavery and postslavery oppression. The word *Black*, with a capital *B*, became accepted as a symbol of liberation from feelings of inferiority. Anthropologists continued to use

the word *Negro* in what they considered a technical, scientific sense, and it is so used in this book without quotation marks. It is occasionally used, too, for the sake of variety, as synonymous with "Black." "*The* Negro" means the caricature.

32. Quoted in Curtin, *Image of Africa*, vol. 1, p. 39.

33. See chapter 10, "Black Caricature: The Roots of Racialism," in James Walvin, *Black and White: The Negro and English Society, 1555–1945* (London: Allen Lane, Penguin Press, 1973).

34. For North American examples of derogatory stereotyping, see Harris Dickson, "The Unknowable Negro," and Frederick Moore, "The Coon's Content," in *Racism at the Turn of the Century*, ed. Donald P. De Nevi and Doris A. Holmes (San Rafael, Calif.: Leswing Press, 1973). For an example of the type of derogatory image making that constantly stereotyped recently freed and enfranchised Blacks after the Civil War in the American South, a book written by northern newspaperman James S. Pike is typical. Its title—*The Prostrate State*—referred to South Carolina. (The book was first published in 1874 by D. Appleton and Co., New York, and reissued in 1968 as a Harper Torchbook by Harper & Row, New York.) Characterizations such as the following occur in the table of contents to describe topics discussed in the thirty-four chapters: "Sambo as a Critic of the White Man"; "The Raw Negro as a Legislator; His Ignorance and Corruption." The general tone of the book was one of patronizing ridicule. A more scurrilous assault is represented by Charles Carroll's "*The Negro a Beast*"; or, "*In the Image of God*," which included extremely derogatory drawings as well as abusive text. An edition of this book was being sold by the American Bible House of St. Louis as recently as 1911. For a comprehensive discussion of this stereotyping process, note Burns, *Colour Prejudice*, chapter 6, "Alleged Inferiority of the Negro."

35. Quoted in Curtin, *Image of Africa*, vol. 1, p. 43.

36. Kenneth Little, *Negroes in Britain* (London: Kegan Paul, Trench, Trubner, 1947), pp. 213–214.

37. Quoted in Léon Poliakov, *The Aryan Myth* (New York: New American Library, 1971), p. 169.

38. Benjamin Quarles, *The Negro in the Making of America* (New York: Collier Books, 1964), pp. 113–118; 123–125.

39. For two important essays on racism by a Marxist historian, see "White Chauvinism: The Struggle Inside the Ranks" and "The History of Anti-Racism in the United States," in Herbert Aptheker, *The Unfolding Drama: Studies in U.S. History* (New York: International Publishers, 1978), pp. 120–129; 129–138. For an excellent discussion of the importance of racism directed at white ethnics in the framing of U.S. immigration laws, see Oscar Handlin, *Race and Nationality in American Life* (Boston: Little, Brown, 1957). For a discussion of the victimization of other colored ethnics, as well as Blacks, see Robert Daniels and Harry H. L. Kitano, *American Racism: Exploration of the Nature of Prejudice* (Englewood Cliffs, N.J.: Prentice-Hall, 1970). Fredrickson, *Black Image*, presents an excellent discussion of the stereotyping of Blacks in the United States immediately after the Civil War. Handlin devotes a chapter—"Prejudice and Capitalist Exploitation"—to a criticism of Oliver Cromwell Cox's Marxist analysis of racism. Cox interprets integration in the United States as an ongoing process within an expanding industrial capitalist system that is inevitably moving toward some form of socialism. See "The Final Logic of Race Relations" in Cox, *Race Relations: Elements of Social Dynamics* (Detroit: Wayne State University Press, 1976), pp. 288–297. Froman, in *Racism*, presents a less optimistic view. That class may be more salient

than race in current black-white relations is the argument advanced by William J. Wilson in *The Declining Significance of Race* (Chicago: University of Chicago Press, 1978).

40. For a discussion of the origins of the Hamitic Hypothesis, see the chapter by St. Clair Drake, "Toward the Evaluation of African Societies," in *Africa as Seen by American Negroes*, ed. John A. Davis (Paris: Librairie Présence Africaine, 1958), and an article—"Détruire le mythe chamitique devoir des hommes cultivés"— in *Présence Africaine; Revue Culturelle du Monde Noir*, n.s., nos. 24–25 (1959): 215–230.

41. See chapter 3, "Social Structure," and chapter 7, "Racial and National Identity," in David Lowenthal, *West Indian Societies* (London: Oxford University Press, 1972); and Magnus Mörner, *Race Mixture in the History of Latin America* (Boston: Little, Brown, 1967), pp. 136–150.

42. The absence of Asians in the top echelons of power in the USSR after sixty years of socialist rule, and what some consider the slow pace of upward mobility of Blacks in Cuba, might be cited. See, however, the optimistic statement by a Cuban journalist made to an Afro-American journalist, as reported in an article by Robert Chrisman, "National Culture in Revolutionary Cuba," *Black Scholar*, Summer (1977): 86–89 (especially sections on "Race and Sex"). There are visible and viable African religious retentions in Cuba, such as the Santería and Shango cults. This complicates the study of the reaction of a Communist government to the black *présence*. Theoretically, it is possible to oppose Africanisms without being prejudiced against Blacks, and vice versa. The question must be raised, from a black perspective, as to how long Blacks who have been impacted at the bottom of the social ladder should be expected to wait until the slow process of education has done its work. Are "affirmative action" programs needed for Blacks in Socialist Cuba? At a Party congress in 1986 Castro called for a special effort to eliminate the last vestiges of color prejudice. The UCLA Center for Afro-American Studies is readying for publication a manuscript by Carlos Moore, "Cuban Race Politics: The Shaping of Castro's Africa Policy" (2 vols.). In that work, Moore examines the impact of the Cuban Revolution and Castro's Africa policy on the Afro-Cuban population and its culture. Another work examining the present status of Blacks in Latin America is *Race, Class, and Power in Brazil*, Pierre-Michel Fontaine, ed. (Los Angeles: UCLA Center for Afro-American Studies, 1986).

43. James Africanus B. Horton, the distinguished West African physician, is reported to have written a book, *Vindication of the African*, in the 1800s, but no publisher or precise date is mentioned (see Christopher Fyfe, *Africanus Horton: West African Scientist and Patriot* [New York: Oxford University Press, 1972], p. 69). Edward Wilmot Blyden's booklet *Vindication of the Negro Race* was published in Monrovia, Liberia, in 1857 by Gaston Killian. Hollis Lynch has written a chapter entitled "Vindicator of the Negro Race," in his biography, *Edward Wilmot Blyden, Pan-Negro Patriot* (London: Oxford University Press, 1967). See also W.E.B. Du Bois, "Possibilities of the Negro: The Advance Guard of the Race," *Booklover's Magazine*, July 1903.

44. See Earl E. Thorpe, *Black Historians: A Critique* (New York: Morrow, 1971); and William Toll, *The Resurgence of Race: Black Social Theory from Reconstruction to the Pan-African Conferences* (Philadelphia: Temple University Press, 1979).

45. Gordon W. Allport, "Prejudice and the Individual," and Thomas Pettigrew, "Prejudice and the Situation," in *The American Negro Reference Book*, ed. John P. Davis (Englewood Cliffs, N.J.: Prentice-Hall, 1966), pp. 706–723.

46. Stokely Carmichael and Charles V. Hamilton, *Black Power* (New York: Random House, 1967), p. 3. Quoted also in John L. Hodge, Donald K. Struckmann, and Lynn Dorland Trost, *Cultural Bases of Racism and Group Oppression* (Berkeley, Calif.: Two Riders Press, 1975), p. 11.
47. See, for example, articles in Joyce A. Ladner, ed., *The Death of White Sociology* (New York: Random House, 1973).
48. Louis L. Knowles and Kenneth Prewitt, eds., *Institutional Racism in America* (Englewood Cliffs, N.J.: Prentice-Hall, 1969). This was the first book to carry the term in its title.
49. Quoted in Davis, *Negro Reference Book*, p. 707.
50. A Harvard-trained Afro-American psychiatrist defines racism as ''a mental health and public health disease characterized by perceptual distortion, contagion, and fatality. The vehicle for these characteristics is the cumulative effect of offensive mechanisms, individually exhibited but collectively approved by the White sector of this society.'' Chester Pierce, ''Offensive Mechanisms,'' in *The Black Seventies*, ed. Floyd B. Barbour (Boston: Porter Sargent, 1970), p. 268.
51. Noel Chabani Manganyi, *Alienation and the Body in Racist Society, a Study of the Society That Invented Soweto* (New York: Nok, 1977), pp. 100–107. This study synthesizes the work of a group of psychiatrists interested in the study of alienation into an effective tool for examining racism in South Africa. Kovel's *White Racism*, to which Manganyi refers, also merits careful study (see note 18).
52. See, for example, Abdul Alkalimat, *A Scientific Approach to Black Liberation* (Nashville, Tenn.: Peoples College, 1974). Compare Haki R. Madhubuti (Don L. Lee), ''The Latest Purge,'' *Black Scholar*, December (1974) with Mark Smith's ''A Response to Haki Madhubuti,'' *Black Scholar*, January–February (1975), and with Kalamu Ya Salaam's ''A Response to Haki Madhubuti,'' in the same issue. The issue also contained one of the first statements by Amiri Baraka (LeRoi Jones)— ''The Congress of Afrikan People: A Position Paper''—as he began his shift from Black Nationalism to Marxism. For an exposition of his position after the shift was completed, see the January 1980 issue of *Forward: Journal of Marxism-Leninism-Mao Zedong Thought*. The entire issue is devoted to Baraka's prose and poetry. The writings of C.L.R. James, George Padmore, Horace Mann Bond, and Ralph Bunche in *A World View of Race* (Washington, D.C.: Associates in Negro Folk Education, 1936), express the position stated by Smith, either implicitly or explicitly.
53. Cox, *Race Relations*, pp. 25–26.
54. Oliver Cromwell Cox, *Caste, Class and Race* (New York: Monthly Review Press, 1959), p. 322.
55. See, for example, the works of Amilcar Cabral, C.L.R. James, George Padmore, Walter Rodney, Clive Y. Thomas, Samir Amin, Sékou Touré, and Kwame Nkrumah. A valuable scholarly discussion is presented in a book by the Director of the Black Studies Center, University of California, Santa Barbara, Dr. Cedric J. Robinson's *Black Marxism: The Making of the Black Radical Tradition* (London: Zed Press, 1983).
56. Margaret Mead expressed these fears of ''reverse racism'' in her introduction to the post–World War II reprint edition of Ruth Benedict's *Race: Science and Politics* (New York: Viking, 1959), pp. viii-ix. Sartre's use of the term *antiracist racism* can be found in his foreword, ''Orphée noir,'' to Leopold Senghor's *Anthologie de la nouvelle poèsie négre et malgache de la langue française* (Paris: Presses Universitaires de France, 1948). This essay was translated by Samuel W. Allen and pub-

lished in 1963 in pamphlet form as *Black Orpheus* for the American Society of African Culture by the publishers of the magazine *Présence Africaine*.

Some powerful factors have operated to discourage racism in colored Third World countries, such as the need for allies during liberation struggles and for financial and technical assistance after victory. It is significant, too, that when the Black Muslims in the United States ventured into large-scale financial operations— importing fish, owning jet planes, planning community development projects, etc.—they stopped calling whites "devils" and eventually opened the Nation of Islam to all races, changing the name of the organization to The World Community of Islam in the West.

In contemporary South Africa, both the Marxist-oriented African National Congress and the United Democratic Front accept members of all races. The Black Consciousness movement does not, and like the Afrikaner government insists its separateness is not racist. In the United States, the Reagan administration is redefining "Affirmative Action" to mean "reverse discrimination" against white males. Some judges are insisting that unless *intent* to discriminate could be proved, structural inequities are not actionable under Civil Rights laws. What Marxists call a heightening of contradictions in black-white relations is evident on a global scale.

CHAPTER 2

1. Myrdal, *An American Dilemma*, vol. 2, appendix 1: "Note on Valuations and Beliefs," pp. 1027–1034; appendix 2: "A Methodological Note on Facts and Valuations in the Social Sciences," pp. 1035–1064; appendix 3: "A Methodological Note on the Principle of Cumulation," pp. 1065–1072; chapter 1, "American Ideals and the American Conscience," pp. 3–25; chapter 3, "Encountering the Crossroads," pp. 997–1024. Historian Herbert Aptheker leveled an additional Marxian criticism, viz., that Myrdal's theory of the vicious circle "suits perfectly a program of excruciating patience, high-level politicking, and the absence of mass action directed at the elimination of real grievances and the achievement of fundamental advances." Herbert Aptheker, *Afro-American History* (Secaucus, N.J.: Citadel Press, 1971), p. 40. For critical, but on the whole favorable, analysis of the Myrdal study by an academic sociologist, see chapter 4, "Gunnar Myrdal's *An American Dilemma*," in Stanford M. Lyman, *The Black American in Sociological Thought: A Failure of Perspective* (New York: Capricorn Books, 1973), pp. 99–120.
2. See St. Clair Drake, "Recent Trends in Research on the Negro in the United States," *International Social Science Journal* 9, 4 (1957), for a detailed summary of the literature in the postwar period and a summary of pre–World War II trends.
3. Myrdal, *American Dilemma*, pp. 1022-1023.
4. Gordon W. Allport, *The Nature of Prejudice* (New York: Doubleday Anchor Books, 1958), chapter 9.
5. For one of the most influential articles affecting decision-making in race relations during the early postwar period, see Joseph D. Lohman and Dietrich C. Reitzes, "Notes on Race Relations in Mass Society," *American Journal of Sociology* 58 (November 1952): 240–246; republished in Raymond W. Mack, ed., *Race, Class and Power* (New York: Van Nostrand Reinhold, 1968). See also Melvin L. Kohn and Robin M. Williams, Jr., "Situational Patterning in Intergroup Relations," in ibid., pp. 152–166; and Allport, *Nature of Prejudice*, chapter 31, "Limitations and Horizons," pp. 463–480.

6. Robert K. Merton, "The Unanticipated Consequences of Social Action," *American Sociological Review* 1 (December 1936): 894–904.

7. H. Hoetink, *Caribbean Race Relations: A Study of Two Variants* (London: Oxford University Press, 1967), p. 88; first published by Oxford University Press for the Institute of Race Relations, London.

8. Ibid., p. 122.

9. Ibid., p. 88.

10. Ibid., p. 89.

11. Quoted in Lyman, *Black American*, p. 46, from an article by Robert E. Park, "Our Racial Frontier on the Pacific," in Everett C. Hughes et al., eds., *Race and Culture*. vol. 1, The Collected Papers of Robert Ezra Park (Glencoe, Ill.: Free Press, 1950), p. 150.

12. Gustav Ichheiser, "Sociopsychological and Cultural Factors in Race Relations," *American Journal of Sociology* 54, 5 (March 1949): 395. An article that follows Ichheiser's in this issue of the journal—Emilio Willems's "Race Attitudes in Brazil"—adds significance to Ichheiser's argument.

13. Ichheiser, "Sociopsychological and Cultural Factors," pp. 395, 396.

14. Ibid., p. 397.

15. Ibid., pp. 398, 397n.

16. Louis Wirth, "Comment," following Ichheiser, "Sociopsychological and Cultural Factors," p. 400.

17. Quoted in Lyman, *Black American*, chapter 2, pp. 41–42. This is from an extended discussion, by Lyman, of some of Park's views under the rubric of "Black Temperament."

18. Ibid., p. 42. The Afro-American novelist Ralph Ellison criticized Park for his "lady of the races" statement in *Shadow and Act* (New York: Random House, 1964), p. 308. Despite Park's belief in special inherited traits, he favored a type of education that would prepare Afro-Americans for assimilation into the middle-class white cultural milieu. For this point of view he was assailed by a young black-militant Ph.D. candidate in sociology during the sixties. See Abdul Hakim Ibn Alkalimat, "The Ideology of Black Social Science," in *The Death of White Sociology*, ed. Joyce A. Ladner (New York: Random House, 1973), pp. 175–181. For the unusual case of a black student (an African at Rutgers, in this case) defending Park's view explicitly and insisting that "black temperament" has a genetic base, see Julius M. Waichugu, "Black Heritage of Genetics, Environment and Continuity," in *Black Life and Culture in the United States*, ed. Rhoda L. Goldstein (New York: Crowell, 1971), pp. 36–48. For a critical discussion of Leopold Senghor's tendency to think of *Négritude* as inherited, see St. Clair Drake, " 'Hide My Face?' On Pan-Africanism and Negritude," in *The Making of Black America*, ed. August Meier and Elliot Rudwick (New York: Atheneum, 1969), pp. 77–78.

19. Ichheiser, "Sociopsychological and Cultural Factors," p. 401.

20. Quoted in Lyman, *Black American*, chapter 2, p. 44.

21. Ibid., p. 44.

22. Louis Wirth, *On Cities and Social Life. Selected Papers*, ed. and with an introduction by Albert J. Reiss, Jr. (Chicago: University of Chicago Press, Phoenix Books, 1964), chapter 18, "Race and Public Policy," pp. 270–291. Quotation from p. 274.

23. Robin M. Williams, Jr., "Prejudice and Society," in *The American Negro Reference Book*, ed. John P. Davis (Englewood Cliffs, N.J.: Prentice-Hall, 1966), pp. 727–728.

24. W. Lloyd Warner et al., *Yankee City*, abridged ed. in one vol., selected and edited

by W. Lloyd Warner (New Haven, Conn.: Yale University Press, 1963), p. 413 and chapter 14, "The Future of American Ethnic and Racial Groups."

25. Allport, *Nature of Prejudice*, chapter 15, "Choice of Scapegoats"; chapter 21, "Frustration."

26. For a statement of the psychoanalytic view, see Bruno Bettelheim and Morris Janowitz, *Dynamics of Prejudice* (New York: Harper and Brothers, 1950), chapter 1, "Dynamic Approach to Intolerance," pp. 1-6; chapter 9, "Reflections, and Applications for Social Action," pp. 162-186. This is a simple but authoritative statement using Jews and Negroes as examples. See also Allport, *Nature of Prejudice*, chapters 12, 15. For the role of black workers as a target, see Robert L. Allen, *Reluctant Reformers* (Washington, D.C.: Howard University Press, 1974), chapter 6, "Organized Labor: From Underdog to Overseer."

27. Robert A. Levine and Donald T. Campbell, *Ethnocentrism: Theories of Conflict, Ethnic Attitudes, and Group Behavior* (New York: John Wiley, 1972), pp. 168-169.

28. For an interesting, unconventional discussion of the possibility of giving impetus to a strong *intellectual* thrust within the Black Consciousness movement in the United States, note African scholar Ali Mazrui's appraisal, "Negritude, the Talmudic Tradition and the Intellectual Performance of Blacks and Jews," *Ethnic and Racial Studies* 1, 1 (January 1978): 19-36.

29. Preface to the Proceedings of the American Academy of Arts and Sciences, Spring 1967, entitled "Color and Race." Published in *Daedalus* 96, 2: iii.

30. Edward Shils, "Color and the Afro-Asian Intellectual," *Daedalus* 96, 2 (Spring 1967): 279-295. Some of the influential contributions to the discussion of the meaning and function of "blackness" during this period were: Claude Lévi-Strauss, *Race et histoire* (Paris: UNESCO, 1952; reissued, Paris: Gonthier, 1970); Frantz Fanon, *Peau noire, masques blancs* (Paris: Seuil, 1952; reissued, New York: Grove Press, 1967, as *Black Skins, White Masks: The Experiences of a Black Man in a White World*; Oliver Cromwell Cox, *Caste, Class and Race* (New York: Monthly Review Press, 1959; originally published in 1948 by Doubleday); Harry Levin, *The Power of Blackness: Hawthorne, Poe, Melville* (New York: Knopf, 1958); Charles Wagley, "On the Concept of Social Race in the Americas," in *Actas del Internacional 33, Congreso Internacional de Americanistas* (San José: Lehmann 1959), vol. 1, pp. 403-417 (reprinted in Dwight B. Heath and Richard N. Adams, *Contemporary Cultures and Societies of Latin America* [New York: Random House, 1965]); Harold R. Isaacs, *The New World of Negro Americans* (Cambridge, Mass.: MIT Press, 1963), part 2, chapter 3, "Black, Stand Back"; C. G. Jung, *Memories, Dreams, Reflections* (New York: Vintage Books, Random House, 1961), chapter 1, "First Year," and pp. 272-274; Mary Ellen Goodman, *Race Awareness in Young Children*, with an introduction by Kenneth Clark (New York: Oxford University Press, 1964; originally published in 1952); Philip D. Curtin, *The Image of Africa: British Ideas and Action, 1780-1850*, 2 vols. (Madison: University of Wisconsin Press, 1964); Roger Bastide, "Dusky Venus, Black Apollo," *Race* 3, 3 (1961); Victor Turner, "Color Classification in Ndembu Ritual: A Problem in Classification," in *The Forest of Symbols* (Ithaca, N.Y.: Cornell University Press, 1967; originally published in *Anthropological Approaches to the Study of Religion*, A.S.A. Monograph No. 3 [London: Tavistock Publications, 1965]); Jordan, *White Over Black*; Hoetink, *Caribbean Race Relations* (London: Oxford University Press, 1967); Carl Degler, *Neither Black nor White: Slavery and Race Relations in Brazil and the United States* (New York: Macmillan, 1971); Bernard Lewis, *Race and Color in Islam* (New York: Harper Torchbook, 1971).

31. Roger Bastide, "Color, Racism and Christianity," in *Color and Race*, ed. and with an introduction by John Hope Franklin (Boston: Houghton Mifflin, 1968), pp. 36–37. See also the articles "Dualism," "Mani," "Manichaeism," and "Zoroastrianism" in the 1963 edition of *Encyclopaedia Britannica* for the original religious conceptualism used, in a secularized metaphorical sense, in the expression "New (or Modern) Manichaeans."

32. Bastide, "Color, Racism and Christianity," p. 37.

33. See the article "Mani" in the 1963 edition of *Encyclopaedia Britannica*, vol. 14.

34. Fanon, *Black Skin, White Masks*, pp. 167, 177, 188–192. Fanon was quite explicit about the black-white polar contrast, writing that "Good-Evil, Beauty-Ugliness, White-Black, such are the characteristic pairings of the phenomenon that, making use of an expression of Dide and Guiraud, we shall call 'Manichaean delirium' " (p. 183).

35. Ibid., p. 40.

36. Jordan, *White Over Black*, p. 248.

37. Ibid., p. 253.

38. Lewis Copeland, "The Negro as a Contrast Conception," in *Race Relations and the Race Problem, a Definition and an Analysis*, ed. Edgar T. Thompson (New York: Greenwood Press, 1968), pp. 152–179; reprinted from a 1939 edition published by Duke University Press.

39. John L. Hodge, Donald K. Struckmann, and Lynn Dorland Trost, *Cultural Bases of Racism and Group Oppression* (Berkeley, Calif.: Three Riders Press, 1975), p. 40.

40. Manichaean symbolism was being used in the United States in the early sixties. In 1963 Harold Isaacs, a professor at MIT, urged some of his graduate students to explore the black-white symbolism in a comparative frame of reference. In reflecting upon the results, he wrote, "In coming to terms with himself, every Negro individual has had in one way or another to cope with the infinity of ways in which 'white' is elevated above 'black' in our culture. The association of white and black with light and dark and the translation of these qualities of light into polarities of 'good' and 'evil' and 'beauty' and 'ugliness' have taken place in the conventions and languages of many cultures, but in few has the conversion of physical facts into religious and esthetic values been worked harder than in our own" (*New World of Negro Americans*, p. 74). Isaacs did not present a theory to account for the presence of the polarity in various cultures. The use of the term *Manichaean* is, of course, a metaphor and does not imply that those who accept the contrast accept the metaphysical explanations once associated with it.

41. Degler, *Neither Black nor White*, p. 211.

42. Ibid., p. 287. Degler's quoting of Hoetink on page 291n is also significant.

43. Kenneth J. Gergen, "The Significance of Skin Color in Human Relations," *Daedalus* 96, 2 (Spring 1967); republished, with an introduction by John Hope Franklin and an additional article by Talcott Parsons, as *Color and Race*, pp. 112–128.

44. Gergen, "Significance of Skin Color," p. 392.

45. Ibid.

46. Ibid.

47. Ibid., n. 6, pp. 403, 404.

48. Ibid., pp. 399–400.

49. Ibid., pp. 395–396.

50. Ibid. It is significant that despite Jung's fixation on the more sinister aspects of "blackness," he did not claim universality for the equivalences white = good,

black = evil. In fact, his concept of archetype is not inconsistent with the structuralist view put forward by some anthropologists. Jung stated: "It is necessary to point out once more that archetypes are not determined as regards their content, but only as regards their form. . . . A primordial image is determined as to its content only when it has become conscious and is therefore filled out with the material of conscious experience" (*Memories, Dreams, Reflections*, pp. 392–393). Yet, Jung referred to "the fear of the 'black man' that is felt by every child" (p. 14). He apparently meant "in Western Christian cultures," if the context of his statement is taken into account.

51. Ibid., p. 398. If one assumes that all children everywhere have the same kind of experiences, then all children will require deliberate "treatment" of their negative conditioning toward darkness if they are not to be prejudiced against Blacks as adults. Logically, in theories based on "deep structures" and archetypes rather than conditioning, such negative attitudes could not be removed. For studies indicating that change is possible, see Judith Porter, *Black Child, White Child: The Development of Racial Attitudes* (Cambridge, Mass.: Harvard University Press, 1971); Mary E. Goodman, *Race Awareness in Young Children*, rev. ed. (New York: Collier Books, 1964).

52. Edmund Leach, *Culture and Communication: The Logic by Which Symbols Are Connected* (Cambridge: Cambridge University, 1976), p. 57. Victor Turner was only incidentally interested in the question of whether negative evaluations of "blackness" carried over into social relations. He was interested primarily in broader theoretical questions in cognitive anthropology. His sampling of cultures, limited though it was, revealed the prevalence of three colors existing within individual cultures: *Red, White*, and *Black*. Repeatedly, he finds the colors *Red* and *White* "paired together against *Black*." Most cultures do not formulate systematic correlations between colors of the triad and values or psychological states.

Turner describes one subculture that contains a group that does, noting some Hindu philosophical systems which refer to three *gunas* that form the "strands" of existence. *White* is the "subtlest" (purity, tranquility, primal energy); *Black* is "coarsest" (darkness, apathy, obstruction, constriction); and *Red* is "medium" (energy that inititates *karma*). Turner combines these color associations from one school of Hindu philosophy with a modified psychoanalytical point of view and states that the colors really symbolize certain "primordial psychobiological experiences" that all people have from birth onward. It is these that Leach contends do not *necessarily* have the connotations of the *gunas*:

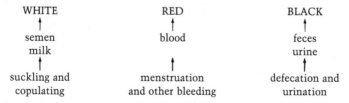

From Turner, "Color Classification in Ndembu Ritual," pp. 88–91.

53. Leach, *Culture and Communication*, p. 74.

54. Turner does not list any negative associations with the color *White*, but reports numerous such associations with *Black*:

WHITE		BLACK	
Moonlight	Ancestors	Darkness	Night
Women	Goodness	Evil	Death
Health	Light	Impurity	Disease
Purity	Hope	Sterility	Misfortune
Public matters	Joy	Hidden matters	Suffering
Power	Good luck	Sorcery	Witchcraft

But, and this is important, Turner also reports some positive associations with *Black*, including marital peace and happiness, sexual satisfaction, cattle, goats, and fowls. Turner then reminds the reader: "I have mentioned the ambivalence of black symbolism among the Ndembu." Degler ignored this ambivalence. Turner comments further that, "in many African societies black has auspicious connotations" (p. 82). He cites a number of instances from central and southern Africa and presents an ingenious ecological explanation to account for the positive affect in some of these cultures: "*My own hypothesis is that black tends to become an auspicious color in regions where water is short, for the black clouds bring fertility and growth (apparently of hair as well [as] of plants!). In regions where water is plentiful and food more or less abundant, black may well be inauspicious*" (pp. 82–83, italics added). Turner also referred to *Black* as symbolizing "mystical or ritual death" necessary for passage from a "lower" to a "higher" status of existence.

In an unpublished paper made available to the author, sociologist Pierre van den Berghe attempts to demonstrate that women become lighter at adolescence—even in sub-Saharan Africa—and this signals readiness to mate. This sociobiological argument sees survival value in sexual dimorphism and the custom of choosing light-skinned mates. He admits it is still an unproved hypothesis.

55. Gergen, p. 399. This less extreme view than Degler's is supported by Turner, who, in his well-conceived and impressive theoretical article, draws a clear distinction between the symbolism of color as it appears in artifact, clothing, and ornament, and the color terms and evaluations people make of each other in their social relations. This is a crucial distinction and one that we also make in each chapter of this volume. Victor Turner found that "*when the colors are considered in abstraction from social and ritual contexts, Ndembu think of white and black as the supreme antitheses in their scheme of reality*" (p. 74). He cites eleven other African ethnic groups in which this same kind of contrast was present at the level of abstract symbolization, but he warns the reader before presenting his data on them and some Asian Amerindian and Australian groups: "Since I have had little opportunity to comb through the literature systematically, what follows must be necessarily somewhat haphazard" (p. 81). For an interesting attempt to deal with this question using the semantic differential technique see Charles E. Osgood, W. H. May, and S. Miron, *Cross-Cultural Universals of Affective Meaning* (Urbana, Ill.: University of Illinois Press, 1975). The results are inconclusive.

56. Gergen, p. 399.

57. Ibid., p. 400.

58. Ibid.

59. Ibid.

60. For a statement by a social scientist who documented the relative absence of racial

conflict in such a system and who stated a preference for such a type, see Hoetink, *Caribbean Race Relations*, "The Socio-Racial Structure of Caribbean Society," pp. 35-55; "Biological Homogenization in the Iberian Variant," pp. 182-190. An anthropologist who described such a system without stating a preference is Julian Pitt-Rivers, in "Race, Color and Class in Central America and the Andes" (*Daedalus* 96, 2). Another anthropologist advanced the interesting hypothesis that where considerable ambiguity exists about the color designation for specific individuals within a society, "noise" is introduced into the communication system which minimizes the formation of groups around such differences. See Marvin Harris, "Referential Ambiguity in the Calculus of Brazilian Racial Identity," in *Afro-American Anthropology*, ed. Norman E. Whitten, Jr., and John F. Szwed (New York: Free Press, 1970), pp. 75-86.

61. Gergen, "Significance of Skin Color," pp. 398-401. A work dealing with this problem among white children in the United States is Porter's *Black Child, White Child* (1971). Gergen's view that black people generally have negative attitudes toward their own physical type is widely shared by both black and white scholars. An extreme statement of this attitude by two black psychiatrists, William H. Grier and Price M. Cobbs, can be found in *Black Rage* (New York: Basic Books, 1968), pp. 160-167; see also an article by black sociologist C. Eric Lincoln, "Color and Group Identity in the United States," *Daedalus* 96, 2. W. C. Kvaraceus, a white scholar, made a similar statement in *Negro Self Concept* (New York: McGraw-Hill, 1965), pp. 1-51. Gergen raised the question in his article (n. 33, p. 408) as to whether or not the Black Consciousness and Black Power movements were likely to alter this situation. Evidence from the individual and collective behavior of Afro-Americans points toward a reversal of attitudes, but there is no controlled research to confirm it. For a persuasive argument that black self-esteem was never so low as most white observers thought it was, see Patricia Guren and Edgar Epps, *Black Consciousness, Identity and Achievement* (New York: John Wiley, 1975), pp. 5-6.

62. Gergen, "Significance of Skin Color," p. 403; Hoetink, *Caribbean Race Relations*, pp. 182-190.

63. Hiroshi Wagatsuma, "The Social Perception of Skin Color in Japan," *Daedalus* 96, 2 (Spring 1967): 407. Incidentally, the word used for *Black* by the Japanese covers a wide range of colors and is applied to tanned or brunette Japanese as well as to Africans. A more precise word was used for the Negro phenotype, and it had pejorative connotations. There is evidence, however, that Blacks were popular in Japan when they came with the first Portuguese traders in the fifteenth century. See Arnold Rubin, *Black Nanban: Africans in Japan during the Sixteenth Century* (Bloomington, Ill.: African Studies Program, Indiana University, 1974), p. 8.

64. Quoted in Wagatsuma, "Social Perception of Skin Color," p. 413.

65. Jordan, *White Over Black*, pp. 27-28.

66. Richard Ligon, *A True and Exact History of the Island of Barbados* (London: Frank Cass, 1970; first published in 1657). He praised some "young Negro virgins" he had met in the Canary Islands and said he liked them because they did not have flat features and thick lips (pp. 15-16).

67. William Shakespeare, *The Complete Works*, with an introduction and glossary by Peter Alexander (London: Collins, Tudor Edition, 1951), pp. 1329, 1330; sonnets 127, 130, 131, 132.

68. Cheikh Anta Diop, in presenting pictures of West African and Egyptian coiffures, stated that they "reflect a constant effort (from Egyptian antiquity to the present) to adapt frizzy hair to feminine grace. The whole aspect of the world would be

changed if black girls had long hair." See Diop, *The African Origin of Civilization* (1974), plate 24, p. 37. Desroches-Noblecourt, on the other hand, stated that Eighteenth-Dynasty women at the Egyptian court wore short, curly-haired "Nubian wigs" to be in fashion. Diop, the West African savant, unconsciously reflected here the values of the French culture in which he was socialized. He may have been reading his own attitudes into the minds of "black girls" throughout history. See Christiane Desroches-Noblecourt, *Tutankhamen: Life and Death of a Pharaoh* (New York: New York Graphic Society, 1963), p. 121. Incidentally, research on "Negroidness" has never been carried out by scholars in the field of comparative esthetics.

69. For a statement of early views on this issue, see Jordan, *White Over Black*, "The Apes of Africa," pp. 28–31; "Negroes, Apes and Beasts," pp. 228–234. An anthropology text published in 1969 contained an illustrated chart showing the "most apelike" and "least apelike" hair and lip forms, degree of prognathism, development of buttocks, heel, brow ridge, arm-body ratio, and amount of hair. Bar graphs showed traits on which each racial group—Caucasian, Mongolian, and Negro— was evaluated on a scale from "most apelike" to "least apelike." The point was made that all races had some "mosts." The author, in another context, stated that primates exhibit a variety of skin-colors. See Herman K. Bleibtrau, *Human Variation* (Beverly Hills, Calif.: Glencoe, 1969, pp. 159, 184). Ashley Montagu, in a pamphlet prepared for mass distribution by the Anti-Defamation League of B'nai B'rith, noted that apes and human beings have a common ancestral stock whose skin-color is unknown, and commented that "since that of the apes is black or dark brown, we may assume that it was dark brown." He went on to imply that the earliest men were probably of this color, and stated further that "the apes have practically no visible lips, they never have kinky hair. . . . In these respects, the white man is 'closer to the apes' than the Negro." In fact, both have evolved very far away from their early common ancestor (Ashley Montagu, *What We Know about "Race,"* in The One Nation Library Series, Anti-Defamation League, New York, n.d. [circa 1960], pp. 10 and 13).

70. Gary Allighan, *Curtain Up on South Africa* (London: Boardman, 1960), p. 29.

71. The classic case of inferring intellectual capacity and character from the possession of "refined" features is the still-persistent use of the Hamitic myth in dealing with the people of Africa. See George Peter Murdock, *Africa: Its People and Their Culture History* (New York: McGraw-Hill, 1959), p. 65. Curtin pointed out that some nineteenth-century Englishmen actually believed that "Negro features" were the result of a "low state of civilization" and would "improve" as the African became more civilized. See Curtin, *Image of Africa*, vol. 1, p. 238.

72. For an exhaustive treatment of the erotic component utilizing a wide range of photographs and including extensive documentation, see Joel A. Rogers's three-volume work *Sex and Race: Negro-Caucasian Mixing in All Ages and All Lands* (vols. 1 and 2 [New York: J. A. Rogers]; vol. 3 [New York: H.M. Rogers, 1942–67]) and his one-volume *Research into the Negro Ancestry of the White Race*, 3d ed. (New York: H. M. Rogers, 1952). (These privately printed works are available in many university libraries and in book shops in black communities.) See also Robert Seidenberg, "The Sexual Basis of Social Prejudice," *Psychoanalytic Review* 38 (1952); Grace Halsell, *Black/White Sex* (New York: Morrow, 1972). For a comparison of the views of a white scholar and a black scholar on the erotic factor in race relations, see Calvin C. Hernton, *Sex and Racism in America* (Garden City, N.J.: Doubleday, 1965); Charles Herbert Stember, *Sexual Racism: The Emotional Barrier to an Integrated Society* (New York: Harper Colophon, 1978).

73. Mandingo and Wolof women from what is now Senegal often became greatly prized as household slaves in the French Caribbean, where they were used as casual sexual partners or as concubines for males in the slave-owning families.

74. Quoted in Degler, *Neither Black nor White*, p. 188.

75. Bastide, "Dusky Venus, Black Apollo," pp. 14-15, 18.

76. John Dollard, *Caste and Class in a Southern Town* (New York: Doubleday-Anchor, 1949), chapter 7, pp. 144-146, 170-172. Stember, *Sexual Racism*, chapter 3, "Explanations of Racial Hostility."

77. Stember, *Sexual Racism*, chapter 7, "Female Sexuality and Response to Black Males." What appears to be a strain of Puritanism in contemporary Islamic fundamentalism in Iran and elsewhere is really an extreme case of the double standard in sexual expression coupled with anti-Western mobilization tactics.

78. See the discussion of *The Arabian Nights* in chapter 5 (volume 2, forthcoming).

79. For a discussion of this philosophy and its origins, see August Meier, *Negro Thought in America, 1880-1915: Racial Ideologies in the Age of Booker T. Washington* (Ann Arbor, Mich.: University of Michigan Press, 1963), p. 88. The founder of Hampton Institute was said to have believed that "the colored races were slothful, backward, lascivious, and inferior."

80. The association of physical features with mental traits in the popular mind is most readily apparent in the descriptions of individuals in fiction and biographies. Systematic content analyses on this specific point have not yet been made.

81. With the publication of Audrey Shuey's *The Testing of Negro Intelligence* (New York: Social Science Press) in 1958, the pre–World War II controversy about the innate ability of Negroes was reopened. Shuey's book was republished in 1966, and Cyril Burt's article "The Genetic Determination of Differences in Intelligence" appeared the same year in the *British Journal of Psychology* (vol. 57, pp. 137-153). William Shockley of Stanford University, a Nobel Prize–winning physicist, became an ardent popularizer of Burt's heritability findings on the basis of studies carried out on twins. These studies also provided the basis for a "biological interpretation" of Shuey's findings. (See, e.g., Shockley's article in *Phi Delta Kappan*, January 1972, pp. 297-307). The *Harvard Educational Review* (vol. 39 [1969]: 1-123) published an article by University of California, Berkeley, psychologist Arthur Jensen entitled "How Much Can We Boost I.Q. and Scholastic Achievement." His pessimistic answer precipitated a controversy, and the *Review* published rejoinders during the same year (vol. 39, pp. 274-277; pp. 278-300; pp. 523-557; pp. 557-580). Harvard University professor R. Herrnstein evoked widespread discussion with "I.Q." in the *Atlantic* (September 1971), pp. 43-58, 63-64, stating the case for a meritocracy that dooms those with low IQs. Liberal anthropologist Ashley Montagu presented essays by seventeen biologists and social scientists in 1975 criticizing the views of the so-called "hereditarians." See *Race and I.Q.* (New York: Oxford University Press, 1975). For the black "mirror image" of the white hereditarian view, see *Voodoo or I.Q.: an Introduction to African Psychology* by Cedric X (Clark), D. Phillip McGee, Wade Nobles, and Na'im Akbar, published in 1976 by the Institute of Positive Education, Chicago, "What is the Mystery of Melanin," pp. 7-8 and "What is the Nature of Black Intelligence," pp. 10-13.

82. Bettelheim and Janowitz, *Dynamics of Prejudice*, p. 4.

83. Herbert Blumer, "The Nature of Race Prejudice," *Social Process in Hawaii* 18 (1954): 13. This article appeared in a special issue entitled "Race Relations in Hawaii."

84. Allport, *Nature of Prejudice*, pp. 6-8.

85. Blumer, "Nature of Race Prejudice," p. 14. The views presented in this article were

originally published in 1939 and then amplified and extended by the author in "Race Prejudice as a Sense of Group Position," *Pacific Sociological Review* 1 (1958). An influential sociologist writing nearly ten years later referred to "man's need to be in contact with the point and moment of his origin and to experience a sense of affinity with those who share that origin. The needs for connections or relationships of a primordial character will be endemic in human experience as long as biological existence has a value to the individual organism. Ethnic identification, of which color identification is a particular variant, is a manifestation of this need." See Edward Shils, "Color, the Universal Intellectual Community and the Afro-Asian Intellectual," in *Color and Race*, ed. John Hope Franklin (Boston: Houghton Mifflin, 1968), p. 4. Shils felt that color was a primary symbol of this primordial solidarity. Blumer's statement that color *could* be such a symbol was less strong than Shils's.

86. See Blumer, "Nature of Race Prejudice," pp. 13–15, for the discussion from which the hypotheses are abstracted. Oliver Cromwell Cox, in *Race Relations: Elements and Social Dynamics* (Detroit: Wayne State University Press, 1976), pp. 23–24, concurred with Blumer's argument about race prejudice resulting from a "sense of position." An extended discussion of this aspect of Blumer's analysis appeared in Lyman, *Black American*, pp. 137–143, 152.
87. Cox, *Caste, Class, and Race*, pp. 22, 24.
88. Cox, *Race Relations*, p. 275.

BIBLIOGRAPHIC ESSAY

1. Philip Mason, *Patterns of Dominance* (London and New York: Oxford University Press, 1970), p. 30.
2. C. F. Dicken, "Connotative Meaning as a Determinant of Stimulus Generalization," *Psychological Monographs* 72, 1 (1961). See also Kober, *Color Words in the Greek Poets*, pp. 1–12.
3. Winthrop Jordan, in *White Over Black*, cites P. J. Heather, "Colour Symbolism," *Folk Lore* 59 (1948), pp. 169–170, 176–178, 182–183, and *Folk Lore* 60 (1949) pp. 208–216, 266–276; Don Cameron Allen, "Symbolic Color in the Literature of the English Renaissance," *Philological Quarterly* 15 (1936): 81–92; Caroline F. E. Spurgeon, *Shakespeare's Imagery and What It Tells Us* (Boston, 1956), pp. 64, 66–69, 158; Francis B. Gummere, "On the Symbolic Use of the Colors Black and White in Germanic Tradition," *Haverford College Studies* 1 (1889): 112–162. See also Kober, *Color Words*, pp. 1–36, for a discussion of the contrast in ancient Greek usage.
4. A perceptive discussion of this point is developed around the concept of "somatic norm image" in Hoetink, *Caribbean Race Relations* (1968). Basic theoretical questions, however, are left unanswered.
5. Longshore, "Color Connotations" (1979), p. 184.
6. Williams, 1966, p. 482, quoted in Longshore, "Color Connotations" (1979), p. 185.
7. Longshore's final draft of this paper, submitted to the UCLA Department of Sociology in 1975 under the title "The Effect of Black Power Ideology on the Racial Self-Esteem of Black Children and Adults," reports the same conclusions.
8. Longshore, "Color Connotations," 1979, p. 194.
9. Ibid., p. 190.
10. Longshore and Beilin, "Inter-racial Behavior," 1980, p. 107.
11. Thomas F. Pettigrew, "Social Evaluation Theory: Convergences and Applications,"

in David Levine, *Nebraska Symposium on Motivation* (Lincoln: University of Nebraska Press, 1967), pp. 241–311; and Steven Asher and Vernon Allen, "Social Preference and Social Comparison Processes," *Journal of Social Issues* 25 (1969): 157–166. See also C. Garcia and H. Lenson, "Differences Between Blacks' and Whites' Expectation of Control by Chance and Powerful Others." *Psychological Reports* 37 (1975): 563–566.

CHAPTER 3

1. *Memoirs and Poems of Phillis Wheatley*, 3d ed. (Boston: 1838; reprinted by Mnemosyne Publishing Co., Miami, Fla., 1969), p. 48.
2. The full text of this petition is presented in Herbert Aptheker, ed., *A Documentary History of the Negro People in the United States* (Secaucus, N.J.: Citadel Press, 1973), vol. 1., pp. 8–9.
3. For a list of churches bearing the designation "African" and a discussion of the reasons for the shift away from the practice of naming organizations in this manner after 1817, with the word "colored" being preferred, see St. Clair Drake, "Negro Americans and the 'Africa Interest'," in *American Negro Reference Book*, ed. John P. Davis (Englewood Cliffs, N.J.: Prentice-Hall, 1966), pp. 669–673. This chapter also includes a discussion of Afro-American reinterpretations of the doctrine of Providential Design, which some white Christians used to explain why a benevolent deity permitted Africans to be enslaved. They believed that slavery was a means of exposing them to Christianity and "civilization," so that some of them could be prepared to return to Africa to "redeem" and "uplift" their kinsmen.
4. Countee Cullen, *On These I Stand* (New York: Harper and Brothers, 1947), pp. 24–28.
5. See St. Clair Drake, " 'Hide My Face?' On Pan-Africanism and Negritude," in *Soon One Morning*, ed. Herbert Hill (New York: Knopf, 1963), pp. 78–105; and LeRoi Jones, "The Myth of a 'Negro Literature'," in *Home* (New York: Morrow, 1966), 105–115.
6. Winthrop Jordan, *White Over Black* (Baltimore: Penguin, 1969), p. 258.
7. An American anthropologist, writing in the 1950s, stated that Africa was probably the "cradle of mankind," and that "for several decades hardly a year has passed without some exciting new evidence of early man or of manlike apes in East or South Africa to strengthen this conclusion" (George Peter Murdock, *Africa: Its People and Their Culture History* [New York: McGraw-Hill, 1959], p. 7). For an article by the British archaeologist whose research in East Africa revealed some of the earliest hominids, see L.S.B. Leakey, "Adventures in the Search for Man," *National Geographic Magazine* (January 1963), pp. 132–152. Note also J. Desmond Clark, "The Prehistoric Origins of African Culture," in *Papers in African Prehistory*, ed. J. D. Fage and R. A. Oliver (Cambridge: Cambridge University Press, 1970), pp. 3–4. See also "Why Is East Africa Important?" Preface to G. L. Isaac and E. R. McCown (Menlo Park, Calif.: W.A. Benjamin, 1976).
8. For an article emphasizing the non-Negroid character of fossils of early man in the area where it is thought mankind originated, see Sonia Cole, "The Stone Age of East Africa," in *History of East Africa*, vol. 1, ed. R. Oliver and G. Mathew (Oxford: Oxford University Press, 1963), pp. 23–57 (especially pp. 42, 48, and 53–54).
9. The belief that the first men and women were dark skinned is based upon the assumption that melanin provided protection against the ultraviolet rays of the tropical sun. But knowledge that African higher apes have a wide range of skin-color,

and speculation that hominids might have originated in less torrid subtropical Africa, or that cultural and economic factors could be more important than climate in the selection for skin-color within a gene pool where variation was great, have led to some questioning of the older general assumption about the dark skin-color of the earliest humans. For a discussion of these points, see John Buettner-Janusch, *Origins of Man* (New York: Wiley, 1966), pp. 366–377; David Pibeam, *The Ascent of Man: An Introduction to Human Evolution* (New York: Macmillan, 1972), p. 83; Harold F. Blum, "Does the Melanin Pigment of Human Skin Have Adaptive Value?" in *Man in Adaptation: The Biosocial Background*, ed. Yehudi A. Cohen (Chicago: Aldine, 1968), p. 143; and J. F. Downs and H. K. Bleibtreu, *Human Variation* (Beverly Hills, Calif.: Glencoe Press, 1969), pp. 181–188. For an excellent popular exposition see Montagu, *What We Know about "Race."*

Since soft human remnants are unavailable for study when making generalizations about the earliest human beings, and only portions of fossilized skeletal material are available in many cases, comparison with people now classified as belonging to a specific "race" is difficult. Assessment of skeletal remains takes into account nasal index, degree of alveolar prognathism, and certain characteristics of the pelvis and limbs. An ideal-type "Negro" has been abstracted from a statistical model based upon measurements made of individuals living in contemporary African populations, using traits unavailable to archaeologists: skin-color, hair form, shape of lips and nose, in addition to skeletal measurement. The presence of alveolar prognathism, the forward projection of the face below the nasal aperture, is most often cited as the major diagnostic trait. The following discussion of so-called Grimaldi Man in southern Europe illustrates use of this diagnostic concept: "The two skeletons from the lowest level of the Grotte des Enfants belong to a type of shorter stature and with facial prognathism—the race of Grimaldi which R. Verneau considered Negroid and which he thought preceded the Cro-Magnon race in this region. Verneau's ideas are often questioned because no other Negroid fossils have been found in Europe, and it seems that the prognathism of the so-called Negroids was essentially the result of a posthumous deformation." (This is a statement in the 1963 *Encyclopaedia Britannica* article "Grimaldi Fossils" by Professor Henri Victor Vallois.) For another statement about the difference of opinion concerning the Grimaldi finds, see Buettner-Janusch, *Origins of Man*, p. 153, where the author concludes that "the anatomical evidence available is not sufficient, nor is it diagnostic, for relating differences among living human populations to differences found among Pleistocene fossil skulls."

10. A strong statement in favor of the theory of a late appearance of the Negro in human evolution is included as part of a discussion entitled "Early Man in Africa," in Harry A. Gailey, Jr., *History of Africa from Earliest Times to 1800* (New York: Holt, Rinehart and Winston, 1970), p. 19. Carleton Coon, in *The Origin of Races*, states the minority view, viz., that the Negro type is very old and is "evolutionarily retarded" by about 250,000 years. A distinguished Berkeley prehistorian is convinced that "by the end of the Pleistocene, the Bush physical stock was already present in South Africa and it may be postulated that, similarly, by selective processes, the Negroid and Erythriote [i.e., the so-called Hamitic] types had also made their appearance. . . . Because of their blood group relationships, the Bushman and the Negro must be derived from the same African ancestral stock." An "unspecialized Negroid ancestral type" is spoken of as living in the Congo river basin during "the Later Stone Age," but "there is reason to suppose that the origin of the Negro physical stock and its distribution in Africa is linked with the

forest and woodland savannah region" (J. Desmond Clark, "Origins of African Culture," pp. 19-20, 25).

11. For a discussion of climatic changes over long time spans in the Sahara, and of fossils found there that seem to be Negroid, see Clark, "Origins of African Culture," pp. 18-20. See also some observations to the point that "mystery surrounds the origin of the true Negro," in Roland Oliver and J. D. Fage, *A Short History of Africa* (Baltimore: Penguin, 1962), pp. 20-22. For an excellent description of the oldest fossils classified as "Negro" and "Negroid," see Frederick S. Hulse, *The Human Species* (New York: Random House, 1963), pp. 237-239.

12. Oliver and Fage, *Short History of Africa*, pp. 14-16.

13. Coon, *Origin of Races*, p. 658.

14. "On Coon's *The Origin of Races*," in *The Concept of Race*, ed. Ashley Montagu (New York: Collier Books, 1964), pp. 228-241 (especially p. 234).

15. Oliver and Fage, *Short History of Africa*, pp. 21-22.

16. Murdock, *Africa*, chapter 4, "Economy," especially pp. 22-24. This discussion of a Middle Eastern Neolithic period adopts a useful but oversimplified frame of reference from V. Gordon Childe, *Man Makes Himself* (New York: Mentor, 1951), chapter 5, "The Neolithic Revolution." See also V. Gordon Childe, *What Happened in History* (Harmondsworth, England: Penguin, 1967), chapter 3, "Neolithic Barbarism," and chapter 4, "The Higher Barbarism of the Copper Age." A standard account, which argued the case for the introduction of the food-producing revolution into the Nile Valley by Caucasoid people from the Middle East, may be found in Oliver and Fage's *Short History of Africa*. Another scholar examines the arguments of those who oppose this view and gives reasons for his adherence to it (Glyn Daniel, *The First Civilizations* [New York: Crowell, 1968], chapter 1, "Savagery, Barbarism and Civilization"). For a revisionist argument suggesting the possibility that "the agriculture of tropical Africa is original and that of the Middle East derivative," see Christopher Wrigley, "Speculation on the Economic Prehistory of Africa," in *African Prehistory*, ed. Fage and Oliver, pp. 59-74. The late R. Portères did not discuss priority in innovation but concluded that "recent research has confirmed the importance of the Fertile Crescent in the history of world agriculture." He warned, however, against neglecting the roles of other areas, including several in Africa (R. Portères and J. Barrau, "Origins, Development and Expansion of Agriculture," in *A General History of Africa*, vol. 1, ed. J. Ki-Zerbo [Berkeley: University of California Press, 1981], pp. 687-705.)

17. Oliver and Fage, *Short History of Africa*, p. 28.

18. Murdock, *Africa*. A chart comparing the cultivated plants of West Africa with those of Ethiopia, Southwest Asia, Southeast Asia, and America is presented on page 23. A full discussion of Murdock's theory of a separate West African center of plant domestication is presented on pages 64-72, along with an indictment of those who fail to recognize or admit that "the assemblage of cultivated plants ennobled from wild forms in Negro Africa ranks as one of the four major agricultural complexes evolved in the entire course of human history" (pp. 64-65).

19. Joseph Harris, professor of history at Howard University, made these remarks in his excellent *Africans and Their History: A Major Work of Historical Re-evaluation* (New York: Mentor, 1972), p. 30. (This Afrocentric volume serves as a fine complement to Oliver and Fage's Eurocentric *Short History of Africa*.) Professor Portères, in the scholarly article referred to in note 16, does not call Murdock by name but concedes that "in addition to the Abyssinian centre and the African portion of the Mediterranean centre, there existed also a West African centre, and an East

African one" (pp. 693–694). For another scholar who gives some credibility to Murdock's argument, see Wrigley, "Economic Prehistory of Africa," in *African Prehistory*, ed. Fage and Oliver, pp. 61–63. J. Desmond Clark, in his article "The Spread of Food Production in Sub-Saharan Africa" in the same volume, comments that "the archaeological record as yet provides no confirmation for the belief that an independent centre of cereal crop domestication existed in West Africa as suggested by Portères and Murdock" (p. 33). Clark does not discuss the other crops that Murdock contends were domesticated by the Mande Negroes, including cotton and watermelon.

20. Murdock, *Africa*, p. 64. This kind of entrenched attitude can be found in Sir Harry H. Johnston's long and learned article "A Survey of the Ethnography of Africa," *Journal of the Royal Anthropological Institute of Great Britain and Ireland* 43 (1913), pp. 375–421. Sir Harry insisted that iron smelting must have been imported into sub-Saharan Africa, for "I myself require very convincing proof that the pure-blooded Negro ever originated anything" (p. 418). The tautological character of the Hamitic argument is illustrated by the comment of an anthropologist about one African ethnic group that "the rude character" of some of their pottery suggests that they were "well tinctured with Negro blood." Such inference of race from inferior craftsmanship where the physical traits are not Negro occurs less frequently than the explaining of "inferior" culture by the presence of Negroid traits (C. G. Seligman, "Some Aspects of the Hamitic Problem in the Anglo-Egyptian Sudan," *Journal of the Royal Anthropological Institute*, 43 [1913], p. 592).

21. For some excellent photography showing a wide variety of African physical types, accompanied by a group of authoritative articles written by experts for laymen, consult the second volume in the Danbury Press Peoples of the Earth series, *Africa from the Sahara to the Zambesi*, published in 1972. Issues of *National Geographic* containing articles on Africa are excellent for getting acquainted with the wide range of physical types within the African population. These types are the products of millennia of miscegenation operating concurrently with the processes of geographical and social isolation to produce and stabilize a variety of subtypes. Two excellent articles appear as chapters in volume 1 of the UNESCO *General History of Africa*, one by the African editor, J. Ki-Zerbo, "Editorial Note on the 'Races' and History of Africa," and the other by Russian Africanist D. Olderogge, entitled "Migrations and Ethnic and Linguistic Differentiation." Ki-Zerbo concludes that "Today, except for a few dissenting voices, the large majority of scholars agree on the basic genetic unity of peoples south of the Sahara" (p. 268). Cheikh Anta Diop also insists that Africans themselves view this mass of people as *one* population despite the wide range in color and physical features, as do Afro-Americans, West Indians, and Latin Americans when dealing with the descendants of the African slaves in the New World (see Diop, *The African Origin of Civilization: Myth or Reality* [New York: Lawrence Hill, 1974], pp. 48–49). A wide range in color and features, and two types of hair ("smooth" and "frizzy") are considered normal to "Negro" African populations according to Diop. Professional anthropologists insist upon a narrower definition that makes facial architecture crucial (especially degree of prognathism) and does not accept "smooth" or "straight" hair as a Negro trait. Incidentally, Herodotus spoke of "smooth"- and "woolly"-haired Ethiopians.

22. Alan Lomax, "The Homogeneity of African–Afro-American Musical Style," in *Afro-American Anthropology: Contemporary Perspectives*, ed. Norman E. Whitten and John F. Szwed (New York: Free Press, 1970), pp. 191, 193.

23. That skin-color, along with other physical differences, was recognized in early

times is apparent in rock paintings, incised portrayals, and drawings. The nature of the social sentiments associated with the recognition of physical differences, however, is not clear. See Henri Breuil, *The Rock Paintings of South Africa* (London: Trianon Press, 1955); Henri Lhote, *The Search for the Tassili Frescoes: The Story of the Prehistoric Rock Paintings of the Sahara* (London: Hutchinson, 1959); and Jean D. Lajoux, *Rock Paintings of Tassili* (New York: World, 1963).

24. Jacques Maquet, *The Premises of Inequality in Ruanda* (London: Oxford University Press, 1960). This anthropologist analyzes the dynamics of a castelike system that evolved with Pygmies at the bottom. See also Marcel D'Hertefelt, "The Rwanda of Rwanda," in *Peoples of Africa*, ed. James L. Gibbs, Jr. (New York: Holt, Rinehart and Winston, 1965), pp. 403–440. It is difficult to make a plausible guess about the nature of the system of social ranking among Pygmies, Bushmen, and similar hunting and gathering people before they came in contact with agricultural Negroes. These groups today do not have slaves and do not make internal color distinctions. Whether this was true in the remote past we do not know. The study of marginal peoples who have fled into refuge areas is instructive, however, and such groups studied in East Africa do not have slaves or classes.

25. There are legends among the Bunyoro-Kitara people of Uganda that a tall, "red" people called the Bachwezi, who had supernatural powers, came to Uganda. After the reign of a few Bachwezi kings, they disappeared from the area. When the Europeans arrived, some people thought the Bachwezi were returning. See J. W. Nyakatura, *Anatomy of an African Kingdom* (Garden City, N.J.: Doubleday, 1973), chapter 1, "Abachwezi Rule," pp. 21–49, for a careful piecing together of the oral tradition. Among the Kikuyu, light-brown people are sometimes referred to as "red" and as coming from a specific area. They are "Fort Hall Kikuyu." Variations in physical type are wide within this Kenyan ethnic group, however.

26. The first effort at scholarly demolition of the Hamitic theory, accompanied by the charge that it was being used in a racist manner, was carried out by an American anthropologist, Joseph Greenberg. See his *Studies in African Linguistic Classification* (Evanston, Ill.: Northwestern University Press, 1955). For a sophisticated recent critique by another American scholar, see Wyatt MacGaffey, "Concepts of Race in the Historiography of Northeast Africa," *Journal of African History* 7, 1 (1966): 99–115. Greenberg dropped the term entirely in his work. Murdock, however, clung to it for use in classifying languages only, not for designating entire cultures. He then used the term "Cushitic" to apply to some of the Caucasoid peoples who had previously been called Hamites, thus compounding confusion since most scholars and interested laymen use the term "Cushite" to apply to Negroid peoples. Dr. J. Ki-Zerbo, in his Introduction to volume 1 of the UNESCO *General History of Africa*, states that "the excesses of racially prejudiced physical anthropology are now rejected by all serious authors. But the Hamites and other brown races invented to fit the purpose [are] still to be found in the mirages and fantasies produced by otherwise scientific minds" (pp. 21–22). P. Diagne, in the same volume (p. 245), states that the term "Hamite," despite the work of modern linguists and ethnologists, "has still continued to be used as a criterion for discriminating between certain black peoples who are regarded as superior beings, and the rest." The authors in volume 2 of the *General History*, who occasionally use the term, assume that readers take for granted their absence of racist intent.

The history of the use of the term "Hamite" merits thorough study. The article that first gave the Hamitic theory respectability in English-speaking circles was Charles Seligman's "Some Aspects of the Hamitic Problem in the Anglo-Egyptian

Sudan," *Journal of the Royal Anthropological Institute of Great Britain and Ireland* 43 (1913): 593–704 (especially pp. 679–680). Seligman later gave wide currency to the British theory of Hamitic superiority in his book *Races of Africa* (London: Butterworth, 1930). Even the revision of this work in 1957 perpetuated the Hamitic myth and retained a number of offensive passages. The most derogatory statements about "Negroes" as compared with "Hamites" in the British anthropological literature appear in the works of a missionary who became an "expert" on East Africa: John Roscoe (see "Immigrants and Their Influence in the Lake Region of Central Africa" in *The Frazer Lectures, 1922–1932,* ed. Warren R. Dawson [London: Macmillan, 1932], pp. 25–46, and "Bahima: A Cow Tribe of Enkole," *Journal of the Royal Anthropological Institute of Great Britain and Ireland* 37 [1907]: 93–118.

A Belgian anthropologist, Emil Torday, made the first challenge to this group of British scholars in a sarcastic attack on Seligman and his followers that is reprinted in the Introduction to the 1930 edition of Herbert Spencer's *Descriptive Sociology,* published by the Herbert Spencer Trust, London. A very restrained criticism of the Hamitic formulation as being tautological was made by one of Seligman's students after he had become one of Britain's most distinguished anthropologists, E. E. Evans-Pritchard, in his chapter "Ethnological Survey of the Sudan" in *The Anglo-Egyptian Sudan from Within,* ed. J. A. de C. Hamilton (London: Faber and Faber, 1935), pp. 79–93. For more recent discussions see St. Clair Drake, "Destroy the Hamitic Myth," *Présence Africaine* 24–25 (February–May 1959), pp. 228–243, special issue, English edition; and Edith S. Sanders, "The Hamitic Hypothesis: Its Origins and Functions in Time Perspective," *Journal of African History* 10, 4 (1969): 521–532.

27. "At present the arable lands of Egypt and Western Asia are embedded in large tracts of desert. But it seems that in the Ice Age the pressure of cold air over Europe compelled the Atlantic rain storms to travel east by a more southerly track, so that the whole area from the west coast of Africa to the Persian mountains was a continuous belt of park and grassland. . . . [A] change of climate, which started in the Old Stone Age, continued in the New, and very gradually changed living conditions throughout the Near East. . . . Progressive dessication marked the period from perhaps 7000 B.C. onwards, turning the plateaux from grassland into steppe, and, ultimately, into desert, and making the valleys of the great rivers inhabitable" (Henri Frankfort, *The Birth of Civilization in the Near East* [Bloomington: Indiana University Press, 1954], pp. 33–34).

Oliver and Fage, in their *Short History of Africa,* state that "early Egyptian cultivators of the valley margin soon began to suffer from the steady dessication of the climate during the late fifth and early fourth millennia. It was the encroaching drift sand of the desert which stimulated the Tasians and Badarians of Middle Egypt to move down and clear the flood-plain, with results so startling for the history of the world. From that moment onwards the remains of the predynastic period indicate a phenomenal growth of population" (p. 26).

28. Young's *Ethiopian Manifesto* can be found in Sterling Stuckey, *The Ideological Origins of Black Nationalism* (Boston: Beacon Press, 1972), pp. 30–38. See also Stuckey, *Ideological Origins,* pp. 40 and 58, for references to Ethiopia in Walker's *Appeal.* Black plantation religious symbols emphasized the Jewish slave experience in Egypt, with the Exodus, Jordan, and Jericho appearing in songs, sermons, prayers, and testimonials. In contrast, Free Negro ministers, as members of a literate clergy, elaborated the retrospective and prospective myth of "Ethiopianism" based on the prophecy of ultimate vindication for Egypt and Ethiopia in the Psalms. Note St.

Clair Drake's *Black Religion and the Redemption of Africa* (Chicago: Third World Press, 1971); and Albert J. Raboteau's *Slave Religion: The "Invisible Institution" in the Antebellum South* (New York: Oxford University Press, 1978).

29. References to ancient Egypt and Ethiopia appeared in a book published in England but read by Free Negroes in the United States, *A Tribute for the Negro, Being a Vindication of the Moral, Intellectual, and Religious Capabilities of the Coloured Portion of Mankind, with Particular Reference to the African Race* (Manchester, 1848), by William Armstead. "Part First" was entitled "An Inquiry into Claims of the Negro Race to Humanity, and a Vindication of Their Original Equality with the Other Portions of Mankind" and included among the subtopics the following: "Their Origin and Noble Ancestry—Ethiopians and Egyptians Considered." The author, after discussing "this noble ancestry," said that "all Africans" were "fully entitled to claim [it] as their own" (pp. 120–123).

30. Herodotus wrote that he considered the people of the colony of Colchians near the Black Sea to be Egyptians, "because they are black-skinned and have wooly hair," as were the inhabitants of "several other nations." The fact that they also practiced circumcision clinched the matter of their Egyptian origin for him. Frank Snowden, in *Blacks in Antiquity* (Cambridge, Mass.: Harvard University Press, 1971), p. 290, cites a fellow classicist to support the idea that Herodotus meant precisely "black skin and kinky hair": P. T. English, "Cushites, Colchians, and Khazars," *Journal of Near Eastern Studies* 18 (1959): 49–53. Others claim the passage means only "dark skinned and curly haired," not "black and kinky haired."

31. When Egyptian antiquities were first discovered by the scholars who accompanied Napoleon, there was a tendency to credit Negroes with the founding of the Egyptian nation and with its early advances toward civilization. A quick reversal of this view took place, partly because of pressure from proslavery interests (see Diop, *African Origin*, pp. 45–57).

32. J. C. Nott and George R. Gliddon, *Types of Mankind or Ethnological Researches* (Philadelphia: Lippincott, 1855), chapter 5, "African Types"; chapter 8, "Egypt and Egyptians."

33. Quoted in Diop, *African Origin*, pp. 27–28.

34. Vivant Denon, *Travels in Upper and Lower Egypt*, vol. 1 (New York: Arno Press, 1973), pp. 271–272; reprinted from the 1803 edition published by Longman and Reese of London.

35. Quoted from Blyden's *From West Africa to Palestine*, in W.E.B. Du Bois's *The Negro* (London: Oxford University Press, 1970; republication of the original edition published by Henry Holt, 1915), p. 19. Blyden wrote these words after a visit to Egypt.

36. Chancellor Williams, *The Destruction of Black Civilization* (Chicago: Third World Press, 1974), p. 73.

37. Arthur Weigall, *A History of the Pharaohs*, vol. 1 (London: Thornton Butterworth, 1925), p. 177.

38. Note "King Khephren—side view" and "King Khephren—front view," in Cyril Aldred, *The Development of Ancient Egyptian Art from 3,200 to 1,315 B.C.* (London: Alec Tiranti, 1952), plates 17, 18.

39. Arthur Weigall, *Personalities of Antiquity* (Garden City, N.J.: Doran and Co., 1928), chapter 24, "The Exploits of a Nigger King," p. 186.

40. Weigall, *History of the Pharaohs*, vol. 1, p. 177.

41. Du Bois, *Black Folk Then and Now: An Essay in the History and Sociology of the Negro Race* (New York: H. Holt and Co., 1939, 1940).

42. Ibid., p. 148.
43. Ibid., pp. 9, 17.
44. The quotations from the 1974 UNESCO conference are taken from G. Mokhtar, ed., *A General History of Africa*, vol. 2 (Berkeley: University of California Press, 1981), "Introduction," pp. 14, 59–78.
45. Cheikh Anta Diop, "Origin of the Ancient Egyptians," in *General History of Africa*, vol. 2, ed. G. Mokhtar, pp. 50, 51.
46. Roland Oliver, "The African Rediscovery of Africa," *Times Literary Supplement* (March 20, 1981), p. 29.
47. Modern Egyptologists occasionally point out that to translate *"Nehesi"* as "Negro" is misleading. Older Egyptologists invariably did so, thus giving the impression that the Egyptians drew a racial distinction between themselves and the people of Kush. In fact, *Nehesi* was applied to a number of physical types living south of Egypt, including some Blacks, most of whom were Negroid, but not all. It was never applied to Egyptians with Negro facial characteristics. There is some evidence that from the Eighteenth Dynasty on, the "typical" *Nehesi* was thought of as being a Negro although the word was applied to any southerners regardless of physical type. See Diop, *African Origins*, pp. 46–49.
48. Snowden points out, in *Blacks in Antiquity* (p. 112), that Latin writers spoke of both Leucaethiopes and Melanogaetuli in the Sahara, that is, light-skinned Ethiopians and "dark-skinned members of the Gaetuli tribe." They also referred to "Libyans resembling Ethiopians." This suggests that a wide range of physical types were living in "Libya," the vaguely defined area stretching west of Egypt. Some Egyptian paintings portrayed "Libyans" (called Libou, Temehou, Tehenou, and Meshwesto) as "yellow skinned" with distinctive dress and hair styles. Some scholars use the wide range of Negro types portrayed during the Eighteenth Dynasty and after as evidence that Egyptians had not had contact with Blacks above the sixth Nile cataract before that time.
49. One Egyptologist states that, in painting, "Flesh tones were determined more by convention [than by the natural color of the person], the skin of Egyptian men being painted red-brown and that of their womenfolk pale ochre . . . nevertheless there are some departures from these norms, some women being depicted with yellow-brown skins." His statement that "Nubians and Negroes were usually represented as black" ignores the fact that some Egyptians, male and female, were sometimes portrayed as black, too. The conditions under which the conventional representation of Egyptians was ignored is relevant to our inquiry but not discussed (Cyril Aldred, *Egyptian Art in the Days of the Pharaohs, 3100–320 b.c.* [London: Oxford University Press, 1980], p. 30).
50. Du Bois, *The Negro*, p. 17. For a critical analysis of contemporary views about the origins of Egyptian culture, see G. Mokhtar's introduction to *General History of Africa*, vol. 2, p. 21, in which he concludes that "an invasion of civilizing elements from the outside, notably from Mesopotamia, rests only on the flimsiest evidence."
51. Quoted in E. A. Wallis Budge, *Osiris and the Egyptian Resurrection* (New York: Dover, 1973), pp. 338–339.
52. An important research breakthrough occurred in the first quarter of the twentieth century when the British inspector-general of antiquities of the Egyptian government, Arthur Weigall, reconstructed a text of the annals written on a large stone tablet possessed by an Italian museum. He was able to fill in gaps by translations from a fragment of this Palermo Stone that remained in Cairo, and from several

fragments located elsewhere. He then correlated the Palermo Stone dynasties with those of Manetho as well as king lists deciphered from the Turin Papyrus and the Abydos List. Even a layman can share the excitement of this scholarly detective work as reported by the man who carried it out (Weigall, *History of the Pharaohs,* vol. 1, *The First Eleven Dynasties,* pp. xi-42).

53. Ethnocentric partisanship has led to disputes over the question of whether writing was invented first in Egypt or in Mesopotamia. Childe, in *Man Makes Himself,* does not address himself directly to this question but implies independent invention. (See chapter 8, "The Revolution in Human Knowledge"; see especially p. 147, where he states, inter alia, that by 2950 B.C. the Egyptian system of writing was "already more mature than that of the oldest Sumerian documents.") Frankfort, however, is convinced that writing was a Mesopotamian invention borrowed by Egyptians (*Birth of Civilization,* pp. 105-108).

54. Weigall, *History of the Pharaohs,* pp. 80-82.

55. Barbara Mertz, *Red Land, Black Land: Daily Life in Ancient Egypt* (New York: Dodd, Mead, 1978), chapter 2, "The Red and Black Lands," pp. 20-37).

56. Mokhtar, *General History of Africa,* vol. 2, "Introduction," pp. 11-13.

57. John A. Wilson, "The Function of the State," in *Before Philosophy,* ed. Henri Frankfort et al. (Baltimore: Penguin, 1964), pp. 82-83.

58. Cyril Aldred, *Egypt to the End of the Old Kingdom* (New York: McGraw-Hill, 1965), pp. 28-29.

59. Modern observers find it difficult to conceive of a regional difference so pronounced as this not taking on racial overtones if there was a marked difference in skin-color between the southern Egyptians and the northerners. Wilson, who stresses the depth of consciousness of difference, quotes evidence pointing to speech differences, not skin-color differences, as symbolizing differentness. An Egyptian, when in Syria, said, "Your speeches . . . are confused when heard, and there is no interpreter who can unravel them. They are like the words of a man of the Delta marshes with a man of Elephantine [near the first Nile cataract]" (John A. Wilson, *The Burden of Egypt* [Chicago: University of Chicago Press, 1951], p. 266).

60. Professor Frank Snowden, for instance, hews close to the anthropometrists' line in classifying sculptured and painted images according to race (see pp. 7-11 of his *Blacks in Antiquity*). Diop, in *African Origin* and "Origin of the Ancient Egyptians" (pp. 27-57), takes anthropometry seriously, although in the latter work he expresses some doubt about its value in deciding whether the original Egyptians were "Negroes."

61. Diop, "Origin of the Ancient Egyptians," p. 28.

62. Ibid., p. 29.

63. See Giuseppe Sergi, *The Mediterranean Race: A Study of the Origin of European Peoples* (New York: Scribner's, 1901). The entire work is an argument for the fundamental homogeneity of a "Brown Race" living on both sides of the Mediterranean and in parts of the Middle East. General shape of the skull viewed from various positions, rather than minute measurements taken on the skull, as well as skin-color in the living, were used in defining the Brown Race.

64. Aldred, *Old Kingdom,* pp. 16, 22.

65. Murdock, *Africa,* pp. 101, 106.

66. Diop, "Origin of the Ancient Egyptians," "Melanin Dosage Test," p. 35.

67. See the National Geographic Society publication *Ancient Egypt* (1978), color plates on pp. 128-129, 132-133.

68. Diop, *African Origin*, p. 93, and chapter 5.
69. Childe, *Man Makes Himself*, chapter 5, "The Neolithic Revolution," pp. 59–86. (See note 16.)
70. Carleton S. Coon, *The Races of Europe* (New York: Macmillan, 1939), p. 62.
71. Ibid., pp. 92, 95.
72. William C. Hayes, *Most Ancient Egypt* (Chicago: University of Chicago Press, 1965), p. 135.
73. Ibid.
74. Ibid.
75. Arnold J. Toynbee, *A Study of History*, vol. 1 (London: Oxford University Press, 1939), pp. 233, 238. An abridgement of the six-volume *A Study of History*, was published by D. C. Somervell, under auspices of the Royal Institute of International Affairs, in 1947. This was a Book-of-the-Month Club selection. (See p. 54 of the abridged version.)
76. Toynbee, *Study of History*, vol. 1 (1939), pp. 233–235. This is a translation from the French quotation in Toynbee's book taken from M. Delafosse, *Les noirs de l'Afrique* (Paris: Payot, 1922), pp. 156–160. This same idea is expressed in Maurice Delafosse, *The Negroes of Africa: History and Culture*, translated from the French by F. Fligelman and published by an affiliate of the Association for the Study of Negro Life and History, The Associated Publishers, Washington, D.C., 1931.
77. This reference to the Shilluk appears in both editions of *Study of History*, a surprising concession in view of the stress Toynbee places on the Egyptians' not being Black during their early creative period. (See pp. 312–315 in the 1939 edition, from which the quote used by Childe was taken, and pp. 71–72 in the 1947 abridged edition.) For a discussion of the Shilluk, using extensive photographic documentation, see E. E. Evans-Pritchard, "Shilluk-Sudan" in *Africa from the Sahara to the Zambesi*, ed. dir. Tom Stacey (New York: Danbury Press, 1972), pp. 46–53.
78. Aldred, *Old Kingdom*, pp. 31, 34. See also Frankfort, *Birth of Civilization*, pp. 100–111, "The Influence of Mesopotamia on Egypt Towards the End of the Fourth Millennium B.C."
79. Diop, *African Origin*, pp. 87–89. For a discussion of the metallurgy question, based on the available archaeological data and without reference to folklore, see J. Vercoutter, "Discovery and Diffusion of Metals and Development of Social Systems up to the Fifth Century before Our Era," in *General History of Africa* vol. 1, ed. J. Ki-Zerbo, pp. 634–655, 706–729.
80. Flinders Petrie, *The Making of Egypt* (London: Sheldon Press, 1939), chapter 8, "The Dynastic Conquest," pp. 65–68; chapter 12, "The Pyramid Age," pp. 105–112.
81. David O'Connor, "Nubia before the New Kingdom," in *Africa in Antiquity: The Arts of Ancient Nubia and the Sudan*, vol. 1 (Brooklyn: Brooklyn Museum, 1978), pp. 52–53, touches briefly upon the factors that inhibited diffusion northward from Kush, or what is referred to as Upper Nubia. See also the discussion of pottery in volume 2, pp. 38–39.
82. See, e.g., Wilson, *Burden of Egypt*, p. 176. By an ingenious deduction from Eighteenth Dynasty records, one unconventional scholar has attempted to prove that Judea was "Punt" and "God's Land" and that Hatshepsut was the Queen of Sheba who visited both (Immanuel Velikovsky, *Ages in Chaos* [Garden City, N.J.: Doubleday, 1952], pp. 114–129).
83. It has been suggested that in the period prior to the post-Makalian dry phase, which

began in the fourth millennium B.C., the swamps of the Bahr-al-Ghazal and the arid land between the upper Nile and Ethiopia had not cut off the people of the southern Sudan from the civilization of the Nile Valley (Wrigley, "Economic Prehistory of Africa," p. 71).

84. Boyce Rensberger, "Nubian Monarch Called Oldest," *New York Times* (March 1, 1979), pp. A1, A16. See also Bruce Williams, "The Lost Pharaohs of Nubia," *Archaeology* 33, 5 (1980): 12–21.

85. John G. Jackson, *Introduction to African Civilization* (Secaucus, N.J.: Citadel Press, 1974), chapter 2, "Ethiopia and the Origin of Civilization." See chapter 19, "The King of Ethiopia," in Angelo S. Rappoport and Raphael Patai, *Myth and Legend of Ancient Israel*, vol. 2 (New York: KTAV, 1966), pp. 244–249.

86. Petrie, *Making of Egypt*, chapter 8, "The Dynastic Conquest." Petrie begins with a subtitle, "Conflict of Races." He visualizes the Negroid Anu (or Aunu) invading from Asia, subduing Caucasoid and Negroid peoples already there making conquests in Libya and Nubia. Illustrations of sculptured images of Narmer and Teter-Neter are presented. Both have Negroid traits. See reprints of these photographs in Diop, *African Origin*.

87. Ibid., pp. 21, 65, 67. Petrie describes in some detail the conflicts that he interprets as racial. See also Diop, *African Origin*, pp. 131–132, 164–167.

88. Budge, *Osiris*, vol. 1, p. 16.

89. Ibid., p. 16.

90. Ibid., p. 11.

91. The quotation is from H. H. Johnston, *The Negro in the New World* (London: Methuen, 1910), p. 27. For a statement of the case for a wide distribution of black people throughout the Middle East in prehistoric times, see Jackson, *African Civilization*, pp. 66–70. There is very little archaeological evidence to support this view, however. Within historic times some material from Elam is convincing, but attempts by some vindicationists to make the "black-headed" people of Sumer equivalent to a black or Negroid group is not convincing. Gaston Maspero, a French archaeologist, has written of the Elamites that they were brown-skinned and "belonged to that Negritic race which inhabited a considerable part of Asia in prehistoric times" (Gaston Maspero, *History of Egypt*, vol. 4, trans. M. L. McClure [London: Grollier Society, 1903], pp. 45–46). Jackson, as well as other vindicationists, accepts folklore and linguistic studies as proof that the Kushites, the Anu, or some similar groups once inhabited the Middle East as well as Africa. For a recent careful statement of the case by an Afro-American scholar, see Runoko Rashidi, "The African Presence in Sumer and Elam," *Journal of African Civilizations* 4, 2 (November 1982): 137–147.

92. See Gerald Massey, *A Book of the Beginnings*, 2 vols. (London: Williams and Norgate, 1881), and *Ancient Egypt: The Light of the World*, 2 vols. (London: T. Fisher Unwin, 1907); Godfrey Higgins, *Anacalypsis*, 2 vols. (New Hyde Park: University Books, 1965).

93. Budge, *Osiris*, p. 2.

94. Ibid.

95. Ibid., p. 19.

96. James George Frazer, *The Golden Bough* (New York: Book League of America, 1929), p. 363.

97. Ibid.

98. Osiris worship was a complex phenomenon extending over several millennia. The

god meant different things to different people at various times and in various places. From a local god in Upper Egypt near Thebes, Osiris ultimately became a god worshiped throughout the Hellenistic and Roman World, as did his wife, Isis. A succinct statement on the evolution of Osiris worship is presented in chapter 1 of E.A.W. Budge's *Osiris*, a detailed, copiously illustrated two-volume work by the one-time Keeper of Egyptian and Assyrian Antiquities in the British Museum. Originally published in 1911, the book was reprinted as a Dover paperback in 1973 and is readily available, as is Budge's translation of the Book of the Dead.

Budge insists that the Osiris cult was of purely African origin, was in existence long before the dynastic period began in Egypt, and was a beneficent, civilizing influence upon people in northern Egypt. He attempts to reconstruct its earliest form by studying the customs of Africans in the Sudan during the nineteenth century, a method that modern anthropologists look upon with disfavor. Black readers will resent certain fixed ideas about innate traits of Negroes that must be rejected by modern standards of scholarship. Some of Budge's remarks are insulting to the African people about whom he was writing. Nevertheless, despite his patronizing air, he was probably more accurate about the diffusion of religious ideas northward in the Predynastic period than those racists who insisted that a lily-white Egypt spread civilization southward. (For example, see C. G. Seligman, *Egypt and Negro Africa: A Study of Divine Kingship* [London: George Routledge and Sons, Ltd., 1934].) As a source of fact about Osiris worship, Budge's book is invaluable. His observations on the Sudan, however, may be ignored. For an excellent discussion of Osiris that avoids the piling up of tedious detail, has no theoretical axes to grind, and makes no attempt to find modern survivals, see R. T. Rundle Clark, *Myth and Symbol in Ancient Egypt* (London: Thames and Hudson, 1959). See especially chapter 3, "Osiris—Original Scheme"; chapter 4, "Osiris Universalized"; and chapter 5, "Esoteric Osiris." For a discussion of the role of Osiris in Memphite theology, see also Henri Frankfort, *Kingship and the Gods* (Chicago: The University of Chicago Press, 1948), pp. 36–40; 181–197; 286–294.

99. Rundle Clark, *Myth and Symbol*, p. 101.

100. Norma Loore Goodrich, *The Ancient Myths* (New York: Mentor, 1960), p. 28. Budge did not emphasize the dark skin-color of Osiris, but he did note that one of the oldest representations is in the Eighteenth Dynasty Papyrus of Nebseni, which forms part of the Book of the Dead. In the printed representation of this Osiris, he is either white or colorless (Budge, *Osiris*, p. 38). In the Papyrus of Iuau, who lived in the time of Akhenaten's father, Osiris is depicted with skin of "an earthy red color," the conventional color for Egyptian males. A Twenty-second Dynasty papyrus portrays Osiris as black. In the Papyrus of Ani, however, he is painted green. Goodrich does not cite her source for the color symbolism associated with Osiris, but such a point is not inconsistent with Rundle Clark's statement that "for the native Egyptian Osiris is always helpless. He is never represented in movement, but as a swathed figure with black or green face—for he is both a mummy and the life spirit of the earth and vegetation" (*Myth and Symbol*, p. 106). Veronica Irons, in *Egyptian Mythology* (Middlesex: Hamlyn House, 1968), presents black paintings and Negroid sculptures of Osiris (see pp. 127, 128). Budge states (*Osiris*, pp. 15–16) that visual representations of Osiris were very rare before the Twelfth Dynasty, and that there was no painting anywhere of Osiris judging the dead until the Eighteenth. Yet worship of Osiris extended back many centuries before the Twelfth Dynasty. Diop (*African Origin*

of Civilization, p. 89) states categorically that the Book of the Dead teaches that "Isis is a Negro woman, Osiris a Negro man. . . . This we have known since Emile Amelineau [a French Egyptologist]." This seems to be a reference to that Egyptologist's discovery that Osiris worship began in the area near Thebes, close to the borders of Ethiopia, and applies only to Osiris in one of his several aspects. Isis was sometimes given a very European look in Ptolemaic times and thereafter; but as Amelineau pointed out (*Prolegomene*, p. 203), in Upper Egypt, on her home soil, she was portrayed as "reddish black." Her features were sometimes quite Negroid, sometimes not.

101. See note 97. For a discussion of the Isiac cult in Italy and its utilization of Africans in some of the ceremonies, see Snowden, *Blacks in Antiquity*, pp. 189-192. Professor Snowden presents photographs of ceremonies from frescoes at Herculaneum on pages 252-253.

102. Serge Sauneron, *The Priests of Ancient Egypt* (New York: Grove, 1969), pp. 83-84.

103. For statements emphasizing the point that labor for public works and pyramids was done by farmers in their off season and was probably not considered an onerous burden, see Weigall, *History of the Pharaohs* vol. 1, pp. 168-169; Frankfort, *Birth of Civilization*, pp. 90-91.

104. The reason for accepting this position espoused by Cheikh Anta Diop, despite the negative reaction it still evokes from some Egyptian scholars, as well as from most of their European and American counterparts, follows from the analysis presented earlier. See also the report on the symposium entitled "The Peopling of Ancient Egypt," held in Cairo, January 28-February 3, 1974, under the auspices of UNESCO, in *General History of Africa*, vol. 2, ed. Mokhtar, annex to chapter 2, pp. 58-82. The conference concluded that those who opposed the Diop view had not yet done enough serious work to refute it decisively.

105. The best discussion of this question to date, presented by an expert but written in nontechnical language, is Bruce C. Trigger, "Nubian, Negro, Black, Nilotic?" in *Africa in Antiquity*, vol. 1, pp. 26-35 (especially "The Nile Valley Continuum," pp. 27-28).

106. Although Diop and other scholars have made occasional comments about Egyptians, living and dead, based upon photographs, in the study of "Negroidness" no systematic studies exist, based upon careful study of photographs for various time periods and class levels, of the degree of "Negroidness" found in Egyptian populations. I have made a cursory, uncontrolled survey and would suggest that readers make their own in order to acquire a "feel" for the racial types to be found in ancient Egypt. The most useful introduction to such an exercise would be a study of Werner Forman and Bedrich Forman, *Egyptian Art* (London: Peter Nevill, 1962). All of the photographs are from objects in the Cairo Museum, and the total impact of this beautiful collection of photographs is to convey an impression of "Negroidness." The authors selected pieces to demonstrate ancient Egyptian artists' concern with "racial type" as well as with individual traits and stylistic conventions of particular periods. The introductory essay by Dr. Milada Vilimkova is an excellent guide to the Forman method of analysis as well as an art critic's interpretation of the materials. A wider range of objects is presented in Cyril Aldred's *Development of Ancient Egyptian Art* (1952). It would be a rewarding exercise to attempt an evaluation of the pieces in this broad sample using the Forman type of art analysis to supplement Aldred's. In both cases laymen will want to ask, "Would this person be judged 'Negro' or 'Black' in the modern

United States on the evidence of phenotype alone if no other facts were available?" Scientific procedures and panels of judges could be utilized, with controls for race, ethnicity, and class in the selection of judges.

Readers interested in judging independently the claim that the Egyptian population was similar to the modern Afro-American population in degree of "Negroidness" and wide range of physical types might, after examining these two sources, wish to replicate (or to refine) my crude study of the Petrie collection of sculpture in Anthea Page, *Egyptian Sculpture, Archaic to Saite* (London: University College Press, 1959). Of the 109 photographs of heads intact and relatively undamaged, I deemed 28 to have pronounced Negro characteristics, judged by anthropological criteria, and another 50 as likely to be classified as "Negro" by an observer from the United States. Only 31, or about 28 percent, would be classified as "white" by contemporary Americans. It is significant that very few of the statues in the Petrie collection were of servants or slaves. A similar incidence of "Negroidness" is apparent in the photographs in James H. Breasted, Jr., *Egyptian Servant Statues* (Princeton: Princeton University Press, 1948), although a slightly higher proportion may be non-Negro. (This is the son and namesake of the pioneer Egyptologist who included Egyptians in "The Great White Race.")

107. Diop, *African Origin*, pp. 216–218.
108. Walther Wolf, in *The Origins of Western Art* (New York: Universe Books, 1971), p. 33, has stated that "the Egyptian statue itself is not intended as a copy of nature but rather as a symbol. This explains among other things why the flesh of the man is painted a reddish brown while the woman's is yellow." See also Edouard Naville, *The XIth Dynasty Temple at Deir El-Bahari*, part 1, 28th Memoir of the Egypt Exploration Society (London, 1907), p. 56.
109. Aldred, *Old Kingdom*, pp. 41–42.
110. Frankfort, *Birth of Civilization*, p. 82.
111. Weigall describes the dramatic case of Pharaoh Djoser, who, according to the legend, had to make the journey to the first cataract to implore the god Khnum to let the Nile waters rise. He was told by the image of the god that the pharaoh had let the temple run down very badly but that he would grant plenteous harvests "if proper care were taken of him." So an endowment was fixed on the god in the form of land, which later became a subject of dispute between his priests and those of Isis (*History of the Pharaohs*, pp. 148–149).
112. Ibid., pp. 98–101.
113. Ibid., p. 140.
114. Ibid., p. 141.
115. Ibid., p. 143.
116. Frankfort stresses the importance of Mesopotamian influences during the Predynastic Period, especially with regard to the development of writing. However, he concludes that "it would be an error to see the birth of Egyptian civilization as a consequence of contact with Mesopotamia" (*Birth of Civilization*, p. 110).
117. Aldred, *Ancient Egyptian Art*, plates 1–50 in section entitled "Old Kingdom Art in Ancient Egypt."
118. Weigall, *History of the Pharaohs*, "Dynasty III, 2. Tosortho: Thoser Retho Neterkhet 2868–2850 B.C.," pp. 146–151.
119. Ibid., p. 147.
120. Ibid.

121. Aldred, *Old Kingdom*, p. 65.
122. Joel A. Rogers, *World's Great Men of Color*, vol. 1 (New York: Collier Books, 1972), pp. 38–41.
123. Jamieson B. Hurry, *Imhotep* (New York: AMS Press, 1978). This is an excellent, in-depth study of the process by which Djoser's architect became first a demigod and then a god. For the portrait on the wall at Philae, see p. 62 of Hurry's work. This is, however, a Eurocentric study; research on Imhotep from a black perspective is needed to complement it.
124. Weigall, *History of the Pharaohs*, pp. 156–158.
125. Weigall, in *History of the Pharaohs* (pp. 170–172), discusses the charges of cruelty that were lodged, retrospectively, against Cheops during the Persian and Greek periods. He presents Sir Flinders Petrie's defense of the pyramid project and repeats the latter's insistence that it did not involve exploitation of forced and whip-driven labor. The article entitled "Khufu" in *Encyclopaedia Britannica* (1963), written by Dr. Margaret Drower of the University of London, calls the prostitution story "a clearly scandal mongering legend." See also Frankfort, *Birth of Civilization*, pp. 90–92, for an argument against the "slave labor" theory.
126. Sir Flinders Petrie makes specific reference to Djoser, whose statue has been "so much defaced that the type is obscured." As he phrases it, "A breath of life came from the Sudan," and "the Sudany infusion continued in the upper classes." What a different picture he presents from that of Roland Oliver, who as late as 1982 wrote in the *Times Literary Supplement* that "Negroidness" in the Egyptian gene pool came from slaves! Petrie continues, "The southern source was likewise the inspiration of the XIIth, the XVIIIth, and the XXVIth Dynasties" (*Making of Egypt*, p. 105).
127. Photographs of this head and other so-called "reserve heads" may be found in Aldred's *Ancient Egyptian Art*, pp. 21–22; and in his *Egyptian Art in the Days of the Pharaohs*, published thirty-one years later. Although he made no reference to the race of the princess in the 1980 work, Aldred, on page 30 of the earlier book, makes the statement quoted in the text. A former curator of Egyptian art in the museum where the head of the princess is now exhibited reveals what I interpret as esthetic bias in comparing it with the head of another princess: "[it is] of negroid type, with thick lips, wide nostrils and full cheeks. . . . Altogether different is the piquant head of a princess with her delicate features and sharp upturned nose" (William Stevenson Smith, *Ancient Egypt as Represented in the Museum of Fine Arts* [Boston: Boston Museum of Fine Arts, 1952], p. 32). The very use of the term "delicate features" expresses a culturally derived aversion on the American Egyptologist's part to the "thick lips, wide nostrils and full cheeks," an aversion that the Fourth Dynasty prince who married the woman evidently did not have. Both women were his wives!
128. One perceptive critic of Egyptian art, commenting on the statue of Prince Hemon, speaks of his "strikingly thin, bent nose, not unlike a bird's beak, and narrow lips in a full face." He concludes that "the prince's face differs completely from what might be called the Egyptian racial type" (Werner Forman and Bedrich Forman, with text by Milada Vilimkova, *Egyptian Art*, p. 22). Of the combination—racial features, stylized elements, and individual traits—that sculptors tried to express, Dr. Milada Vilimkova felt that it was the latter that was emphasized in the case of Hemon.
129. Aldred does not mention the issue of color for these statues in *Ancient Egyptian*

Art. The quotation is from Forman and Forman, *Egyptian Art*, pp. 21–22, 43. An attractive reproduction of this husband-and-wife statue appears on page 56 of *Ancient Egypt: Discovering Its Splendors* (Washington, D.C.: National Geographic Society, 1978).

130. See Aldred, *Ancient Egyptian Art*, "Old Kingdom Art," plates 11, 12, 13, 14, 37, 42.
131. Weigall, *History of the Pharaohs*, p. 177.
132. Aldred, *Old Kingdom*, pp. 48–50.
133. Wilson, "Function of the State," pp. 89–90 for the quotations on water; pp. 108, 109 on self-reliance. See also Frankfort, *Birth of Civilization*, p. 99.
134. Wilson, "Values of Life," p. 111.
135. Ibid., pp. 110–111.
136. Weigall, *History of the Pharaohs*, pp. 222–250.
137. Frankfort, *Birth of Civilization*, pp. 90, 140.
138. Wilson, "The Nature of the Universe," in *Before Philosophy*, ed. H. Frankfort et al., pp. 41–42.
139. Mertz, *Red Land, Black Land*, pp. 34–35.
140. Diop, *African Origin*, p. 205.
141. Weigall, *History of the Pharaohs*, p. 283.
142. Quoted in Weigall, *History of the Pharaohs*, pp. 282, 283–284.
143. Ibid., p. 291.
144. Wilson, "The Values of Life," in *Before Philosophy*, ed. H. Frankfort et al., pp. 120, 115.
145. Ibid., p. 120.
146. Weigall, *History of the Pharaohs*, p. 295.
147. Naville, *Deir El-Bahari*, part 1, p. 56.
148. Weigall, *History of the Pharaohs*, p. 295.
149. Aldred, *Egyptian Art*, p. 213.
150. Ibid., pp. 113, 124.
151. Weigall, *History of the Pharaohs*, p. 296.
152. Ibid., p. 298.
153. Naville, *Deir El-Bahari*, p. 55. This Egyptologist states that a skull presumed to be Kemsit's had Negro characteristics. Mrs. Naville copied the tomb paintings and rendered blue as black. Naville states that this was the convention for the period.
154. H. E. Winlock, *Excavations at Deir el-Bahari, 1911–1931* (New York: Macmillan, 1942), p. 129. Weigall discusses the six princesses, and cites both Naville and Winlock. He does not mention their color (*History of the Pharaohs*, pp. 296–298).
155. Winlock, *Excavations*, pp. 129–130.
156. Ibid., p. 130.
157. William Y. Adams, *Nubia: Corridor to Africa* (Princeton, N.J.: Princeton University Press, 1977), pp. 175–195.
158. Walter B. Emery, *Egypt in Nubia* (London: Hutchinson, 1965), pp. 157, 159.
159. E. A. Wallis Budge, *Annals of Nubian Kings*, vol. 2 (London: Kegan Paul, Trench, Trubner and Co., 1912). Appendix I, pp. 170–176, passim.
160. Wilson, "Values of Life," p. 121.
161. Gailey, *History of Africa*, pp. 34–35.
162. Chancellor Williams, *Destruction of Black Civilization*, pp. 84–91 (especially p. 87); Aldred, *Egyptian Art*, p. 139.

163. Aldred, *Egyptian Art*, pp. 139–140.

164. William Whiston, trans., *The Genuine Works of Flavius Josephus, the Jewish Historian* (London: J. and F. Tallis, n.d.), pp. 547–548.

165. Rudolph A. Windsor, *From Babylon to Timbuctoo: A History of the Ancient Black Races, Including the Black Hebrews* (New York: Exposition Press, 1969), pp. 61–63.

166. Aldred, *Egyptian Art*, p. 139.

167. W. H. McNeill, *The Rise of the West* (New York: Mentor, 1965), pp. 96–97.

168. Wilson, "Values of Life," pp. 121, 123.

169. See Diop, *African Origin*, plate 31.

170. For some excellent, readily accessible photographs, see the National Geographic Society publication *Ancient Egypt*, pp. 58–72.

171. See Diop, *African Origin*, p. 214. Although the basic thrust of Chancellor Williams's interpretation is in terms of race, he writes, "The compelling reason for the reconquest of the Delta was always economic. In fact 'race' itself was an economic factor" (*Destruction of Black Civilization*, p. 87, in "Black Egypt Turning Brown and White," pp. 83–91).

172. An interesting account of how the decision was made to attack the Hyksos was found on a schoolboy's tablet and later confirmed by a stele. Although Kamose's council advised against it, the king overruled them, saying, "No man can settle down, being despoiled by the imposts of the Asiatics. I will grapple with him that I may cut open his belly. My wish is to save Egypt and to smite the Asiatics." Some of the more cautious advisers protested, "We are at ease in our part of Egypt." Kamose answered, "He who divides the land with me will not respect me." So, he sailed down the Nile with a large fleet, using soldiers from the eastern desert, the Madjoi, as scouts and landing parties. In this description of the capture of a city, one can see clearly how Kamose was able to assemble an army: "I broke down his walls. I killed his people. I made his wife come down to the riverbank [i.e., the wife of the ruler of the town]. My soldiers were as lions are, with their spoil, having serfs, cattle, milk, fat, and honey, dividing up their property, their hearts gay" (James B. Pritchard, ed., *Ancient Near Eastern Texts Relating to the Old Testament* [Princeton, N.J.: Princeton University Press, 1950], pp. 22–23).

173. The quotations are used in a narrative account by Lerone Bennett in *Before the Mayflower* (Chicago: Johnson Publishing Co., 1962), pp. 5–10. The text is accompanied by a reproduction of a tomb painting of Nefertari and her husband (p. 9). See also the statement by Petrie in *Making of Egypt* (p. 155), where, after calling Nefertari "a black queen . . . not in the least prognathous," he claims, "a possibility of the black being symbolic has been suggested." He does not, however, indicate who was unwilling to take the representation at its face value. See also the reproduction of a tomb fresco in *Journal of African Civilizations* 4, 2 (November 1982): 89.

174. Wilson, "Values of Life," p. 122.

175. Ibid.

176. Ibid., p. 123.

177. Rogers, *Great Men of Color*, vol. 1, "Hatshepsut," pp. 43–51.

178. Ibid., p. 54, quoted from Weigall, *Personalities of Antiquity*, pp. 169–176. Thutmose III is lauded by Weigall in this book as a military tactician and as also "the kindest and most gentle of men, notorious for the generous manner in which he

pardoned his captured enemies, adored by his countrymen, and reverenced as the ideal pharaoh for hundreds of years." He describes his mummy in detail but makes no remarks about his probable race.

179. James H. Breasted, *A History of Egypt* (New York: Scribner's, 1924). An article by Breasted on Akhenaten, which uses these same laudatory phrases, also appears in *Encyclopaedia Britannica* (1963).

180. Quoted in Rogers, *Great Men of Color*, vol. 1, p. 62. The chapter entitled "Akhenaten" (pages 57–66) contains an excellent bibliography and selection of quotations.

181. Arthur Weigall, *Life and Times of Akhnaton* (London: Thornton and Butterworth, 1910), pp. 250–251. Although some of the pictures that Weigall uses portray Akhenaten as quite Negroid, he never suggests in the text that the pharaoh might be Black. (See plates between pages 176, and 177 and between 232 and 233.) One of the most Negroid photos is really that of a daughter, Meryt-Aten, whose likeness is erroneously presented as that of Akhenaten (see plate between pages 80 and 81).

182. See, e.g., Rostovtzeff, *History of the Ancient World*, vol. 1, p. 78.

183. Sigmund Freud, *Moses and Monotheism* (New York: Knopf, 1939), p. 27. This statement serves as a preface to an extensive sympathetic discussion of Amenhotep IV (i.e., Akhenaten).

184. Aldred has devoted an entire book to the pharaoh, *Akhenaten, Pharaoh of Egypt—A New Study* (New York: McGraw-Hill, 1968). This straightforward, scholarly account of the pharaoh does not discuss his race. In trying to account for the pharaoh's misshapen torso, Aldred suggests that he may have been suffering from Frölich's Syndrome (see pp. 134–135, 136). When, however, he uses this to explain the Negroid configuration of facial features (pp. 144–145), a distinct impression is conveyed of trying to "explain away" Akhenaten's "Negroidness." Five years later, when working with Bernard W. Bothmer at the Brooklyn Museum, a subtle shift is apparent in Aldred's approach to the pharaoh's "Negroidness." He still does not mention his race, but he presents photographs of him in such a way as to emphasize the "normality" of his facial features in a number of the representations. His "Negroidness" needs no verbal comment.

185. Immanuel Velikovsky, *Oedipus and Akhenaten* (New York: Doubleday, 1960). This fascinating bit of speculation suggests that the Oedipus story of the Greeks was actually based upon the life of Amenhotep IV (Akhenaten), who, suffering an injury to his leg as Oedipus did to his foot, married his mother, Queen Tiye, bringing tragedy to his relations with Nefertiti and, eventually, suffering to Egypt. Velikovsky explicitly states his lack of respect for the pharaoh. A recent novel about the Eighteenth Dynasty exploits the alleged mother-son incest theme as an explanation of what most Egyptologists assume was a rift that occurred between Queen Tiye and Nefertiti. See Pauline Gedge, *The Twelfth Transforming* (New York: Harper and Row, 1984).

186. Yosef ben-Jochannan, *The Black Man's Religion and Extracts and Comments from the Holy Black Bible* (New York: Alekebu-lan Books Associates, 1974), pp. 70, 72. The caption to one picture of Akhenaten calls him "The First Christ of the World."

187. Williams, *Destruction of Black Civilization*, p. 116.

188. Diop, *African Origin*, p. 211.

189. Wilson, *Burden of Egypt*, p. 224.

190. Cyril Aldred, *Akhenaten and Nefertiti* (New York: Brooklyn Museum, in association with Viking Press, 1973), pp. 199, 94.

191. Christiane Desroches-Noblecourt, *Ancient Egypt* (Greenwich, Conn.: New York Graphic Society, 1960), plate 10.
192. Rogers, *Great Men of Color*, vol. 1, p. 63. These remarks are included in a chapter entitled "Akhenaton," pp. 57–66.
193. Aldred, *Akhenaten*, pp. 43–44.
194. Christiane Desroches-Noblecourt, *Tutankhamen* (New York: New York Graphic Society, 1963), p. 121.
195. Mertz, *Red Land, Black Land*, p. 13. Disagreement about Queen Tiye's origin and physical type has not been confined to Egyptologists. Pauline Gedge published a highly imaginative fictionalized account of palace intrigue from the reign of Akhenaten to the end of the Eighteenth Dynasty (see note 185). Domineering and crafty, manipulating royal matings based upon brother-sister incest, and willing to seduce her own son, Tiye is presented not as a Nubian but as a Mitanni wife of Amenhotep III, of "sallow complexion" with "red brown hair" and "clear blue eyes." She is invested with the same psychological traits by Finnish novelist Mika Waltari in *The Egyptian*, a 1949 Book-of-the-Month Club selection, source of the 20th Century Fox movie of 1954, and published in fourteen languages. But Waltari describes Tiye as "very dark" and comments that it was said that she "had Negro blood in her veins" and had "thick lips." A "merciless plotter," all Thebes called her "the black witch" who took counsel with sorcerers from her Nubian homeland. After the Aten worship was installed in Thebes through her influence, "court ladies . . . enjoyed the virility of the black man." Gedge exhibits racism by refusing to recognize Tiye as Black; Waltari, by stereotyping her as a Negro sorcerer.
196. Aldred, *Akhenaten*, plates 69, 70, p. 175.
197. Adams, *Nubia*, p. 8.
198. Desroches-Noblecourt, *Tutankhamen*, pp. 120–121. The quotations are from an extensive discussion of Kap.
199. This brief summary of the post-Akhenaten period is based upon the account in ibid., pp. 165–288.
200. Diop, *African Origin*, p. 211.
201. Childe, making an assessment from a Marxist perspective, comments that "the first boast of an Oriental conqueror in his inscriptions is the booty in animals, metal, jewels, and slaves that he has brought home. Such plunder did not increase the wealth for total enjoyment. . . . It meant transferring wealth from poorer societies to courts already glutted with a superfluity. . . . In a general way the empires thus established were mere tribute collecting machines." He points out that such behavior inevitably led to revolts by the exploited peoples (*Man Makes Himself*, p. 185). An account by an Egyptian general of how he captured a town in what is now Palestine is given in William Kelly Simpson, ed., *The Literature of Ancient Egypt* (New Haven and London: Yale University Press, 1972), "The Capture of Joppa," pp. 81–84.
202. Letters on record in the Amarna Correspondence, written by Burnaburia of Babylon to Naphururiya (Akhenaten), complain that the latter had not been as generous as Amenhotep III had been: "When the weather improves, a messenger of mine who will leave later on will bring many fine presents to my brother. My brother should also write to me for what he needs. . . . I am engaged in a special undertaking and therefore I send this message to my brother; my brother should send me much fine gold. . . . Ever since my fathers and your fathers arranged friendly relations with each other they have sent fine presents to each other and have not refused each other any reasonable demand. But now my brother has sent only two

pounds of gold as a present for me. Indeed if there is much gold in Egypt do send me as much as your fathers did, in case there is little gold send me half of what your fathers did, but why in the world did you send only two pounds of gold to me?'' (A. Leo Oppenheim, trans., *Letters from Mesopotamia* [Chicago: University of Chicago Press, 1967], pp. 114–115).

203. Bustenay Oded, *Mass Deportations and Deportees in the Neo-Assyrian Empire* (Wiesbaden: Ludwig Reichert Verlag, 1979). For references to African deportees, see pp. 41, 72.

204. See the article entitled ''Jews'' in *Encyclopaedia Britannica* (1963), pp. 42E, 42F. For a comprehensive account of population movements in the Middle East and the role of the Hebrews, consult Colin McEvedy, *The Penguin Atlas of Ancient History* (Harmondsworth: Penguin, 1967), pp. 22, 28, 30.

205. Josephus thought the Exodus occurred when the Hyksos were expelled from Egypt. Since he wrote, there has been continuous discussion about a probable date for this event. The currently most popular theory is that Rameses II was the pharaoh ''who knew not Joseph'' and enslaved the Hebrews who had previously been a guest people in Egypt. The biblical account suggests that a Rameses was the pharaoh of the extreme oppression that led to the Exodus but does not mention which one. See Exodus 1:11 and 12:37.

206. The biblical statement of the claim to the Land of Canaan, based on Jehovah's covenant with Abraham, is given in Genesis 15 and 17. An account is given, in Numbers 3, of the spies who were sent out, after forty years of wandering in the Sinai Desert, to ''search the land of Canaan'' before embarking upon the war of conquest against the tribes then inhabiting the area.

207. For legends about Solomon and his kingdom, see 1 Kings 4; for a reference to a palace Solomon built for the pharaoh's daughter, to whom he was married, see 1 Kings 7. For an account of the division of the kingdom, see 1 Kings 11 and 12.

208. Wilson, ''Values of Life,'' p. 122.

209. Ibid., p. 123.

210. Sauneron, *Priests of Ancient Egypt*, p. 186.

211. Diop, *African Origin*, pp. 213–216; McNeill, *Rise of the West*, pp. 312–321. M. Rostovtzeff, speaking of the ''natives'' under the Ptolemies, writes: ''they were no longer at home in Egypt, but were expected to be obedient tools in the hands of foreigners'' (*Social and Economic History of the Hellenistic World* [Oxford: Clarendon Press, 1941], p. 413).

212. See ''Hymn of Victory of Mer-ne-Ptah'' (the ''Israel Stela''), in James B. Pritchard, ed., *Ancient Near Eastern Texts Relating to the Old Testament*, pp. 377–378.

213. Diop, *African Origin*, p. 214.

214. Ibid., pp. 217–218.

215. Emanuel bin Gorion, ed., *Mimekor Yisrael, Classical Jewish Folktales* (Bloomington: Indiana University Press, 1976), pp. 324–327, 330–334.

216. Quoted in George S. Goodspeed, *A History of the Babylonians and Assyrians* (New York: Scribner's, 1902), pp. 193–194.

217. Ibid., pp. 237–238.

218. Ibid., p. 245.

219. bin Gorion, *Jewish Folktales*, pp. 324–327, 330–334.

220. Goodspeed, *History of the Babylonians and Assyrians*, pp. 247–248.

221. Diop, *African Origin*, p. 146.

222. Margaret Shinnie, *Ancient African Kingdoms* (New York: St. Martin's, 1965), pp. 23–24.

223. Weigall, *Personalities of Antiquity*, p. 175.

224. Ibid., p. 186.
225. Snowden, *Blacks in Antiquity*, p. 144.
226. Weigall, *Personalities of Antiquity*, pp. 188-189, in chapter 24, "The Exploits of a Nigger King."
227. Rogers, *Great Men of Color*, vol. 1, p. 92.
228. E.A.W. Budge, *Annals of Nubian Kings*, p. lxxix.
229. Diop, *African Origin*, pp. 219-220.
230. Goodspeed, *History of the Babylonians and Assyrians*, pp. 249-250. The story of relations between the Hebrew kingdoms, Egypt/Ethiopia, and Assyria is told in a well-researched and lively fashion by E.A.W. Budge, in *A History of Ethiopia, Nubia, and Abyssinia* (London: Methuen, 1928), vol. 1, pp. 30-45.
231. Goodspeed, in developing his theme of Egyptian actions that provoked attacks by Assyria, describes the plotting, attacks, and counterattacks, and occasionally quotes from the Assyrian chronicles. See Sennacharib's boastful account of his victory, from which Goodspeed quotes (*History of the Babylonians and Assyrians*, p. 270).
232. Ibid., p. 272. See also 2 Chronicles 32 and 2 Kings 18 and 19, especially references to Taharka in 19. The episode forms the basis for the poem by Lord George Gordon Byron, "The Destruction of Sennacherib," beginning with the words, "The Assyrian came down like the wolf on the fold."
233. Goodspeed, *History of the Babylonians and Assyrians*, p. 272.
234. Both Goodspeed and Budge consider the actions of Egyptian plotting to be an "interference" that inevitably drew Assyrian reprisals.
235. Budge compliments Taharka and other Kushite kings of the Twenty-fifth Dynasty on their fighting prowess in conquering Egypt, but he believes they sacrificed the welfare of Egypt and Ethiopia to the interests of the priests of Amon in trying to "take on" Assyria, a great power they could not expect to defeat.
236. Goodspeed, *History of the Babylonians and Assyrians*, pp. 286-297.
237. Diop, *African Origin*, pp. 215-221.
238. Goodspeed, *History of the Babylonians and Assyrians*, p. 303.
239. For a suggestion that Taharka was murdered, see E.A.W. Budge, *Egyptian Literature: Legends of the Gods*, vol. 2 (London: Kegan Paul, Trench, Trubner, 1912), p. xxxi.
240. Ibid., p. xxix.
241. Williams, *Destruction of Black Civilization*, p. 95.
242. Diop, *African Origin*, p. 221.
243. Williams, *Destruction of Black Civilization*, pp. 98, 99.
244. Aldred, *Egyptian Art*, p. 215. See also Forman and Forman, *Egyptian Art* (p. 10), in which the curator of the Egyptian Museum in Cairo states that "art steadily declined until the time of the Ethiopian monarchs when a new school arose."
245. Snowden, *Blacks in Antiquity*, pp. 103, 122.
246. McNeill, *Rise of the West*, p. 136.
247. Aldred, *Egyptian Art*, p. 225.
248. See the article entitled "Psammetichus" in *Encyclopaedia Britannica* (1963). For meanings associated with the term "Libyan" in antiquity, see Diop, *African Origin*, pp. 64-65; Snowden, *Blacks in Antiquity*, pp. 104-105.
249. Aldred, *Egyptian Art*, p. 228.
250. Snowden, *Blacks in Antiquity*, plates 20, 91, 92; pp. 103-104, 159-160. See also the striking "Heracles and Busiris," plate 60, in M. Rostovtzeff, *A History of the Ancient World*, vol. 2 (Oxford: Clarendon Press, 1926).
251. Goodspeed, *History of the Babylonians and Assyrians*, p. 339.

252. For an account of these events, see ibid., pp. 340-352.
253. See the article entitled "Ahmose" in *Encyclopaedia Britannica* (1963); Snowden, *Blacks in Antiquity*, p. 145.
254. McNeill, *Rise of the West*, p. 143.
255. For an account of Cambyses's relations with the king of Kush, see Snowden, *Blacks in Antiquity*, pp. 105, 123, 125, 145-147.
256. Under the Fatimid Caliphate of Cairo, between A.D. 969 and A.D. 1171, Syria, along with Palestine, was usually ruled as a province of Egypt. Black rulers and soldiers played an important part in the Fatimid regime.
257. For an exhaustive analysis of this process, see the chapter "The Balance of Power," in M. Rostovtzeff, *History of the Hellenistic World*, pp. 260-500.
258. Aldred, *Egyptian Art*, p. 233.
259. Ibid.
260. See photographs in Hurry, *Imhotep*, with special attention to votive images and the mural at Philae on page 62.
261. Rogers, *Great Men of Color*, vol. 1, pp. 119-121.
262. Irons, *Egyptian Mythology* (London: Hamlyn, 1968), p. 110. See the photograph of Min in Jules Taylor, "The Black Image in Egyptian Art." *Journal of African Civilizations* 1 (1979): 27.
263. Sauneron, *Priests of Ancient Egypt*, p. 180.
264. For the reference to Hatshepsut, see Rogers, *Great Men of Color*, vol. 1, p. 47. Sauneron notes that "Amon gave out his decrees regarding everything; the political weakness of the priestly sovereigns hid itself behind the scarecrow of the divine oracle" (*Priests of Ancient Egypt*, p. 186).
265. Sauneron, *Priests of Ancient Egypt*, p. 173.
266. See the article entitled "Serapis" in *Encyclopaedia Britannica* (1963). For a comparison of Serapis and the Aten disc as examples of "the calculated manufacture" of new religions by Egyptian rulers, see Toynbee, *History* (1947 edition), p. 492.
267. Diop, "Origin of the Ancient Egyptians," p. 43; see Budge, *Osiris*, p. 324, and also p. 398 for a reference to Apis as "a black bull . . . living image of Osiris."
268. Budge, in *Osiris*, and Irons, in *Egyptian Mythology*, mention these variations in color in the course of their discussions of Osiris. See also Budge, *Egyptian Literature*, vol. 2, p. 241.
269. Rundle Clark, *Myth and Symbol*, pp. 17, 117; Irons, *Egyptian Mythology*, pp. 55-58.
270. The Greek god Hermes was assimilated to the Egyptian god Thoth, who was reputed to be the source of esoteric "Hermetic" knowledge.
271. Victor Turner, *The Forest of Symbols* (Ithaca, N.Y.: Cornell University Press, 1967), chapter 3, "Color Classification in Ndembu Ritual: A Problem in Primitive Classification"; see especially "White and Red as a Binary System," pp. 79-81.
272. Budge, *Osiris*, p. 324; Frankfort, *Birth of Civilization*, p. 11.
273. For a discussion of the white bull in the annual festivals at various Min cult centers, see Irons, *Egyptian Mythology*, p. 110.
274. Ibid., pp. 198-205, 211, 212; see also Snowden, *Blacks in Antiquity*, pp. 198-205, 211, 212.
275. Weigall, *History of the Pharaohs*, pp. 109-115.
276. An interpretation of Seth as desert encroaching upon the fertile land (Osiris) may be found in Rundle Clark, *Myth and Symbol*, p. 115.
277. Budge, *Osiris*, pp. 210-212.

278. Faber Birren, *The Story of Color* (Westport, Conn.: Crimson Press, 1941), pp. 18, 54.

279. Sauneron describes the reported visit of Pythagoras to Egypt between 568 B.C. and 526 B.C. and his reputed instruction by priests over a period of fifteen years (*Priests of Ancient Egypt*, p. 115).

280. Birren, *Story of Color*, pp. 41–43.

281. Diop, "Origin of the Ancient Egyptians," pp. 41–43.

282. Jules Taylor, "The Black Image in Egyptian Art," *Journal of African Civilizations* 1, 1 (April 1979): 38.

283. Williams, *Destruction of Black Civilization*, p. 98.

284. Snowden, *Blacks in Antiquity*, chapter 4, "Greek Encounters with Ethiopian Warriors," pp. 121–129.

285. Ibid., chapter 6, "Ethiopians in Classical Mythology," pp. 144–155.

286. Ibid., p. 152.

287. Prior to the New Kingdom, the term "Ta-Meri" was used in Egypt with reference to the organized kingdoms south of the first Nile cataract. It meant "People of the Bow." "Kush" gained general usage during the Eighteenth Dynasty. The Hebrews had been using it before that. See the entry for "Cush" in *Encyclopedia Judaica* (1961).

288. Adams, *Nubia*, pp. 334–338. Here is described, in some detail, the relations between Kushite rulers and the Ptolemies, involving the Dodekaschoenos and the Isis shrine at Philae.

289. Snowden, *Blacks in Antiquity*, p. 128.

290. Ibid., p. 105.

291. Ibid., p. 143.

292. Ibid. See plates 78, 103, 113, 114, 42, 43, 64, 67, 71, 109.

293. Adams, *Nubia*, p. 338.

294. For discussion of the Blemmyes, see Snowden, *Blacks in Antiquity*, pp. 136, and Adams, *Nubia*, pp. 389–392, 422–429, 454; for relevant sculpture, see Snowden, plates 64, 65, 67, 115, 116.

295. Snowden, *Blacks in Antiquity*, pp. 110–113, 135.

296. J. Leclant, "The Empire of Kush: Napata and Meroe," in *General History of Africa*, vol. 2, ed. G. Mokhtar, p. 293.

297. Shinnie, *African Kingdoms*, p. 35.

298. Ibid., pp. 25–28, includes a map of the Meroë area. See also Oliver and Fage, *Short History of Africa*, for a succinct account of Meroë's ecological setting (pp. 40–43). See M. Rostovtzeff, *The Social and Economic History of the Roman Empire*, vol. 1 (Oxford: Clarendon Press, 1957), pp. 301–307.

299. A. A. Hakem, "The Civilization of Napata and Meroe," in *General History of Africa*, vol. 2, ed. G. Mokhtar, pp. 298–325.

300. Ibid., with special reference to pp. 311–313, "The Problem of Iron Working." See also Williams, *Destruction of Black Civilization*, pp. 132–134.

301. Leclant, "Empire of Kush," pp. 278–297; Hakem, "Civilization of Napata and Meroe," especially p. 318.

302. Leclant, "Empire of Kush," pp. 278–297.

303. Hakem, "Civilization of Napata and Meroe," pp. 301–302, and discussion of "The Candace: The Role of the Queen Mother," pp. 303–305; see also Adams, *Nubia*, "The Royal Succession," pp. 259–260.

304. Hakem, "Civilization of Napata and Meroe," p. 302.

305. Ibid., p. 303.

306. Ibid., p. 304.
307. Ibid.
308. Snowden, *Blacks in Antiquity*, p. 120.
309. Petrie, *Making of Egypt*, p. 155; Oliver and Fage, *Short History of Africa*, pp. 40–41.
310. B. V. Bothmer, "Egyptian Sculpture of the Late Period, 700 B.C. to A.D. 100" (New York: Brooklyn Museum, 1960), p. xviii; quoted in *Africa in Antiquity: The Arts of Ancient Nubia and the Sudan*, vol. 2, *The Catalogue*, ed. Steffen Wenig (New York: Brooklyn Museum, 1978), p. 49. Compare, in Wenig, the "brutal realism" of the granite head of King Shebitqo (fig. 25, p. 51) with the "softer" treatment of King Taharqo in the same medium (fig. 26, p. 51). For an example of what I call "aggressive masculinity," see the bas-relief of "Prince Arikarkharer Smiting Enemies" on page 203.
311. Ibid. Note text on page 87 and the following plates: 90, "Swimming Girl with Basin"; 127, "Funerary Stela of a Woman and a Man"; 129, "Funerary Stela of Lapakhidaye"; 144, "Female Torso"; and 151, "*Ba*-Statue of a Woman."
312. Shinnie, *African Kingdoms*, p. 31.
313. Wenig, *Africa in Antiquity*, vol. 2, p. 70. Note fig. 50, "Pylon of the Apedemak Temple of Natakamani at Naqa, Meroitic Period, early first century A.D."; Fig. 39, "Kandake Amanitore before the ram-headed Amun, from Temple M720 at Meroe, Meroitic Period, early first century A.D., Khartoum Sudan National Museum"; Fig. 46, "Queen Amanitore on the rear outside wall of the Apedemak Temple at Naqa, Meroitic Period, early first century A.D., Khartoum Sudan National Museum"; Fig. 46, "Queen Amanitore on the rear outside wall of the Apedemak Temple at Naqa, Meroitic Period, early first century A.D."
314. A reference to pendulous breasts occurs frequently in descriptions of African women. Carleton Coon, in a gratuitously offensive comment, contrasts the "high conical breasts" of what he calls the "handsome Somali women" with the "pendulous Negroid udders" of some other tribes (*Races of Europe*, p. 456). A more perceptive Baron Denon spoke of it as a trait of old Egyptian women (*Travels in Upper and Lower Egypt*, p. 221). To speak of this characteristic as an inherited "racial" trait is somewhat less than scientific and ignores the factors of age, nursing practices, and other possible explanations.
315. Wenig, *Africa in Antiquity*, vol. 2, pp. 79, 88.
316. Ibid., p. 212; see also plates 13, 16, 103, 134.
317. Ibid., fig. 52, p. 77.
318. Ibid., fig. 59, "Incised Drawing of a Man and a Woman, Great Enclosure at Musawwarat-es-Sufra, Meroitic Period, probably second century B.C.," p. 81.
319. Ibid., fig. 68, p. 87; fig. 61, p. 82.
320. Ibid., p. 87.
321. Ibid., fig. 161, p. 235.
322. Jacques Maquet, *Africanity* (London: Oxford University Press, 1972), pp. 4–14, 114–131.
323. Diop, *African Origin*, chapter 7, "Arguments Supporting a Negro Origin," pp. 134–155.
324. Williams, *Destruction of Black Civilization*, chapter 8, "The Scattering of the People: Routes to Death and Resurrection," pp. 187–222.
325. Budge, in *Osiris*, mentions human sacrifice at the death of members of the Eleventh Dynasty royal family (pp. 224–225). That this was still occurring in Kush during Egyptian Eighteenth Dynasty times seems clear from studies of the Kerma Culture burials near the third cataract, according to Adams (see *Nubia*, pp. 198–

199) as well as in post-Meroitic times immediately prior to Christianization (see *Nubia*, p. 407).

326. Wenig, *Africa in Antiquity*, vol. 2, fig. 55, "Block found at Meroe with representation of a royal head bearing marks of scarification, Meroitic Period, first century B.C. to third century A.D.," p. 80. Note the photographs in E. E. Evans-Pritchard, *The Nuer* (Oxford: Clarendon Press, 1947), pp. 222, 257.

327. Adams, *Nubia*, pp. 441-443, 473-481.

328. Ibid., p. 505.

329. Leclant, "Empire of Kush," p. 292.

330. Adams, *Nubia*, "The Meroitic Decline and Fall," pp. 383-389.

331. Hakem, "Civilization of Napata and Meroe," p. 317.

332. Leclant, "Empire of Kush," p. 293.

333. Basil Davidson, *Lost Cities of Africa* (Boston: Little, Brown, 1970), pp. 25-70.

334. Note chapter 4, "The Sudanic Civilization," of Oliver and Fage, *Short History of Africa*.

335. Leclant, "Empire of Kush," p. 293.

336. See the article entitled "Ethiopia" in *Encyclopaedia Britannica* (1963).

337. Snowden, "Blacks in Antiquity," pp. 206-207.

338. Ibid., p. 188, where the tradition that Piankhy was Black is mentioned.

339. Bruce C. Trigger, "The Ballana Culture and the Coming of Christianity," in *Africa in Antiquity*, vol. 2., ed. S. Wenig, p. 117.

340. Adams, *Nubia*, p. 435.

341. Chancellor Williams, *Destruction of Black Civilization*, pp. 143-158.

342. See the article entitled "Hypatia" in *Encyclopaedia Britannica* (1963).

343. Trigger, "Ballana Culture," pp. 117-118.

344. Williams, *Destruction of Black Civilization*, p. 148.

345. For an extended discussion of this conflict, see Adams, *Nubia*, "The Crown and the Cross," pp. 459-507.

346. Williams, *Destruction of Black Civilization*, p. 149.

347. Wenig, *Africa in Antiquity*, vol. 2, pp. 110, 112, 326.

348. W. Y. Adams, "Medieval Nubia," in *Africa in Antiquity*, vol. 1, ed. S. Wenig, p. 121, and photograph on p. 125. See also, in volume 2, plate 292 (p. 326), "Bishop Petros under the Protection of the Apostle Peter." Adams also discusses the art of Christian Nubia at some length in his book *Nubia*, "Religious Art and Literature," pp. 482-487 (especially p. 484).

349. Bernard Lewis, *Race and Color in Islam* (New York: Harper, 1971), p. 73.

350. Simpson, *The Literature of Ancient Egypt*, p. 28.

351. Ibid., p. 244.

352. Ibid., "Hymn to the Aten," pp. 292-293.

353. Ibid., p. 300.

354. Ibid., p. 311.

355. Ibid., p. 324.

356. Snowden, *Blacks in Antiquity*, pp. 177-178. An extended account of this legendary visit to the Candace, which stresses the myth that Alexander was the son of Nectanebus, last Pharaoh of Egypt, does not mention such a remark but does speak of her great beauty (E.A.W. Budge, *The History of Alexander the Great*, English translation of the Syriac version of *Pseudo-Callisthenes* and original text [Amsterdam: Philo Press, 1976, reprint of 1889 Cambridge University Press edition]). Snowden is quoting from one Latin and one Greek source of *Pseudo-Callisthenes*.

357. Quoted in Snowden, *Blacks in Antiquity*, notes 17, 18, pp. 331-332.

358. Whiston, *Works of Flavius Josephus*, "How Moses Made War with the Ethiopians," pp. 33–34.
359. Ibid., "How Solomon . . . Entertained the Queen of Egypt and Ethiopia," pp. 166–168.
360. Ibid., p. 167. Whiston wrote: "That this queen of Sheba was a queen of Sabea in southern Arabia and not of Egypt and Ethiopia as Josephus here asserts is, I suppose, now generally agreed." The King James version of the Bible calls her Queen of Sheba. Josephus does not mention Sheba.
361. Examples might be cited from Africa and the West Indies of movements that have insisted upon a revalorization of "blackness."
362. *Plutarch's Lives*, translated from the Greek by John Langhorne, D.D. and William Langhorne, A.M. (Cincinnati: Applegate and Co., 1856), pp. 452–453. The episode of Clitus saving Alexander's life is given on p. 439. These authors do not translate the original as "Clitus called the Black," as other versions do, but rather as "the celebrated Clitus." The standard English version, called the Dryden Plutarch, rendered it "Clitus called the Black Clitus." See volume 2 of A. H. Clough's revised version of the Dryden edition (Boston: Little, Brown and Co., 1881), p. 677. A London version of the Langhorne translation, published in 1826, comments that while there was some discussion about the matter, "Plutarch *probably* wrote 'black'." The standard French version of *Plutarch's Lives* says the murdered man was called Clitus the Black to distinguish him from another of Alexander's soldiers called "the White Clitus," and cites classical Roman scholars on this point.

INDEX

Authors and titles cited only in the bibliographic essays are not indexed

ABOUT THE AUTHOR

St. Clair Drake is Professor Emeritus at Stanford University, where he taught anthropology and sociology and organized and directed the African and Afro-American studies program from 1969 until his retirement in 1976. Among the institutions at which he has also taught are Dillard University, Roosevelt University, the University of Chicago, Boston University, Columbia University, and the University of Liberia. From 1958 to 1961 Drake was head of the sociology department of the University of Ghana. Soon after the end of World War II, while doing field-work in England and Wales for a dissertation on race relations in Britain, he met and worked with the organizers of the Pan-African Federation, among them, George Padmore and Kwame Nkrumah.

Drake's works include *Black Metropolis* (1945, 1962, and 1970), which he co-authored with Horace Cayton; *Race Relations in a Time of Rapid Social Change* (1966); *Our Urban Poor* (1967); and *The Redemption of Africa and Black Religion* (1970). He has also contributed numerous poems and articles to professional journals and other publications, including *Présence Africaine, Daedalus,* and *Crisis,* as well as chapters to edited volumes.

He obtained his Ph.D. in Social Anthropology with an emphasis on African studies from the University of Chicago in 1954, and was elected an Honorary Fellow of the Royal Anthropological Institute of Great Britain and Ireland in 1986. A symposium was held in his honor at the annual meeting of the American Anthropological Association in 1985. Among many other honors, he has received the Anisfeld Wolf Award in 1945 for *Black Metropolis,* a Ford Foundation fellowship for research in West Africa (1954–1955), and a Social Science Research Council fellowship for studies in Ghana (1965). In 1973, he was the recipient of the Du Bois-Johnson-Frazier Award of the American Sociological Association while serving as a Fellow of the Center for the Study of Multi-Racial Societies at the University of the West Indies. He received a National Endowment for the Humanities Fellowship in 1977.

906034